Illegitimacy in Medieval Scotland
1100–1500

SCOTTISH HISTORICAL REVIEW MONOGRAPH SERIES

SCOTTISH HISTORICAL REVIEW MONOGRAPH SECOND SERIES

The Scottish Historical Review Monograph Second Series aims to promote major works of scholarly research covering any aspect or period of Scottish History. The series seeks, in particular, to support the work of early-career scholars active in the discipline. Its volumes are selected in partnership with the Trustees of the *Scottish Historical Review*.

Proposals or queries may be sent directly to the series editor at the address given below; all submissions will receive prompt attention before being sent to expert readers.

Professor Steve Boardman, School of History, Classics and Archaeology, William Robertson Wing, Doorway 4, Teviot Place, University of Edinburgh, EH8 9AG.

Details of volumes in the first series are available from Edinburgh University Press.

Previous volumes in the second series:

1. *The Scots in Australia, 1788–1938*, Benjamin Wilkie (2017)

2. *Ghosts in Enlightenment Scotland*, Martha McGill (2018)

Illegitimacy in Medieval Scotland
1100–1500

Susan Marshall

THE BOYDELL PRESS

Illegitimacy in Medieval Scotland
1100–1500

Susan Marshall

THE BOYDELL PRESS

First published 2021
The Boydell Press, Woodbridge

ISBN 978-1-78327-588-5

The Boydell Press is an imprint of Boydell & Brewer Ltd
PO Box 9, Woodbridge, Suffolk IP12 3DF, UK
and of Boydell & Brewer Inc.
668 Mt Hope Avenue, Rochester, NY 14620–2731, USA
website: www.boydellandbrewer.com

A catalogue record for this book is available from the British Library

This publication is printed on acid-free paper

i.m.

Malcolm MacDonald Marshall

and Jessie Davidson (née Fraser),

ministrators of love's austere and lonely offices.

Tha an saoghal fhathast àlainn
ged nach eil thu ann.

The world is still beautiful
though you are not in it.

Sorley MacLean, 'Elegy for Calum I. MacLean',

in *Sorley MacLean: Collected Poems*,

ed. Christopher Whyte and Emma Dymock (Manchester, 2011)

reprinted with kind permission from Carcanet Press Ltd.

Contents

Tables

Preface

Illegitimacy in medieval Scotland has never been the subject of a book-length study. There is no Scottish equivalent of Given-Wilson and Curteis's 1984 book on illegitimate offspring of English medieval kings.[1] Sara McDougall's more recent work, *Royal Bastards*, examines that topic in a number of Europe's developing royal dynasties, but does not include Scotland.[2] Where scholarship on illegitimacy focuses on the Scottish situation, relatively little of it concerns the medieval era, the general exception being in the field of research into the papal archives. Even so, this tends to concentrate either on illegitimacy, with some reference to Scotland, or on Scotland, with some reference to illegitimacy.[3] References to illegitimates in royal, noble and ecclesiastical life abound in Scottish historiography, but usually – where it is not scattered and piecemeal – as a subsidiary element of an investigation into something else.[4]

1 C. Given-Wilson and A. Curteis, *The Royal Bastards of Medieval England* (London, 1984).

2 S. McDougall, *Royal Bastards. The Birth of Illegitimacy, 800–1230* (Oxford, 2017).

3 The important research on Scottish clerics mentioned in papal penitentiary material, undertaken by J. R. McDonald (see bibliography for some of these), looks almost exclusively at the period 1449–1542. S. Thomas examines fourteenth- and fifteenth-century cases in 'Clerical Illegitimacy in the Diocese of Sodor – Exception or Rule in the Late Medieval Church?', in A. P. Roach and J. R. Simpson, ed., *Heresy and the Making of European Culture: Medieval and Modern Perspectives* (Farnham, 2013), 313–31. Published papal records relating exclusively to Scotland, which include some content pertaining to illegitimacy, include *CSSR*; C. Burns, *Calendar of Papal Letters to Scotland of Clement VII of Avignon, 1378–1394* (Edinburgh, 1976); F. McGurk, *Calendar of Papal Letters to Scotland of Benedict XIII, 1394–1419* (Edinburgh, 1976); *The Apostolic Camera and Scottish Benefices 1418–1488*, ed. A. I. Cameron, (London, 1934). Other collections include Scottish material, some of which touches on illegitimacy, alongside that of other parts of Britain and Ireland: *CPL*; *CPP*; *Vetera Monumenta Hibernorum et Scotorum Historiam Illustrantia*, ed. A. Theiner (Rome, 1864).

4 For example, I. G. MacDonald, *Clerics and Clansmen. The Diocese of Argyll between the Twelfth and Sixteenth Centuries* (Leiden, 2013) includes a valuable discussion of illegitimacy among the clergy of Argyll. A notable exception is Sandy Grant's extended essay, 'Royal and Magnate Bastards in the Later Middle Ages: The View from Scotland', in É. Bousmar and others, ed., *La Bâtardise et L'Exercice du Pouvoir en Europe du XIIIe au Debut du XVIe Siècle. Revue du Nord. Hors Série. Collection Histoire N° 31* (Lille, 2015), 313–67. This considers the careers of illegitimate men in political life in the fourteenth and fifteenth centuries.

Acknowledgements

The writing of this book has been much aided by the support and kindness of many people. It has taken rather too long to produce, and so my thanks are due firstly to Steve Boardman and Caroline Palmer for their forbearance.

Lisa Collinson, Clare Downham, Helen Lynch, Aly Macdonald, Melanie Marshall and Alice Taylor gave generously of their time and expertise to read and re-read draft chapters. Their insights, comments and questions have saved me from many errors: those that remain are entirely my own. I would also like to thank the publisher's anonymous readers for their helpful and stimulating remarks. I have benefited from discussions on medieval law with Alice Taylor, Andrew Simpson, and with the late David Lessels. I am grateful to Michael Schmidt at Carcanet Press, who responded with warmth and generosity to my request to use lines by Sorley MacLean in the book's dedication.

I owe the largest debt of gratitude to my family: John Tomlinson, Melanie Marshall, Mark Edwards, Sean Burke, Cristina Vercesi, and Alessandra, Francesca and Agatha Burke. Each has contributed uniquely and irreplaceably to my work and to my life. Special thanks, too, to my spiritual kindred: my god-daughter Mia, her mother, Miriam, and grandmother, Helen.

Preface

Illegitimacy in medieval Scotland has never been the subject of a book-length study. There is no Scottish equivalent of Given-Wilson and Curteis's 1984 book on illegitimate offspring of English medieval kings.[1] Sara McDougall's more recent work, *Royal Bastards*, examines that topic in a number of Europe's developing royal dynasties, but does not include Scotland.[2] Where scholarship on illegitimacy focuses on the Scottish situation, relatively little of it concerns the medieval era, the general exception being in the field of research into the papal archives. Even so, this tends to concentrate either on illegitimacy, with some reference to Scotland, or on Scotland, with some reference to illegitimacy.[3] References to illegitimates in royal, noble and ecclesiastical life abound in Scottish historiography, but usually – where it is not scattered and piecemeal – as a subsidiary element of an investigation into something else.[4]

1 C. Given-Wilson and A. Curteis, *The Royal Bastards of Medieval England* (London, 1984).

2 S. McDougall, *Royal Bastards. The Birth of Illegitimacy, 800–1230* (Oxford, 2017).

3 The important research on Scottish clerics mentioned in papal penitentiary material, undertaken by J. R. McDonald (see bibliography for some of these), looks almost exclusively at the period 1449–1542. S. Thomas examines fourteenth- and fifteenth-century cases in 'Clerical Illegitimacy in the Diocese of Sodor – Exception or Rule in the Late Medieval Church?', in A. P. Roach and J. R. Simpson, ed., *Heresy and the Making of European Culture: Medieval and Modern Perspectives* (Farnham, 2013), 313–31. Published papal records relating exclusively to Scotland, which include some content pertaining to illegitimacy, include *CSSR*; C. Burns, *Calendar of Papal Letters to Scotland of Clement VII of Avignon, 1378–1394* (Edinburgh, 1976); F. McGurk, *Calendar of Papal Letters to Scotland of Benedict XIII, 1394–1419* (Edinburgh, 1976); *The Apostolic Camera and Scottish Benefices 1418–1488*, ed. A. I. Cameron, (London, 1934). Other collections include Scottish material, some of which touches on illegitimacy, alongside that of other parts of Britain and Ireland: *CPL*; *CPP*; *Vetera Monumenta Hibernorum et Scotorum Historiam Illustrantia*, ed. A. Theiner (Rome, 1864).

4 For example, I. G. MacDonald, *Clerics and Clansmen. The Diocese of Argyll between the Twelfth and Sixteenth Centuries* (Leiden, 2013) includes a valuable discussion of illegitimacy among the clergy of Argyll. A notable exception is Sandy Grant's extended essay, 'Royal and Magnate Bastards in the Later Middle Ages: The View from Scotland', in É. Bousmar and others, ed., *La Bâtardise et L'Exercice du Pouvoir en Europe du XIIIe au Debut du XVIe Siècle. Revue du Nord. Hors Série. Collection Histoire N° 31* (Lille, 2015), 313–67. This considers the careers of illegitimate men in political life in the fourteenth and fifteenth centuries.

As an undergraduate, stray references to medieval Scottish bastards and bastardy in my reading intrigued and frustrated in equal measure. It appeared that a person believing herself to be legitimate could find in an instant she was not, or an illegitimate person could just as rapidly have her status reversed. Bastards could not be heirs, but a few did inherit; illegitimate people were discriminated against in law, but some families apparently operated a 'no bastards left behind' policy. The Church was clear that the child should not be punished for the sins of the father, but equally certain that illicit sex left an imprint of sin on the character of the resulting offspring. Illegitimacy was a 'defect' rendering a person unfit for ecclesiastical office, but did not stop some from attaining the episcopate. Historians could not agree whether being illegitimate was a degraded and problematic status or a quotidian irrelevance, and rarely took the time to justify either position. The texts themselves were just as contradictory. '[T]his is customarily often distressing and shameful,' wrote Bower of illegitimacy, but, 'I see the cause for joy, but none for sorrow,' said the future Pope Pius II of his illegitimate son.[5] In writing this book, I have kept in mind my younger self; and if I have not have resolved all the contradictions, I have at least gathered together and set in context some of the diverse and fragmentary material relating to the Scottish experience of bastardy.

Quantifying the incidence of illegitimacy in medieval Scotland is not possible, partly because of poor record survival, but also because pertinent data concerning marriages and births were not routinely recorded in the first place. Even papal material, among the more abundant of our sources, has significant gaps and problems, though even if it did not, we would still know more about illegitimacy only in relation to the Church's particular field of operations. Given that much of the other surviving material concerns transmission of lands, and bastards were not usually heirs, many illegitimate men and women from noble families would not have made it into the records. We know of some inheritance disputes turning on allegations of bastardy, but we cannot know what proportion of the overall number these survivals represent. The lives of the majority of the population, whose resources were few, are as obscure in respect of illegitimacy as they are in much else.

Though it is not possible to state the prevalence of illegitimacy, what *is* possible is to bring together some of the existing evidence for illegitimacy in various spheres of medieval Scottish life, in an effort to shed further light on its political and social importance. Since the term 'illegitimate' was a legal one, applied to offspring whose parents were not married to each other at the time of their birth, the first two chapters of this book explore this legal definition and its consequences. The next two consider the relationship between

5 *Chron. Bower*, vii, 321; *Reject Aeneas, Accept Pius: Selected Letters of Aeneas Sylvius Piccolomini (Pope Pius II)*, ed. T. Izbicki and others (Washington, DC, 2006), no. 30.

illegitimacy and royal succession, a relationship which in Scotland was neither independent of the law nor bound strictly by it. The situation of elite women who were illegitimate, or who were mothers of illegitimate children, is discussed in Chapter 5. The Church – the arbiter of who was and was not legitimate – kept a watchful eye on its illegitimate clergy, whose careers are considered in Chapter 6. The final chapter looks at illegitimacy, social status and political power, especially in relation to the possession of earldoms and lordships.

In addressing multiple aspects of this subject in what is a relatively short book, the balance struck between breadth and depth is unlikely to content all readers. Much more could be said about much more. Although I have occasionally made comparisons between a Scottish situation and a broad equivalent elsewhere, I have focused on Scotland to the virtual exclusion of international perspectives, to allow for as much exploration of the Scottish experience as possible. A systematic contextualisation of Scottish bastardy within the wider European picture has yet to be attempted. A more thorough understanding of the Scottish experience is an essential first step towards such a goal. The scope of this study, which examines illegitimacy across both a lengthy time period and a range of sectors within Scotland, is deliberately wide, and seeks to fill what is a substantial gap in Scottish historiography. I hope it will contribute to the wider picture of medieval bastardy being assembled by scholars examining the subject in other geographical and cultural settings, and from a variety of perspectives.

Acknowledgements

The writing of this book has been much aided by the support and kindness of many people. It has taken rather too long to produce, and so my thanks are due firstly to Steve Boardman and Caroline Palmer for their forbearance.

Lisa Collinson, Clare Downham, Helen Lynch, Aly Macdonald, Melanie Marshall and Alice Taylor gave generously of their time and expertise to read and re-read draft chapters. Their insights, comments and questions have saved me from many errors: those that remain are entirely my own. I would also like to thank the publisher's anonymous readers for their helpful and stimulating remarks. I have benefited from discussions on medieval law with Alice Taylor, Andrew Simpson, and with the late David Lessels. I am grateful to Michael Schmidt at Carcanet Press, who responded with warmth and generosity to my request to use lines by Sorley MacLean in the book's dedication.

I owe the largest debt of gratitude to my family: John Tomlinson, Melanie Marshall, Mark Edwards, Sean Burke, Cristina Vercesi, and Alessandra, Francesca and Agatha Burke. Each has contributed uniquely and irreplaceably to my work and to my life. Special thanks, too, to my spiritual kindred: my god-daughter Mia, her mother, Miriam, and grandmother, Helen.

Abbreviations

ADC	*The Acts of the Lords of Council in Civil Causes*, ed. T. Thomson and others (Edinburgh, 1839 and 1918–)
ADCP	*Acts of the Lords of Council in Public Affairs 1501–1554: Selections from Acta Dominorum Concilii*, ed. R. K. Hannay (Edinburgh, 1932)
APS	*The Acts of the Parliaments of Scotland*, ed. T. Thomson and C. Innes (Edinburgh, 1814–75)
CDS	*Calendar of Documents relating to Scotland*, ed. J. Bain, 4 vols (Edinburgh, 1881–8); ed. G. G. Simpson and J. D. Galbraith, vol. 5 (Edinburgh, 1986)
Chron. Bower	*Scotichronicon by Walter Bower*, in Latin and English, ed. D. E. R. Watt and others, 9 vols (Aberdeen, 1987–98)
Chron. Melrose	*The Chronicle of Melrose (Facsimile Edition)*, ed. A. O. Anderson and others (London, 1936)
Chron. Holyrood	*A Scottish Chronicle Known as the Chronicle of Holyrood*, ed. M. O. Anderson and A. O. Anderson (SHS, 1938)
Chron. Howden	*Chronica Magistri Rogeri de Hovedene*, ed. W. Stubbs, 4 vols (Rolls Series, 1868–71)
Chron. Lanercost	*Chronicon de Lanercost* (Maitland Club, 1839)
Chron. Wyntoun	*Androw of Wyntoun, The Orygynale Cronykil of Scotland*, ed. D. Laing, 3 vols (Edinburgh, 1872–9)
CP	*Complete Peerage*, ed. G. E. Cokayne and V. Gibbs, Second Edition, 14 vols (London, 1910–1998)
CPL	*Calendar of Entries in the Papal Registers Relating to Great Britain and Ireland: Papal Letters*, ed. W. H. Bliss and others (London, 1893–1998)
CPP	*Calendar of Entries in the Papal Registers Relating to Great Britain and Ireland: Petitions to the Pope*, ed. W. H. Bliss (London, 1896)
CSSR	*Calendar of Scottish Supplications to Rome*, ed. A. I. Dunlop and others, 5 vols (SHS, 1934–97), vol 6 (SRS, 2017)

ER	*The Exchequer Rolls of Scotland*, ed. J. Stuart and others (Edinburgh, 1878–1908)
ESSH	*Early Sources of Scottish History 500–1286*, ed. A. O. Anderson, 2 vols (Edinburgh, 1922)
Foedera	*Foedera, Conventiones, Litterae et Cuiuscunque Generis Acta Publica*, ed. T. Rymer, Record Commission edition, 4 vols in 7 parts (London, 1816–69)
Gratian	*Decretum Gratiani, in Corpus iuris canonici*, ed. E. L. Richter, revised by E. Friedburg, 2 vols (Leipzig, 1879; repr. Graz, 1959)
Hist. MSS. Comm.	*Reports of the Royal Commission on Historical Manuscripts* (London, 1870–)
IR	*Innes Review*
JMH	*Journal of Medieval History*
JR	*Juridical Review*
Mansi	*Sacrorum Conciliorum nova et amplissima collectio*, ed. G. D. Mansi, 53 vols (Florence, 1759–98)
Nov.	*Corpus Iuris Civilis: Novellae leges*, ed. R. Schöll and W. Kroll (Berlin, 1895)
ODNB	*Oxford Dictionary of National Biography* [www.oxforddnb.com]
PL	*Patrologia Latina*, ed. J.-P. Migne and others, 221 vols (Paris, 1844–64)
PoMS	*The People of Medieval Scotland, 1093–1314*, ed. A. Beam, J. Bradley, D. Broun, J. R. Davies, M. Hammond and M. Pasin, with others (Glasgow and London, 2010 and 2012) [www.poms.ac.uk]
PSAS	*Proceedings of the Society of Antiquaries of Scotland*
RM	*Regiam Majestatem and Quoniam Attachiamenta*, ed. Lord Cooper (Stair Society, 1947)
RMS	*Registrum Magni Sigilli Regum Scotorum*, ed. J. M. Thomson and others (Edinburgh, 1882–1914)
RPS	*The Records of the Parliaments of Scotland to 1707*, ed. K. M. Brown and others (St Andrews, 2007–09) [www.rps.ac.uk]
RRS	*Regesta Regum Scottorum*, ed. G. W. S. Barrow and others (Edinburgh, 1960–)
RSS	*Registrum Secreti Sigilli Regum Scotorum*, ed. M. Livingstone and others (Edinburgh, 1908–)

Rot. Scot.	*Rotuli Scotiae in Turri Londinensi et in Domo Capitulari Westmonasteriensi Asservati*, ed. D. Macpherson and others (1814–19)
RSCHS	*Records of the Scottish Church History Society*
Skene, *Fordun*	*Johannis de Fordun Chronica Gentis Scotorum*, ed. W. F. Skene, transl. F. Skene, 2 vols (Edinburgh, 1871–2)
SHR	*Scottish Historical Review*
SHS	Scottish History Society
SP	*The Scots Peerage*, ed. Sir J. Balfour Paul, 9 vols (Edinburgh, 1904–14)
SRS	Scottish Record Society
TA	*Accounts of the Lord High Treasurer of Scotland*, ed. T. Dickson and Sir J. Balfour Paul (Edinburgh, 1877–1916)
TCWAAS	*Transactions of the Cumberland and Westmorland Antiquarian and Archaeological Society* (1870–)
TRHS	*Transactions of the Royal Historical Society*
TDGNHAS	*Transactions of the Dumfriesshire and Galloway Natural History and Antiquarian Society*
TGSI	*Transactions of the Gaelic Society of Inverness*
X	*Liber Extra (= Decretales Gregorii IX) in Corpus iuris canonici*, ed. E. L. Richter, revised by E. Friedburg, 2 vols (Leipzig, 1879; repr. Graz, 1959)

Introduction

In the twelfth and early thirteenth centuries, the Church succeeded in gaining jurisdiction over marriage and transforming it from a largely private arrangement between families to the expression of a Christian ideal, subject to a codified system of regulation shaped by theological concerns. The conception of marriage as an earthly expression of the bond between Christ and the faithful, of the family as a microcosm of wider social polities reflective of the heavenly regime, and of both as a means of maintaining a peaceful and well-ordered society, combined to produce in authorities both secular and ecclesiastical a belief that marriage contracted according to the laws of the Church was the only acceptable context for the founding of a family.

Previously, kingdoms and the population groups within them had their own definitions and rules of what constituted marriage, and, independently of this, which children could be heirs. In many early medieval societies the offspring of more than one woman might be heirs to their father.[1] It is not unreasonable to suppose that in at least some cases 'legitimacy' worked backwards – those children selected by their fathers as heirs, or for other honours such as prestigious marriages, may have been deemed 'legitimate' by the fact of being selected, not by the pre-existing nature of the relationship between their parents.[2]

Only with a clear definition of marriage can offspring be identified as legitimate or illegitimate. Still, the meanings attached to these terms, the consequences of being legitimate or not, depend on how society decides to acknowledge the distinction, or on whether it does so at all. Scotland, along with many other kingdoms, enshrined in secular legislation the legal disability

1 For Ireland as an example, see D. Ó Cróinín, *Early Medieval Ireland 400–1200* (London, 1995), 70–1 (selection of kings); F. Kelly, *A Guide to Early Irish Law* (Dublin, 2015), 102–4 (inheritance of land).

2 Jan Rüdiger, 'Married Couples in the Middle Ages? The Case of the Devil's Advocate', in P. Andersen and others, ed., *Law and Marriage in Medieval and Early Modern Times. Proceedings of the Eighth Carlsberg Academy Conference on Medieval Legal History 2011* (Copenhagen, 2012), 103. Rüdiger argues that the moral distinction between marital (correct and lawful) and non-marital (imperfect and 'basically libidinous') relationships was a construct of St Augustine (354–430), based on the teachings of St Paul; this became a pervasive dichotomy in the literature of the Church, and did not reflect the complexity of social organisation in late Antiquity and the early middle ages.

of bastardy: the principle that illegitimate people may not be heirs, nor have heirs other than their own, lawfully procreated, offspring. Wealth, power, prestige – or, in many cases, subsistence and the hope of future improvement to material circumstances – rested on the precise nature of an individual's relationship to land and property. To be barred from inheriting land, and the income derived from it, was to suffer serious disadvantage. The prohibition on inheritance was not imposed on Scottish society by the Church, which, though vigorous in promoting monogamous marriage, was not interested in penalising illegitimates among the laity. Ecclesiastical authorities were concerned to prevent priestly offspring, necessarily illegitimate once clerical marriage was outlawed, having heirship rights in respect of Church livings and property, but lay inheritance was outwith its jurisdiction. The penalty of non-heirship, imposed by secular authorities on children born outside marriage, demonstrated wider society's endorsement of the Church's stance on sexual morality.

The gravity with which the procreation of illegitimate children was regarded varied according to the particular circumstances concerned, and who was doing the regarding. In the fifteenth century, the abbot Walter Bower described it as 'a crime', adding that, for reasons to do with their upbringing, such offspring were likely to be 'insolent, degenerate and depraved' as adults.[3] His view owes something to canonistic theories about the character of the illegitimate child being affected at conception by the sinfulness of the act by which he or she was created. The more reprehensible the union, the greater was the resulting child's propensity to corruption: without a strict corrective in early life, moral catastrophe beckoned.

Most Scots seem to have taken a rather more pragmatic view. Excluding illegitimates from inheritance served a useful political function in regulating access to estates and above all to the crown, but in medieval Scotland there was a persistent tension between the demands of legitimate primogeniture and a native tradition of heirship (including throne-worthiness) being vested in something other, or additional to, the roulette-wheel of birth circumstance. Reluctance to see offspring excluded from some share of the family wealth led to the creation of remedies for the legal disability, and beyond this, Scots maintained a distinctly ambivalent attitude to illegitimacy. If it was true, as the Church claimed, that the character of a child conceived outside the sacred bond of marriage was contaminated by his parents' evil-doing, it was also true that other, highly desirable, qualities might equally be transmitted by his pedigree. Lineage mattered, and did not stop mattering throughout the Scottish middle ages, even as the significance of illegitimate birth changed.

In the late eleventh century, Donnchad II became king of Scots; over thirty years after his death, he was described as illegitimate. Whether this was

3 *Chron. Bower*, vii, 321.

a statement of fact, or whether it was a lie intended to discredit anticipated royal pretensions of his descendants, is a matter for conjecture; it did not prevent his grandson and later generations of his line insisting that they had a right to the throne, and gaining support from enough of the Scottish nobility to present a credible threat. Donnchad's illegitimate nephew Mael Coluim, the son of Alexander I, also sought the crown; he and his line, along with their supporters, saw no reason why being born of a non-marital relationship should vitiate the rights conferred by his lineage.

In the thirteenth century, the developing legal culture of Scotland confirmed and strengthened the incompatibility of bastardy and inheritance. Although legitimacy was by now widely understood to be a precondition of royal succession in Scotland, there are hints at both ends of this century – a king-list of 1198x1214, and the proceedings of the Great Cause in 1291–2 – that the legitimacy of claimants or their ancestors might be a highly important, but not an indispensable, qualification for kingship.

The imputation of illegitimacy was a useful weapon in the propaganda armoury of the middle ages, casting doubt on the entitlement of a king to rule. The correlation between legitimacy and legitimate kingship was firmly established, though in Scotland, unlike in England, a son did not have to be born legitimate to become king, nor to become an heir to lesser estates. The experience of Robert III, born a bastard and later legitimated by his parents' decision to marry each other, may have been singular among kings of Scots, but it was far from unique among the wider Scottish community. The canon law doctrine by which pre-nuptial children were recognised as legitimate in the eyes of the Church was based on the same ideology of marriage that rendered illegitimate those born of liaisons that did not meet the stringent criteria for a valid marital union. The immense spiritual power attached to properly constituted and legally binding marriage could, according to this doctrine, reach back in time to correct the status of those born before it; where legal marriage between two people was impossible, a child procreated between them could rarely receive this grace. Fortunately for some in this situation, later medieval Scottish kings stood ready to offer, for a price, royal legitimations which, though lacking the transcendent authority of divine law, sufficed to allow inheritance of a parental estate or to enable the nomination of heirs.

The idea that being conceived through a wrongful sexual encounter blemished the resulting person's character was an appealing one when seeking to highlight the villainy of a political enemy who happened to be illegitimate. It also justified the Church's policy of monitoring the careers of illegitimate clergy, who could obtain benefices with cure of souls only if they were dispensed from their illegitimacy, a process which required them to declare whether they were the product of adultery, incest, fornication, or some other offence against chastity. In the main, however, no firm correspondence was drawn between legitimate birth and a person's capacity for valour or excellence, nor between legitimacy and the affection and esteem in which someone was held, or the bonds of social obligation by which they might prosper. Some men of illegitimate birth in later medieval Scotland obtained estates and titles, either through their own efforts or the desire of family members to provide for them. High office in the Church and in government was not beyond their grasp; among the laity, marriages to people of rank were possible.

The extent to which illegitimacy was a source of shame or embarrassment, for illegitimate people themselves or for their parents, depended on their individual circumstances. The use of 'bastard' to describe something counterfeit, adulterated or inferior was well-known in the middle ages, and makes clear the scope for associating illegitimate birth with negative characteristics. Couples who had children, and later sought a dispensation to marry, sometimes asked for it to be granted so that the mother 'may not remain defamed', suggesting that a degree of stigma attached to founding a family outside of marriage. Requests for dispensations not unusually exaggerated the harmful consequences likely to ensue from refusal, and so the magnitude of defamation may not always have been very great: still, that such appeals were made indicates a shared understanding that the women concerned were vulnerable to denigration on account of their status as unmarried mothers. This would hardly be surprising, given the Church's teaching on the matter. In these dispensations, it is always the mother's character which is said to be at risk of disparagement. Fathers appear not to have attracted much reputational damage in this respect, although they might do indirectly, if they seduced a woman without the consent of her male guardian. James III's sister is the only medieval Scottish princess we know to have had an illegitimate child, an event which apparently rendered her unmarriageable. The relative obscurity of women's lives in our sources makes it difficult to assess the consequences for women of other ranks in this regard, but certainly some, and probably many, went on to marry.[4] The frequency with which illegitimate people appear in our sources, the formulation of laws concerning it, and the variety of remedies devised to circumvent its legal implications, suggest it was part of everyday life in medieval Scotland. Mothers of these children, therefore, were not a category of women set apart from ordinary society, but were family members, friends and neighbours, living in communities where attitudes to illegitimate children were shaped not only by Christian teaching (which included messages about forgiveness and the innocence of children, as well as about marriage and sexual conduct), but also by traditions concerning kinship, and a host of other ideas and beliefs touching on human behaviour and social *mores*.

[4] Some mothers were already married. Children born to a married woman were, in law, the husband's children, whoever may have fathered them; a husband who suspected otherwise needed compelling evidence to overturn the legal presumption of paternity. Women who had children with priests or others in holy orders sometimes did so in concubinage: stable and often long-term relationships with the men concerned.

A letter by Aeneas Silvius Piccolomini (1405–64), the Italian papal diplomat and poet who fathered an illegitimate child in Scotland, and who later (in 1458) became Pope Pius II, sheds some light on the complexities of medieval attitudes to illegitimacy. His Scottish child, born in 1436, died in infancy; Aeneas went on to have another son, following an affair with a married woman called Elizabeth he met in Strasbourg in 1442.[5] The following year Aeneas wrote to his father, asking him to take the baby in and raise him while Aeneas pursued his career.[6] The future pope's letter refers to earlier correspondence from his father, who had evidently expressed disapproval. 'Father, you write that you are uncertain whether to rejoice or mourn that the Lord has given me progeny… you say I should bewail my crime – that I begot my son in sin.' Aeneas is unequivocal: 'I see the cause for joy, but do not see one for sorrow', adding that fatherhood is 'an enormous pleasure', since 'what is sweeter for a human being than to beget someone similar to himself…?' Aeneas appeals to nature, to classical heroes, to biblical precedent, to literary characters and even to personal virtue ('I am no hypocrite, wishing to seem, rather than to be, good') in justifying his actions. His attraction to Elizabeth, he says, put him in mind of Julius Caesar's attraction to Cleopatra, and of Boccaccio's tale of Zima (who, through ardour and native wit, succeeds in seducing the wife of a nobleman).[7] In acting on his attraction, he is no worse than David and Solomon, two of the mightiest kings of the Old Testament. 'This fault [lust] is ancient and entrenched, but I do not know anyone who lacks it. It is quite clear that this plague, if it is a plague to use nature's gifts – although I do not see why sexual intercourse ought to be condemned so much – is broadly compatible with nature, which does nothing wrongly.'

The urge to procreate being intrinsic to all living creatures, suggests Aeneas (after the legal commentator Teutonicus), it belongs to the realm of natural law.[8] He acknowledges that adultery is a breach of natural law and so that aspect of the affair was wrong, but then so too was King David (both a prefiguration and ancestor of Christ) wrong to have committed adultery. It is an artful piece of rhetoric, reliant on his knowledge of canon law and scholastic arguments concerning justice and equity. But its force lies in its appeal to shared human experience: sexual desire as a normal part of life, the love of

5 Izbicki and others, *Reject Aeneas*, no. 53 (in which he mentions the Scottish child who died); R. J. Mitchell, *The Laurels and the Tiara: Pope Pius II, 1458–1464* (London, 1962), 71, 91–4.

6 Izbicki and others, *Reject Aeneas*, no. 30. The quotes in this section are taken from this letter.

7 Piccolomini strove in various ways to present himself as the new Caesar. E. O'Brien, 'Arms and Letters: Julius Caesar, the Commentaries of Pope Pius II, and the Politicization of Papal Imagery', *Renaissance Quarterly* 62 (2009), 1057–97.

8 Z. von Martels, 'The Fruit of Love: Aeneas Silvius Piccolomini About his Illegitimate Child', in Z. von Martels and A. Vanderjagt, ed., *Pius II, 'El Più Expeditivo Pontefice': Selected Studies on Aeneas Silvius Piccolomini (1405–1464)* (Leiden, 2003), 240–1.

Notwithstanding St Paul's judgement that marriage existed as a concession to human weakness and was inferior to celibacy, the Church supported marriage both in principle and in practice, and this was reflected in its laws. By the end of the eleventh century, the Church had come to see marriage as something exclusively for the laity, but a vocation nonetheless, a way of life that had its own place in the divine order. In its legal judgements, the Church sought to uphold the principle of *favor maritalis*, a bias in favour of endorsing the marriage wherever it was feasible to do so, and exercised a similar bias in respect of offspring, who benefited from a presumption of legitimacy.

The Church courts

Ecclesiastical courts were organised on a diocesan basis and each was presided over by an 'official', the chief legal officer of the bishop, assisted where required by other legal officers called commissaries. In large dioceses, such as Glasgow, where the volume of business in the courts was great, a commissary general might act as a deputy to the official.[5] Exactly when the Church court system was established in Scotland is not certain, but there were diocesan officials operating in ecclesiastical courts in Aberdeen, Glasgow and St Andrews in the twelfth century, and almost every diocese in Scotland had its own official by the second half of the thirteenth century, though the absence of an appointed official did not imply that ecclesiastical jurisdiction was lacking.[6] From time to time special judges-delegate were appointed by Rome to resolve particular disputes, including those concerning legitimacy.[7] The use of judges-delegate in Scotland was known from 1125, and increased from the end of the twelfth century.[8] Between 1192 and 1472 Scotland was a 'special daughter' of the papacy, having neither a metropolitan see of its own nor, as far as the vast majority

5 G. Donaldson, *Scottish Church History* (Edinburgh, 1985), 41.

6 S. Ollivant, *The Court of the Official in Pre-Reformation Scotland*, Stair Society 34 (Edinburgh, 1982), 22–4, 43; H. L. MacQueen, 'Canon Law, Custom and Legislation: Law in the Reign of Alexander II', in R. Oram, ed., *The Reign of Alexander II, 1214–49* (Leiden, 2005), 229–30, 235. Papal bulls to Bishop Jocelyn of Glasgow (1175–99), answering his questions on points of canon law, show that the Scottish Church was closely in touch with the development of ecclesiastical law at this time. M. Morgan, 'The Organisation of the Scottish Church in the Twelfth Century', *TRHS* 29 (1947), 139 n. 2 citing *Registrum Episcopatus Glasguensis* (Bannatyne and Maitland Clubs, 1843), i, nos 58–61, 63–5, 67–8.

7 W. D. H. Sellar, 'A Historical Perspective', in M. C. Meston and others, *The Scottish Legal Tradition*, ed. S. C. Styles (Edinburgh, 1991), 40; Ollivant, *Court of the Official*, 3; L. J. Macfarlane, *William Elphinstone and the Kingdom of Scotland 1431–1514: The Struggle for Order* (Aberdeen, 1995), 54, 69.

8 H. MacQueen, 'Expectations of the Law in 12th and 13th Century Scotland', *Tijdschrift voor Rechtsgeschiedenis* 70 (2002), 281–2; P. C. Ferguson, *Medieval Papal Representatives in Scotland: Legates, Nuncios, and Judges-Delegate, 1125–1286* (Edinburgh, 1997), 29, 120–2.

of dioceses were concerned, being answerable to an English metropolitan.[9] Appeals against the decisions of Scottish spiritual courts before 1472 could be made only to the papacy.[10] This militated against the Scottish courts arriving at judgements contrary to canon law as it was disseminated by Rome. The Scottish Church was granted the right to establish its own provincial council in 1225. Surviving statutes of this body show that it was concerned to ensure marriage was conducted in accordance with canon law.[11]

Taxonomy

The canon law of the middle ages recognised two broad categories of illegitimates: natural children, born to parents who were free to intermarry but who had not done so, and spurious children, whose parents could not marry because of a legal impediment preventing matrimony between them. This division pre-dated canon law, though the terms applied to rather different legal and cultural conditions. Roman law had distinguished between children procreated with a concubine, and those fathered on certain other categories of women. Concubinage was a broadly acceptable non-marital sexual relationship, very often an enduring relationship between a high-status man and a woman whose status was too far below his to allow legal marriage between them.[12] In Roman law, offspring of concubines were natural children (*naturales*). Spurious children (*spurii*) were those born from liaisons with women who could never marry, such as slaves or prostitutes. Neither *naturales* nor *spurii* had an automatic right to inherit from their fathers, and they were not under *patria potestas*, although fathers could leave the *naturales* a proportion of their

9 Pope Celestine III's bull *Cum universi* in 1192 declared the Scottish Church answerable only to the Holy See. Galloway (Whithorn) was the exception, being ecclesiastically subject to York. Sodor and Man (the Isles) and Orkney (including Shetland) were under the jurisdiction of Trondheim, but were incorporated into the Scottish Church, along with Whithorn, when St Andrews was raised to a metropolitan see in 1472. A. Mackay, ed., with D. Ditchburn, *Atlas of Medieval Europe* (London, 1997), 110. Glasgow became a metropolitan see in 1492.

10 Macfarlane, *William Elphinstone*, 54. He points out that even after Scotland had its first metropolitan see in 1472, there was a preference for appeals to continue to be directed to Rome. The bishop of Aberdeen was the first to seek an exemption for his diocese, freeing it from the requirement to be subject to St Andrews. *Statutes of the Scottish Church 1225–1559*, ed. D. Patrick (SHS, 1907), lxxxvi. A determination of the birth status of Christina Sutherland, alleged bastard, was under appeal at Rome in 1494. *ADC*, i, 376.

11 Patrick, *Statutes*, 39, 44, 63–4, 71–3.

12 J. Evans Grubbs, *Women and the Law in the Roman Empire* (London, 2002), 150–3; Brundage, *Law, Sex, and Christian Society*, 23–5, 40–4. The severity of the sin entailed by concubinage was something that divided twelfth-century canonists. Gratian had no great objection to someone having a concubine instead of a wife, as long as this was his only sexual relationship. Gratian, C. 32 q. 2 c. 5. Concubinage was later firmly prohibited in canon law.

wealth or property if they so wished.[13] In the later Roman Empire, the term *spurii* began to be applied to those children resulting from unions which were regarded as iniquitous or disgraceful, especially incest.[14]

The principle of dividing extra-marital offspring into two groups – those born of morally reprehensible relationships and those resulting from other, still wrongful but less disreputable, liaisons – lived on in the canon law of the middle ages. Although the Church formally regarded all extra-marital sexual relationships as sinful, some were deemed more sinful than others, with concomitant effects on the status of the children procreated of them. The category of spurious children contained a number of sub-divisions.[15] 'Merely spurious' children resulted from unions that were forbidden because of a technical impediment such as age (women had to be twelve and men fourteen to marry), or any one of a number of positive laws created by the Church to regulate matrimony.[16] The breach of such rules was serious, but slightly more innocuous than the violations that resulted in children belonging to the classes of 'infamous' or 'heinous' illegitimates, who were considered to have been conceived *ex damnato coitu* (of a condemned union). These included children resulting from adultery, prostitution, incest or other violations against the natural law (law that was deemed to arise out of an innate sense of morality shared by humankind and so to be universal).[17] The birth of some offspring entailed offences against the sacraments and so breached spiritual law, as well as the positive laws of the Church and the natural law.[18] Examples of these 'sacrilegious' bastards were children resulting from the union of a godparent to a godchild, or of a Christian to a non-Christian.[19] Also sacrilegious bastards were the *filii presbyterorum*, born of a parent or parents in religious life: the offspring of nuns, monks, and those in the secular clergy.[20] Categorising illegitimates in this way enabled decisions as to which illegitimate men and

13 J. Evans Grubbs, *Law and Family in Late Antiquity: The Emperor Constantine's Marriage Legislation* (Oxford, 1999), 295–6; Brundage, *Law, Sex, and Christian Society*, 408.

14 L. Wertheimer, 'Children of Disorder: Clerical Parentage, Illegitimacy, and Reform in the Middle Ages', *Journal of the History of Sexuality* 15 (2006), 385–6.

15 J. Witte Jr, *The Sins of the Fathers: The Law and Theology of Illegitimacy Reconsidered* (Cambridge, 2009), 89–95.

16 Witte, *Sins of the Fathers*, 90–1.

17 Ibid., 92–3.

18 Ibid., 93.

19 The sexual unions of non-Christians were deemed outside the purview of the laws of the Church, and so whether they had married according to their own laws or not, their offspring required to be baptised into the Christian faith to be regarded as legitimate for matters governed by law in a Christian society. The child of a Christian and a non-Christian was not legitimate under canon law, which did not recognise such unions as valid marriages. Witte, *Sins of the Fathers*, 87–8, 93.

20 Witte, *Sins of the Fathers*, 93–4.

women should be furnished with dispensations permitting them to pursue careers in the Church.[21]

Offspring who were conceived and born after a valid marriage which had been contracted publicly were undoubtedly legitimate, but canon law also recognised as legitimate children born from a range of unions, some of which did not meet this ideal of marriage as promulgated by the Church. Children conceived before, but born after, a marriage contracted in front of witnesses were legitimate; so too were children conceived and born after a valid marriage which had been contracted clandestinely (without anyone else present).[22] Offspring resulting from an invalid, but publicly contracted, marriage in which at least one of the parties had been unaware of the impediment at the time of the wedding were also legitimate.[23] Those who were baptised as Christians, having been born of a union between non-Christians, were legitimate.[24]

The purpose of these categorisations, too, was to facilitate Church processes; in this case, to enable rulings in cases where the legitimacy of an individual was called into question. A legal dispute in which a putative heir was alleged to be illegitimate on the grounds that his or her parents' marriage was invalid could turn on whether or not both parents were aware of the impediment. If his or her parents had married clandestinely, further investigation may be warranted, since this suggested awareness of an impediment and the desire to conceal it. The classification system provided a rule of thumb, by which someone's legitimacy or otherwise could be inferred, and it flagged up where there was a need for confirmatory evidence. The intention of the Church was to endorse the legitimacy of children wherever it could do so compatibly with maintaining the rules of marriage.

The various synonyms for 'illegitimate' in canon law each had a specific legal meaning, but these meanings changed over time or according to the authority consulted. Isidore of Seville (570–636) used the Latin term *nothus* to denote the mother of the illegitimate person being of an inferior rank to the father, and this is also how Bede (673x4–735) defined it.[25] For Hostiensis (d. 1271), a *nothus* was born of adultery.[26] As is clear from the canonical categories of illegitimacy,

[21] See pp. 152 and 171–2 for a discussion of papal considerations in respect of parentage of illegitimate supplicants for Church benefices.

[22] X 4.17.2, 9.

[23] X 4.17.11.

[24] X 4.17.15.

[25] '*Nothus dicitur qui de patre nobili et matre ignobili gignitur, sicut ex concubine.*' Isidore of Seville, *Etymologiae*, IX.23, in *PL* 82, 356. He goes on to explain (at IX.24) that a *spurius* is someone born of a noble mother and low-ranking father, or where the identity of the father is uncertain. Bede's definition is set out in *In Samuelem Prophetam, id est, librum primum, Allegorica Expositio*, in J. A. Giles, ed., *The Complete Works of the Venerable Bede* (London, 1843–4), viii, 90.

[26] Hostiensis (Henricus de Segusio), *Summa Aurea* (Venice, 1570), 59 ('*De filiis presbyterorum*', 3).

'Incest' and illegitimacy

The impediment most likely to create a barrier to lawful marriage in medieval Scotland was endogamy: kinship (very widely defined) between the two parties to the intended marriage. Prior to the establishment of the Christian Church, incest had been prohibited under Roman law, and regarded as taboo. Diocletian's (C.E. 245–313) horror on discovering that the Egyptians married close relatives prompted him to restate the law on this, and describe those guilty of it as like 'cattle or wild beasts'; accusations of incest were not uncommonly a form of slander in Roman society.[39] These attitudes were later reinforced by highly influential patristic writers such as Ambrose and Augustine.[40] In early medieval Scotland kin marriage may not have been particularly unusual. Turgot (c. 1050–1115) gave an account of attempts by Margaret of Scotland (d. 1093) to bring religious practices of the Scots into line with those of the Church elsewhere. According to this, her reforms of the early 1070s included banning marriage between men and their stepmothers, and between men and their brothers' widows, 'both of which customs had hitherto prevailed in the country'.[41] Turgot tells us that 'she showed how utterly abominable, and to be shunned by the faithful as death itself' such marriage practices were.[42] The unusually strong language employed by Turgot here (none of the other Scottish infringements excites anything like the same degree of repulsion) gives a hint of the contemporary Church's attitude to incest, which informed the stringent laws of forbidden degrees.[43] Medieval Irish culture similarly attracted the

39 Evans Grubbs, *Women and the Law*, 140–3; S. Treggiari, *Roman Marriage* (Oxford, 1991), 105, 294, 315–16, 480.

40 *The Letters of St Ambrose, Bishop of Milan* (Devonport Society, 1881), no. 60; Augustine, *Concerning the City of God against the Pagans*, transl. H. Bettenson with an introduction by D. Knowles (Harmondsworth, 1972), 623–6; Evans Grubbs, *Women and the Law*, 123, 136–43, 161–6; E. Archibald, *Incest and the Medieval Imagination* (Oxford, 2001), 24–6.

41 Turgot, 'Life of Margaret', in *Ancient Lives of the Scottish Saints*, transl. W. M. Metcalfe (Paisley, 1895), 309. This forms part of a wider imputation of promiscuity associated with the 'barbaric nature' of the Scots according to some contemporary stereotypes. In the twelfth century, Ailred of Rievaulx made the somewhat extravagant claim that the people of Galloway were so inclined to put aside their spouses in pursuit of new amorous adventures that women who changed their husbands only every month were considered chaste. *The Life of Ailred of Rievaulx by Walter Daniels*, ed. F. M. Powicke (London, 1950), 45. Anglo-Saxon kings sometimes married their fathers' widows, a practice that also existed in Denmark and other parts of Europe. W. A. Chaney, *The Cult of Kingship in Anglo-Saxon England* (Manchester, 1970), 25–8.

42 Turgot, 'Life of Margaret', 309.

43 Brundage, *Law, Sex, and Christian Society*, 191–2. See also Archibald, *Incest and the Medieval Imagination*; E. Archibald, '"The appalling dangers of family life": Incest in Medieval Literature', in C. J. Itnyre, ed., *Medieval Family Roles: a Book of Essays* (New York, 2000), 157–71; M. Gelting, 'Marriage, Peace and the Canonical Incest Prohibitions: Making Sense of an Absurdity?', in M. Korpiola, ed., *Nordic Perspectives on Medieval Canon Law* (Saarijärvi, 1999), 93–124; M. Mitterauer, 'Christianity and Endogamy', *Continuity and Change* 6 (1991), 295–333.

A letter by Aeneas Silvius Piccolomini (1405–64), the Italian papal diplomat and poet who fathered an illegitimate child in Scotland, and who later (in 1458) became Pope Pius II, sheds some light on the complexities of medieval attitudes to illegitimacy. His Scottish child, born in 1436, died in infancy; Aeneas went on to have another son, following an affair with a married woman called Elizabeth he met in Strasbourg in 1442.[5] The following year Aeneas wrote to his father, asking him to take the baby in and raise him while Aeneas pursued his career.[6] The future pope's letter refers to earlier correspondence from his father, who had evidently expressed disapproval. 'Father, you write that you are uncertain whether to rejoice or mourn that the Lord has given me progeny… you say I should bewail my crime – that I begot my son in sin.' Aeneas is unequivocal: 'I see the cause for joy, but do not see one for sorrow', adding that fatherhood is 'an enormous pleasure', since 'what is sweeter for a human being than to beget someone similar to himself…?' Aeneas appeals to nature, to classical heroes, to biblical precedent, to literary characters and even to personal virtue ('I am no hypocrite, wishing to seem, rather than to be, good') in justifying his actions. His attraction to Elizabeth, he says, put him in mind of Julius Caesar's attraction to Cleopatra, and of Boccaccio's tale of Zima (who, through ardour and native wit, succeeds in seducing the wife of a nobleman).[7] In acting on his attraction, he is no worse than David and Solomon, two of the mightiest kings of the Old Testament. 'This fault [lust] is ancient and entrenched, but I do not know anyone who lacks it. It is quite clear that this plague, if it is a plague to use nature's gifts – although I do not see why sexual intercourse ought to be condemned so much – is broadly compatible with nature, which does nothing wrongly.'

The urge to procreate being intrinsic to all living creatures, suggests Aeneas (after the legal commentator Teutonicus), it belongs to the realm of natural law.[8] He acknowledges that adultery is a breach of natural law and so that aspect of the affair was wrong, but then so too was King David (both a prefiguration and ancestor of Christ) wrong to have committed adultery. It is an artful piece of rhetoric, reliant on his knowledge of canon law and scholastic arguments concerning justice and equity. But its force lies in its appeal to shared human experience: sexual desire as a normal part of life, the love of

5 Izbicki and others, *Reject Aeneas*, no. 53 (in which he mentions the Scottish child who died); R. J. Mitchell, *The Laurels and the Tiara: Pope Pius II, 1458–1464* (London, 1962), 71, 91–4.

6 Izbicki and others, *Reject Aeneas*, no. 30. The quotes in this section are taken from this letter.

7 Piccolomini strove in various ways to present himself as the new Caesar. E. O'Brien, 'Arms and Letters: Julius Caesar, the Commentaries of Pope Pius II, and the Politicization of Papal Imagery', *Renaissance Quarterly* 62 (2009), 1057–97.

8 Z. von Martels, 'The Fruit of Love: Aeneas Silvius Piccolomini About his Illegitimate Child', in Z. von Martels and A. Vanderjagt, ed., *Pius II, 'El Più Expeditivo Pontefice': Selected Studies on Aeneas Silvius Piccolomini (1405–1464)* (Leiden, 2003), 240–1.

parents for their children, the satisfaction of knowing that some part of us lives on after our death. Aeneas's letter is a statement that laws may seek to regulate this, and determine the circumstances in which children should be born, but its efforts to do so could never be wholly successful when the biological and psychological imperatives behind the creation of children were so powerful.

The very power of these instincts and feelings required the establishment of laws to discourage people acting on them when doing so might harm the way society was, or should be, organised. The laws themselves acknowledged this. A man who had heritage lands (that is, lands he inherited, as opposed to those he acquired in his own lifetime) to pass on to his heir, expected to be his eldest surviving son, could give only a small portion of them away to a younger son without the heir's consent. This protection was needed, we are told, because otherwise, 'it would be a common occurrence for elder sons to be disinherited by reason of the greater affection fathers usually feel for their younger sons'.[9] No part of heritage lands may be given to an illegitimate son, because permitting this could result in an illegitimate son being in a better position than a younger son born in marriage, 'and this is not the law'.[10] Unstated, but clearly implied, is the understanding that fathers love their illegitimate children as much as their legitimate ones. Heritage lands should pass down through a family line via the heir in each generation: this is how society ought to work; but to ensure that it did, heirs had to be given protections in law from the anticipated actions of fathers who might love their non-heirs, including bastard offspring, as much as their eldest legitimate sons.

As far as illegitimate offspring were concerned, canon law and secular law alike sought to uphold a set of ethics thought essential to a virtuous and peaceful society, while making a few, strictly limited, concessions to the fact that not everyone found themselves able or willing to meet the standards of ideal conduct the laws endeavoured to promote. The two legal systems operated alongside each other in the Scottish middle ages, intersecting nowhere more conspicuously than in relation to illegitimacy. How bastardy was conceptualised in law, and how these ideas played out in legal contexts, underpinned much of its political and social significance. This book begins, therefore, by considering illegitimacy as a legal phenomenon in medieval Scotland.

9 *RM*, ii, ch. 19.

10 Ibid. *Regiam Majestatem* directly contradicts its English counterpart *Glanvill* on this point. *Glanvill* says, 'But, it may be asked, whether a man, having a Son and Heir, can give any part of his Inheritance to his illegitimate son? If he can, it follows, that the condition of the illegitimate son would, in this respect, be preferable to that of the younger son born in Wedlock; and yet the Law is so.' Hudson suggests that this may have been a response to the particular circumstances of the English royal family when *Glanvill* was written: either Henry II's grant of Appleby to his illegitimate son William Longespée or, perhaps, in relation to the future King John. J. Hudson, 'Emotions in the Early Common Law (*c.* 1166–1215)', *The Journal of Legal History* 38 (2017), 133. John was the father of at least seven illegitimate children.

1

Church law and Scottish families

For [quhay-sa] falt has in his natiuitie,
In his conditioun fa[l]tles sal nocht be[1]

During the twelfth century the Church succeeded in claiming jurisdiction over marriage and established a body of canon law, further refined in the thirteenth century, setting out rules for what constituted valid marriage.[2] Determination of legitimacy was also the province of the Church, since it depended on determination of marital status.[3] The law of the Church came to be collected in the *Corpus Iuris Canonici* (c. 1586). Its constituent elements include the work known as Gratian's *Decretum* (c. 1140) which set out important principles concerning lawful marriage and discussed various kinds of illegal relationship, but had relatively little to say about illegitimacy; the *Liber Extra* (1234), which examined both marriage and illegitimacy in more detail, especially the circumstances in which offspring were and were not legitimate; and the *Liber Sextus* (1298), a compilation of decretals produced under the aegis of Pope Boniface VIII intended to supplement the *Liber Extra*.[4]

1 *The Buik of King Alexander the Conquerour by Gilbert Hay*, ed. J. Cartwright, STS 4th series, 16, 18 (Edinburgh, 1986 and Aberdeen, 1990) (hereafter *King Alexander*), lines 10126–7. Hay may not have been the author.

2 J. A. Brundage, *Law, Sex, and Christian Society in Medieval Europe* (Chicago, IL, 1990), 183–4, 225–8, 414–16.

3 Two decretals by Pope Alexander III (1159–81) denied the competency of secular tribunals to determine legitimacy. X 4.17.5, 7.

4 These three works form a significant proportion of the *Corpus Iuris Canonici* but do not comprise the whole. For the authorship and development of the *Decretum*, see A. Winroth, *The Making of Gratian's Decretum* (Cambridge, 2000). The *Decretum* notes that offspring of clergy and of certain types of relationship are illegitimate and stained by their parents' sin (though they should not be blamed for this), but aside from occasionally commenting on implications for the offspring's rights in respect of ordination, he does not explore illegitimacy in any detail. For example: D. 26 c.3; D. 56; C. 28 q. 2 d. a. c. 1. The contents of Book Four of the *Liber Extra* concern marriage and children, with illegitimacy discussed at X 4.17, '*Qui filii sint legitimi*'. Illegitimate clergy and the offspring of priests are treated at X 1.11 and X 1.17. The *Liber Sextus* concerns itself with illegitimacy in relation to clerical offices at VI 1.11. The foregoing is not an exhaustive list of *Corpus Iuris Canonici* material relating to marriage and illegitimate offspring.

Notwithstanding St Paul's judgement that marriage existed as a concession to human weakness and was inferior to celibacy, the Church supported marriage both in principle and in practice, and this was reflected in its laws. By the end of the eleventh century, the Church had come to see marriage as something exclusively for the laity, but a vocation nonetheless, a way of life that had its own place in the divine order. In its legal judgements, the Church sought to uphold the principle of *favor maritalis*, a bias in favour of endorsing the marriage wherever it was feasible to do so, and exercised a similar bias in respect of offspring, who benefited from a presumption of legitimacy.

The Church courts

Ecclesiastical courts were organised on a diocesan basis and each was presided over by an 'official', the chief legal officer of the bishop, assisted where required by other legal officers called commissaries. In large dioceses, such as Glasgow, where the volume of business in the courts was great, a commissary general might act as a deputy to the official.[5] Exactly when the Church court system was established in Scotland is not certain, but there were diocesan officials operating in ecclesiastical courts in Aberdeen, Glasgow and St Andrews in the twelfth century, and almost every diocese in Scotland had its own official by the second half of the thirteenth century, though the absence of an appointed official did not imply that ecclesiastical jurisdiction was lacking.[6] From time to time special judges-delegate were appointed by Rome to resolve particular disputes, including those concerning legitimacy.[7] The use of judges-delegate in Scotland was known from 1125, and increased from the end of the twelfth century.[8] Between 1192 and 1472 Scotland was a 'special daughter' of the papacy, having neither a metropolitan see of its own nor, as far as the vast majority

5 G. Donaldson, *Scottish Church History* (Edinburgh, 1985), 41.

6 S. Ollivant, *The Court of the Official in Pre-Reformation Scotland*, Stair Society 34 (Edinburgh, 1982), 22–4, 43; H. L. MacQueen, 'Canon Law, Custom and Legislation: Law in the Reign of Alexander II', in R. Oram, ed., *The Reign of Alexander II, 1214–49* (Leiden, 2005), 229–30, 235. Papal bulls to Bishop Jocelyn of Glasgow (1175–99), answering his questions on points of canon law, show that the Scottish Church was closely in touch with the development of ecclesiastical law at this time. M. Morgan, 'The Organisation of the Scottish Church in the Twelfth Century', *TRHS* 29 (1947), 139 n. 2 citing *Registrum Episcopatus Glasguensis* (Bannatyne and Maitland Clubs, 1843), i, nos 58–61, 63–5, 67–8.

7 W. D. H. Sellar, 'A Historical Perspective', in M. C. Meston and others, *The Scottish Legal Tradition*, ed. S. C. Styles (Edinburgh, 1991), 40; Ollivant, *Court of the Official*, 3; L. J. Macfarlane, *William Elphinstone and the Kingdom of Scotland 1431–1514: The Struggle for Order* (Aberdeen, 1995), 54, 69.

8 H. MacQueen, 'Expectations of the Law in 12th and 13th Century Scotland', *Tijdschrift voor Rechtsgeschiedenis* 70 (2002), 281–2; P. C. Ferguson, *Medieval Papal Representatives in Scotland: Legates, Nuncios, and Judges-Delegate, 1125–1286* (Edinburgh, 1997), 29, 120–2.

of dioceses were concerned, being answerable to an English metropolitan.[9] Appeals against the decisions of Scottish spiritual courts before 1472 could be made only to the papacy.[10] This militated against the Scottish courts arriving at judgements contrary to canon law as it was disseminated by Rome. The Scottish Church was granted the right to establish its own provincial council in 1225. Surviving statutes of this body show that it was concerned to ensure marriage was conducted in accordance with canon law.[11]

Taxonomy

The canon law of the middle ages recognised two broad categories of illegitimates: natural children, born to parents who were free to intermarry but who had not done so, and spurious children, whose parents could not marry because of a legal impediment preventing matrimony between them. This division pre-dated canon law, though the terms applied to rather different legal and cultural conditions. Roman law had distinguished between children procreated with a concubine, and those fathered on certain other categories of women. Concubinage was a broadly acceptable non-marital sexual relationship, very often an enduring relationship between a high-status man and a woman whose status was too far below his to allow legal marriage between them.[12] In Roman law, offspring of concubines were natural children (*naturales*). Spurious children (*spurii*) were those born from liaisons with women who could never marry, such as slaves or prostitutes. Neither *naturales* nor *spurii* had an automatic right to inherit from their fathers, and they were not under *patria potestas*, although fathers could leave the *naturales* a proportion of their

9 Pope Celestine III's bull *Cum universi* in 1192 declared the Scottish Church answerable only to the Holy See. Galloway (Whithorn) was the exception, being ecclesiastically subject to York. Sodor and Man (the Isles) and Orkney (including Shetland) were under the jurisdiction of Trondheim, but were incorporated into the Scottish Church, along with Whithorn, when St Andrews was raised to a metropolitan see in 1472. A. Mackay, ed., with D. Ditchburn, *Atlas of Medieval Europe* (London, 1997), 110. Glasgow became a metropolitan see in 1492.

10 Macfarlane, *William Elphinstone*, 54. He points out that even after Scotland had its first metropolitan see in 1472, there was a preference for appeals to continue to be directed to Rome. The bishop of Aberdeen was the first to seek an exemption for his diocese, freeing it from the requirement to be subject to St Andrews. *Statutes of the Scottish Church 1225–1559*, ed. D. Patrick (SHS, 1907), lxxxvi. A determination of the birth status of Christina Sutherland, alleged bastard, was under appeal at Rome in 1494. *ADC*, i, 376.

11 Patrick, *Statutes*, 39, 44, 63–4, 71–3.

12 J. Evans Grubbs, *Women and the Law in the Roman Empire* (London, 2002), 150–3; Brundage, *Law, Sex, and Christian Society*, 23–5, 40–4. The severity of the sin entailed by concubinage was something that divided twelfth-century canonists. Gratian had no great objection to someone having a concubine instead of a wife, as long as this was his only sexual relationship. Gratian, C. 32 q. 2 c. 5. Concubinage was later firmly prohibited in canon law.

wealth or property if they so wished.[13] In the later Roman Empire, the term *spurii* began to be applied to those children resulting from unions which were regarded as iniquitous or disgraceful, especially incest.[14]

The principle of dividing extra-marital offspring into two groups – those born of morally reprehensible relationships and those resulting from other, still wrongful but less disreputable, liaisons – lived on in the canon law of the middle ages. Although the Church formally regarded all extra-marital sexual relationships as sinful, some were deemed more sinful than others, with concomitant effects on the status of the children procreated of them. The category of spurious children contained a number of sub-divisions.[15] 'Merely spurious' children resulted from unions that were forbidden because of a technical impediment such as age (women had to be twelve and men fourteen to marry), or any one of a number of positive laws created by the Church to regulate matrimony.[16] The breach of such rules was serious, but slightly more innocuous than the violations that resulted in children belonging to the classes of 'infamous' or 'heinous' illegitimates, who were considered to have been conceived *ex damnato coitu* (of a condemned union). These included children resulting from adultery, prostitution, incest or other violations against the natural law (law that was deemed to arise out of an innate sense of morality shared by humankind and so to be universal).[17] The birth of some offspring entailed offences against the sacraments and so breached spiritual law, as well as the positive laws of the Church and the natural law.[18] Examples of these 'sacrilegious' bastards were children resulting from the union of a godparent to a godchild, or of a Christian to a non-Christian.[19] Also sacrilegious bastards were the *filii presbyterorum*, born of a parent or parents in religious life: the offspring of nuns, monks, and those in the secular clergy.[20] Categorising illegitimates in this way enabled decisions as to which illegitimate men and

13 J. Evans Grubbs, *Law and Family in Late Antiquity: The Emperor Constantine's Marriage Legislation* (Oxford, 1999), 295–6; Brundage, *Law, Sex, and Christian Society*, 408.

14 L. Wertheimer, 'Children of Disorder: Clerical Parentage, Illegitimacy, and Reform in the Middle Ages', *Journal of the History of Sexuality* 15 (2006), 385–6.

15 J. Witte Jr, *The Sins of the Fathers: The Law and Theology of Illegitimacy Reconsidered* (Cambridge, 2009), 89–95.

16 Witte, *Sins of the Fathers*, 90–1.

17 Ibid., 92–3.

18 Ibid., 93.

19 The sexual unions of non-Christians were deemed outside the purview of the laws of the Church, and so whether they had married according to their own laws or not, their offspring required to be baptised into the Christian faith to be regarded as legitimate for matters governed by law in a Christian society. The child of a Christian and a non-Christian was not legitimate under canon law, which did not recognise such unions as valid marriages. Witte, *Sins of the Fathers*, 87–8, 93.

20 Witte, *Sins of the Fathers*, 93–4.

women should be furnished with dispensations permitting them to pursue careers in the Church.[21]

Offspring who were conceived and born after a valid marriage which had been contracted publicly were undoubtedly legitimate, but canon law also recognised as legitimate children born from a range of unions, some of which did not meet this ideal of marriage as promulgated by the Church. Children conceived before, but born after, a marriage contracted in front of witnesses were legitimate; so too were children conceived and born after a valid marriage which had been contracted clandestinely (without anyone else present).[22] Offspring resulting from an invalid, but publicly contracted, marriage in which at least one of the parties had been unaware of the impediment at the time of the wedding were also legitimate.[23] Those who were baptised as Christians, having been born of a union between non-Christians, were legitimate.[24]

The purpose of these categorisations, too, was to facilitate Church processes; in this case, to enable rulings in cases where the legitimacy of an individual was called into question. A legal dispute in which a putative heir was alleged to be illegitimate on the grounds that his or her parents' marriage was invalid could turn on whether or not both parents were aware of the impediment. If his or her parents had married clandestinely, further investigation may be warranted, since this suggested awareness of an impediment and the desire to conceal it. The classification system provided a rule of thumb, by which someone's legitimacy or otherwise could be inferred, and it flagged up where there was a need for confirmatory evidence. The intention of the Church was to endorse the legitimacy of children wherever it could do so compatibly with maintaining the rules of marriage.

The various synonyms for 'illegitimate' in canon law each had a specific legal meaning, but these meanings changed over time or according to the authority consulted. Isidore of Seville (570–636) used the Latin term *nothus* to denote the mother of the illegitimate person being of an inferior rank to the father, and this is also how Bede (673x4–735) defined it.[25] For Hostiensis (d. 1271), a *nothus* was born of adultery.[26] As is clear from the canonical categories of illegitimacy,

21 See pp. 152 and 171–2 for a discussion of papal considerations in respect of parentage of illegitimate supplicants for Church benefices.

22 X 4.17.2, 9.

23 X 4.17.11.

24 X 4.17.15.

25 '*Nothus dicitur qui de patre nobili et matre ignobili gignitur, sicut ex concubine*.' Isidore of Seville, *Etymologiae*, IX.23, in *PL* 82, 356. He goes on to explain (at IX.24) that a *spurius* is someone born of a noble mother and low-ranking father, or where the identity of the father is uncertain. Bede's definition is set out in *In Samuelem Prophetam, id est, librum primum, Allegorica Expositio*, in J. A. Giles, ed., *The Complete Works of the Venerable Bede* (London, 1843–4), viii, 90.

26 Hostiensis (Henricus de Segusio), *Summa Aurea* (Venice, 1570), 59 ('*De filiis presbyterorum*', 3).

'Incest' and illegitimacy

The impediment most likely to create a barrier to lawful marriage in medieval Scotland was endogamy: kinship (very widely defined) between the two parties to the intended marriage. Prior to the establishment of the Christian Church, incest had been prohibited under Roman law, and regarded as taboo. Diocletian's (C.E. 245–313) horror on discovering that the Egyptians married close relatives prompted him to restate the law on this, and describe those guilty of it as like 'cattle or wild beasts'; accusations of incest were not uncommonly a form of slander in Roman society.[39] These attitudes were later reinforced by highly influential patristic writers such as Ambrose and Augustine.[40] In early medieval Scotland kin marriage may not have been particularly unusual. Turgot (c. 1050–1115) gave an account of attempts by Margaret of Scotland (d. 1093) to bring religious practices of the Scots into line with those of the Church elsewhere. According to this, her reforms of the early 1070s included banning marriage between men and their stepmothers, and between men and their brothers' widows, 'both of which customs had hitherto prevailed in the country'.[41] Turgot tells us that 'she showed how utterly abominable, and to be shunned by the faithful as death itself' such marriage practices were.[42] The unusually strong language employed by Turgot here (none of the other Scottish infringements excites anything like the same degree of repulsion) gives a hint of the contemporary Church's attitude to incest, which informed the stringent laws of forbidden degrees.[43] Medieval Irish culture similarly attracted the

39 Evans Grubbs, *Women and the Law*, 140–3; S. Treggiari, *Roman Marriage* (Oxford, 1991), 105, 294, 315–16, 480.

40 *The Letters of St Ambrose, Bishop of Milan* (Devonport Society, 1881), no. 60; Augustine, *Concerning the City of God against the Pagans*, transl. H. Bettenson with an introduction by D. Knowles (Harmondsworth, 1972), 623–6; Evans Grubbs, *Women and the Law*, 123, 136–43, 161–6; E. Archibald, *Incest and the Medieval Imagination* (Oxford, 2001), 24–6.

41 Turgot, 'Life of Margaret', in *Ancient Lives of the Scottish Saints*, transl. W. M. Metcalfe (Paisley, 1895), 309. This forms part of a wider imputation of promiscuity associated with the 'barbaric nature' of the Scots according to some contemporary stereotypes. In the twelfth century, Ailred of Rievaulx made the somewhat extravagant claim that the people of Galloway were so inclined to put aside their spouses in pursuit of new amorous adventures that women who changed their husbands only every month were considered chaste. *The Life of Ailred of Rievaulx by Walter Daniels*, ed. F. M. Powicke (London, 1950), 45. Anglo-Saxon kings sometimes married their fathers' widows, a practice that also existed in Denmark and other parts of Europe. W. A. Chaney, *The Cult of Kingship in Anglo-Saxon England* (Manchester, 1970), 25–8.

42 Turgot, 'Life of Margaret', 309.

43 Brundage, *Law, Sex, and Christian Society*, 191–2. See also Archibald, *Incest and the Medieval Imagination*; E. Archibald, '"The appalling dangers of family life": Incest in Medieval Literature', in C. J. Itnyre, ed., *Medieval Family Roles: a Book of Essays* (New York, 2000), 157–71; M. Gelting, 'Marriage, Peace and the Canonical Incest Prohibitions: Making Sense of an Absurdity?', in M. Korpiola, ed., *Nordic Perspectives on Medieval Canon Law* (Saarijärvi, 1999), 93–124; M. Mitterauer, 'Christianity and Endogamy', *Continuity and Change* 6 (1991), 295–333.

women should be furnished with dispensations permitting them to pursue careers in the Church.[21]

Offspring who were conceived and born after a valid marriage which had been contracted publicly were undoubtedly legitimate, but canon law also recognised as legitimate children born from a range of unions, some of which did not meet this ideal of marriage as promulgated by the Church. Children conceived before, but born after, a marriage contracted in front of witnesses were legitimate; so too were children conceived and born after a valid marriage which had been contracted clandestinely (without anyone else present).[22] Offspring resulting from an invalid, but publicly contracted, marriage in which at least one of the parties had been unaware of the impediment at the time of the wedding were also legitimate.[23] Those who were baptised as Christians, having been born of a union between non-Christians, were legitimate.[24]

The purpose of these categorisations, too, was to facilitate Church processes; in this case, to enable rulings in cases where the legitimacy of an individual was called into question. A legal dispute in which a putative heir was alleged to be illegitimate on the grounds that his or her parents' marriage was invalid could turn on whether or not both parents were aware of the impediment. If his or her parents had married clandestinely, further investigation may be warranted, since this suggested awareness of an impediment and the desire to conceal it. The classification system provided a rule of thumb, by which someone's legitimacy or otherwise could be inferred, and it flagged up where there was a need for confirmatory evidence. The intention of the Church was to endorse the legitimacy of children wherever it could do so compatibly with maintaining the rules of marriage.

The various synonyms for 'illegitimate' in canon law each had a specific legal meaning, but these meanings changed over time or according to the authority consulted. Isidore of Seville (570–636) used the Latin term *nothus* to denote the mother of the illegitimate person being of an inferior rank to the father, and this is also how Bede (673x4–735) defined it.[25] For Hostiensis (d. 1271), a *nothus* was born of adultery.[26] As is clear from the canonical categories of illegitimacy,

21 See pp. 152 and 171–2 for a discussion of papal considerations in respect of parentage of illegitimate supplicants for Church benefices.

22 X 4.17.2, 9.

23 X 4.17.11.

24 X 4.17.15.

25 '*Nothus dicitur qui de patre nobili et matre ignobili gignitur, sicut ex concubine*.' Isidore of Seville, *Etymologiae*, IX.23, in *PL* 82, 356. He goes on to explain (at IX.24) that a *spurius* is someone born of a noble mother and low-ranking father, or where the identity of the father is uncertain. Bede's definition is set out in *In Samuelem Prophetam, id est, librum primum, Allegorica Expositio*, in J. A. Giles, ed., *The Complete Works of the Venerable Bede* (London, 1843–4), viii, 90.

26 Hostiensis (Henricus de Segusio), *Summa Aurea* (Venice, 1570), 59 ('*De filiis presbyterorum*', 3).

a 'natural' child was not the same as a 'spurious' one, but the term 'natural' son or daughter was very commonly used for illegitimate offspring without regard for whether they were natural or spurious according to canon law. The term 'natural and legitimate (or 'lawful') son' is also occasionally encountered in our sources, and so 'natural' could also denote a child of the person's own body, as opposed to a stepchild, foster-child or godchild. The addition of 'and legitimate' or 'lawful' in the phrase is significant, the obvious interpretation being that it would not have been necessary unless the writer was aware that 'natural' usually meant 'not legitimate'. John, lord Carlyle (d. 1501) composed a will in which he named among his executors James, 'his son natural and lawful' and Robert, 'his son natural'.[27] Robert was illegitimate, while James was a son of Carlyle's marriage.[28] Similarly, the term 'carnal' applied to a son or daughter could mean illegitimate, though this was not invariably the case. In his *Lectures*, the academic theologian William Hay (d. 1542) defined a carnal son as being one born of his father's body, and so a carnal child may be either legitimate or illegitimate.[29] This is borne out in our sources. Robert Lawder, 'carnal son' of Gilbert Lawder, was illegitimate: following his death, Robert's lands escheated to the king by reason of bastardy.[30] A charter of James IV refers to the certainly illegitimate James, earl of Moray, as his 'carnal son', and Robert, second lord Lyle, describes his illegitimate son John as his 'carnal son' in a charter granting him lands.[31] But Colin MacAlexander describes his legitimate son, Gilbert MacAlexander, as his 'carnal son' (*'dilecto suo et carnali necnon apparenti heredi')*; William Gordon was a 'carnal son' procreated between his father and his father's spouse; and John Stewart of Balvany, the legitimate son of Joan Beaufort, widow of James I, with her second husband, Sir James Stewart, is given as 'carnal brother' of James II.[32] Like 'natural', 'carnal' is occasionally paired with 'and legitimate', but where 'carnal' appears without further elaboration, it is often difficult to know what was intended.[33] In commonplace Scottish legal parlance, 'bastard' was used for anyone who was illegitimate. A legal 'action of bastardy' (or 'bastardry/bastardrie') against

27 *Hist. MSS. Comm., Fifteenth Report*, App. Pt. viii (1897), no. 97.

28 *SP*, ii, 386.

29 William Hay, *Lectures on Marriage*, transl. J. C. Barry (Edinburgh, 1967), 235. Hay was sub-principal of the University of Aberdeen under Hector Boece (d. 1536).

30 *RMS*, ii, no. 2596.

31 Ibid., ii, nos 3639, 2061.

32 Ibid., ii, nos 371, 2551, 1503; see also nos 2267, 1465.

33 After the fourth duke of Roxburgh died in 1805, inheritance of the title and estates of the dukedom was disputed by five rivals. One of the early arguments in a lengthy case was that an ancestor of one of the claimants had been styled *carnalis* and so, it was argued, was illegitimate. J. Bain, 'Notes on a Dispensation for the Marriage of Johanna Beaufort with the Black Knight of Lorn', *PSAS* 16 (1881–2), 170. In the end the case was settled on other grounds. The arguments and appeals are found in *Reports of Cases Decided in the House of Lords, Upon Appeal from Scotland, from 1726 to 1822* (Edinburgh, 1849–56), v, 320–482.

someone, or an escheat of lands to the crown 'by reason of bastardy' was simply an acknowledgement that the individual concerned was illegitimate and so was unable to have heirs other than his or her own legitimate children.[34]

As this suggests, the distinctions may have been important to lawyers but the various synonyms for 'illegitimate' were used interchangeably in ordinary life. Walter Bower in *Scotichronicon*, for example, describes the same person, Thomas of Galloway, as *filius naturalis*, *filius nothus* and *bastardus filius*.[35] That each had a separate (and possibly incompatible) definition was not important: he and his audiences knew that those terms meant illegitimate. A charter of 1426 refers to a John Carruthers as being 'of bastard and illegitimate birth', suggesting either that the writer understood the terms were not strictly synonymous and the distinction was relevant to the context of the charter, or merely that he wanted to place a special emphasis on Carruthers's illegitimacy.[36]

Making and unmaking bastards

A person was illegitimate if born of a union deemed by the Church to be something other than lawful matrimony. The Church's rules for what constituted a legally valid marriage were such that it was possible to 'marry' – make vows according to the required form and live together afterwards – and yet not be lawfully married, because of a legal impediment to the union. Some impediments were diriment, making a valid marriage impossible. Among the diriment impediments were 'non-age' (being below the legal age for marriage), being in holy orders, and being married to someone else. It was possible, if exceptional, for diriment impediments to be set aside by means of papal mandate. Popes might do so if it furthered some political aim with a moral dimension, such as bringing about peace, or preventing war.[37] Other impediments were not diriment but impedient, and could be rectified by means of a papal dispensation to marry (if the couple sought a dispensation before going through with the wedding) or to remain in the union (if the impediment had come to light only after the marriage had been contracted): in either case, the impediment was understood to be nullified and the union lawful.[38] Marriage dispensations routinely included a statement that the children resulting from it were legitimate.

34 For the terms 'bastard *eigné*' and '*mulier puisné*', see pp. 32–3 and 36.

35 *Chron. Bower*, v, 147, 151. Bower may well have known the technical distinctions but had stylistic or other reasons for using three different terms when discussing the illegitimate in question.

36 *RMS*, ii, no. 85.

37 O. F. Robinson, 'Canon Law and Marriage', *JR* 29 (1984), 33. An example is the dispensation granted in 1307 to allow the marriage of Donnchad (IV), earl of Fife, to the nine-year-old Mary de Monthermer, a granddaughter of Edward I (via his daughter Joan of Acre and her husband Ralph de Monthermer). Theiner, *Vet. Mon.*, no. 383.

38 Brundage, *Law, Sex, and Christian Society*, 289, 355–6.

'Incest' and illegitimacy

The impediment most likely to create a barrier to lawful marriage in medieval Scotland was endogamy: kinship (very widely defined) between the two parties to the intended marriage. Prior to the establishment of the Christian Church, incest had been prohibited under Roman law, and regarded as taboo. Diocletian's (C.E. 245–313) horror on discovering that the Egyptians married close relatives prompted him to restate the law on this, and describe those guilty of it as like 'cattle or wild beasts'; accusations of incest were not uncommonly a form of slander in Roman society.[39] These attitudes were later reinforced by highly influential patristic writers such as Ambrose and Augustine.[40] In early medieval Scotland kin marriage may not have been particularly unusual. Turgot (c. 1050–1115) gave an account of attempts by Margaret of Scotland (d. 1093) to bring religious practices of the Scots into line with those of the Church elsewhere. According to this, her reforms of the early 1070s included banning marriage between men and their stepmothers, and between men and their brothers' widows, 'both of which customs had hitherto prevailed in the country'.[41] Turgot tells us that 'she showed how utterly abominable, and to be shunned by the faithful as death itself' such marriage practices were.[42] The unusually strong language employed by Turgot here (none of the other Scottish infringements excites anything like the same degree of repulsion) gives a hint of the contemporary Church's attitude to incest, which informed the stringent laws of forbidden degrees.[43] Medieval Irish culture similarly attracted the

39 Evans Grubbs, *Women and the Law*, 140–3; S. Treggiari, *Roman Marriage* (Oxford, 1991), 105, 294, 315–16, 480.

40 *The Letters of St Ambrose, Bishop of Milan* (Devonport Society, 1881), no. 60; Augustine, *Concerning the City of God against the Pagans*, transl. H. Bettenson with an introduction by D. Knowles (Harmondsworth, 1972), 623–6; Evans Grubbs, *Women and the Law*, 123, 136–43, 161–6; E. Archibald, *Incest and the Medieval Imagination* (Oxford, 2001), 24–6.

41 Turgot, 'Life of Margaret', in *Ancient Lives of the Scottish Saints*, transl. W. M. Metcalfe (Paisley, 1895), 309. This forms part of a wider imputation of promiscuity associated with the 'barbaric nature' of the Scots according to some contemporary stereotypes. In the twelfth century, Ailred of Rievaulx made the somewhat extravagant claim that the people of Galloway were so inclined to put aside their spouses in pursuit of new amorous adventures that women who changed their husbands only every month were considered chaste. *The Life of Ailred of Rievaulx by Walter Daniels*, ed. F. M. Powicke (London, 1950), 45. Anglo-Saxon kings sometimes married their fathers' widows, a practice that also existed in Denmark and other parts of Europe. W. A. Chaney, *The Cult of Kingship in Anglo-Saxon England* (Manchester, 1970), 25–8.

42 Turgot, 'Life of Margaret', 309.

43 Brundage, *Law, Sex, and Christian Society*, 191–2. See also Archibald, *Incest and the Medieval Imagination*; E. Archibald, '"The appalling dangers of family life": Incest in Medieval Literature', in C. J. Itnyre, ed., *Medieval Family Roles: a Book of Essays* (New York, 2000), 157–71; M. Gelting, 'Marriage, Peace and the Canonical Incest Prohibitions: Making Sense of an Absurdity?', in M. Korpiola, ed., *Nordic Perspectives on Medieval Canon Law* (Saarijärvi, 1999), 93–124; M. Mitterauer, 'Christianity and Endogamy', *Continuity and Change* 6 (1991), 295–333.

opprobrium of eleventh- and twelfth-century Churchmen in response to kin marriage practices.[44]

Endogamy was problematic because of how the canon law defined who was and was not related to each other. A relationship prohibiting marriage was created not only by having a common ancestor (consanguinity), but also by an earlier marriage or sexual relationship (affinity), which rendered other people in the former lover's family off-limits to the intended spouse. Additionally, marriage-prohibiting spiritual kinships were established by godparenthood or standing as sponsor to someone at confirmation.[45] Betrothal that did not lead on to marriage also created a set of relationships which prevented lawful matrimony, since to marry the relative of a former fiancé(e) was deemed an offence against public decency (*iustitia publicae honestatis*).[46] The network of forbidden relationships was governed by rules that dictated how far through the family tree (and the family tree of former partners, godchildren and so on) one would have to travel before encountering a legal mate. These rules required a calculation to be made that established the number of prohibited degrees between the two parties intending to marry, based on their distance from a common ancestor or from another individual whose kinship created the impediment. The calculation was usually expressed in terms that stated the distance each partner was from the 'link' person (since the number of steps may differ in each partner's case). For example, a couple may have been said to be in the third and fourth degree, or the fourth and fourth degree, of consanguinity. Not all the dispensations stated the relationship, though it must have been standard practice for supplications to include sufficient details of the parties' respective family trees to allow the papacy to determine the case.

Prior to 1215, the range of forbidden contacts could be very extensive indeed, depending on what method of computation was used, theoretically

44 *The Letters of Lanfranc Archbishop of Canterbury*, ed. H. Clover and M. Gibson (Oxford, 1979), no. 10; *Pontificia Hibernica: Medieval Papal Chancery Documents Concerning Ireland*, 640–1261, ed. M. Sheehy (Dublin, 1962–5), i, 21–2; F. J. Byrne, 'The Trembling Sod: Ireland in 1169', in A. Cosgrove, ed., A *New History of Ireland: II Medieval Ireland* (Oxford, 1987), 41–2.

45 Hay, *Lectures*, 221–9. See J. H. Lynch, 'Spiritual Kinship and Sexual Prohibitions in Early Medieval Europe', in S. Kuttner and K. Pennington, ed., *Proceedings of the Sixth International Congress of Medieval Canon Law* (Vatican City, 1985), 271–88 for the development of the theology of, and strength of feeling regarding, spiritual kinship that shaped later canon law; and J. Bossy, 'Blood and Baptism: Kinship, Community and Christianity in Western Europe from the Fourteenth to the Seventeenth Centuries', in D. Baker, ed., *Sanctity and Secularity: the Church and the World. Studies in Church History 10* (Oxford, 1973), 129–43, for a discussion of its social functions.

46 J. D. Scanlan, 'Husband and Wife: Pre-Reformation Canon Law of Marriage of the Officials' Courts', in *An Introduction to Scottish Legal History*, Stair Society 20 (Edinburgh, 1958), 80. A non-consummated marriage was treated similarly.

excluding even sixth cousins from inter-marriage.[47] The Fourth Lateran Council in that year formally reduced the number of prohibited degrees from seven to four, which widened the field of possible marriage partners somewhat.[48] Nonetheless, there remained considerable scope for a 'marriage' contracted in good faith to be rendered null on grounds of endogamy. The system of papal dispensations provided a recourse by which many were able to marry, or to remain in a marriage that was technically void. Dispensations could be granted to those related in the third or fourth degrees, although occasionally it was possible to obtain a dispensation for a relationship in the second degree.[49] There are Scottish examples of dispensations granted to men seeking to marry women previously betrothed to the intended spouse's brother, but these were granted on the basis that the young woman concerned had not had *carnal copula* with her previous fiancé.[50] If she had, she would be related in the first degree to the surviving brother: because the sexual act made her 'one flesh' with her previous consort, in canonical terms she would have been sister to her prospective spouse.[51]

In a small and, in places, sparsely populated country such as Scotland, where it was common for marriage alliances to be forged with neighbouring families, often as a tactic for extending domains, complying with the rules of exogamy could present significant difficulties.[52] A papal letter of 1353 containing a marriage dispensation for Scots nobleman David Graham and

47 Regulations concerning prohibited degrees were in place from the fourth century; they fluctuated over time and according to country or region. Until the eleventh century, when a single method of computation was agreed, two distinct methods – the Roman and the Germanic – were in use, with the latter resulting in a greater number of excluded kin members than the former. J. Goody, *The Development of the Family and Marriage in Europe* (Cambridge, 1983), 134–46; Brundage, *Law, Sex, and Christian Society*, 140–1, 355–6. Although the prohibited degrees were formally determined by the Church, they were sometimes reinforced by secular laws. Royal legislation issued by Cnut the Great (d. 1035) between 1020 and 1023, for example, forbade marriage within six degrees of relationship. *The Laws of the Kings of England from Edmund to Henry I*, ed. and transl. A. J. Robertson (Cambridge, 1925), 163. Various arguments have been propounded to explain the Church's stance on exogamy. An overview and discussion of them can be found in Mitterauer, 'Christianity and Endogamy'.

48 Fourth Lateran Council, c. 50. *Decrees of the Ecumenical Councils*, ed. N. P. Tanner (Washington, DC, 1990), 257–8; Patrick, *Statutes*, 39.

49 A late fifteenth-century papal tariff states that marriage within the second degree should be to be restricted to magnates only. W. E. Lunt, *Papal Revenues in the Middle Ages* (New York, 1934), ii, 526. In the fifteenth century Jean, count of Armagnac (d. 1473), 'married' his sister Isabelle: Pope Nicholas V refused to provide a dispensation but, Armagnac having paid 24,000 ducats to a bishop to arrange it, a forgery was obtained from a Vatican scriptor. *I Commentari di Enea Silvio Piccolomini*, ed. G. Bernetti, (Milan, 1981), ii, 370–6. Jean and Isabelle had three children.

50 *CSSR* i, 143–4; ii, 210–11. The men to whom the women had been betrothed were now dead, which was probably important to the pope's decision in each case.

51 Hence Turgot's antipathy to men marrying their brothers' widows.

52 R. A. Dodgshon, *Land and Society in Early Scotland* (Oxford, 1981), 107.

his intended spouse, Helen Chene, illustrates the problem. Graham's petition claimed that the combination of the Church's rules concerning prohibited degrees, the relative lack of noble families in the region, and the great number of blood relations in such families as there were, meant that it was scarcely possible for anyone of rank to find a social equal with whom to contract a legal marriage.[53] Additional restrictions reducing the pool of marriageable partners still further are cited in a Scottish marriage petition of 1366. Mariota Campbell and John Campbell of Argyll, related in the fourth degree of kindred, sought dispensation to marry each other, since those living in the highlands of Scotland, as they did, rarely married anyone from the lowlands because of the language difference, and, to make matters worse, the combination of war and plague had reduced the number of nobles available as marriage partners to such an extent that 'it is hard for them to marry except within the prohibited degrees'.[54]

In seeking marriage dispensations, petitioners sometimes sought to strengthen their case by appealing to the Church's assumed function as a promotor of peace not just between kingdoms but also within them. Many Scottish requests for marriage dispensations included a claim that the marriage was important for the purposes of fostering or increasing friendship between the two kin groups and their associates.[55] Not uncommonly, petitions went further and claimed that a marriage was necessary to end or prevent violence, feuding and dissent between the families. In 1341, a dispensation to allow marriage between John Barclay and Margaret Graham, widow of Hugh, earl of Ross, was sought on the basis that it would end long-standing, bitter discord between their families and friends.[56] A similar appeal had been included in the 1329 appeal by Margaret and her first husband to be dispensed, but in this case the marriage had already been contracted in ignorance of an impediment, and the conflict they sought to avert was that expected to ensue if the union was declared null.[57] Dispensations granted in response to pleas of this kind routinely included a statement that the pope was granting the petition out

53 Theiner, *Vet. Mon.*, no. 613. The same complaint was made in 1554 by John Hamilton (born illegitimate), archbishop of St Andrews. Hay, *Lectures*, xlvii–iii.

54 *CPL*, iv, 56. The Black Death had struck Scotland in 1349–50, and a further major pestilence occurred in 1361; Scotland was at war during all but ten of the sixty years before 1357, and had been badly affected by a worsening climate contributing to famine. M. Brown, *The Wars of Scotland, 1214–1371* (Edinburgh, 2012), 318.

55 For example, Theiner, *Vet. Mon.*, no. 673; *CSSR*, i, 304.

56 Theiner, *Vet. Mon.*, no. 549. Marriage between the offspring of two families in dispute was often one component of conflict resolution, usually along with other measures. J. Armstrong, 'The "Fyre of Ire Kyndild" in the Fifteenth-Century Scottish Marches', in S. A. Throop and P. R. Hyams, edd., *Vengeance in the Middle Ages* (Farnham, 2010), 51–84, esp. 63, 78–9.

57 Theiner, *Vet. Mon.*, no. 490. Margaret Graham and Hugh, earl of Ross, were the parents of Euphemia, who married as her second husband Robert the Steward, later Robert II. Euphemia may have been born before her parents' marriage dispensation was granted.

of a desire to avert conflict, and to maintain peace and harmony among the faithful. How true such claims by petitioners were is open to question: while some marriages were intended to repair relationships between families at odds with each other, and others possibly to forestall bad relations from developing, it is likely that the stakes were exaggerated, if not sometimes invented, in an effort to encourage a favourable outcome to the supplication. Petitioners of the noble classes occasionally obtained the backing of royal figures, adding clout to a plea.[58] That royal endorsement and appeals to the peace of the realm were invoked in support of dispensations suggest that papal approval was not a foregone conclusion.

'Handfasting', clandestine marriage and illegitimacy

Consent to marriage had to be stated in vows of present consent (*per verba de presenti*), that is, in wording to the effect that each partner takes the other, in the present tense, as his or her spouse. A vow of future consent (*per verba de futuro*; one 'will take' the other at some later point) was not a marriage but a betrothal, but if the couple subsequently engaged in sexual intercourse (*carnali copula subsecuta*), they were legally married. Handfasting is often described as a traditional, secular form of marriage ceremony, but it was a promise to marry in future: in other words, a betrothal, not a wedding.[59] The distinction between handfasting and marriage is made explicit in an agreement of 1432 between William Carlyle of Torthorwald and Thomas of Kirkpatrick, lord of Closeburn, by which the son of the former was to marry the daughter of the latter:

> the saidis Jone and Elisabeth sail be handfast, as the oys is, in haly Kyrk at the enterchanging of thir present indenturis, but langer delay, and at the next opin and lachful tyme folowand, the matrimone to be complete and fulfillet betwixt thaim, as oys is, in haly kirk, but langer delay, fraud or gille.[60]

Similarly, in 1483, George Clephane of Carslogie in Fife sought to prevent James III from exercising his prerogative to provide a husband for Margaret Barclay, who had been in Clephane's care since her father died, on the grounds that Margaret was his daughter-in-law, showing as evidence 'a contract of marriage to be made and an instrument of handfasting'.[61] This wording alone shows that handfasting did not constitute marriage, and confirmation lies in James III ordering Clephane to deliver the young woman either to him or to the man he

58 Theiner, *Vet. Mon.*, nos 579, 613.

59 A. E. Anton, '"Handfasting' in Scotland', *SHR* 37 (1958), 91; W. D. H. Sellar, 'Marriage, Divorce and Concubinage in Gaelic Scotland', *TGSI* 51 (1978–80), 466. It was also practised in other countries, including England and France. C. Donahue Jr, *Law, Marriage and Society* in *the Middle Ages: Arguments About Marriage in Five Courts* (Cambridge, 2007), 105, 154–6, 197, 199, 202–4, 210, 212–13, 216, 286, 334, 340, 365–6, 376.

60 *Hist. MSS. Comm, Fifteenth Report*, App. part viii, no. 81.

61 *RPS*, 1483/3/129.

had chosen for her.[62] The king could not give a married woman to another man without this second union being bigamous and null. If Margaret Barclay and Clephane's son had had sexual intercourse following their betrothal, however, then they were married. Perhaps they had, and this is why Clephane called Margaret his daughter-in-law rather than his son's fiancée – though he may have been misrepresenting the relationship in a bid to keep her in his family. But no marriage ceremony had yet taken place, which allowed James III to consider her single. If Margaret and the younger Clephane had slept together, then telling the king that the union was now a canonically valid marriage ought to have decided the matter, but it might have been worse for Clephane to admit he had allowed his ward to be deflowered when the right to give her in marriage belonged to the king.

As is clear from these two examples, handfasting was not an alternative to Church-approved, legal marriage. The Carlyle and Kirkpatrick handfasting was to take place in church and involve a ritual exchange of legal documents, while the Barclay and Clephane handfasting was recorded in writing for the avoidance of future doubt. The use of written instruments was doubtless useful, but couples could also become betrothed simply by stating their intention to marry.[63] However the betrothal was accomplished, if the couple afterwards became lovers they were legally, if irregularly, married (unless there was an impediment to the marriage), and their children were legitimate. In Church law, a child born to a handfasted couple was illegitimate if either party had a living spouse due to an earlier handfasting which had been followed by sexual intercourse, as this made the current partnership bigamous.

Since consent appropriately expressed was what made marriage, any man and woman could marry each other independently of witnesses, formal ceremony or priestly blessing. An espousal performed without witnesses was a clandestine marriage, and while such marriages were valid (assuming there was no impediment), they were actively discouraged by the Church, largely because it was often very difficult to prove later that the marriage had taken place.[64] Clandestine marriages by definition were not subject to reading of banns, so defied the attempts of local clergy to uncover possible impediments. In addition, either party might later deny they had exchanged vows with his or her supposed spouse. In both these circumstances the lack of witnesses often made it impossible to know whether the couple was actually married.

62 If Clephane failed to comply, he was to pay the king or the prospective husband the value of the marriage, under pain of imprisonment.

63 Hay, *Lectures*, 7. 'Handsel' was sometimes given: money or an object of value given in pledge as a form of surety.

64 Fourth Lateran Council, c. 51. Tanner, *Decrees*, 258; Patrick, *Statutes*, 39, 64, 72–3. It was not until the establishment of the decree *Tametsi* (Council of Trent, 1545–63), that the presence of clergy became formally necessary to the validity of a marriage. Brundage, *Law, Sex, and Christian Society*, 563–4.

The validity of clandestine marriages made it possible that any supposed marriage – contracted publicly or otherwise – might be subject to claims of pre-contract: that is, a third party might allege that one of the spouses had previously married him or her clandestinely, rendering the later marriage, though apparently contracted licitly, invalid. These considerations could easily obscure the birth status of children, making judgements as to their legitimacy very difficult.

Annulments and illegitimacy

Not all couples who contracted an invalid marriage wanted to be dispensed to continue in it. *Divortium a vinculo* (divorce from the bond) was not divorce as we know it now, but an annulment: official recognition that there had been no marriage in the first place. The only other form of legal separation, *divortium a mensa et thoro* (divorce from bed and board), was permitted in exceptional circumstances, but it did not license either party to make a new marriage as long as his or her spouse was living. As a result, annulments were frequently the only means, aside from the death of a spouse, by which people could escape an unwanted union and marry someone else without committing bigamy.[65] Canonical incest seems often to have been useful in this regard. Just as some couples may have been aghast to discover they were not legally married, others may have gone to some lengths to establish that their 'marriage' was a *de facto* one, that is, not a marriage at all.

If one, or both, parents were ignorant of the impediment, then the *bona fides* (good faith) of the partner(s) was enough to ensure the legitimacy of the children.[66] A union of this kind was called a putative marriage, and from at least the thirteenth century canon law allowed that offspring of putative marriages were legitimate, providing the marriage had been contracted publicly (the exchange of vows was expected to take place *in facie ecclesie*: 'in the face of the church'; usually, at a church door).[67] A marriage contracted clandestinely, however, was considered evidence of *mala fides* (bad faith) on the part of both. The assumption behind this was that the couple had known of the impediment and deliberately sought to exclude the local community from knowledge of the marriage, out of fear that others who also knew they were forbidden to marry could forestall the union. Children born to a couple in this situation were illegitimate, unless their parents obtained a papal dispensation

65 C. Rolker, 'Kings, Bishops and Incest: Extension and Subversion of the Ecclesiastical Marriage Jursidiction around 1100', in K. Cooper, and J. Gregory, ed., *Discipline and Diversity* (Woodbridge, 2007), 160.

66 X 4.17.2; Hay, *Lectures*, 31, 235.

67 A. Esmein, *Le Mariage en Droit Canonique* (Paris, 1929–35), ii, 34.

that expressly declared them legitimate.[68] The 'discovery' of an impediment may have been useful to those who had no heirs with their spouse and hoped for better luck with another. Alexander, second lord Home (d. 1506) obtained an annulment ending his childless marriage with Isobel Douglas, to whom he was related within the prohibited degrees, though the 'incest' was not close and an application for a dispensation was likely to have been successful. With his second wife Nichola Ker he had ten children.[69]

Obtaining a dispensation

Fees were levied for the administrative costs of preparing letters of dispensation.[70] Formal fees, or Chancery taxes, were in operation from at least the pontificate of Innocent III (1198–1216) and the system was much expanded towards the end of the thirteenth century and in the first half of the fourteenth century.[71] The very poorest supplicants might, in theory at least, receive their letters of dispensation free of charge, while the charges paid by others could vary according to the financial standing of the petitioners and the length and degree of complexity of the letters; the official rate might be considerably increased by bribes, tips, or by the need to engage legal assistance.[72] The *Calendar of Scottish Entries in Registers of Introitus et Exitus*, mainly listing payments for annates or common service, includes details of a small number – twenty-one in total – of marriage dispensation payments.[73] These are all concentrated in the period between late 1465 and 1471. According to this, Scottish couples paid anything between three and twelve florins 'gold of the *camera*' (g.c.) to be dispensed. The lowest amount, of three florins g.c., appears only once, as does the highest sum of twelve florins g.c.: the most frequently levelled fee (ten times) is six florins g.c. At the end of the fourteenth century, the value in exchange of such a

68 Canon 51 of the Fourth Lateran Council (1215) formally decreed that children born of a putative and clandestine marriage were illegitimate, even if one or both parents were unaware of the impediment. Tanner, *Decrees*, i, 258. Regularisation could still be obtained by dispensation, however: an Elizabeth Stewart and George Campbell of Glasgow married clandestinely (without banns) and knowing that they were related, but were granted a dispensation (with salutary penance and temporary separation order), and their children were declared legitimate. *CPL*, xii, 490.

69 *SP*, iv, 453–4. Roger (III) Bigod, earl of Norfolk, husband of Isabella, a legitimate daughter of William the Lion, cited consanguinity in his unsuccessful attempt to have their childless marriage annulled after twenty years. R. C. Stacey, 'Bigod, Roger, Fourth Earl of Norfolk (ca. 1212–1270), Magnate and Courtier', *ODNB*, 12 January 2019.

70 K. Salonen and L. Schmugge, *A Sip from the "Well of Grace": Medieval Texts from the Apostolic Penitentiary* (Washington, DC, 2009), 78.

71 Lunt, *Papal Revenues*, i, 126.

72 L. Schmugge, 'Cleansing on Consciences: Some Observations Regarding the Fifteenth-century Registers of the Papal Penitentiary', *Viator* 29 (1998), 353–4; Lunt, *Papal Revenues*, i, 125–7.

73 Cameron, *Apostolic Camera*, 281–7.

florin was two shillings and eightpence or two shillings and ninepence.[74] Using the late fourteenth-century value of 2s 8/9d, six florins g.c. amounted to 16s or 16s 6d. In the mid-fifteenth century, this was the price of a cow in Scotland.[75] Gemmill and Mayhew suggest that such a sum was not easy for most people to find in the ordinary course of their lives.[76] The amount generally charged at this time (1465–71) has also been described as 'a heavy sum roughly equal to the annual income of an artisan'.[77] The amounts paid by Scots for marriage dispensations are broadly equivalent to those of German supplicants, who also commonly paid a sum corresponding to the value of a cow.[78]

The information contained in the calendar entries is too scanty to explain why some of these couples were charged more than others. A couple who obtained a retrospective dispensation for a marriage they had contracted knowing that they were related within the forbidden degrees of consanguinity was charged the standard six florins g.c., so on the basis of this small sample, there did not seem to be an additional financial penalty for deliberately flouting the canonical rules, as opposed to innocently contracting a marriage, the forbidden status of which came to light later.[79] All the dispensations granted were to couples related in the third or fourth degree of either consanguinity or affinity (in one instance both), so the variation in fees cannot be explained in these cases solely by the differences in distance between the couples and their shared ancestor or impediment-creating relationship. This was one factor the papal penitentiary usually took into account in calculating the fees, but it was not the only one.[80] That the better-off paid more for their marriage dispensations than others is borne out by evidence from the late fifteenth century showing that Maximilian I, duke of Austria and Burgundy (d. 1519), paid 2,250 ducats for a dispensation to marry Mary of Burgundy in 1477.[81]

74 'J. Dowden, *The Medieval Church in Scotland: Its Constitution, Organisation and Law* (Glasgow, 1910), 329.

75 A cow cost 16s 7d. E. Gemmill and N. Mayhew, *Changing Values in Medieval Scotland: A Study of Prices, Money, and Weights and Measures* (Cambridge, 1995), 249.

76 Ibid.

77 L. Schmugge, 'Female Petitioners in the Papal Penitentiary', *Gender and History* 12 (2000), 695–6.

78 L. Schmugge, *Marriage on Trial. Late Medieval German Couples at the Papal Court*, transl. A. A. Larson (Washington, DC, 2012), 18. Schmugge provides a table of fees and compositions for marriage dispensations between 1450 and 1513 at 353–4. He also gives examples of dispensations provided free of charge to couples who swore on oath to their poverty. Ibid., 44.

79 Cameron, *Apostolic Camera*, 287.

80 Schmugge, 'Cleansing on Consciences', 354; Lunt, *Papal Revenues*, i, 126–7; for a fifteenth-century list of taxes by the penitentiary, setting out charges for marital dispensations, see Lunt, *Papal Revenues*, ii, 524–6.

81 Lunt, *Papal Revenues*, ii, 525. In 1488, the value of a ducat (of unspecified origin) in Scottish money was 16s. P. Spufford, *Handbook of Medieval Exchange* (London, 1986), 211.

The papacy sometimes empowered its representatives – often bishops or legates – to grant a fixed number of marriage dispensations on its behalf. This meant that some couples could obtain their marriage dispensation locally instead of having to apply to Rome; depending on what fee the bishop wished to levy, it was probably a more affordable option. Lawyers concerned in a Scottish marriage dispute of 1471 heard testimony concerning the sale of a marriage dispensation by one bishop to another.[82] The marriage, which had taken place in Glasgow some seventeen years previously, was between Walter Turnbull, nephew of the then bishop of Glasgow, and a Margaret Gargunnock, related to Walter within the prohibited degrees. The dispensation allowing the marriage to proceed had been written by the bishop of St Andrews, who, according to one witness, 'wished to have twenty nobles (ca. £30) for the dispensation, but the bishop of Glasgow refused to give more than ten merks (ca. £6 13s 4d), so that the dispensation was obtained for that sum'.[83] What the bishop of St Andrews would have sought to charge someone with fewer resources than a fellow prelate is unknown.

Some indirect evidence that the cost of a dispensation might be quite substantial can be found in a contract of marriage made in the last quarter of the fifteenth century. William, thane of Cawdor, sought to marry his daughter Margery to Alexander Fraser in 1487, but 'thai mane haf licence and be dispensit of our haly father the Pape' as the groom was 'god brother to the saide Margeory Caldor and scho gode sister to him'.[84] William undertook to pay for the dispensation himself, on the basis that Alexander would reimburse him once he had been vested in his lands of Philorth. The sum involved was clearly not so insignificant that William was prepared to write it off, and repaying it required the groom to have possession of estates.

If six florins g.c., or the equivalent cost of a cow or annual income of an artisan, was a typical fee for a dispensation, many, probably most, people would have needed to rely on the generosity of the papacy in reducing the fees to match their circumstances. Even so, the associated costs, for example of lawyers or clerks and their expenses, which may include travel to Rome (or a contribution toward this, as one courier would take multiple items), would often have been prohibitive, resulting in a widespread inability, or at least reluctance, to apply for a dispensation. Dowden remarks that dispensations 'were not to be had by the poor', although the power of local bishops to dispense for marriage may have reduced costs for some; and Sellar notes that the wealthiest were at an advantage 'because petitioning for a dispensation could be a very expensive

82 Macfarlane, *William Elphinstone*, 61–3.

83 Gemmill and Mayhew, *Changing Values*, 385.

84 *The Book of the Thanes of Cawdor: A Series of Papers Selected from the Charter Room at Cawdor 1236–1742* (Spalding Club, 1859), 69.

process'.[85] Given that there was no guarantee of a petition being successful, some couples may have felt it unwise to draw the Church's attention to an impediment, especially if doing so left them significantly out of pocket. Better, perhaps, to contract a 'marriage' they knew to be invalid and pass themselves off as legally wed, hoping that their children's legitimacy would not be challenged later. The exchange of marriage vows between couples who knew quite well they were not legally eligible to marry each other happened in Scotland as elsewhere in western Christendom, sometimes with the connivance of local clergy.[86] Such a couple might gamble on the impediment not coming to light but if it did, then they could throw themselves on the mercy of the papacy and only in those circumstances incur the costs of a dispensation. Sellar remarks that the rules governing forbidden degrees were regarded with some cynicism in late medieval Scotland and encouraged a 'marry first and dispense later' attitude.[87]

It is indeed extremely unlikely that all retrospectively issued dispensations were given to couples whose claim that they had married in ignorance of the impediment between them was genuine. The terms of the dispensation given by Pope Eugenius IV (1431–47) to Joan Beaufort, widow of James I, and her second husband, Sir James Stewart of Lorne, hint that the papacy did not believe they had, as they claimed, discovered only after the marriage that they were related within the forbidden degrees.[88] For one thing, the survivor of the two was forbidden from marrying again, and for another, they were required to separate for a period of time (to be determined by the bishop to whom the letter was addressed) before entering into their properly canonical marriage. These penalties may have been exacted because of Joan and James's admission that they had continued to live as husband and wife after the impediment came to light – for which they were additionally required to seek an absolution from excommunication – though the inclusion of not one but two punitive clauses suggests the papal authority concerned took an exceptionally dim

85 Dowden, *The Medieval Church*, 269; D. Sellar, 'The Family', in E. J. Cowan and L. Henderson, ed., *A History of Everyday Life in Medieval Scotland, 1000 to 1600* (Edinburgh, 2011), 99. Concerning local powers of dispensation, Dowden is commenting on the sixteenth century, but the pope delegated dispensatory powers to clergy and legates in earlier centuries too: for example, *CPL*, ii, 283 (in 1328), and see pp. 152–3. The haggling between the bishops of St Andrews and Glasgow over the cost of the 1471 dispensation suggests that bishops with delegated powers of dispensation had some freedom in determining what to charge for them.

86 Brundage, *Law, Sex, and Christian Society*, 443. Clerics did have discretion when it came to publicising a forthcoming marriage: there were circumstances in which the banns might lawfully be omitted. Hay, *Lectures*, 31–3; Brundage, *Law, Sex, and Christian Society*, 442–3. Knowingly allowing a couple to marry without banns probably laid a heavier burden of responsibility on the clergy to ensure the couple was legally entitled to marry.

87 Sellar, 'The Family', 99.

88 The dispensation is printed in Bain, 'Notes on a Dispensation', at 171–2.

view of the infringement. Joan's remarriage after the death of James I was highly unpopular in Scotland, and it is possible that widespread disapproval of the union also influenced Eugenius IV's response. The letter is addressed to the bishop of Dunkeld and not the bishop of the couple's own diocese, St Andrews, since the latter is said to be *suspectus*.[89] This implies a perception that the cleric concerned was complicit in a wrongful marriage. The sanction of Church-enforced separation was routinely, though not invariably, used in cases where a couple had applied for a dispensation but then proceeded with the marriage before the papal letter arrived. The penalty for this transgression was sometimes more severe than a temporary separation: Sir Alexander Home (d. 1461), and his spouse Marion Lauder married before their expected dispensation turned up; their marriage ('if marriage it ought to be called', noted the official of St Andrews) was declared null and they were obliged to separate before going to the trouble and expense of a second dispensation.[90]

In cases where one partner seemed to be genuinely ignorant of the impediment, the spouse who had concealed it might incur a penance. In 1344, John of Douglas, of the diocese of St Andrews, was required to found two chaplaincies, with annual endowments to them, as a punishment for having hidden from his wife, Agnes Graham, that before their marriage he had cohabited with her niece.[91] John and Agnes were dispensed to remain in marriage and their children were declared legitimate. But there appears to be little consistency in the application of penalties. Responding to Scottish couples, (Anti-)Pope Benedict XIII (d. 1423), for example, applied the penalty of temporary separation to an apparently childless couple who had contracted a marriage they knew to be invalid and lived together; a penalty in the form of payment of a sum of money, the amount to be determined by their bishop, to 'a holy place or to the poor of Christ' to a similarly childless couple who knew they could not marry because of the impediment between them and were simply cohabiting; the same penalty to a couple who are not stated to be cohabiting, but who had known each other carnally and had a child; and the twin penalties of temporary separation and a payment were imposed on a childless couple who had contracted an invalid marriage 'in full awareness' that they were related by consanguinity, and were now living together.[92] But some couples, who as far as can be judged from the records had done nothing untoward, were obliged to make a donation (in addition to whatever payment they had made to obtain the dispensation) as a condition of their dispensation being granted: in 1394 Angus Goffredson and Anna, daughter of Lachlan MacLean, sought permission to marry and had to pay one silver

89 Bain, 'Notes on a Dispensation', 172, 174.

90 *Hist. MSS. Comm.*, *Twelfth Report*, App. Pt. viii (1891), 122–3.

91 *CPL*, iii, 165; *CPP*, i, 79; Theiner, *Vet. Mon.*, no. 563. The case is discussed further at pp. 37–8.

92 McGurk, *Letters of Benedict XIII*, 150, 171, 199, 245.

merk each to the church of Glasgow and the Cistercian monastery at Saddell; and in 1406 John Stewart and Elizabeth Lennox had to pay 10 francs of gold for the ornamentation of their parish church.[93] In 1403, Lachlan MacLean sought a dispensation to marry a woman who had previously been betrothed, successively, to two of his kinsmen.[94] The dispensation was granted on condition that the couple donate a sum of money towards the reconstruction of the collapsed monastery on Iona. Some couples who had contracted marriage in good faith and lived together, unaware of any impediment, and who now asked for a dispensation, were required to pay alms, while others were not.[95] However, no penalties were apparently applied to a couple who knew they were related by affinity but who were in a sexual relationship and had a child; nor to a childless couple who were guilty of fornication 'on several occasions' and now wanted to marry; nor to a further three unmarried couples who each had a child together.[96] Presumably the full details of each case, not recorded in the mandates, influenced Benedict's decisions. No matter what the parents' offence or error, in each of these instances the children born or yet to be born were declared legitimate, and so although parents might sometimes incur a penalty, no penalty was inflicted on the innocent offspring. But if the marriage was entered into with both parties knowing they were forbidden to marry, and no dispensation was granted, the children were not legitimate.

Legitimation *per subsequens matrimonium*

The redemptive power of marriage was so great, Pope Alexander III ruled in his 1172 decretal, *Tanta*, that it was even effective retroactively, and so was capable of legitimising children born to a couple prior to their marriage: '*Tanta est vis matrimonii ut, qui antea sunt geniti, post contractum matrimonium legitimi habeantur*' (such is the power of matrimony, that those who are born before marriage are held to be legitimate after it).[97] This clear inducement to couples to regularise their domestic relationships in line with Church rules sat alongside the common law prohibition on illegitimate inheritance. Not all parents were free to marry each other, but the opportunity offered by the decretal for at least some to rehabilitate the status of their children was

93 Ibid., 55, 155.

94 Ibid., 103.

95 Ibid., 148, 236, 237, 303.

96 Ibid., 237, 288, 324–5, 373, 374.

97 X 4.17.6. Legitimation by subsequent marriage had been known in Roman law (introduced by Constantine in the fourth century and further refined by Justinian in the sixth), though its justification was not based on theological considerations; it was not introduced into Church law before the twelfth century. *Nov.* 12.4, 18.11, 78.4, 89.11; R. Génestal, *Histoire de la Légitimation des Enfants Naturels en Droit Canonique* (Paris, 1905), 137.

accepted in Scotland, as it was in most of Europe, but not in England.[98] The doctrine attracted controversy when it came to children of adulterous or other forbidden relationships, that is, *spurii* rather than *naturales*.[99] Canonists were divided as to whether the retroactive legitimating power of marriage was sufficient to erase the fault involved in an encounter or liaison that was not merely irregular but criminal, resulting in *spurii*.[100] In the end, the ruling that entered canon law was that only *naturales*, not *spurii*, could be legitimated by their parents' subsequent marriage.[101] Which is to say that only *naturales* could be automatically legitimated: *spurii* were not necessarily debarred from legitimation, but their parents would require a marital dispensation for these children to be legitimate, rather than legitimacy being an immediate consequence of their parents' marriage.

This was the law according to the Church. English common law, uniquely in western Europe, did not accept the canon law of legitimation *per subsequens matrimonium*. In 1236, the English barons considered the provision and declared that, 'We do not wish to change the laws of England'.[102] Scotland, by contrast, did accept legitimation *per subsequens matrimonium* into the common law of the realm. When this came about, and the relationship of the doctrine to inheritance law, is discussed in the next chapter.

98 M. M. Sheehan, 'The European Family and Canon Law', *Continuity and Change* 6 (1991), 354.

99 L. Mayali, 'Legitimization by Subsequent Marriage from Alexander III to Innocent III', in L. Mayali and S. A. J. Tibbetts, ed., *The Two Laws: Studies in Medieval Legal History Dedicated to Stephan Kuttner* (Washington, DC, 1990), 62. Roman law under Justinian similarly restricted legitimation by subsequent marriage to *naturales*, the children of couples who were free to marry at the time the child was conceived, and excluded *spurii*, the offspring of forbidden relationships. G. Mousourakis, *Fundamentals of Roman Private Law* (Berlin, 2012), 95.

100 Mayali, 'Legitimization by Subsequent Marriage', 62–3.

101 '*Naturales legitimantur per subsequens parentum coniugium, spurii vero non*.' X 4.17.6. See also X 4.17.1.

102 'The So-called Statute of Merton', in *English Historical Documents*, ed. H. Rothwell (London, 1975), 353–4. Shortly beforehand, a letter of Robert Grosseteste, bishop of Lincoln, to William of Raleigh, chief justice of the king's court, argued at considerable length for pre-nuptial children to be considered legitimate for inheritance purposes in the English royal courts. *The Letters of Robert Grosseteste, Bishop of Lincoln*, ed. F. A. C. Mantello and J. Goering (Toronto, 2010), no. 23.

2

Illegitimacy and inheritance

Off wrangus get cummis wrang successioun.[1]

In canon law, 'defect of birth' established a barrier to the holding of Church offices with cure of souls, but illegitimacy also created a legal disability in secular law. In theory, the legal disability of bastardy prevented illegitimate people from holding high public offices, though there is little evidence that this was enforced in medieval Scotland.[2] More critically, and certainly more widely implemented, illegitimacy was a bar to inheritance. Further, bastards could have no heirs except for their own legitimately procreated children – a nephew, for example, would be unable to succeed to an illegitimate person, even though nearest in kin. Ownership and transmission of land was the province of the secular law system and disputes came under the jurisdiction of courts other than those of the Church. Where doubt existed as to a person's legitimacy, and the dispelling of this doubt was required for secular law purposes (most often to confirm or deny inheritance rights), the usual procedure was for the spiritual courts to adjudicate as to the birth status of the person concerned, and for the civil courts to award heirship to the appropriate claimant.

There was an important and apparently irreconcilable difference with respect to illegitimacy between the canon law of the Church, and the common law of Scotland as expressed in *Regiam Majestatem* (*RM*), the earliest surviving secular law treatise for Scotland.[3] The substantive difference between them

1 R. Henryson, 'The Taill of the Sone and Air of the foirsaid Foxe, callit Father wer: Alswa the Parliament of Fourfuttit Beistis, haldin be the Lyoun', in *Robert Henryson: The Poems*, ed. D. Fox (Oxford, 1987), line 806.

2 For example, it certainly did not prevent illegitimates from becoming chancellor of the kingdom. Illegitimate men who held this post include Robert Kenleith, abbot of Melrose (d. 1272), Gamelin, bishop of St Andrews (d. 1271), Adam Murray, bishop of Brechin (d. 1349x50), Andrew Stewart, Lord Avondale (d. 1488), and William Elphinstone, bishop of Aberdeen (d. 1514). E. B. Fryde and others, ed., *Handbook of British Chronology*, 3rd edn. (London, 1986), 180–2.

3 *RM* was heavily reliant on the *Tractatus de legibus et consuetudinibus regni Anglie* (1187x9; commonly called *Glanvill*) and the Romano-canonical *Summa* of Goffredus de Trano (1240s), with some additional Scottish material. *RM*'s accompanying text, *Quoniam Attachiamenta* (also known as *Leges Baronum*), provided guidance on laws and procedures to be used in the aristocratic courts. It has traditionally been dated to

centred on what each understood to be the effects of one form of canonical legitimation. In canon law, those legitimated according to their parents' later intermarriage (legitimation *per subsequens matrimonium*) – were fully legitimate, and so by implication should not suffer the legal disability of bastardy in respect of inheritance.[4] That canon law regarded those legitimated *per subsequens matrimonium* as heirs to heritage is acknowledged in *RM*, which then goes on to deny this right under the common law:

> Arising out of this subject the question has been put whether a person begotten or born before his father married his mother is a lawful heir if his father subsequently marries his mother. Although the Canon Law and the Roman Law treat such a person as a lawful heir, nevertheless, according to the law of this realm, he cannot under any circumstances be treated as an heir or allowed to claim the inheritance.[5]

The law-book instructs that where this is the matter at issue, the ecclesiastical courts are required to provide a ruling on whether a litigant was born before or after the marriage of his parents and to relay this information to the king's court, which would then award or refuse the inheritance according to common law. In this circumstance, it appears that the Church courts would not be asked to confirm whether or not someone was legitimate, but to answer a different question: did his birth precede his parents' marriage, or not?

The common law as presented in *RM* in essence recognised two distinct categories of alleged bastard: the pre-nuptial child, who could never inherit, and those children born of other liaisons, who could, providing the Church courts deemed them legitimate. That in many, perhaps most, instances canon law would consider a pre-nuptial child legitimate (because of the doctrine of legitimation *per subsequens matrimonium*) accounts for the instruction that if pre-nuptiality is alleged, the ecclesiastical courts were to advise on the timing of someone's birth, not on legitimacy *per se*.

---

around 1318 but for a discussion of its relationship to this date, see A. Taylor, *Laws of Medieval Scotland*, Stair Society 66 (Edinburgh, 2019), 274–80. Work on a new, standard print edition of *RM*, based on analysis of the earliest manuscripts of the text, is being undertaken currently by Dr Alice Taylor and Dr John Reuben Davies as part of the AHRC-project 'The Community of the Realm in Scotland, 1249–1424: History, Law and Charters in a Recreated Kingdom' (www.cotr.ac.uk). My thanks to Dr Alice Taylor for advising me of the *RM* project and giving me advance notice of her Stair Society volume.

4 X 4.17.1, 6. The decretal (*Tanta*) containing this doctrine was in circulation from 1172, over six decades before the compilation of the *Liber Extra*. The power of papal authority to legitimate for royal succession was established in 1201 by Pope Innocent III when he legitimated the children of Agnès of Meran and Philip II 'Augustus', king of France. Pope Alexander III (1159–81) had earlier insisted that those who were legitimate according to canon law, including those legitimated *per subsequens matrimonium*, were legitimate in the secular forum and had full inheritance rights. Brundage, *Law, Sex, and Christian Society*, 344.

5 *RM*, ii, Ch. 51. Dr Alice Taylor advises that the earliest manuscripts say '*secundum ius et consuetudinem regni*'.

Where an inheritance dispute being heard in the civil court turned on the matter of bastardy, its legal officers were to sist (pause) proceedings in that forum, and remit to the ecclesiastical courts a decision as to the legitimacy or otherwise of the person concerned; only once a verdict was reached on this matter could the civil case be resumed and a judgement given as to the inheritance.[6]

RM provides an example of the wording of the brieve to be used for this:

> The form of brieve addressed to the bishop in such a case runs as follows:-
>
> "THE KING to the Bishop of … Greeting. M. has appeared before me (or before my justiciars), claiming against his brother N. the fourth part of a knight's fee in the township of … as his right, to which the said M. has no right because, according to the allegation of the said N., he was born before the marriage of their mother.[7]
>
> And since it is not for my Court to enquire concerning bastardy, I send the parties to you commanding you that you shall do in the Court Christian that which pertains to its jurisdiction. And when the action has been carried to a conclusion before you, certiorate me by writing under your hand what action you have taken in the matter."[8]

This closely resembles the text of a corresponding writ in the English law-compilation, *Glanvill*.[9] The Scottish formulary known as TCa contains a brieve (TCa42), the wording of which is very similar to the template forms found in *RM* and *Glanvill*.[10] All three begin by outlining the case of uterine brothers, one of whom denies the other has inheritance rights on the grounds that the brother is illegitimate because born before the marriage of their mother. The wording of the second part of the brieve is sufficiently vague that it can be used in cases concerning any type of illegitimacy: doing 'that which pertains to [the Christian Court's] jurisdiction' could mean determining legitimacy or establishing whether the claimant's birth preceded his parents' marriage, and could be adjusted *mutatis mutandis* as the particular circumstances dictated.

6 There are certainly instances of people being served heir by means of a brieve before the consistorial courts had reached a decision as to the legitimacy of a claimant (see pp. 44–5 below), but the fact that objections were usually raised when this happened indicates that Church courts were understood to have rights of jurisdiction.

7 '*M. bastardus natus est ante matrimonium matris eorum*.' *RM*, ii, ch. 50. Cooper translates the final four words as 'before the marriage between his parents'.

8 *RM*, ii, ch. 50. The Latin of earlier manuscripts differs slightly (Taylor).

9 *The treatise on the laws and customs of the realm of England commonly called Glanvill*, ed. and transl. G. D. G. Hall (London, 1965), book vii, chapters 13 and 14.

10 TCa42, in *Scottish Formularies*, ed. A. A. M. Duncan, Stair Society 58 (Edinburgh, 2011), 201–2. The date of the brieve is not certain: Duncan says (at 175–6) that the formulary in question was probably compiled early in the reign of James IV with some forms belonging to the time of James III, and that the final document in it is datable to 1510x12.

The case outlined in the first half of the brieve foregrounds pre-nuptiality.[11] Given that the same scenario is described in all three texts, it is apparently one that was felt to be relevant to the English and Scottish situations alike. This supports, and is supported by, the very next chapter of *RM*, which sets out the law denying pre-nuptial children rights of inheritance. But was it true that pre-nuptial offspring formed a special category of bastard, who could never inherit? It is worth looking at the brieve and its contexts in more detail.[12] It appears as a writ in *Glanvill*, compiled while the decretal *Tanta* (containing the doctrine of legitimation *per subsequens matrimonium*) was still being debated by canonists. It was then, and would remain (until 1926), the law of England: given the opportunity to amend it in line with ecclesiastical law after *Tanta* had been incorporated into the *Liber Extra*, the barons of thirteenth-century England rejected this.[13]

The use of the term 'born before the marriage of their mother' implies that the two men had different fathers. If so, the situation is one of a son born in marriage alleging that his half-brother, born of a non-marital liaison between their mother and a previous consort, has no right to the estate. If the lands being contested descended through the younger son's father, then it is difficult to see what claim the older could have on them anyway, without a blood relationship to the deceased. The scenario is more plausible if the lands descended through the mother, though since this occurred much less often it is a slightly odd choice for inclusion in a law-book. Another possibility exists. It may be that the lands did descend through the father and the phrase 'born before the marriage of their mother' was used because of a peculiarity of English law relating to inheritance and illegitimacy. In England, a pre-nuptial child whose parents subsequently married was a bastard *eigné* or 'bastard elder', while a child born after that couple's marriage was a *mulier puisné*.[14] Only the latter was legitimate for inheritance purposes, and so the terms were needed to distinguish between full siblings, not all of whom had inheritance rights. A post-nuptial son was also sometimes known as a *filius mulieratus*, *mulier* younger, or simply a *mulier*; references can be found in English medieval sources to letters or certificates *mulier*, that is, documentation confirming that the bearer was born after the marriage and not before, and is a legitimate heir.[15] The terminology centres on legitimacy being understood to

[11] This brieve, dealing with a claim based on pre-nuptiality, occurs in the chapter titled 'A Bastard Cannot Be an Heir', and not in the following chapter, which denies pre-nuptial offspring a right of inheritance.

[12] I would like to record my thanks to Dr Alice Taylor for discussing this brieve with me and sharing her expertise so generously.

[13] See p. 27.

[14] F. Pollock and F. W. Maitland, *The History of English Law before the Time of Edward I* (Cambridge, 1923), ii, 382.

[15] *Rotuli Parliamentorum; ut et Petitiones, et Placita in Parliamento*, ed. J. Strachey and others (London, 1767–77), iv, 375–6; H. Lovelich, *The History of the Holy Grail*, ed. J. F.

relate primarily to the status of the mother as married or not: in this context, *mulier* means 'wife', not simply 'woman'. The phrase 'born before the marriage of their mother' therefore would imply to an English court not that the men had different fathers, but that they had the same father (and mother), with one brother born before the marriage and the other after it. Since the fact of most significance to the legitimacy of either brother was whether or not his mother was a wife when he was born, 'the marriage of their mother' is foregrounded as the salient factor in the decision as to which brother had a right to the estate.

If this is accepted, then it becomes clearer that the brieve was simply copied from *Glanvill* into *RM* without regard for its relevance to Scotland. The terms bastard *eigné* and *mulier puisné* are not found in Scottish sources and neither are there references to letters or certificates *mulier*, and so the brieve as it stands makes sense only for the rather niche scenario in Scotland of lands descending through a woman, who has one son allegedly born out of wedlock and another born in marriage. It is much more likely that the brieve was incorporated into *RM* not because the situation it outlines was a typical occurrence in Scotland, but because the compiler, working from *Glanvill*, had it in front of him.[16] Taylor suggests that *RM* in its entirety is unfinished: the compiler based the work on *Glanvill*, and adopted a range of editing techniques which he applied to greater and lesser degrees throughout *RM*, but he did not complete the editing work.[17] This makes it very difficult to determine whether any part of the treatise as it stands is in the final form intended by the compiler, who may have been planning to make further changes.[18] The first fourteen chapters of book two have been more significantly altered than the latter section containing the chapters on illegitimacy and inheritance (chapters fifty to fifty-two).[19] It is possible he intended to return to the remaining chapters at some point to continue editing. The brieve remitting determination of bastardy to the ecclesiastical authorities is one of only two *Glanvill* writs to appear in *RM*, as the compiler removed the other writ formulae and any reference to them.[20] Possibly he intended to do the same to the remaining two, although this is not certain. The wording in the second half of the writ or brieve, containing the instruction to the ecclesiastical authorities, was applicable to both England and Scotland, and perhaps the compiler felt this was worth preserving. If it was not his intention to remove the writ entirely, as he did with almost all the others, he may have intended to amend the first part to reflect a more typically

Furnivall (London, 1877), xxxix, line 543.

16 Dr Alice Taylor, phone conversation, 25 June 2018.

17 Further thanks to Dr Alice Taylor for sharing her unpublished paper, 'What Does *Regiam Maiestatem* Actually Say (and What Does It Mean)?'. Duncan also notes that *RM* is unfinished. Duncan, *Scottish Formularies*, xiii.

18 Taylor, 'What Does *Regiam Maiestatem* Actually Say?'.

19 Ibid.

20 Ibid. The other Glanvill writ in *RM*, concerning *dos*, is also in book two, at chapter sixteen.

Scottish scenario. He did 'Scotticise' earlier sections of *RM*, especially book one and the first part of book two, rewriting his source material to fit with the Scottish situation (or so it seems), and to include Scottish material.[21]

The appearance of the brieve in a sixteenth-century Scottish formulary, complete with a virtually identical scenario – in TCa42, 'one-quarter of a knight's fee' is changed to 'one-quarter of a feu', and the initials of the litigants are different – is most probably attributable to the status of *RM* at this time, rather than it being reflective of Scottish legal practice. The authority of *RM* increased significantly from the second half of the fifteenth century.[22] Once having been incorporated into the Scottish treatise, the legal scenario in the first half of the brieve did not have to have shown itself to be useful or relevant for it to have acquired, by association, the reputational weight accorded to the law-book as a whole.[23] That its preservation in *RM* led to its later inclusion in a formulary is not altogether surprising. However, because it appears in not one but two Scottish texts, it gives the false impression of having been relevant to the Scottish situation.

What of the very next item in *RM*, the law concerning the inability of pre-nuptial children to inherit? This provision is unequivocal – 'he cannot under any circumstances be treated as an heir or allowed to claim the inheritance' – and is not attached to a complex inheritance dispute scenario. Certainly, historians have understood it to have been applied in the practice of law concerning inheritance in Scotland. Grant, for example, cites it in his argument that John of Carrick, eldest son of Robert the Steward and Elizabeth Mure, born before their marriage, was preferred by some former supporters of David II to succeed in 1371, instead of Robert.[24] But, 'the law, as stated in *Regiam Majestatem*, denied John any inheritance rights, and therefore he could never become king; instead Robert's heirs would be the sons of his second marriage'.[25] John's eventual succession to the throne is seen as an instance of a royal edict overriding the provision of common law which would normally apply, and the disinheritance of the rightful heirs of Robert II, his sons (born in marriage) with Euphemia of Ross.[26]

RM book two, chapter fifty-one, which acknowledges that legitimation *per subsequens matrimonium* is permitted under canon law but then explicitly

[21] Taylor, 'What Does *Regiam Maiestatem* Actually Say?'; Duncan, *Scottish Formularies*, xiii.

[22] Taylor, 25 June 2018.

[23] Taylor, 25 June 2018. Writing in 1958, Anton remarked that, 'there is no trace of the employment of this writ in Scotland', and thinks it likely that litigants simply seized the Church courts themselves. A. E. Anton, 'Parent and Child', in *Introduction to Scottish Legal History*, 116.

[24] Grant, 'Royal and Magnate Bastards', 322–3. Brown suggests something similar, saying that 'Carrick was the acceptable face of the Stewart dynasty.' M. Brown, *The Black Douglases* (East Linton, 1998), 69.

[25] Grant, 'Royal and Magnate Bastards', 323.

[26] This is discussed in more detail at pp. 110–14.

denies pre-nuptial offspring any inheritance rights under common law, was also copied from *Glanvill*. Again, the unfinished nature of *RM* may account for its inclusion, since it fits with English legal practice but appears to be much less congruent with that of Scotland. In *RM*, the two separate categories of people born outside marriage are not simply two categories of non-heirs, but two categories of bastard, with pre-nuptiality being a more disadvantageous category when it came to inheritance, because it is the circumstance which *RM* expressly states to be a disqualification for heirship. Under such a two-tier system, there would have been a materially better chance of gaining an inheritance by alleging the pre-nuptiality of a rival heir, as opposed to a generic allegation of bastardy.

If the common law provision was indeed in force, then it might be argued that the dispensations were sought to ensure that later children, the post-dispensation offspring, could be heirs while their older siblings would simply be excluded, but if this were the case we would expect to see more evidence of first-born sons having their inheritance challenged by younger brothers.[27] Surviving records of bastardy cases rarely mention the grounds on which someone's legitimacy was considered doubtful, or why a claimant failed to obtain an inheritance. A litigant in fifteenth-century Glasgow, for example, says his rival can be shown to be illegitimate 'by the laws of the realm', but whether this refers to canon law, or common law as expressed in *RM*, is not explained.[28] Theiner's compilation of papal mandates contains an instruction issued in 1257 ordering that the legitimacy or otherwise of the father and grandfather of the earl of Mar is to be investigated, but does not specify whether pre-nuptiality is alleged against either man, neither does it instruct the clerics charged with carrying out the investigation to ascertain whether the birth of either man preceded his parents' marriage, as opposed to simply establishing their legitimacy.[29] The mandate includes a reference to 'certain letters', now lost, which may have contained more details of the grounds on which the allegation of bastardy rested.

It may be that pre-nuptiality was sometimes (or often) alleged in bastardy cases concerning inheritance, but if it was not standard practice to record on what grounds someone was alleged, or found, to be a non-heir, or if such records are now lost, then the distinction is understandably not visible.[30] Equally, it may be that the lack of visibility of a two-tier system indicates pre-nuptiality was not the insurmountable barrier to inheritance suggested by *RM*,

27 An older brother was made to yield the earldom of Menteith to a younger in the early thirteenth century (see pp. 173–4) but the details are so scant it is impossible to know whether the brothers had the same mother.

28 RPS, 1472/24. Discussed below, pp. 44–5.

29 Theiner, *Vet. Mon.*, no. 196.

30 Details occasionally survive: in 1498 Muriel of Cawdor's legitimacy was challenged (unsuccessfully) on the grounds that she was not the child of her mother's husband. *Cawdor Book*, 92–126.

and that as long as the canon law regarded a person as legitimate, the common law did as well. The existence of a two-tier system in England is evident from the use of the legal terms bastard *eigné* and *mulier puisné* and their variants, along with the evidence for letters *mulier*. The absence of similar terms in Scottish legal parlance is a strong indication that the distinction did not exist in the kingdom's legal practice.

The surviving statutes of the Scottish Church dating from 1225 are silent on this, but overall they indicate a Church keen to implement the canon law as promulgated by Rome, which is suggestive of the doctrine of legitimation by subsequent marriage being accepted in Scotland following the incorporation of the decretal *Tanta* into the canon law (possibly between its promulgation in the 1170s and its inclusion in the *Liber Extra* in 1234, but perhaps after the *Liber Extra* was disseminated).[31] Since we have no Scottish equivalent of the Statute of Merton, which for England provides us with a date when the doctrine was considered (and rejected) by the political community, the question of when legitimation by subsequent marriage was accepted in Scotland has not been answered.

According to Maitland Thomson, the case of Robert II's sons with Elizabeth Mure may have been the legal turning point. He conjectured that the decretal *Tanta* was accepted into Scottish common law only after, and in fact because of, the 1371 Parliamentary acceptance of John (later Robert III), the eldest son of Robert and Elizabeth, as heir to the throne.[32] He highlights the role of parliament as a legislative as well as a judicial body, and the difficulty later generations may have had in separating out those two functions. He concludes by suggesting that the parliamentary ruling that John was heir to his father effectively set a legal precedent by which all offspring born before their parents' marriage could now claim to be legitimate.

John had been retrospectively legitimated by the marriage of Robert and Elizabeth in the late 1340s, when John and his siblings were children. The marriage had been made possible by a papal dispensation, since Elizabeth and Robert were related by both consanguinity and affinity and were not free to intermarry. These impediments are not why they did not get married before the birth of their children: in their eventual petition to be dispensed, they claimed they had been ignorant of the double connection between them.[33] The only contemporary chronicle account of the marriage suggests that they simply entered into a sexual relationship and after a number of years decided to marry.[34]

This is confirmed by the terms of their papal dispensation. It sets out that Robert had had carnal knowledge first of Elizabeth's kinswoman, Isabella

31 X 4.17.1, 6.

32 J. Maitland Thomson, preface to J. R. Mylne, *The Canon Law* (Edinburgh, 1912), xvi–ii.

33 Theiner, *Vet. Mon.*, no. 577.

34 *Gesta Annalia II* in Skene, *Fordun*, i, 317.

Boutellier, and later of Elizabeth, with whom he had been cohabiting 'for a long time', producing 'numerous children of both sexes'.[35] Now Robert and Elizabeth wished to marry. This was rather different from most petitions, which usually related that the parents had contracted a marriage, often publicly, which was faulty, and which they now wished to make good. Robert and Elizabeth's was not a putative marriage requiring convalidation, but a more serious breach of the rules governing Christian conduct: the children had been deliberately procreated outwith marriage, by fornication.[36] Pope Clement VI granted Robert and Elizabeth permission to marry and he declared their children legitimate, but Robert had to pay a penance in the form of founding one or more chaplaincies.

If this was an instance of legitimation *per subsequens matrimonium* by a couple who had not contracted a marriage (even a faulty one) before the birth of their children, but had later married, by which act their offspring had been legitimated, it was not the first in Scotland. John of Douglas, knight, who obtained a dispensation to marry Agnes Graham in 1344, had similarly had carnal knowledge of a kinswoman of hers before cohabiting with Agnes (for three years) and having children.[37] He had told Agnes before they started living together that 'if he contracted marriage he would do so with her before doing so with any other woman, and promised to make her his wife'. His petition claimed that his prior attachment, which had recently come to light, was likely to be the cause of scandals among the families and friends of the two women, unless he and Agnes married. His previous consort was in fact Agnes's niece, a circumstance of which Agnes had been (or claimed to have been) unaware; John also claimed he did not know of it until latterly, when a friend of Agnes pointed it out to him. As he would later do for Robert and Elizabeth, Clement allowed the couple to marry and declared the children legitimate, but imposed on John an obligation to found two chaplaincies in two years, endowed with 10 merks annually. A further penalty was levied: if Agnes died first, John was not permitted to remarry.[38]

In canon law, a couple who exchanged vows of future consent and subsequently engaged in sexual intercourse were married, although irregularly. But the papal mandate does not say that John and Agnes exchanged vows, only that John had made a promise to Agnes: nothing is mentioned of Agnes making a promise in return. Further, John's statement that *if* he was ever to

35 Theiner, *Vet. Mon.*, no. 577.

36 I am grateful to the publisher's anonymous reader for suggesting that this distinction is significant.

37 Theiner, *Vet. Mon.*, no. 563; *CPP*, i, 79; *CPL*, iii, 165.

38 Possibly the pope did not impose the latter prohibition on Robert because he was heir presumptive to the throne, and dynastic considerations might make this impossible to fulfil. Or it may be Clement considered John to have acted particularly badly, since he convinced Agnes to set up home with him by suggesting he might marry her one day, when it appeared that was not his real intention.

marry, it would be to her, was a slippery one in legal terms, since it was not a straightforward pledge but a conditional one. Clement certainly does not treat John and Agnes's relationship as an irregular or putative marriage which can be made good with a dispensation, but as fornication. He does not say that they are given leave to remain in the faulty marriage they have contracted, now dispensed so that the fault is removed, but instead that they are dispensed to contract a marriage freely. The papal register notes the petitioners' claim that, 'unless they marry, scandals may arise', clearly indicating they were not considered to be married already.

John and Agnes's eldest son, James Douglas (d. 1420), was named in a tailzie of 1351 as heir to his uncle William's estates of Dalkeith and of Aberdour in Fife.[39] It took him a number of years to gain possession, since his uncle's killer, William, first earl of Douglas, seized them.[40] In 1367 the lands, or some part of them, were in the possession of James's cousin Mary. When she died in childbirth, James sought to obtain the lands as the rightful heir; Mary's husband, Thomas Erskine, argued that he had the right to them.[41] The matter was settled by a compromise agreement brokered by David II, in which James was awarded the lands, with Thomas to receive a sum of money. Prior to David's intervention, the two disputants had acquired weapons and armoury in preparation for a trial by combat to decide the heirship, revealing very considerable determination on the part of both men to possess the lands.[42] Despite this strength of feeling, Thomas Erskine did not cast any aspersions on James's legitimacy. James's right to the lands was not challenged on grounds of being illegitimate, although he was born before the dispensation granted by Clement which allowed his parents to marry, a consideration which according to *RM* should have made him ineligible to inherit.[43]

His status as a legitimate heir was tested again in 1368, when James brought an action against Roger and Isabel Carruthers, arguing that they unjustly detained lands which had belonged to his uncle and were tailzied on James.[44] Three justiciars were instructed by means of a brieve of mortancestor

39 *Registrum Honoris de Morton*, ed. T. Thomson and others (Bannatyne Club, 1853), ii, nos 70 and 71. James is not described as illegitimate in these. A tailzie was a legal instrument securing the descent of a heritable estate to series of heirs or substitutes, as named by the maker of the tailzie.

40 M. Brown, 'Douglas, Sir James, of Dalkeith (d. 1420), Magnate', *ODNB*, 14 January 2019.

41 The law allowed Erskine rights in the land only if Mary's child had been born alive; his claim to this effect was contested by Douglas.

42 The dispute following Mary's death is discussed in W. D. H. Sellar, 'Courtesy, Battle and the Brieve of Right, 1368 – A Story Continued', in Sellar, ed., *Miscellany II*, Stair Society 35 (Edinburgh, 1984), 1–12. The tale is narrated in *Gesta Annalia II* in Skene, *Fordun*, i, 370 n. 12.

43 He was in his eighties when he died in 1420; the dispensation was dated 1344. Brown, 'Douglas, Sir James'.

44 *RRS*, vi, no. 417; H. MacQueen, 'Dissasine and Mortancestor in Scots Law', *Journal of Legal History* 4 (2007), 34, 37; *SP*, vi, 341–3; *The Douglas Book*, ed. W. Fraser (Edinburgh, 1885), i, 253–4.

to find out whether or not James was the lawful and nearest heir of the most recent person to have died vest and saised in the lands.[45] A recognition of 'good and faithful elder men of the neighbourhood', presumably those old enough to recall the people and relationships concerned, found that he was. In this contest, too, no allegation was made by his opponents that James was not legitimate, despite this being an obvious tack to attempt in the circumstances, given the provision in *RM* to this effect. If it was the case in the 1360s that no person born before the marriage of his parents could be an heir, then even if Roger and Isabel Carruthers did not suggest this applied to James, it should have entered into the considerations of the crown's legal officers during their attempt to establish whether or not James was a lawful heir. In short, James, born before the marriage of his parents, was not regarded in 1367 or 1368 – some three to four years before John of Carrick was accepted as heir to the throne – as a non-heir according to common law.[46]

The case of James Douglas of Dalkeith undermines the premise that legitimation *per subsequens matrimonium* was not accepted before 1371. It was apparently already accepted in the 1340s, otherwise there would have been little point in Robert the Steward using a papal marriage dispensation to alter the status of his children with Elizabeth Mure: he was heir presumptive to David II and likely to become king, and if he was not confident that the marriage would legitimate his sons for royal succession it would have made more sense for him to cut his losses with Elizabeth and marry someone else.[47]

In fact, there is evidence that legitimation *per subsequens matrimonium* was accepted long before this. In 1281 Hugh of Abernethy sought and received a papal dispensation to remain in an invalidly contracted marriage to Mary of Argyll, from which a number of children had already been born.[48] The eldest of these children, Alexander (d. 1315x17), was not yet of age in 1293 but could not have been a child either, since he swore fealty to Edward I in 1291.[49] He cannot, therefore, have been born after the dispensation of 1281 and must have been one of the offspring born before it. In the Balliol parliament of February 1293, 'the lands of Alexander de Abernethy' were given in wardship to Alexander of Menteith.[50] His mother had been asked a few days before if there was any reason why he should not inherit, but there seems to be no suggestion that he was thought of as illegitimate: if he had been, the lands would have

45 MacQueen, 'Dissasine and Mortancestor', 34.

46 He became an immensely wealthy magnate, marrying, shortly after David II's death, that king's mistress and intended third wife Agnes Dunbar; his second wife was Egidia, sister of Robert II. His son with Agnes married Elizabeth, daughter of John, earl of Carrick, later Robert III.

47 See also pp. 101–2 and 105.

48 Theiner, *Vet. Mon.*, no. 277.

49 *Instrumenta Publica sive Processus super Fidelitatibus et Homagiis Scotorum Domino Regi Angliae Factis 1291–96*, ed. T. Thomson (Bannatyne Club, 1834), 157.

50 *RPS*, 1293/2/14.

been described as 'of Hugh de Abernethy', not as 'of Alexander' (they are, further, described as Alexander's 'heritage') and his possessions would not have been held in ward for him but would have descended to a sibling born after the dispensation, or some other family member, or else they would have escheated to the king.[51] Alexander later took possession of the lands as lord of Abernethy. This being the case, and taken with the example of James Douglas, the provision in *RM* denying pre-nuptial children rights of inheritance was evidently not a statement of pre-existing law in Scotland, neither was it a law that was introduced to Scotland through *RM* and not revoked or robbed of force until 1371 when John of Carrick was recognised as heir to the throne.

Underlying Maitland Thomson's argument is the premise that acceptance of legitimation *per subsequens matrimonium* must have taken place after the production of *RM*, which forbids inheritance by pre-nuptial children. He was of course not privy to the argument made much more recently, that *RM* is an unfinished work and so may well be quite unreliable on this point. But independently of this, positive evidence that pre-nuptial children were in fact denied heirship, either before or after *RM* was compiled, is lacking. The argument that they were, and that this was later reversed, depends on, firstly, accepting that *Glanvill*'s provision to this effect was copied into *RM* because it was true of Scots law as well as of English, and, secondly, attempting to reconcile this using the evidence of the later fourteenth century, when people born before the marriages of their parents were in fact recognised as heirs. Maitland Thomson and other historians have looked for a change in the law in the place they expected to find it: *after* the first quarter of the fourteenth century (the assumed date of *RM*'s production), because otherwise they would have to discount this provision in *RM* as part of legal practice at that time. But it is by no means certain that it was. The weight of circumstantial evidence tends to point against it having been implemented in Scotland, and recent work by Taylor raises the possibility that it may not have been intended to form part of a finalised text of *RM*. There seems to be no good reason why couples would go to the trouble and expense of obtaining papal dispensations either to convalidate their putative marriages or to enter into marriages with partners canonically forbidden to them, unless regularising their unions ensured their offspring became their heirs. These dispensations were sought both before and after *RM* was compiled; the codification of a law denying pre-marital children heirship appears to have made little difference to the couples concerned.

Given the lack of positive evidence for the enactment of the provision, it is more credible that legitimation *per subsequens matrimonium* was accepted – perhaps actively welcomed – from the time it gained traction among the legal authorities of the Church, either in the late twelfth century or in the first half of the thirteenth. The doctrine applied to those who needed no dispensation to

[51] *RPS*, 1293/2/10.

wed, but who had embarked on a sexual relationship with someone they were free to marry. Such couples do not appear in papal records, and so we do not know how numerous they may have been. In a society with a long-standing tradition of accepting all offspring into a kin group, the facility to remedy with comparative ease the status of a child born before the marriage of his parents is likely to have been readily embraced. The decretal *Tanta* was being introduced, debated, incorporated into canon law and disseminated at the same time (late-twelfth to mid-thirteenth century) as primogeniture and the exclusion of illegitimate sons from inheritance was becoming more prevalent. The remedy offered by the doctrine may well have eased the transition, and from the Church's point of view provided what was probably the best means possible of furthering its aim of encouraging ecclesiastically sanctioned marriage in replacement of the irregular marriage practices it was seeking to eliminate.

Enforcing the legal disability

By the middle of the thirteenth century, developments in both the systemisation of canon law and professionalisation of its implementation meant that Church law was being dispensed with some degree of consistency throughout western Christendom.[52] In Scotland, the process was aided by the creation in 1225 of a provincial council. Its surviving statutes (1225–1559) reflect an organisation seeking to promote conformity to contemporary Church doctrine and teaching.[53] The establishment of the provincial council, providing a forum for Churchmen to meet regularly for the purpose of developing and issuing legislation to be implemented in their dioceses, appears to have been influential on the development of the common law in Scotland. It was not long after its foundation that Alexander II began to make important innovations in royal law, some of which suggest he took a particular interest in rightful succession.[54] Taylor argues that the Church's provincial council provided a model for Alexander to adopt, 'and left a gap for secular power to develop concurrently'.[55]

Royal brieves – formulaic letters initiating a legal process – were known in the twelfth century, but Alexander II introduced new forms of these, which allowed more people to bring actions, within royal jurisdiction but independently of royal favour, to be recognised as rightful heirs or possessors

52 G. Dolezalek, 'The Court of Session as a *Ius Commune* Court – Witnessed by "Sinclair's Practicks", 1540–1549', in H. L. MacQueen, ed., *Miscellany IV*, Stair Society 49 (Edinburgh, 2002), 54; MacQueen, 'Canon Law, Custom and Legislation', 229–30, 235.

53 They do not include any discussion of the legal consequences of illegitimacy, but they do repeatedly exhort clerics to desist from entering into sexual relationships with their parishioners and others. Patrick, *Statutes*, 14, 16, 28–9, 37, 44, 51, 59–60, 68–9 (all pre-1500).

54 A. Taylor, *The Shape of the State in Medieval Scotland 1124–1290* (Oxford, 2016), 296.

55 Ibid., 348.

of land.[56] Brieves of inquest, in particular, were an accessible means of identifying the nearest lawful heir.[57] Once a claimant had purchased a brieve of inquest, it was issued to an appropriate authority – usually a sheriff – who was obliged to conduct an investigation which sought to establish, on behalf of the 'bearer' (purchaser) of the brieve, his or her rights in the land or other heritable property in question. This entailed gathering information from those with pertinent knowledge of the lands and families concerned.[58] Findings were reported back to the king's *capella* (writing office) for judgement and for the issuing of instructions as to the awarding of sasine (possession).[59] The development and use of brieves expanded significantly over the course of the reign of Alexander II (1214–49) and that of his son Alexander III (1249–86).[60] This had significant implications for inheritance disputes in which bastardy was alleged against a putative heir, since it enabled litigants to launch or reopen actions and settle disputes under royal jurisdiction where that might be felt to offer some advantage.[61] Some late medieval Scottish bastardy disputes illustrate the utility of brieves in this regard.

Henry Carruthers, son of Simon, had either succeeded, or was poised to succeed, to Simon's lands in Annandale, but his kinsman Archibald Carruthers of Mouswald brought an action of bastardy against him.[62] This action had been remitted to the consistory court in Glasgow but had not progressed to a decision. At some point in the process, Henry purchased a brieve of inquest

56 On the development and use of brieves in medieval Scotland, see Taylor, *Shape of the State* (esp. Chapter 5); H. L. MacQueen, *Common Law & Feudal Society in Medieval Scotland* (Edinburgh, 1993); H. L. MacQueen, 'Pleadable Brieves, Pleading, and the Development of Scots Law', *Law and History Review* 4 (1986), 403–22; H. L. MacQueen, 'The Brieve of Right in Scots Law', *The Journal of Legal History* 3 (1982), 52–70; D. Broun, 'The Adoption of Brieves in Scotland', in M. T. Flanagan and J. A. Green, ed., *Charters and Charter Scholarship in Britain and Ireland* (Basingstoke, 2005), 164–83; I. D. Willock, *The Origins and Development of the Jury in Scotland*, Stair Society 23 (Edinburgh, 1966); A. Harding, 'The Medieval Brieves of Protection and the Development of the Common Law', *JR* 11 (1966), 115–49; H. McKechnie, *Judicial Process upon Brieves, 1219–1532* (Glasgow, 1956).

57 The inquest process existed before the development of a brieve for it. Brieves of mortancestry, of recognition, of right, and of novel dissasine were all concerned with identifying the correct heir or owner of land, and might be used according to the circumstances, but the latter three were less accessible than those of mortancestry or inquest. Taylor, *Shape of the State*, 291–3; 308–19.

58 Willock, *The Jury in Scotland*, 109–14; Taylor, *Shape of the State*, 301–4, 323–6.

59 Ibid., 307, 325–6. This was the process in brieves served by sheriffs; justiciars, more commonly used for brieves other than inquests, could deliver judgements and award sasine.

60 Taylor, *Shape of the State*, 321–3; MacQueen, 'Canon Law, Custom and Legislation', 244–51.

61 Taylor, *Shape of the State*, 326, 328–30.

62 *RPS*, 1484/2/80 and 1484/2/119. Archibald was laird of Mouswald and occurs often in the records, but Henry is more obscure. The name Simon is frequently found in the Carruthers family; Henry may have been Archibald's nephew or grand-nephew. Several Carruthers are named as having lands or offices in Annandale in the fifteenth century, but this seems to be the only mention of Henry.

on the lands. The brieve in this case was served by the sheriff of Dumfries, Robert Crichton of Sanquhar, and his deputy, Edward Crichton. Archibald responded by bringing an action against the sheriff and his depute for their 'wrongful and improper proceedings' in doing so. On 20 February 1484, the lords auditors of causes and complaints gave Archibald a week to prove that he had 'done his diligence' in the Church court, and to demonstrate that it was not his fault the case was still pending, by showing that he had 'brought sufficient testimonial' for the spiritual court to reach a decision. On 27 February, the lords auditors concluded that Robert and Edward had 'done no wrong in serving the said brieve purchased by the said Henry on the said lands, because the said Archibald has not done his diligence in pursuing the said action of bastardry and its process to an end, as was shown before the lords'.

In 1482 Margaret Maitland pursued a similar action against sheriffs who had executed a brieve of inquest 'purchased by one William called Maitland', and served him heir.[63] Margaret was the daughter of William Maitland of Lethington, after whose death in 1471 his lands in the Dumfries barony of Tibbers, and in Roxburgh and Berwick, were in the hands of the other party in the dispute, his grandson William Maitland, styled 'of Lethington', evidently under age at his grandfather's death as his curator acted for him in property matters in 1471 and 1476.[64] Margaret's action of bastardy against him concluded in December 1482 with the decision to censure the sheriffs, Michael Balfour of Burleigh and Alexander Spens, and to set aside the brieve. Margaret thereby obtained the family lands: in 1483, she had sasine of Fairnington in Roxburgh and Tibbers in Dumfries.[65] But William was back in possession by 1505, presumably having established his legitimacy.[66]

The reason given for setting aside the brieve in 1482 was that 'the action of bastardry proposed by the said Margaret against the said William was pending undecided in the spiritual court'. This looks very similar to the reason given for the opposite outcome in the Carruthers case. Evidently, however, the sheriffs serving the brieve for William Maitland were held to have acted pre-emptively, while in the Carruthers dispute, the lords auditors decided there was an undue delay at the consistory court. Possibly they thought the delay was caused by Archibald having no proper grounds for his allegation that Henry was illegitimate. In any case, they put the onus on Archibald to

63 *RPS*, 1482/12/19.

64 *Hist. MSS Comm. Fifteenth Report*, App. Pt. viii (1897), nos 58 and 59; *ER*, ix, 678; *RPS*, 1471/8/9 and 1476/7/35. William senior is also given as 'of Thirlestone'.

65 *ER*, ix, 682. Some lands of the latter she gave in tack to her kinsman Robert Maitland of Queensberry. *RPS*, 1483/10/74.

66 *ER*, xii, 717–18; ER, xiii, 658; *Protocol Book of James Young 1485–1515*, ed. G. Donaldson (SRS, 1952), nos 1689–91; *Hist. MSS. Comm. Fifteenth Report*, App. Pt. viii, no. 59. In 1509 he sold Tibbers to Sir William Douglas of Drumlanrig. Ibid., no. 11.

prove that he had complied with the requirements of the court in producing evidentiary material in support of his claim within seven days; Archibald being unable to do so, his allegation was dismissed. This does not mean that Henry was certainly legitimate, only that Archibald was unable to show otherwise. Similarly, Margaret's success in having her nephew William's brieve set aside was achieved independently of confirmation of his actual birth status, which in due course was established either by the Church courts or by some other means, resulting in the lands being returned to him. William's purchasing of a brieve may or may not have been seen as an attempt to pre-empt or obviate the judgement of the consistory court, but the sheriffs' execution of the brieve before due time had elapsed for the court to make a ruling was understood to have had this effect, a subversion of accepted legal procedure.

In each of these two cases, the lords auditors took a view on what was a reasonable timescale for the Church courts to reach a judgement, as must have been usual in cases in which the two jurisdictions intersected. Formally, canon law applied a presumption in favour of legitimacy, so that, as Archibald Carruthers found, in cases where there was doubt, 'sufficient testimonial' had to be brought to overturn the presumption. It is probable that the judicial processes of the Church worked too slowly for some disputants, who seized on the opportunity offered by royal brieves to settle the matter in weeks rather than months or even years.[67] But purchasing a brieve of inquest may also have been a means of avoiding ecclesiastical examination of birth status. Two crown officers, James MacCulloch of Cardoness (Galloway) and his bailie, Thomas MacCulloch, conducted an inquest on behalf of Archibald Muir, which resulted in Archibald being given possession of six merks of land at Auchenflower.[68] They had done so despite the protests of Andrew Agnew, acting for Alexander Muir of Bardrochat, who alleged that Archibald was a bastard, showing this 'by the laws of the realm' and challenging Archibald to prove otherwise. What evidence was adduced to demonstrate the bastardy is not described. Archibald having obtained the lands, Alexander responded by bringing an action against James and Thomas MacCulloch, 'for their unfair and improper proceeding [and] serving of an inquest'. No mention is made of any consultation with the spiritual courts to determine the bastardy or otherwise of Archibald. Possibly he was indeed illegitimate and was wary of subjecting his birth circumstances to the scrutiny of the diocesan official. The lords auditors ruled that James and Thomas 'did err in the serving of the said inquest and that the possession given to the said Archibald thereupon is of no value, force or effect'. James was fined 40 shillings and Thomas, who did not appear for judgement, was instructed by letter to make himself a ward of Edinburgh castle. The surviving record of this

[67] Taylor, *Shape of the State*, 324–5, 326, 332.
[68] *RPS*, 1472/24.

case suggests not that the two jurisdictions worked hand-in-hand to identify the rightful heir and award him his heritage, but that a brieve was used to steal a march on a rival and claim the lands by the quickest and most direct method possible. Similarly, Gilla Críst Megor purchased a brieve of inquest to be served heir to the late Donnchad Megor.[69] Donnchad's brother, Domnall, raised an action against the sheriff for wrongful pursuing of the brieve, 'because there was bastardy proponit against Gilchrist'. The lords of council judged that, 'for aucht that they can yet understand', the sheriff had acted lawfully. This suggests that the inquest had been conducted in accordance with proper procedure and so the sheriff had done no wrong, but also that the matter of heirship was not completely laid to rest, since information may yet emerge to support the allegation of bastardy.

Someone's birth status might be open to reasonable doubt but incapable of proof, resulting in the two sides becoming deadlocked.[70] In such instances the legal authority concerned might force a conclusion by imposing a decree-arbitral on the litigants. The thirteenth-century inheritance dispute in which John of Kinross alleged Ailwin of Callendar to be illegitimate continued for five years before the papacy halted it by declaring in favour of Ailwin and requiring John to abide by its judgement under penalty of ecclesiastical censure, a massive £1,000 fine should John or his heirs fail to comply, and a legal prohibition against him reopening the action in any forum.[71] The severity of these terms hints at a degree of exasperation on the part of the Church, but given what was often at stake in these disputes, it is not surprising that litigants contested them vigorously, and by fair means or foul.[72] Legal professionals were sometimes complicit in wrongful succession, whether through calculated deceit or lack of expertise. Legislation in the reign of James IV called for a programme of rigorous examination of notaries, since the dishonesty of some was putting inheritances in doubt.[73]

69 *ADC*, 88*.

70 'Inevitably, some legitimacy disputes were so complex and intractable, and the evidence so conflicting, that it was difficult for the pope to reach a verdict completely consonant with the law.' C. Duggan, 'Equity and Compassion in Papal Marriage Decretals to England', in C. Duggan, *Decretals and the Creation of 'New Law' in the Twelfth Century. Judges, Judgements, Equity and Law* (Aldershot, 1998), 77.

71 This well-known case is discussed in T. Cooper, *Select Scottish Cases of the Thirteenth Century* (Edinburgh, 1944), 61–5 and in Ferguson, *Medieval Papal Representatives*, 158, 251. The documents pertaining to it may also be found on *PoMS*, www.poms.ac.uk/record/person/2148/.

72 Ailwin concealed the fact that the case was already under appeal when he sought papal mandates to have it heard by new judges-delegate. See also the discussion of Alan Durward's attempt to acquire the earldom of Mar, at pp. 178–80.

73 *RPS*, A1504/3/108.

Secular law remedies for the legal disability

Someone whose illegitimate status could not be rectified by the provisions of canon law might have recourse to means in the secular realm by which the legal effects of bastardy were reduced, or vacated altogether.

The lands of an illegitimate person who died without legitimate issue escheated to the king *ratione bastardie* (by reason of bastardy), because an illegitimate person could have no heirs other than those of his body, legitimately procreated. But kings could waive this right and use their royal authority to allow an illegitimate person to dispone his lands freely; by the same token, they could allow illegitimates to inherit certain lands. The granting of privileges in respect of land transmission, or 'bending the rules' to determine the descent of estates, was part and parcel of ordinary crown patronage in medieval Scotland.[74] Sometime between 1271 and 1285, Alexander III allowed that if William of Badby should die without legitimate heirs then 'his bastard son John' was to hold the lands.[75] But if John too died without legitimate issue, the property reverted to the crown. Robert II issued a letter to William Dunbar, burgess of Aberdeen, in 1384, permitting him to dispone freely any of his lands, rents, tenements and possessions, notwithstanding William's bastardy.[76]

Where an estate escheated *ratione bastardie* to the king he often granted it to a favoured individual.[77] Sometimes this 'gift of bastardy' was made to a relative of the deceased illegitimate, who could not ordinarily inherit from him or her. On the death of the illegitimate Archibald Crichton with no heirs of his body legitimately procreated, his lands escheated to James IV, who granted them to Archibald's brother Andrew and his heirs, whom failing to Andrew's sisters Margaret and Mariota and their heirs, in turn.[78] Or a king might instead retain a portion of escheated lands to use for his own purposes, while allowing the rest to pass from one illegitimate family member to another. When Gilbert Lauder in Whitslaid, Berwick, died, he left only illegitimate sons, one of whom, Robert, later died in possession of a substantial estate. In a charter of James IV, to whom the estate escheated, Robert is variously described as Gilbert's son (without a qualifier), his natural son, his carnal son, and as someone 'born a

74 A. Grant, 'Crown and Nobility in Late Medieval Britain', in R. A. Mason, ed., *Scotland and England 1286–1815* (Edinburgh, 1987), 42. Kings could also provide such dispensations to legitimately born individuals whose rights of succession were compromised either by their youth – those under the age of twenty-one could not succeed – or whose ancestor had died in a state of enmity with the crown. Willock, *Origins of the Jury*, 114. These too were waivers of royal rights in matters of succession.

75 *RMS*, i, App. 1, no. 95; *RRS*, iv, no. 166.

76 Ibid., i, no. 768.

77 Ibid., i, nos 160, 242, 639, App. 2 nos 1360, 1392, 1778; ii, nos 79, 83, 85, 160, 173, 488, 748, 803, 828, 890, 929, 975, 1144, 1218, 1263, 1565, 1697, 1764, 1917, 1926, 2022, 2083, 2096, 2344, 2449, 2450, 2585.

78 Ibid., ii, no. 2069.

bastard and dying without legitimate heirs of his body'.[79] James granted the bulk of the property to another son of Gilbert, Robert's brother Jasper, who was also illegitimate, and to Jasper's lawful heirs, whom failing to Jasper's brother David and his heirs, whom failing to their brother George and his heirs, whom failing to the lawful and nearest heirs of the brothers. But James reserved some of Robert's lands and tenements to grant to others in the locality.[80] Feudal superiors could similarly direct the destination of land held by their tenants, allowing a tenant's illegitimate offspring to succeed, or making grants of lands escheated to them by the death of an illegitimate tenant without lawful heirs of his body.[81]

As this shows, some illegitimate people in medieval Scotland were able to inherit through a tailzie, a legal document by which heritable property was settled on a specified line of heirs or substitutes (the latter known as remainders). The use of tailzies was well-established by the middle of the thirteenth century.[82] A 1378 charter of Robert Stewart, earl of Fife, son of Robert II, makes a grant of a portion of his estates in Fife (all his lands of 'the two Rossies') to his (legitimate) kinsman Sir Alexander Lindsay of Glenesk.[83] The charter tailzies the lands on Alexander's legitimate male heirs with his wife (Lady Marjorie Stewart), whom failing, in turn, Alexander's brother and his legitimate male heirs, Alexander's nephew and his legitimate male heirs, then Alexander's illegitimate son, John Lindsay, and his legitimate male heirs. If all those lines failed, the land was to pass to the 'nearest males by blood and kinship' bearing the name and arms of Lindsay. Similarly, a tailzie of 1342 permitted Archibald the Grim Douglas to inherit the earldom of Douglas some forty-seven years later: it too nominated a sequence of heirs, of which Archibald, the only bastard in the list, was the last named.[84] His (legitimate) son, Archibald, fourth earl of Douglas, duke of Touraine, made charters of tailzie to kinsmen of his Douglas lands which were to be inherited by lawful sons but in the absence of these by the grantees' illegitimate sons.[85]

A charter of John Haliburton, confirmed by the king in 1463, grants lands in the barony of Dirleton (Haddington) to Richard Congalton ('de Congiltoun') and his legitimate sons, with remainders to Richard's brother Edward, then Edward's brother John and John's brother Drew, and their legitimate sons, in

79 Ibid., ii, no. 2595.

80 Ibid., ii, nos 2596 and 2597.

81 Ibid., ii, no. 85; A. Grant, 'Acts of Lordship: The Records of Archibald, Fourth Earl of Douglas', in T. Brotherstone and D. Ditchburn, ed., *Freedom and Authority. Scotland* c. *1050*–c. *1650* (East Linton, 2000), 263, 268.

82 A brieve of 1250 refers to 'writings, charters, tailzies, etc' ('*scriptis cartis taliis decetero*'). *Calendar of Writs Preserved at Yester House 1166–1503*, ed. C. C. H. Harvey and J. Macleod (SRS, 1930), no. 15.

83 *RPS*, 1378/2.

84 *RRS*, vi, no. 51.

85 Grant, 'Records of the Fourth Earl of Douglas', nos 2, 3, 33, 64, 71.

turn; there follows a further two remainders to illegitimate brothers Thomas and Mark and their legitimate sons, after which another two brothers (Edmund and Archibald), not given as illegitimate, stood in line to inherit with their sons; the next remainder is to Archibald's kinsman Roger and his male heirs, and finally, in the event of all those lines failing, then William, uncle of Richard, the original grantee, should obtain the lands.[86] This is an extreme example, but those using tailzies usually ensured that illegitimate kin stood to inherit only if one or more legitimate line(s) failed, so that the nearest legitimate heir, at least, was not excluded. An exception is found in a charter of 1469, by which John, lord of the Isles, gave various lands to his brother Hugh, to be held by Hugh and his male heirs, legitimate or illegitimate ('*legitime sive illegitime*'), procreated between him and Fionnula, daughter of Alexander MacIain of Ardnamurchan, whom failing by sons of Hugh begotten with any other woman after Fionnula's death.[87] Some royal grants of offices were also tailzied on illegitimates: James II appointed Andrew Agnew sheriff of Wigtown for life, which post was heritable by Agnew's heir (also Andrew) and his legitimate sons, whom failing by Andrew senior's illegitimate sons Patrick and Gilbert in turn, with reversion to the crown.[88]

Tailzies released landowners from the restrictions imposed by legitimate primogeniture, which not only excluded bastards from heirship, but also required that the estate of a landholder dying without legitimate sons should descend to legitimate daughters. Where a landholder left more than one daughter, the feu might be divided between them; an undesirable state of affairs for many Scottish landowners, who did not want their estates to be split up and absorbed into the holdings of their sons-in-law's families. 'Male-tails', by which estates were handed on to male kin only, were a regular feature of Scottish land conveyancing from the fourteenth century. Some excluded female heirs entirely, while others allowed inheritance by any lawful heir (implicitly including daughters) in the event of the failure of male heirs in the nominated lines, which may or may not include illegitimate kin. Although tailzies may sometimes have been drawn up to ensure illegitimate members of the family stood some chance of obtaining an inheritance, it is also likely that for some, the real attraction lay in preventing female inheritance while keeping lands within the kindred.

Letters of legitimation

Permission from the king for a bastard to inherit named lands, or to have heirs other than legitimate offspring, was not a legitimation, but kings did also

86 *RMS*, ii, no. 759.

87 *Acts of the Lords of the Isles 1336–1493*, ed. J. Munro and R. W. Munro, SHS 22 (Edinburgh, 1986), no. 96; a confirmation charter was issued in 1495: *RMS*, ii, no. 2286.

88 *RMS*, ii, no. 447.

issue these. Legitimation by rescript was established by the Emperor Justinian in the sixth century C.E.[89] The case of Scots notary-public Alexander Rait issuing a legitimation under imperial authority in the 1470s suggests that some illegitimate people in Scotland had recourse to this means of being legitimated, but James III's adverse response to Rait's actions, along with legislation enacted in 1469 to bring legitimations more securely under royal purview, may have led to an increase in legitimation petitions being sent to the royal chancery instead.[90] Some Scottish royal legitimations are recorded in the register of the great seal but many more were issued under the king's own privy seal. Since the register of the latter begins in 1488, it is difficult to evaluate the impact of the 1469 legislation, or the action against Rait, on requests for royal legitimations. As far as papal legitimations are concerned, the *Liber Extra* (1234) advised that popes should avoid, in general, legitimising children in lands other than those over which the Church exercised temporal power.[91] This was because such rescripts were understood to legitimate their recipients for temporal (inheritance) purposes, and so had the potential to affect the jurisdiction and rights of others. Papal legitimation by rescript was relatively new at the time the *Liber Extra* was compiled. Its first known use is by Pope Innocent III (1198–1216) in 1201, when he legitimated 'by special grace' the children of Philip II 'Augustus', king of France, and Agnès of Meran.[92] 'Special grace' was deployed because, in a first for the papacy, a child's status as legitimate was established not as a consequence of the pope recognising the parents' relationship as a marriage, but quite independently of this; the union of Philip and Agnès was unequivocally not a valid marriage, but the children were granted legitimacy anyway. The following year, in the decretal *Per venerabilem*, the same pope denied legitimation to the offspring of William VIII, count of Montpellier, and Agnes of Castile, saying that the count had a higher temporal authority (that is, the king) capable of legitimating his children, whereas Philip had no such recourse.[93]

89 *Nov.* 74.2; *Nov.* 89.9. The laws of Justinian also provided that children born to an unmarried couple who were free to intermarry were legitimated by the parents' subsequent marriage. Rescripts were intended for use in some cases in which the parents could not marry.

90 *RPS*, 1469/20, discussed in at pp. 186–7.

91 X 4.17.13.

92 *PL* 214, 1191–4 (Innocent III legitimates the French king's offspring *de speciali gratia*, on the grounds that the kingdom required heirs). A letter of Pope Innocent II (1130–43) in 1131 refers to the existence of this power in imperial law, but in the context of ordination rather than of inheritance or of the laity, and there is no record of it being used before 1201. *PL* 179, 99–101; McDougall, *Royal Bastards*, 40.

93 X 4.17.13 (*Per venerabilem*). The scholarship on these two judgements is extensive. See, for example, D. Courtney-Batson, '*Per venerabilem*: From Practical Necessity to Judicial Supremacy', in *Pope Innocent III and His World*, ed. J. C. Moore (Aldershot, 1999), 287–303; J. A. Watt, *The Theory of Papal Monarchy in the Thirteenth Century: The Contribution of the Canonists* (New York, 1965), 35–45, 52–6, 108–17; B. Tierney,

Papal letters of legitimation seem not to have been common in medieval Scotland. A rare example, dated 1445 and issued by Pope Eugenius IV, legitimates (again, 'by special grace') Hugh, Alexander and Donald, three sons of Alexander MacDonald, earl of Ross and lord of the Isles, stating that they thereby have the right to inherit from or succeed to their father.[94] Royal letters of legitimation similarly include wording to the effect that their recipients are made as fully able to exercise legal rights and hold offices as anyone born legitimate, usually including an explicit statement that they may have heirs other than those of their body, presumably for avoidance of doubt after the death of the bearer.[95] When royal letters of legitimation became more numerous in the fifteenth century, compositions were payable to the crown for them, although kings might still have issued some as a sign of royal favour, without a fee being levied. Such payments seem to have been formally introduced through a parliamentary act of 1534.[96] However, well before 1500, royal houses did a brisk trade in payments for the granting of charters and privileges, as well as for remissions of crime, and letters of legitimation were unlikely to have been produced and issued *gratis*.[97] The papal penitentiary also imposed a composition for certain kinds of papal graces, including those concerning bastardy.[98]

James III provided a legitimation on 2 July 1480 to William and John Ruthven, sons of William, first lord Ruthven.[99] The letter specifically enables the sons to inherit their father's estates. Ten days later, the king granted to William junior the lands of the barony of Ruthven, resigned by lord Ruthven in favour of his recently legitimated son.[100] The younger William's mother (who

'"*Tria Quippe Distinguit Iudicia…*' A Note on Innocent III's Decretal *Per Venerabilem*', *Speculum* 37 (1962), 48–59; C. M. Rousseau, 'Innocent III, Defender of the Innocents and the Law: Children and Papal Policy (1198–1216)', *Archivum Historiae Pontificiae* 32 (1994), 31–42; K. Pennington, *Popes, Canonists and Texts, 1150–1550* (Aldershot, 1993), 1–25. For Innocent III's refusal to recognise the relationship between Philip II and Agnès of Meran as a marriage, see D. L. D'Avray, *Dissolving Royal Marriages. A Documentary History, 860–1600* (Cambridge, 2014), 58–68; F. Pedersen, 'Adventures in Law: The Danes and the Marriage Breakup of Philip II of France', in P. Brand and others, ed., *Adventures of the Law. Proceedings of the Sixteenth British Legal History Conference, Dublin, 2003* (Dublin, 2005), 54–69.

94 *Highland Papers*, ed. J. R. N. MacPhail (Edinburgh, 1914–20), i, 92–3. Another papal letter dated nine months later, at the petition of Alexander's wife Elizabeth, censured Alexander for keeping Christina Maclaid as his concubine. Ibid., 93–5.

95 Two fourteenth-century royal letters of legitimation are discussed in Chapter 4 at pp. 97–9.

96 *ADCP*, 414–15.

97 *TA*, i, lxxix, 2–12, 312–18; J. M. Brown, 'The Exercise of Power', in J. M. Brown, ed., *Scottish Society in the Fifteenth Century* (London, 1977), 63; R. Nicholson, *Scotland: The Later Middle Ages* (Edinburgh, 1974), 499.

98 Lunt, *Papal Revenues*, i, 132. These payments were additional to the charges levied by the chancery for the administrative functions involved. Ibid., 129.

99 *RMS*, ii, no. 1442.

100 Ibid., ii, no. 1445.

was also the mother of John) is given as Isabel Livingston, wife of the late Walter Lindsay of Beaufort, making it plain that she was not married to her sons' father. Later that year she and William senior did intermarry.[101] Their sons would have been legitimated automatically on the marriage, according to the doctrine of legimation *per subsequens matrimonium*, and so if William had waited until after his marriage to resign his lands in favour of his son, a royal legitimation ought to have been unnecessary. Lachlan MacLean, 'sone naturall' of Hector MacLean of Duart, similarly obtained a letter of legitimation under the privy seal of James IV, on 3 October 1496; five days later the king granted to Lachlan the estates resigned in Lachlan's favour by Hector.[102] Both of these legitimations were clearly undertaken for the express purpose of ensuring a son born illegitimate was able to succeed to the family estates.

Some royal letters of legitimation were for two or more bastards from the same family. A letter of James IV legitimated Robert Waus or Patrikson and also his sister Marjorie; another made the brothers John, Alexander and Patrick Hepburn legitimate; and a third granted legitimations to Robert, William, Malcolm, John, another William, and David Drummond, 'bastardis and brether'.[103] In 1500, the king issued a letter of legitimation to David Hamilton, illegitimate son of Alexander Hamilton of 'Birnwod' (Bruntwood), which also legitimated David's own bastard sons David and George.[104]

No Scottish king in our period appears to have legitimated his own illegitimate offspring by means of a royal rescript, although legitimations for members of the extended family are known. James III legitimated Andrew lord Avondale and Avondale's two brothers Arthur and Walter Stewart.[105] James IV legitimated in 1489 James Stewart, illegitimate son of James, earl of Buchan.[106] The legitimated James was a grandson of Joan Beaufort, queen of James I of Scotland, from her second marriage (to Sir James Stewart of Lorne); James IV was the great-grandson of Joan and James I. James IV also

101 M. A. Penman, 'Ruthven, William, of that Ilk, First Lord Ruthven (b. in or before 1448, d. 1528), Landowner and Administrator', *ODNB*, 9 February 2018.

102 *RSS*, i, no. 68; *RMS*, ii, nos 2327 and 2329. Lachlan was later forfeited by the same king for assorted treasonous acts, among which was his declaring as Lord of the Isles Donald Dubh MacDonald, grandson of the John MacDonald Lord of the Isles forfeited by James IV in 1493. In the judicial proceedings against Lachlan, Donald Dubh is described as the bastard son of a bastard son. *RPS*, 1504/3/73 and 1506/2/3.

103 *RSS*, i, nos 423, 449, 467.

104 Ibid., i, no. 576.

105 *RMS*, ii, nos 1066–8, 1425. Andrew is discussed in Chapter 7 at pp. 185–6.

106 Ibid., ii, no. 1830; *RSS*, i, no. 340 is a precept of charter in which lands of Alexander earl of Buchan are tailzied on the earl's legitimate sons, with remainders to: the earl of Atholl (Buchan's uncle); two named sons of Atholl and their legitimate sons, in turn; Atholl's other legitimate sons; then James, 'son of the late James Stewart earl of Buchan with Margaret Murray and made lawful by the king' and his legitimate sons; and finally to the nearest lawful male heirs of Buchan.

legitimated David and Katherine Panter, the children of his illegitimate first cousin, Margaret Crichton.[107]

RM sets out that although an illegitimate son cannot inherit any part of his father's heritage lands (those which the holder inherited) if the father has legitimate sons, a father with both heritage and conquest lands (those acquired in his lifetime) may hand over some or all of the latter to anyone he pleases, by *inter vivos* gift (a gift made from one living person to another, rather than in the form of a legacy).[108] If he has only conquest lands, he may alienate part of them, but not all, since he must not disinherit his (legitimate) offspring.[109] This law was exploited by parents of means in urban society as well as by the nobility. Protocol books, in which notaries-public recorded transactions and other legal matters in the course of their practice, include instances of property being gifted to illegitimate offspring. Henry Richardson, burgess of Stirling, gave his 'son natural', Richard, his tenement; John Quareour of Edinburgh similarly made an *inter vivos* gift of his tenement to his illegitimate son George, as did Richard Waldy and his wife Jonet to Richard's natural son James.[110]

Sources for the operation of the law concerning marriage and illegitimacy are not as rich for medieval Scotland as they are for some other countries; nonetheless, it is clear that Scottish legal culture in the later middle ages was concerned to both discourage procreation outside of marriage and, to a greater extent than in England, to allow some of those so procreated to escape the legal consequences of their parents' actions. Canon laws protecting the legitimacy of children born to those who had unwittingly contracted an invalid marriage, and the availability of dispensations legitimising the children of couples who had done so knowingly or otherwise, suggest a degree of willingness on the part of the Church not to disadvantage offspring where this could reasonably be avoided. The legal disability of illegitimacy, because of its implications for possession and transmission of property, was sufficiently momentous to justify the Church's stance in this regard, and also helps to explain the development of civil law remedies in respect of illegitimacy. Royal legitimations and waivers of right, tailzies and *inter vivos* gifts, were lawful means of reducing or eliminating that disadvantage.

From the thirteenth century, royal brieves and their attendant legal processes opened up new possibilities: their intended use in bastardy cases, as in others, was to identify lawful heirs so that inheritances passed only to

107 *RMS*, xiv, no. 2072. Table 13.

108 *RM*, ii, chs 19 and 20.

109 Ibid., ii, ch. 20. The distinction was in effect from at least the twelfth century and the right of the holder to dispose of his conquest lands to whomever he wished was retained by later burgh law and survived in Scots law until 1874. MacQueen, *Common Law and Feudal Society*, 173.

110 *Abstract of Protocol Book of the Burgh of Stirling, A.D. 1469–1484*, ed. A. W. C. Hallen (Edinburgh, 1896), 21; *Protocol Book of James Young*, nos 932, 116.

those with a legal entitlement to them. The evidence of those cases which escalated to higher courts, or were especially protracted, unsurprisingly suggest the system was not immune from misuse, error and manipulation: they may not have been typical, but do give an indication of the importance of bastardy to the economic and social fabric of medieval Scotland. Even where the competence and probity of litigants and their legal representatives was not in question, identifying a lawful heir was sometimes exceptionally difficult. At a time before marriage and birth certificates, the truth of a person's birth status might be irredeemably obscure, and reliance on the memory (and honesty) of local people, whose knowledge of the family might be incomplete to begin with, may not always have guaranteed justice.

In the matter of bastard-born children whose parents subsequently intermarried, Scottish historiography has routinely posited a tension between Church law, which regarded such offspring as legitimate and so capable of inheritance, and the common law of Scotland, in the form of the statement in *Regiam Majestatem* declaring that such children could never be heirs. This apparent tension ceases to exist if it is accepted that, as far as this provision is concerned, *Regiam Majestatem* does not represent Scottish legal practice in the medieval era. A willingness to accept legitimation *per subsequens matrimonium* as sufficient to erase the legal disability concerning inheritance set the country apart from its southern neighbour.

The various measures, in canon law and in common law alike, to mitigate or vacate the legal effects of illegitimacy did not undermine the premise that legitimacy was required for inheritance so much as reinforce it. Their use underscored the principle that illegitimate people could not succeed to estates or share family wealth without them.

3

Illegitimacy and royal succession I: before the Great Cause

Quhow euir it be, a kingis sone am I,
Suppois I gottin was onlauchfullie[1]

In 787, a council of Anglo-Saxon and Carolingian clergy at Chelsea agreed that kingship was a special vocation from which men born of adultery or incest were disqualified.[2] The Church's power to enforce this stance on the polities of western Christendom was limited, not least because a settled definition of what constituted lawful marriage (on which a reliable definition of illegitimacy depended) took centuries to develop. Neither did the Church appear to have any will to impose legitimate succession on royal houses before the late twelfth century.[3] Its promotion of Christian marriage was, initially at least, a separate matter from that of a kingdom's own rules and traditions concerning who was throne-worthy, and how royal succession was to be decided. Kings in Scotland, as elsewhere, contracted marriages which, we may presume, were recognised in their realm as valid marital unions. These may or may not have conformed to contemporary Church rules for lawful wedlock, but certainly could not be expected to anticipate the eventual form of those rules. The difficulty is encapsulated in Turgot's claim that the marriage of Mael Coluim III (d. 1093) and Margaret in 1069x70 was the first lawful marriage in

1 *King Alexander*, lines 2131–2.

2 *Councils and Ecclesiastical Documents*, ed. A. W. Haddan and W. Stubbs (Oxford, 1869–78), iii, 453.

3 McDougall, *Royal Bastards*, 4, 6–7, 191. She also points out (at p. 178) that 'Numerous marriages among European royalty up to, and including, the twelfth century were invalid on grounds of consanguinity and no dispensation was sought for most of them, but there was no question of descendants of these unions being excluded from succession.' See also J. Martindale, 'Succession and Politics in the Romance-speaking World, *ca.* 1000–1140', in M. Jones and M. Vale, ed., *England and Her Neighbours, 1066–1453* (London, 1989), 19–41.

Scotland.[4] This would make Mael Coluim, along with all previous kings of (or in) Scotland, and virtually the whole population of the country, illegitimate.

The first Scottish king-list to describe any ruler of or in the kingdom as illegitimate was produced between 1198 and 1214.[5] Being born of a union recognised by contemporaries as a marriage (perhaps a separate matter from whether or not it met the Church's criteria for marriage) may have been a qualification for kingship in Scotland before the twelfth century, but the paucity and brevity of our sources make it impossible to know for certain. The evidence of royal succession in Scotland before the twelfth century suggests that membership of the royal dynasty was a prerequisite for kingship, along with maleness and, almost certainly, adulthood.[6] Kings might be succeeded by collaterals as much as by lineal descendants. Being someone defined as illegitimate according to Church rules of marriage is likely to have mattered less than descent from a king, being an adult male with experience of war, and personal excellence, or 'worth' (*febas*). This latter quality probably encompassed some combination of leadership ability, especially in military contexts, and whatever other aptitudes and proficiencies were valued or required at the particular time that consideration was being given to who would replace the incumbent or late king.[7]

Political clout and military success could tip the balance in favour of a member of the royal dynasty who might not be the obvious heir, including those who were illegitimate.[8] In the eleventh century, famously, the throne of

4 A. Taylor, 'Robert de Londres, Illegitimate Son of William, King of Scots, *c.* 1170–1225', *Haskins Society Journal: Studies in Medieval History* 19 (2008), 109, citing (n. 66) Madrid, Biblioteca Real, MS II 2097, fo. 8vb. A transcription and translation of Turgot's *vita* of Margaret contained in this MS (also known as the Dunfermline compilation) is provided in C. Keene, *Saint Margaret, Queen of Scots. A Life in Perspective* (New York, 2013). The relevant section reads '*Hoc itaque exemplo nu(lli) ex gente illa scoticana ab illa cito coniugio huc usque ibidem hab(itum) recesserunt, seseque legalibus matrimoniis constrixerunt.*'

5 D. Broun, 'Contemporary Perspectives on Alexander II's Succession: The Evidence of King-Lists', in R. Oram, ed., *The Reign of Alexander II, 1214–49* (Leiden, 2005), 91; *Chron. Melrose*, 25. The scholarship on king-lists is extensive. See D. N. Dumville, 'The Chronicle of the Kings of Alba', in S. Taylor, ed., *Kings, Clerics and Chronicles in Scotland, 500–1297* (Dublin, 2000), 73–86; D. Broun, *The Irish Identity of the Kingdom of the Scots in the Twelfth and Thirteenth Centuries* (Woodbridge, 1999), Chapters VII and VIII; M. Anderson, *Kings and Kingship in Early Scotland* (Edinburgh, 1980).

6 Before Scotland existed as a political entity, north Britain comprised kingdoms of Picts, Gaels, Britons, English and Scandinavians, whose succession practices were not identical. For royal succession in Scotland before 1100, see A. Woolf, *From Pictland to Alba, 789–1070* (Edinburgh, 2007), 27–32; and A. Woolf, 'The "Moray Question" and the Kingship of Alba in the Tenth and Eleventh Centuries', *SHR* 79 (2000), 145–69.

7 A brief discussion of designation of heirs is at pp. 106–8.

8 Illegitimates who became kings in Europe in the middle ages include Tancred of Lecce, king of Sicily (r. 1190–4); Fernando III of Castile (r. 1217–52), and João I (John of Aviz), king of Portugal (r. 1385–1433). Between 1130 and 1240, forty-six men presented themselves as candidates for the kingship of Norway, of whom only twelve or thirteen

England was seized by William the Bastard (r. 1066–87), duke of Normandy.[9] His contemporary on the Scottish throne, Mael Coluim III, presided over a kingdom in which primogeniture was not yet established and being a male, adult member of the ruling kindred who could summon the support of influential men was arguably more significant than being born of a valid marriage, whether defined by the Church or by contemporary social criteria. This is clear from the recorded attempts by members of the Scottish royal kindred who were illegitimate, or descended from illegitimates, to claim the throne over the course of the twelfth and early thirteenth centuries; attempts which, though ultimately unsuccessful, gained the support of enough leading men to pose a real threat to the royal incumbents.

The grandsons of Mael Coluim III

The two principal lines challenging the reigning dynasty for over a century from 1124 were those descending from Donnchad II (d. 1094) and from Alexander I (d. 1124), sons of Mael Coluim III by, respectively, his first wife, said to be Ingibjǫrg, and his second, Margaret.[10] Although Donnchad II was the elder, Alexander's line was first to contest the kingship. Alexander had no known children with his wife Sybilla (d. 1122), one of the numerous bastard daughters of King Henry I of England. Alexander did, however, have an illegitimate son, Mael Coluim.[11] This Mael Coluim and his supporters came into conflict with the Scottish crown from 1124, shortly after Alexander I died and was succeeded by his brother, David I.[12] Mael Coluim pursued his claim to the kingdom in the decade that followed, his illegitimate status not a barrier to the kingship as far as his supporters were concerned. Along with his kinsman Óengus of Moray, possibly also a royal pretender, Mael Coluim was involved in a rebellion against the crown in 1130, when Óengus was killed, and again in 1134, this time with other members of his kindred, at which point he was

were legitimate; only five of the twenty-four men who did rule were legitimate. J. M. Jochens, 'The Politics of Reproduction: Medieval Norwegian Kingship', *The American Historical Review* 92 (1987), 332, 335, 340, 342–3.

9 William's paternal grandfather was the brother of Emma of Normandy (d. 1052), queen to Æthelred II (d. 1016) and mother of Edward the Confessor (d. 1066).

10 Table 1.

11 The identity of the royal pretender Mael Coluim has long been disputed by historians. Alasdair Ross provides an assessment of the competing claims, and concludes that Mael Coluim was the illegitimate son of Alexander I, in A. Ross, 'The Identity of the "Prisoner of Roxburgh": Malcolm Son of Alexander or Malcolm MacHeth?', in S. Arbuthnot and K. Hollo, ed., *Fil súil nglais: A Grey Eye Looks Back. A Festschrift in Honour of Colm Ó Baoill* (Ceann Drochaid, 2007), 269–82. See also A. A. M. Duncan, *The Kingship of the Scots 842–1292: Succession and Independence* (Edinburgh, 2002), 65, 66–7, 71.

12 *The Ecclesiastical History of Orderic Vitalis*, ed. and transl. M. Chibnall (Oxford, 1969–80), iv, 277.

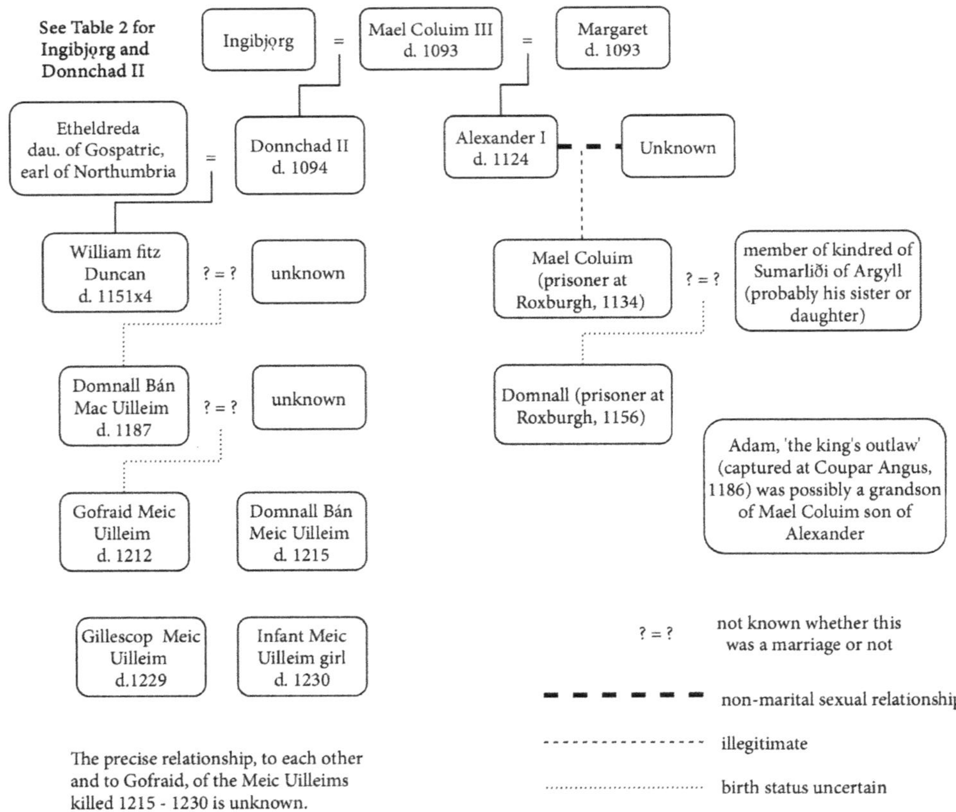

Table 1. Dynastic rebels descending from Mael Coluim III

captured and imprisoned.[13] Mael Coluim's descendants renewed their claim to the throne following the death of David in 1153. *The Chronicle of Holyrood* records that in that year the sons of Mael Coluim joined with their kinsman Sumarliði of Argyll (Mael Coluim's sons are given as Sumarliði's *nepotes* – nephews or grandsons), allying themselves with 'many others', to rise against Mael Coluim IV, then a boy of eleven, creating disturbance and disquiet in a large part of Scotland.[14] Their motive seems to have been to install Mael Coluim son of Alexander's line as rulers of Scotland. In 1156 Domnall, a son of Mael Coluim, was captured in Galloway and brought to the king before joining his father in prison.[15] It is possible that at least one other descendant of Mael Coluim persisted in the claim subsequently. A certain Adam, 'the king's outlaw', who was captured at Coupar Angus abbey in 1186, may have been a grandson of Mael Coluim son of Alexander.[16]

The accession of eleven-year-old Mael Coluim IV may also have had a role to play in provoking descendants of Donnchad II to challenge the throne. During his lifetime, no contemporary source described Donnchad, son of Mael Coluim III by his first wife, as illegitimate.[17] The charter of 1094 in which he styles himself 'hereditably certain king of Scotland' is witnessed by his half-brother Edgar, implying acceptance of his right by a potentially rival claimant.[18]

13 *Chron. Melrose*, 33; Chibnall, *Orderic Vitalis*, iv, 277; Ailred of Rievaulx, *Relatio de Standardo* in *Chronicles of the Reigns of Stephen, Henry II, and Richard I*, ed. R. Howlett (London, 1884–9), iii, 193; Robert of Torigni, *Chronica*, in Howlett, *Chronicles of the Reigns*, iv, 118; R. Oram, *Domination and Lordship: Scotland 1070–1230* (Edinburgh, 2011), 70–2, 86–7, 88; A. Ross, *The Kings of Alba c. 1000–c. 1130* (Edinburgh, 2011), 197–205. The support in the north and west for the claim to the throne by Mael Coluim son of Alexander I in 1130 'suggests that the discrimination between lawful and illegitimate sons, widely accepted in lowland society by this date, had not penetrated the Gàidhealtachd'. Duncan, *Kingship*, 67.

14 *Chron. Holyrood*, 124–5. Mael Coluim may have been married to a sister of Sumarliði, as Ross contends; Woolf says it is also possible Mael Coluim was married to Sumarliði's daughter, or that Mael Coluim and Sumarliði had the same mother. Ross, *Kings of Alba*, 203, 217; A. Woolf, 'The Song of the Death of Somerled and the Destruction of Glasgow in 1153', *Journal of the Sydney Society for Scottish History* 14 (2013), 3.

15 *Chron. Holyrood*, 128; *Chron. Melrose*, 35.

16 *Chron. Holyrood*, 170–1; Ross, 'Prisoner of Roxburgh', 280–2.

17 This is no guarantee of legitimacy, as royal offspring known to be illegitimate were routinely referred to as 'the king's son/daughter', without qualification: see p. 70 below. Duncan considers Donnchad II's legitimacy to be confirmed by the fact that he was a hostage of the English king William the Bastard (d. 1087), who was 'unlikely to have taken an illegitimate son'. A. A. M. Duncan, 'Duncan II (b. before 1072, d. 1094)', *ODNB*, 10 March 2019. But illegitimate family members were sometimes taken as hostages. *CDS*, i, no. 545. This is not to say that Donnchad was in fact illegitimate, only that these grounds do not constitute proof of legitimacy. Mael Coluim may have had other sons, perhaps also by his first wife, namely Domnall: *Annals of Ulster (to AD 1131)*, ed. and transl. S. Mac Airt and G. Mac Niocaill (Dublin, 1983), s.a. 1085; and Mael Coluim: A. C. Lawrie, *Early Scottish Charters* (Glasgow, 1905), no. 12. See Ross, *Kings of Alba*, 160–3 for these men.

18 Duncan, 'Yes, the Earliest Scottish Charters', *SHR* 78 (1999), 8; Duncan, *Kingship*, 55.

The first to call Donnchad illegitimate was William of Malmesbury (d. in or after 1142), writing in, or not long before, 1126.[19] He has Donnchad as a *nothus* (bastard) son of Mael Coluim.[20] Isidore of Seville (570–636) used the term *nothus* to denote the mother of the illegitimate person being of an inferior rank to the father.[21] Given how influential Isidore's writings were on medieval authors, William of Malmesbury's use of it here could have been intended primarily to disparage Ingibjǫrg, presumed mother of Donnchad. Certainly, William conspicuously, and unsurprisingly, favours the line of Margaret, who was not only West Saxon royalty, but the mother of Matilda, queen of Henry I, father of William's patron, Robert, earl of Gloucester.

The chronicler's assertion calls to mind Turgot's claim that Mael Coluim's marriage to Margaret was the first canonically valid marriage in Scotland.[22] Elsewhere, Turgot portrays Margaret as a keen proponent of Church-sanctioned marriage, and so she seems to have been used by him as a mouthpiece for contemporary Church messages in respect of marriage reform.[23] But possibly there was more to Turgot's claim about Mael Coluim's nuptials than zealous promotion of canon law. Making Mael Coluim's second marriage the first legally valid one in Scotland automatically casts doubt on the legitimacy of the offspring of his first. Another English source says that Mael Coluim nominated as heir to the kingdom Edward, his eldest son with Margaret; if true, this sidelined Donnchad and any other sons he had before he married Margaret.[24]

The question of Donnchad II's legitimacy rests on the status of the union between his parents. According to the *Orkneyinga saga*, the only source which mentions Mael Coluim III's first wife, she was Ingibjǫrg, widow of Þorfinnr 'the Mighty' Sigurðarson, earl of Orkney.[25] Some modern historians

19 William of Malmesbury, *Gesta Regum Anglorum*, ed. and transl. R. A. B. Mynors and others (Oxford, 1998), i, xxii–iii.

20 '[Henry I] ...*ille Dunecanum, filium Malcolmi nothum* ...'. William of Malmesbury, *Gesta Regum*, i, 725.

21 See p. 11 and p. 184 n.55.

22 The *Anglo-Saxon Chronicle* stresses that her marriage to Mael Coluim was divinely mandated, implying not only its legality, but also its status as a form of religious vocation. *The Anglo-Saxon Chronicle*, ed. G. N. Garmonsway (London, 1972), D, s.a. 1067.

23 See p. 14 for his depiction of her efforts to extirpate endogamous marriage practices among the Scots. Marriage law was something in which Turgot is known to have taken an interest. R. Bartlett, 'Turgot (c. 1050–1115), Author and Bishop of St Andrews', *ODNB*, 19 June 2019.

24 *Symeonis Monachi Opera Omnia*, ed. T. Arnold (Rolls Series, 1882–5), ii, 222.

25 *Orkneyinga saga. The History of the Earls of Orkney*, ed. and transl. H. Pálsson and P. Edwards (London, 1978), 76. The year of Þorfinnr's death is often given as ca. 1065, on the basis that the *Orkneyinga saga* says it occurred 'in the later days of king Haraldr', but Woolf argues this phrase has been interpreted very narrowly and there is no reason why it could not mean the late 1050s. Woolf, *Pictland to Alba*, 267. Duncan goes further and says Þorfinnr 'probably died in the early 1050s'. Duncan, *Kingship*, 42 n.63.

have suggested she may instead have been his daughter.[26] Woolf points out that a marriage between Mael Coluim and Ingibjǫrg is not recorded in the *Arnmæðlingartal*, a Norwegian genealogical tract.[27] This tract does mention her marriage to Þorfinnr, and provides details of their two sons, but there is no reference to a daughter or a second marriage. Duncan points to a twelfth-century entry in the *Liber Vitae Ecclesiae Dunelmensis* commemorating an 'Ingeberga comitissa' as evidence of a marriage between Mael Coluim III and Ingibjǫrg.[28] The entry is listed alongside the names of late eleventh-century monks, whose lives would have been contemporaneous with hers. The strong association between the monks of Durham and Mael Coluim III and his family make it plausible that the commemoration related to Mael Coluim's first wife, though she is not designated as such in these commemorations. Duncan says that 'no other identity is really possible' for 'Ingeberga'.[29]

The *Orkneyinga saga* also says that Þorfinnr's father, Sigurðr (II) Hlöðvisson (d. 1014) married a daughter of Mael Coluim, 'King of Scotland'.[30] This Mael Coluim has traditionally been identified as Mael Coluim II (d. 1034).[31] If this is accepted, then Þorfinnr was a grandson of Mael Coluim II. If Mael Coluim III married the widow of Þorfinnr, the couple were related by affinity, since her late husband Þorfinnr was first cousin to Mael Coluim III's father, Donnchad I. If Ingibjǫrg was, instead, Þorfinnr's daughter, she and Mael Coluim were related by consanguinity: they shared the same great-grandfather in Mael Coluim II (Table 2). Before 1215, when the Church formally reduced to four the number of forbidden degrees within which marriage was not legally possible, the reach of the prohibition across a kindred was far greater, and generally not fewer than six degrees.[32] In 1059, Pope Nicholas II (d. 1061) used an encyclical to enforce the illegality of marriage contracted within seven degrees.[33] If the number of degrees was fixed at either six or seven, and if the relationships are as described in the *Orkneyinga saga*, and if the Mael Coluim whose daughter

26 Duncan and Woolf both think it more likely she was Þorfinnr's widow; Ross suggests she was his daughter. Duncan, *Kingship*, 42; Woolf, *Pictland to Alba*, 268; Ross, *Kings of Alba*, 130.

27 Woolf, *Pictland to Alba*, 268; *Fagrskinna, a Catalogue of the Kings of Norway: a Translation with Introduction and Notes*, ed. and transl. A. Finlay (Leiden, 2004), 302.

28 *Liber Vitae Ecclesiae Dunelmensis* (Surtees Society, 1841), 141; Duncan, *Kingship*, 42–3 (wherein he notes that her marriages 'were real enough'). The name in the *Liber* is not accompanied by any family information.

29 The names of those commemorated in the pages of the *Liber Vitae Ecclesiae Dunelmensis* include Mael Coluim and Donnchad, 'kings of Scots', Alexander (I), his queen Sybilla and his sister Matilda, and other members of the Scottish royal family, including Margaret, who is given as 'Margareta regina'.

30 *Orkneyinga saga*, ed. Pálsson and Edwards, 38.

31 B. E. Crawford, 'Thorfinn Sigurdson (II) [Þorfinnr Sigurðarson, Þorfinnr inn Ríki] (c. 1009–c. 1065), Earl of Orkney', *ODNB*, 5 May 2020.

32 Discussed at pp. 15–16.

33 Goody, *Development of the family*, 35.

married Sigurðr Hlöðvisson was Mael Coluim II, then Mael Coluim III and Ingibjǫrg's union was not a canonically valid marriage and Donnchad II was not, after all, legitimate.

The problems inherent in using the *Orkneyinga saga* as a source for the facts of Scottish history are well-known. Written in Iceland in the early thirteenth century, its composer may not have had reliable information about eleventh-century figures, and even if he did, need not have prioritised historical accuracy over the spinning of a good yarn. Parts of it are clearly invented; most of it must be treated with considerable caution. The account of Þorfinnr seems to be largely a work of fiction, but not every detail can be discounted: his marriage to Ingibjǫrg, for example, being attested elsewhere, appears reliable.[34] The accuracy of the other relationships described in the saga have to be taken on a case-by-case basis; the lack of independent corroboration for some may indicate that they are dubious, but, equally, may represent nothing more than that evidence for them has been lost.

An important point in all of this is that even if Donnchad was illegitimate according to canon law, this need not have affected his throne-worthiness in the eyes of his contemporaries. The claim that his father Mael Coluim III designated Edward, Margaret's eldest son, his heir in preference to Donnchad reflects Margaret's prestige. If the claim is unfounded, it suggests the English chronicler who made it assumed Edward to have an obviously superior right because his mother was a West Saxon princess; if the claim is well-founded, it probably suggests that Mael Coluim was of a similar opinion. An heir who united the royal lines of England and Scotland was better than one who did not; this did not mean that Donnchad was a non-heir, only that Edward's lineage made him a more desirable one. Had Mael Coluim not married Margaret, Donnchad's status as his father's heir may have been compromised by his long exile in Normandy and England as a hostage of the English king William the Bastard, which resulted in the effective disconnection of Donnchad from the culture and leading men of Scotland, but not, almost certainly, by his parents' union falling foul of consanguinity regulations – if, indeed, it did.[35] Any impediment to the marriage of his parents may have permitted commentators such as Turgot to imply, and William of Malmesbury to state, that Donnchad was illegitimate, which in turn provided a pretext for later writers to deny he had any right to the kingship. Ultimately it may never be known whether there was any basis in fact for the imputation of bastardy to Donnchad. But in Donnchad's lifetime, the relationship between canonical legitimacy and throne-worthiness was far from straightforward.[36]

34 Woolf, *Pictland to Alba*, 243–4 (for a summary of some serious problems in the saga's account of Þorfinnr).

35 McDougall, *Royal Bastards*, 8–9.

36 This is clear from the way he is discussed by William of Malmesbury.

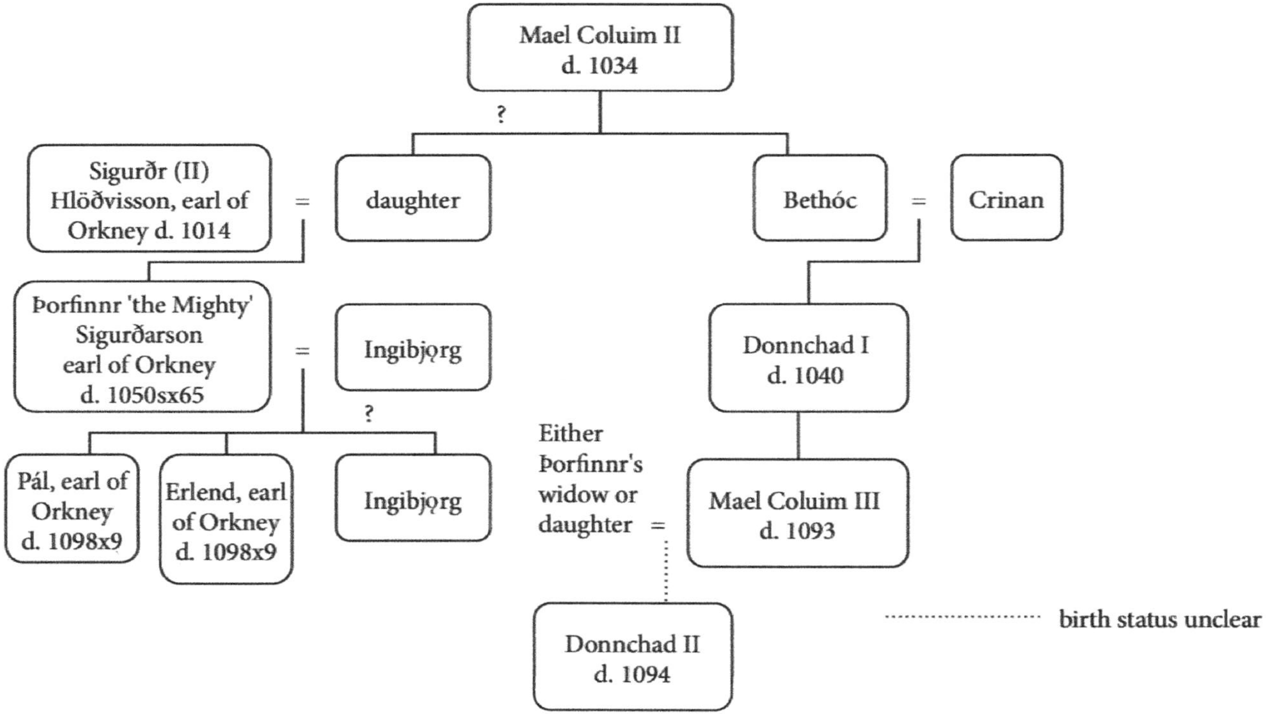

If the identification of either woman is not as given in the chart above, the impediments to lawful marriage between Ingibjǫrg and Mael Coluim III, discussed in this chapter, did not exist. In this case, the women's identities are not known, and so some other impediment cannot be ruled out.

Table 2. Possible lineage of Donnchad II

It has been argued that William of Malmesbury's description of Donnchad as a bastard was invented to discredit claims to the throne stemming from descent from him.[37] As far as we know, none of Donnchad II's progeny had pressed such a claim by 1126 (when William of Malmesbury wrote that Donnchad was a *nothus*), but it may be significant that the chronicler was writing within a year or two of the challenge to the Scottish crown by the illegitimate Mael Coluim, son of Alexander I.[38] Although William of Malmesbury was the first to use the term *nothus* as a descriptor of Donnchad, the ground had already been laid through the depiction of his mother Ingibjǫrg as a non-wife of Mael Coluim, in contrast to his irreproachably 'legal' wife.[39]

Nonetheless, there is nothing in Malmesbury's account which suggests there was anything wrong with a bastard becoming king of Scotland. According to Malmesbury, William II Rufus made the illegitimate Donnchad a knight and, after Mael Coluim III's death, established him as king of Scots.[40] His murder at the hands of his uncle Domnall is described by Malmesbury as an act of treachery, and Edmund's involvement in the killing of his half-brother depicted as a crime for which he spent the rest of his life repenting.[41] Edmund is imprisoned, and the chronicler has him instruct that he be buried with his chains, 'admitting he was rightly punished for the crime of his brother's murder'.[42] If it was the writer's intention to show that Donnchad was a wrongful king on the grounds of his bastardy, the actions of Domnall and Edmund might be lauded, or at least not reviled. Given the chronicle's Anglocentric, royalist viewpoint, Domnall and Edmund's crime may have been as much to do with refusing to accept the English crown's decision as to who should be Scotland's king as it was about kin-slaying or regicide *per se*, but in any case, the story does not suggest Donnchad ought to have been excluded from the throne on grounds of bastardy.

It is difficult to know what the studied neutrality of William Malmesbury's depiction of illegitimate succession reflects. If the portrayal of Donnchad II as a bastard was indeed intended to discredit his line, that Malmesbury does not labour the point may suggest that elaboration was not necessary – his

37 Oram, *Domination and Lordship*, 64.

38 Ross, *Kings of Alba*, 170–1. Ross's view is that it was 'probably no coincidence' and that it may have been English propaganda intended to further the claims of Margaret's offspring at the expense of other segments of the royal kindred.

39 See also V. Wall, 'Queen Margaret of Scotland (1070–93): Burying the Past, Enshrining the Future', in A. Duggan, ed., *Queens and Queenship in Medieval Europe* (Woodbridge, 1997), 29–35 for a brief discussion of contemporary portrayals of Donnchad, Ingibjǫrg and Margaret which subtly but clearly subordinate the status of Mael Coluim's first wife and, by extension, of Donnchad.

40 '...*militem fecit et regem Scottorum mortuo patre constituit*.' William of Malmesbury, *Gesta Regum*, i, 724–5.

41 Ibid., 727.

42 Ibid., 727.

audiences knew that he was not a rightful king if illegitimate. His decision not to comment negatively on it may indicate nothing more than a wariness of emphasising to his patron, a bastard son of a king, that bastard sons of kings were unfit for kingship. In Malmesbury's account, his patron's uncle, William II Rufus, was responsible for placing a known illegitimate on the throne of Scotland, but it would be surprising if the chronicler hesitated to condemn illegitimate succession merely because of this family connection, given how very critical he could be of William II and his kingship.[43] As far as the king's actions concerning Donnchad are concerned, the writer offers no adverse comment. Elsewhere, the same chronicler is clear that illegitimacy was regarded as a barrier to royal succession, although not always an insurmountable one. He says that Aldfrith (d. 704x5), son of King Oswiu of Northumbria (d. 670), was 'rejected as a bastard' on Oswiu's death, while Aldfrith's brother Ecgfrith, 'being legitimate, succeeded'.[44] Retiring to Gaeldom, Aldfrith acquired an education and though 'being illegitimate … [he] had been regarded by the nobles … as unworthy of the throne', his scholarly achievements resulted in him being 'considered more suitable for the reins of power', and he duly succeeded the childless Ecgfrith.[45] The actual reasons for Ecgfrith being preferred to Aldfrith may have been quite other, and Malmesbury is almost certainly imposing twelfth-century English attitudes to illegitimate succession on his knowledge of seventh- and eighth-century events. But here, too, Malmesbury's treatment of illegitimate succession does not betray any horror at the practice.

That William of Malmesbury's patron may have been considered throne-worthy despite his illegitimacy is suggested by another English chronicle. The writer of the *Gesta Stephani* says that Robert of Gloucester was advised by some to claim the throne when his father died in 1135.[46] The chronicler relates that Robert declined to do so, 'saying it was fairer to yield it to his sister's son, to whom it more justly belonged, than presumptuously to arrogate it to himself'.[47] Implicit in this account is that Robert's right to the crown, though

43 Ibid., 555–65, 571, 573–7; B. Weiler, 'William of Malmesbury on Kingship', *History* 90 (2005), 7–8, 10–11, 12, 14–15, 17, 20, 22.

44 William of Malmesbury, *Gesta Regum*, i, 79. Bede (d. 735) described Aldfrith as an illegitimate (*nothus*) son, without any suggestion that he should not have been king. Bede, 'Life of Cuthbert in Prose', in *The Biographical Writings and Letters of Venerable Bede*, ed. J. A. Giles (London, 1845), 48. Adomnán (d. 704) also writes about his friend King Aldfrith, but does not mention his bastardy; and the same is true of Alcuin (d. 804). *Adomnán of Iona. The Life of St Columba*, ed. and transl. R. Sharpe (London, 1991), 203; Alcuin, *The Bishop, Kings and Saints of York*, ed. P. Godman (Oxford, 1982), 71.

45 William of Malmesbury, *Gesta Regum*, i, 81.

46 Gloucester is given as '*filius regis Henrici, sed nothus*'. *Gesta Stephani*, ed. and transl. K. R. Potter, with introduction and notes by R. H. C. Davis (Oxford, 1976), 12. The incident occurs in the first section of the work, written 'in about 1148'. Ibid., xxi. See also Given-Wilson and Curteis, *Royal Bastards*, 77–8.

47 *Gesta Stephani*, 13–15. Robert's status as a leading man of the realm, bastardy notwithstanding, is emphasised by the writer having many of those who had initially

weaker than that of Henry's legitimate grandson, was not non-existent. The writer is using Robert's supposed eligibility for the throne to point up the rightness of Stephen's kingship: Robert accepting Stephen's rule (as he is shown to do shortly afterwards) becomes a more powerful endorsement of Stephen if Robert himself is a contender for the kingship. We should be wary of accepting this account as either true or as evidence for a generalised acceptance of illegitimate succession.[48] However, that the writer of *Gesta Stephani* includes it does suggest that audiences in the first half of the twelfth century would not have thought it wholly preposterous that a bastard of royal blood, with the right political and martial credentials, could gain some support to claim the throne. This is mirrored in the situation of Scotland from the 1120s until at least the 1150s, when Mael Coluim, son of Alexander I, and his descendants were able to muster enough backing to pose a serious threat to the royal incumbents. Later in the twelfth century, the line of Donnchad II, characterised as illegitimate, was similarly able to muster support from subjects of the Scottish king.

Whatever William of Malmesbury's intentions in describing Donnchad as illegitimate, the identification of him as a bastard gained ground over time. A king-list of 1198x1214 inserted into the *Chronicle of Melrose* gives Donnchad as an illegitimate (*nothus*) son of Mael Coluim; this same information is found in the *Chronicle of Huntingdon*, and the *Chronicle of Worcester*.[49] *Gesta Annalia I*, attributed to John of Fordun but actually drawn from an earlier, and now lost, history of the Scots, calls him 'Duncan the bastard'.[50] Fordun also gives him as Mael Coluim III's illegitimate son (*filius nothus*), while the sons of Margaret are Mael Coluim's lawful heirs (*legittimis heredibus*).[51] Wyntoun (d. ca. 1422) describes Donnchad as being born 'off purchas/ That Malcolmys bastard sowne…'.[52] Bower (d. 1449) calls him 'Duncan the Bastard'

resisted Stephen's authority submitting to the new king once Robert had done so.

48 Of the account of advisors urging Gloucester to claim the throne, Crouch comments: 'It is difficult to accept that this happened.' D. Crouch, *The Reign of King Stephen 1135–1154* (Harlow, 2000), 34. Hollister rejects the notion that Gloucester was seriously considered for the throne, citing his bastardy as a definitive disqualification. C. W. Hollister, 'The Anglo-Norman Succession Debate of 1126: Prelude to Stephen's Anarchy', *JMH* 1 (1975), 24.

49 *Chron. Melrose*, 25; *Chronicles of the Picts: Chronicles of the Scots*, ed. W. F. Skene, (London, 1867), 211; *The Chronicle of Florence of Worcester*, ed. B. Thorpe (London, 1849), ii, 253; *ESSH*, ii, 89; Broun, 'Contemporary Perspectives', 93 n.56.

50 *Gesta Annalia I* in Skene, *Fordun*, i, 268. *Gesta Annalia I*, completed by 9 April 1285, formed part of a larger work which was one of the main sources used by Fordun (d. 1363) in his *Chronica*. D. Broun, *Scottish Independence and the Idea of Britain: From the Picts to Alexander III* (Edinburgh, 2007), 215–34; A. Taylor, 'Historical Writing in Twelfth- and Thirteenth-century Scotland: the Dunfermline Compilation', *Historical Research* 83 (2010), 234 n.39.

51 Skene, *Fordun*, i, 223.

52 *Chron. Wyntoun*, ii, 166. 'off purchase' = out of wedlock. For good measure, he has Mael Coluim III illegitimate as well, born of Donnchad I and a miller's daughter, and goes on to point out that therefore 'mony a famowse gret persowne', including the Empress

in his account of the rebellion by Donnchad's descendant, Domnall Bán mac Uilleim; and 'the bastard son of Malcolm', twice: first when describing him as one of a number of usurpers in Scottish history who had ruled 'during certain corrupt periods', and when describing the adoption of Donnchad as king in place of Mael Coluim's 'lawful heirs' (the sons of Margaret), while they were in England.[53] Elsewhere, however, he refers to Donnchad as the son of Mael Coluim, without any descriptor indicating illegitimacy.[54] The Asloan MS version of the *Brevis Cronica*, written in the fifteenth century, relates that Domnall 'was put away be Duncan, a bastard son of King Malcolmmis', while the Advocates MS witness of this chronicle gives Donnchad as 'bastarde sone to King Malcolme'.[55] Both versions claim additionally that Donnchad and his uncle Domnall were wrongful and bad kings: 'Thir twa regnit wranguisly five yeris without richt' (Asloan), and their governance was 'to þe greit truble of þe pepill' (Advocates).[56] In some texts they are simply unworthy of the throne: the *Nomina omnium regum Scotorum* calls Donnchad a 'notorious son', while Domnall is a usurper; and says the two men 'reigned wickedly'.[57] The version of the *Verse Chronicle* in the *Chronicle of Melrose* says of Donnchad that, 'because he lived badly, the whole people crushed him'.[58] The depictions of Donnchad as illegitimate and/or unworthy of the kingship suggest a deliberate smear campaign aimed at portraying his descendants as ineligible for kingship, a campaign perhaps initiated in the early part of the twelfth century to advance the claims of Mael Coluim's sons with Margaret at the expense of his sons with Ingibjǫrg, and perpetuated because Donnchad's descendants sought to claim the throne and gained the support of many in doing so. Portraying Donnchad as a bad king whose rule was damaging to the realm may have been understood to be a natural corollary of his illegitimate status, or it may have served as another reason to reject the claims of his descendants, for those inclined to attach little weight to his supposed bastardy.

At the time of Donnchad's death in 1094, his legitimate son, William fitz Duncan (d. 1151x4), made no bid for the Scottish throne. As Donnchad was older than Mael Coluim III's sons with Margaret, William probably had a stronger claim than her sons, but he may have been a child, or a hostage, or both, at the time of his father's murder.[59] The relationship between David I and

Matilda, kings of England, and Pope Clement VII are lineally descended from a Forteviot miller. Ibid., 120–2.

53 *Chron. Bower*, iv, 337; ii, 399–401; iii, 85.

54 Ibid., iii, 69; vi, 117, 153.

55 D. Embree and others, ed., *Short Scottish Prose Chronicles* (Woodbridge, 2012), 201, 200.

56 Embree, *Prose Chronicles*, 201, 200.

57 Ibid., 201. The word used of Donnchad is *notus*.

58 *Chron. Melrose*, 29; Broun, 'Contemporary Perspectives', 87.

59 Duncan makes a tentative argument that Donnchad II's son William may at one time have been the intended successor to Alexander I, and that this might explain the determination of his descendants to gain the throne. Duncan, *Kingship*, 59–60, 65. Broun

his nephew William, with whom he had shared a similar, aristocratic, Anglo-Norman upbringing, appears for the most part to have been one of close collaboration: William fitz Duncan was a frequent witness to David's (and his son Henry's) charters, fought in his battles, and was instrumental in bringing significant territories in northern England under Scottish domination.[60] But in the final years of his life, he was engaged in a conflict or quarrel with David significant enough to be termed a war.[61] Grant suggests the turning point was the death in 1152 of Earl Henry, David's only son, at the age of around thirty-seven. David had previously taken steps to ensure a smooth succession by Henry, formally proclaiming him his heir (Henry was styled '*rex designatus*' from the early 1140s) and giving him a prominent role in the government of the kingdom.[62] Following Henry's unexpected death, David attempted to replicate in modified form the arrangement, declaring that Henry's eldest son, Mael Coluim, who had recently turned eleven years old, was now the heir to the kingdom. By this time William was an experienced political and military leader in his sixties or seventies, with at least one son. Grant contends that fitz Duncan likely outlived Henry (the date of William's death is uncertain but he was alive in 1152 and may have lived into 1154), and although he had had no apparent objection to Henry's succession, he drew the line at the kingship passing to a child – an unknown practice in Scotland at that time – rather than to himself as the only surviving grandson of Mael Coluim III.[63]

The argument that succession by a child was an unwelcome novelty, emboldening other claimants to the throne, may be given additional weight by the fact that it was also in 1153 that Sumarliði, king of the Hebrides and ruler of Argyll and Kintyre, joined with Domnall, son of the bastard Mael Coluim

points out that merely because William did not press a claim to the throne this does not mean that his claim did not exist. Broun, 'Contemporary Perspectives', 88 n.38. Woolf suggests that Bishop Wimund (the Isles diocese), who justified his invasion of Scotland during David I's reign by claiming that he was attempting to regain his patrimony, was a son of William fitz Duncan. A. Woolf, 'The Diocese of the Suðreyar', in S. Imsen, ed., *Ecclesia Nidrosiensis 1153–1537: søkelys på Nidaroskirkens og Nidarosprovinsens historie* (Trondheim, 2003), 173–4.

60 A. Grant, 'The St Bees Lord and Lady, and their Lineage', in K. J. Stringer, ed., *North-West England from the Romans to the Tudors. Essays in Memory of John McNair Todd*, CWAAS Extra Series 41 (2014), 173; *The Charters of King David I*, ed. G. W. S Barrow (Woodbridge, 1999), nos 14, 15, 52–4, 56, 68–70, 83, 120, 121, 126, 130, 139, 147 (with one exception, William is among the first four witnesses); G. W. S Barrow, 'King David, Earl Henry and Cumbria', *TCWAAS* Series 2 99 (1999), 120–1; P. Dalton, *Conquest, Anarchy and Lordship: Yorkshire 1066–1154* (Cambridge, 1994), 189–90, 227–8.

61 Grant, 'The St Bees Lord and Lady', 174; *CDS*, ii, 16–17 (no. 64); *The Register of the Priory of St Bees* (Durham, 1915), 532–3 ('The Lucy Memorandum'): '... *propter guerram motam inter Regem Scocie et ipsum Willelmum filium Duncan* ...'; and '... *tempore quo guerra mota fuit inter regem Scocie et Willelmum filium Duncan* ...'.

62 Lawrie, *Early Scottish Charters*, no. 162; Barrow, *Charters of David I*, nos 126, 129; Duncan, *Kingship*, 69.

63 Grant, 'The St Bees Lord and Lady', 175.

(Alexander I's son), in an uprising against the Scottish crown.[64] The rebellion may have been merely opportunistic, taking advantage of the liminal period following the death of the old king, when his young and inexperienced heir might be vulnerable, but it could also have reflected a sense that an untested child commanding the kingdom, in defiance of customary practice, was at least improper and perhaps quite unacceptable, when adult males belonging to the royal kindred were available. Illegitimate succession may have been seen as no worse, at least, than the situation which obtained. The prohibition against children being raised to the throne was probably of longer standing than that against men born of a non-marital union: if customary practice was to be breached by allowing a child to succeed, then insisting on other prohibitions, such as bastardy, was hard to justify.[65]

If this was the source of the conflict attested in the memorandum, it may have helped give confidence to the next generation in William fitz Duncan's line, which was to prove the most troublesome to David's heirs. William fitz Duncan was dead by 1154 and his son, William of Egremont, died childless between 1163 and 1165, in the wardship of Henry II and without having pressed a claim to the throne. But a serious bid for the crown was launched in the reign of Mael Coluim IV's brother, William the Lion, by another son of William fitz Duncan, Domnall Bán mac Uilleim (d. 1187), whose lineage continued to assert a right to the kingship for the next fifty years.

The reign of William the Lion (1165–1214)

Historians disagree over whether Domnall Bán mac Uilleim was illegitimate.[66] His father's only known marriage was to Alice de Rumilly, by whom he had William of Egremont (d. in/after 1163) and three daughters. Since Alice and William's son predeceased them, their lands were divided between the daughters. This has been offered as evidence that Domnall must have been illegitimate as otherwise he would have been the heir.[67] It is possible, however, that the lands were heritable by Alice's heirs alone since they descended from her family, or that intervention by a feudal superior ensured Domnall's exclusion. Another twelfth-century case illustrates the point: when Mael Coluim III and Margaret's son David married Maud de Senlis (d. 1131), he had the custody and administration of her estate until her sons by her first husband came of age. Following Maud's death, David refused to relinquish certain lands, including the Honour of Huntingdon, to her eldest son, Simon

64 See above, pp. 57–9.

65 In the early eighth century, Northumbria is known to have had a king – the Bernician Osred I (696x8–716) – who succeeded at the age of eight, but no other instances of royal minority in Britain are recorded before the twelfth century.

66 Duncan, *Kingship*, 6; Oram, *Domination and Lordship*, 78.

67 Duncan, *Kingship*, 102.

(II) de Senlis; Simon was eventually successful in regaining his patrimony, but it took several years.[68] The particulars of this case were complicated by the fact that successive English kings intervened to dictate the destination of the estate, but this seems not to have been an unusual state of affairs among elite families. That a feudal superior could redirect an inheritance is an indication that succession to estates depended on matters other than, or additional to, hereditary right; and Domnall's right to Rumilly lands (which were in England) may in any case have been weak, or non-existent, since he was not a son of Alice. There are other examples from the twelfth century of English lands being designated heritable only by the offspring of a particular wife.[69] No inference as to Domnall's birth status can be made with confidence from his failure to inherit this estate.

It has been speculated that William fitz Duncan had contracted an earlier, unrecorded marriage, but who Domnall's mother was, and whether she was ever married to William fitz Duncan, is now unknowable.[70] Oram points out that no contemporary source describes Domnall as illegitimate and considers the stigmatising of his descendants to be a thirteenth-century development.[71] As with Donnchad, the fact that no contemporary sources describe Domnall as illegitimate should not be taken as evidence that he was legitimate: contemporary sources routinely described William the Lion's illegitimate son Robert of London (ca. 1170–1225) as 'the king's son' without indicating his illegitimacy, nor was this unusual.[72] Given William fitz Duncan's status as the son of a former king, nephew of another three kings, a leading man of the

[68] *CP*, vi, 640–7; K. J. Stringer, 'A Cistercian Archive: The Earliest Charters of Sawtry Abbey', *Journal of the Society of Archivists* 6 (1980), 326–30; K. J. Stringer, 'Senlis, Simon (II) de, earl of Northampton and earl of Huntingdon (d. 1153)', *ODNB*, 21 Oct 2018.

[69] J. Hudson, *Land, Law, and Lordship in Anglo-Norman England* (Oxford, 1994), 113. There are also examples in later centuries of Scottish lands being made to descend to a wife's heirs in place of a husband's: Robert I granted lands to Colbán of Glen and Anabilla his spouse, heritable by their legitimately procreated heirs, whom failing by Anabilla's heirs, not Colbán's. *RRS*, v, no. 334.

[70] Oram, *Domination and Lordship*, 78 and 141, cites G. W. S. Barrow, *Kingship and Unity: Scotland 1000–1306* (Edinburgh, 1981), 51–2 and *RRS*, ii, 12–13, for the proposition that William had an unrecorded marriage prior to marrying Alice de Rumilly. His mother is often said to have come from a prominent Moray family, but this has been disputed by Ross: *Kings of Alba*, 81–2 and 108–10.

[71] Oram, *Domination and Lordship*, 78.

[72] He is 'my son' twenty times out of fifty-seven appearances as a witness to William's charters; he is 'son of the King' and 'son of the lord King' once each. Others, including the papacy, referred to him as the king's son, without reference to his illegitimacy. *Records of the Priory of the Isle of May*, ed. J. Stuart (Edinburgh, 1868), no. 24; *Registrum de Dunfermelyn* (Bannatyne Club, 1842), no. 249; *Chartulary of the Abbey of Lindores* (SHS, 1903), no. 93. Similarly, his illegitimate cousin Ada is called 'daughter' of Earl David and 'sister' of Earl John, also without qualification. *Lind. Cart.*, nos 15, 36; *PoMS*, www.poms.ac.uk/record/person/1848/. There are numerous like examples concerning other illegitimate offspring.

kingdom in the reign of David I, and someone who was politically prominent in the north of England as well as Scotland, the invisibility of a supposed earlier wife is a little surprising.

The earliest recorded attack by Domnall Bán mac Uilleim took place in 1179, some fourteen years into the reign of William the Lion, and was sufficiently well-supported to require the Scottish king and his brother David to raise 'a great army' to confront him in Ross.[73] A Meic Uilleim incursion of 1181, according to Howden (d. 1201x2) one of several, was carried out under 'the mandate of certain powerful men of the kingdom'.[74] Howden records another attack under the year 1187 in which Domnall Bán mac Uilleim asserted that he was of the royal line and, claiming the throne by hereditary right, is said to have acted 'through the consent and counsel of the earls and barons of the kingdom of Scotland'.[75] Bower describes this invasion, which again necessitated the raising of 'a very large army' to repel, as aided by 'some disloyal subjects'.[76] The 1187 campaign ended with Domnall Bán being killed and his head sent to the king.[77]

From 1211 Domnall's son Gofraid took up the claim, causing William to launch two expeditions against him in that and the following year. The level of backing that Gofraid was able to achieve – one account describes his challenge as being made with 'the agreement of certain Scottish magnates' – made it necessary for William to seek assistance from King John of England, who sent Brabantine mercenaries to aid William and his son Alexander.[78] The *Barnwell Chronicle*, which says that William turned to John for help because the Scottish king was now elderly and unable to maintain peace in the interior districts of the country, says Gofraid mac Domnaill meic Uilleim was of the ancient line of Scottish kings, and was assisted by the Scots and Irish.[79] Bower's account makes no mention of English help nor of Scottish magnates' complicity, but says that William sent a 'huge army together with all the nobles of his kingdom' against Gofraid.[80] The *Melrose Chronicle* notes the destruction William was obliged to wreak in his campaign against Gofraid in Ross that year.[81] In 1212, Gofraid was captured and hanged.[82] This was not, however, the end of the Meic Uilleim

73 *Gesta Annalia I*, in Skene, *Fordun*, i, 268; *Chron. Bower*, iv, 337.

74 Howden, *Gesta Regis Henrici Secundi Benedicti Abbatis*, ed. W. Stubbs (London, 1867), i, 277–8.

75 '... *per consensum et consilium comitum et baronum regni Scotiæ*.' Howden, *Gesta Regis Henrici*, ii, 8.

76 *Chron. Bower*, iv, 337.

77 Howden, *Gesta Regis Henrici*, ii, 8; *Chron Bower*, iv, 337.

78 *Memorials of St Edmund's Abbey*, ed. T. Arnold (London, 1890–6), ii, 20 ('*de assensu quorundam magnatum Scotie*'); *Gesta Annalia I* in Skene, *Fordun*, i, 278–9.

79 *Memoriale Fratris Walteri de Coventria*, ed. W. Stubbs (London, 1872–3), ii, 206.

80 *Chron. Bower*, iv, 465.

81 *Chron. Melrose*, 56.

82 *Memoriale Fratris Walteri de Conventria*, ii, 206; *Chron. Bower*, iv, 467.

efforts to obtain the throne, which were next taken up by his kinsman, another Domnall Bán Meic Uilleim, not long after William the Lion's death.[83]

Setting aside Bower's much later account, these contemporary sources show the Meic Uilleim claims had the approval of at least some, and perhaps many, important figures within the kingdom. Howden's account of the uprising of 1187 strongly suggests that a significant number of the chief men preferred Domnall Bán mac Uilleim to the king, to the extent that those who 'loved the king not at all' were numerous enough to succeed in temporarily halting the progress of the royal army sent to deal with the Meic Uilleim insurgents.[84] Combined with his account of the 1181 attacks, which he suggests were carried out on the instructions, or with the connivance, of powerful figures, it appears that Domnall Bán mac Uilleim's probable illegitimacy was not considered a barrier to kingship by at least some, perhaps many, leading men late in the twelfth century.[85] Any propaganda suggesting his grandfather, Donnchad II, had been illegitimate (a claim first known to have been made in or by 1126) was similarly disregarded, either because it was disbelieved, or because illegitimacy was not considered important. We do not know the birth status of other members of the Meic Uilleim kindred, but it may well be that for a significant section of Scottish society, this mattered less than their descent from the eldest known son of Mael Coluim III, or perhaps than the fact that they did not belong to the segment placed on the throne by English intervention.

In 1195, William the Lion became seriously ill. He had been married for nine years and had at least one daughter, Margaret, with his wife Ermengarde. During his illness he sought to have Margaret accepted as his heir. William understood legitimacy to be a necessary qualification for succession, since the political community was unlikely to consider a female child an appealing prospect as ruler, yet he did not offer his adult, experienced, but illegitimate, son instead. Robert of London was well-known to the leading men of the kingdom, having been involved in William's government for around a decade by that point.[86] Walter Bower's fifteenth-century account of this event has William's magnates agree to Margaret being heir to the throne, but according to Howden, William's barons were divided.[87] A faction led by Patrick, earl of Dunbar, objected to the proposal, citing the custom that a brother should inherit the throne in preference to a daughter.[88] The brother in question, David, earl of Huntingdon (d. 1219), had seen both of his older brothers accede to the throne in turn. He was the grandson of the youngest of four brothers who had

[83] See p. 77.

[84] Howden, *Gesta Regis Henrici*, ii, 8.

[85] Howden, *Gesta Regis Henrici*, i, 277–8; *Gesta Annalia I* in Skene, *Fordun*, i, 268.

[86] His life is discussed in Taylor, 'Robert de Londres'.

[87] *Chron. Howden*, iii, 298–9; *Chron. Bower*, iv, 411. Bower mistakenly identifies this Margaret as one of William's illegitimate daughters, also Margaret.

[88] *Chron. Howden*, iii, 299.

held the throne, three of them successively, and the great-grandson of a king (Mael Coluim III) who had been succeeded by his brother (Domnall III Bán). David no doubt expected, throughout the many years during which the king remained without a son born in marriage, to follow William in the kingship.

Only six years later, in 1201, the king of France, Philip II Augustus, would successfully obtain papal legitimations for his two bastard children with Agnès of Meran, specifying their right to inherit the throne of France.[89] William was highly unlikely to have attempted such a manoeuvre, for a number of reasons. To begin with, legitimation by rescript was not used by the papacy before 1201, and so it is most doubtful that it would have crossed the king's mind as a possibility.[90] Even if it had, making Robert legitimate would have impinged on the assumed rights of David. Altering Robert's status to make him an heir would have been a highly divisive step, forcing the nobility to declare their support for one at the expense of the other. In addition, it seems that William had not given up hope of having a son in marriage.[91] As long as he believed there was a chance of this, the king was highly unlikely to have sought to legitimate an older, more experienced son whose existence would, at best, further complicate the succession and who might prove a formidable rival to a much younger brother. In 1195 William was in his fifties; the chances were high that a legitimate son yet to be born would be a child or adolescent at William's death. Another reason not to make Robert of London heir to the throne has been suggested by Taylor. She argues that William pursued a deliberate strategy of 'displaying' Robert as his eldest son while simultaneously making it clear his illegitimacy denied him any claim to the throne, in an effort to stress the necessity of legitimacy as a prerequisite for kingship at a time when the Meic Uilleim line – members of which either were, or were portrayed as being, illegitimate – was posing a threat to his rule.[92]

The appeal by William to have Margaret accepted as his heir in 1195 has a broad parallel in the situation of England in 1127. At the start of that year, Henry I sought and apparently obtained the agreement of his barons that his only surviving legitimate child, Matilda, should inherit the throne. Like William, Henry I had a first-born, adult, politically prominent, but bastard, son: Robert of Gloucester. He seems not to have been a serious contender for the throne either but, unlike Robert of London, is at least mentioned in a narrative

[89] See p. 49. Innocent III's legitimation of Philip's children with Agnès occurred some thirteen years before William's death. The papal assertion that the children were capable of inheriting the throne was never tested since Philip had an elder, legitimate, son (later crowned Louis VIII), who in turn had legitimate sons of his own.

[90] The usual route to legitimation was papal recognition of the parents' union as a valid marriage (this is what Philip II sought and failed to obtain), which seems not to have been an option in the case of Robert of London's mother and the Scottish king.

[91] Howden claims the plan to have Margaret recognised as heir was dropped because William became aware that Ermengarde was pregnant. *Chron. Howden*, iii, 308.

[92] Taylor, 'Robert de Londres', 109–10.

account which suggests he was considered throne-worthy by some.[93] Henry had a brother, Robert Curthose, but relations between them at this point ruled out the possibility of fraternal inheritance of the English throne, in spite of their 1101 agreement to this effect.[94]

In her discussion of the case of Henry I proposing Matilda as his heir, McDougall argues that preference for a legitimate daughter does not imply, at this time at least, that a bastard son was unable to inherit.[95] The most significant difference between the Empress Matilda and Robert of Gloucester, she contends, was not that the former was legitimate and the other not, but primarily concerned their respective maternal lineages. Matilda was descended from Anglo-Saxon royalty through her mother, also Matilda, the daughter of Margaret of Scotland, granddaughter of Edmund II Ironside (making Margaret a direct descendant of Æthelstan II, the first king of all England, and of Alfred the Great). Robert of Gloucester's mother came from a landowning family in Oxfordshire: aristocratic, but not royal.[96]

Maternal lineage and legitimacy, as McDougall acknowledges, are rarely easy to separate since a king, or heir to the throne, is likely to marry a woman with a royal or aristocratic pedigree. A king's legitimate children will therefore tend to have a better maternal lineage than his illegitimate ones, at least in part because the very highest-ranking unmarried daughters were not customarily available as sexual partners except through marriage. But if maternal lineage was an important consideration for a king in selecting an heir, other considerations were accorded equal or greater weight by a community when its king died, as is clear from the fact that Matilda's exemplary maternal lineage was not enough to secure her the throne in 1135, when her kinsman Stephen asserted a right to the crown and garnered enough support to take and hold it.

The fact that William, like Henry I before him, had to seek specific assent to Margaret's heirship indicates that primogeniture was still some way off being accepted as the governing principle of succession. The strength of feeling against female rule was considerable. In recognition of this, William had proposed that Margaret be married to Otto of Brunswick, the future Emperor Otto IV, a nephew and ally of Richard I, and the brother of the woman William had once hoped to marry.[97] Although Margaret would inherit the throne, the extent to which she would be expected to exercise personal rule would be limited at best, and probably non-existent. Marriage being essential, the choice

93 *Gesta Stephani*, see pp. 65–6.

94 K. Thompson, 'Robert [called Robert Curthose], Duke of Normandy', *ODNB*, 10 March 2019; C. W. Hollister, *Henry I*, ed. A. C. Frost (New Haven, CT, 2001), 142. Curthose was older than Henry I and his only legitimate son, William Clito, would have had a claim to the throne, but he died in 1128.

95 McDougall, *Royal Bastards*, 137.

96 D. Crouch, 'Robert of Gloucester's Mother and Sexual Politics in Norman Oxfordshire', *Bulletin of the Institute of Historical Research* 72 (1999), 323–33.

97 See Table 9.

of husband was crucial, as he would be the *de facto* king. The prospect of being ruled by the German king may have been behind at least some of the resistance to Margaret as heir.[98] An independent queen regnant was largely unthinkable. In the thirteenth century, Scotland would twice agree to accept a female heir to the kingdom – once in principle only, concerning an unborn child, and once in respect of the only surviving direct descendant of Alexander III.[99] In the latter instance (the Maid of Norway), her betrothal was of paramount concern. In 1315, when the only child of the king (Robert I) was female, the king's brother was named as his heir ahead of her, and if this brother should predecease her she could accede only if she married someone of whom the political community approved.[100]

The matter of Margaret's heirship was resolved by her brother Alexander being born in 1198. If William the Lion had died in 1195 his brother David would almost certainly have succeeded, but if David had predeceased William, would the Scots have accepted Margaret as queen, or might they have turned instead to Robert of London? A king-list produced sometime between 1198 and 1214, apparently written to present primogeniture as the only correct guiding principle for royal succession, describes Donnchad II as illegitimate, yet not a usurper: it is Domnall III Bán, a brother (of Mael Coluim III) who took the throne that ought to have been held by a son, who is presented as a villain.[101] The text allows that Donnchad was not a lawful heir, but notes without apparent disapproval that he was 'received as king' when he deposed Domnall, whose two reigns are both defined as usurpations.[102] Donnchad was not justly killed for holding the throne illegally, but 'wickedly murdered'. Following the death of Domnall, Edgar 'received the kingdom of Scotland by hereditary right'. The language here is instructive: Edgar 'received' (*suscepit*) the kingdom, an active verb, and one suggesting that he took hold of something presented to him as by right. Donnchad 'was received' (*susceptus est*) as king, a passive verb, but suggesting peaceful acceptance of his authority. The two sons of Mael Coluim are aligned by the same verb being used in relation to their rule. The verb associated with Domnall, by contrast, is *invasere*, violent seizure or entry by an outsider. The text therefore presents a hierarchy of entitlement to the kingship: at the top is the legitimate son Edgar; next, and rhetorically paralleled with him to some extent, is the 'illegitimate' son Donnchad (who lacks the 'hereditary

98 Duncan considers unwillingness to be ruled by Otto the principal motive behind the rejection of William's proposal. Duncan, *Kingship*, 106.

99 *CDS*, i, no. 2229. Discussed at pp. 106–7.

100 *RPS*, 1315/1.

101 Broun, 'Contemporary Perspectives', 91–5. In the Great Cause, the petition for Bruce included an argument that a king's younger brother should inherit the throne ahead of the king's son; Balliol's response was to call Domnall III Bán a usurper, and point out that William the Lion was succeeded by Alexander II and not Earl David. Duncan, *Kingship*, 269–70.

102 Broun, 'Contemporary Perspectives', 94–5.

right' of Edgar, but is not actively wrongful), and the contender with no proper entitlement is the legitimate brother of the deceased king.

The principle of brothers having no rights of succession would not have been recognised by the contemporaries of Domnall III Bán and Donnchad and so, Broun points out, the king-list is evidently calculated to assert the right of the infant or youthful Alexander in the face of an anticipated claim to the throne by his uncle David.[103] To make this point, its author adopts the position that sons should always be preferred to brothers when it comes to the succession, and in doing so commits itself to the stance that illegitimate succession is not an unequivocal evil; it is preferable to at least one alternative, that of succession by a brother when a son is available. As a piece of rhetoric expressing support for Alexander's kingship, the king-list cannot be said to be advocating illegitimate succession, but evidently its creator – and, by implication, at least some among its audience – cared less about legitimacy than about lineal succession.

Margaret offered both lineal descent and legitimacy, but these advantages were offset by her sex. She was still a minor, and although the precedent of a child inheriting the throne had been set in 1153 with the accession of Mael Coluim IV, Robert of London's age and experience would have counted in his favour when weighed against what Margaret had to offer. The period immediately following the deaths of both David I and Mael Coluim IV had seen vigorous attempts by disinherited lines to claim the kingdom, and in 1195 the Meic Uilleim threat was still very much alive – it would be another 35 years before it was eradicated. An adult male with experience of war was a much better proposition as king than a female child. Given the strength of feeling against female succession, and given that purportedly (and actually) bastard claimants had been able to muster significant support for their bids for the crown in the twelfth century, it is possible to envisage Robert of London being preferred to Margaret by at least some of the political community. On balance, however, it is most likely that if William had died brotherless in 1195, a swift marriage would have been arranged between Margaret and someone chosen by the kingdom's magnates – a leading noble, or a prince more acceptable to the Scots than Otto – who would have ruled in right of his wife. Robert of London's position as a bastard son defending the throne against claimants whose right was denied on the grounds they were descended from bastards, actual or supposed, would have been incongruous, to say the least.

The attempts in 1211 and 1212 of Gofraid mac Domnaill meic Uilleim to usurp William the Lion were clearly alarming enough for William to have serious concerns about what might happen were he to die while his only legitimate son, Alexander (1198–1249), was a minor. In 1212 he entered into a pact with King John of England (d. 1216) that each would protect the rights of

[103] Broun, 'Contemporary Perspectives', 94.

the other's heir should they encounter opposition to their succession.[104] No-one knew better than John that a youthful heir might never make it to the throne: he had succeeded in becoming king despite the claim of Arthur of Brittany (1187–1203), son of John's deceased older brother Geoffrey.[105] Broun contends that primogeniture became fixed for inheritance to the throne in Scotland not during the twelfth century, when the child Mael Coluim IV succeeded his grandfather, but only when Alexander II ascended the throne without opposition, in 1214.[106] He points out that the haste with which Alexander was inaugurated as king – within twenty-four hours of William the Lion's death – suggests that right up until that moment there was concern that his status as the next king was not secure. Scottish magnates had sworn fealty to three-year-old Alexander in 1201, with his uncle, earl David, following suit four years later.[107]

If 1214 was a turning-point, it should be borne in mind that primogeniture – which insists on lineal inheritance at the expense of collaterals – might still be set aside when it was likely to yield an undesirable outcome, as it was with the tailzie of 1315 by which Robert I's daughter was ranked below his brother in the succession.[108]

The reign of Alexander II (1214–49)

In 1215, the year following Alexander II's succession, another Domnall Bán Meic Uilleim resumed his line's claim to the throne with an invasion of Moray.[109] He was killed that same year by Ferchar Maccintsacairt, and his head, like that of his namesake, was presented to the king.[110] Gillescop Meic Uilleim and his sons maintained pressure on Alexander in the 1220s, meeting a similar fate in 1229.[111]

104 *Gesta Annalia I* in Skene, *Fordun*, i, 277–8; *Chron. Bower*, iv, 467–9; A. A. M. Duncan, 'John King of England and the Kings of Scots', in S. D. Church, ed., *King John: New Interpretations* (Woodbridge, 1999), 263–4.

105 J. C. Holt, 'King John and Arthur of Brittany', *Nottingham Medieval Studies* 44 (2000), 82–103, discusses the merits of Arthur's claim compared to that of John (both may have been said to have had rights) and the evidence for John's culpability in Arthur's death.

106 Broun, 'Contemporary Perspectives', 82, 90–1.

107 *Chron. Melrose*, 51, 52; Broun, 'Contemporary Perspectives', 90.

108 *RPS*, 1315/1. See p. 95.

109 *Chron. Melrose*, 59. Two Scottish raids on Ulster, in 1212 and 1214, may have been intended to attack a Meic Uilleim base there. A. Ross, 'Moray, Ulster and the MacWilliams', in S. Duffy, ed., *The World of the Galloglass. Kings, Warlords and Warriors in Ireland and Scotland, 1200–1600* (Dublin, 2007), 38.

110 *Chron. Melrose*, 59; *Gesta Annalia I* in Skene, *Fordun*, i, 282–3; R. A. McDonald, 'Old and New in the Far North: Ferchar Maccintsacairt and the Early Earls of Ross, 1200–1274', in S. Boardman and A. Ross, ed., *The Exercise of Power in Medieval Scotland c. 1200–1500* (Dublin, 2005), 278.

111 *Gesta Annalia I* in Skene, *Fordun*, i, 290; *Chron. Bower*, v, 117, 143. The precise relationship of these kinsmen to each other is not known. W. W. Scott, 'Macwilliam Family (per. c.

The conviction of the Meic Uilleim that they had a right to the throne and a chance of obtaining it ended only with the extinction of their line in 1230, when the female infant who was the last Meic Uilleim was publicly killed.[112] The writer of the *Lanercost Chronicle* is condemnatory of the execution of the child, on the grounds that it is '*contra dicente Domine, "non occidentur filii pro patribus"*' (Deut. 24:16: 'Fathers shall not be put to death for their children, nor children put to death for their fathers; each is to die for his own sin'). This verse was also used by some Church Fathers and canonists to argue against the stigmatisation of illegitimate children.[113]

Alexander II married twice: his first marriage, to Joan, daughter of King John of England, was childless, while his second, to Marie de Coucy, resulted in the birth of his only legitimate child, Alexander, in 1241. He also fathered an illegitimate daughter, Marjorie, whose mother is unknown. Alexander gave her in marriage, probably around 1244, to Alan Durward, the son of Thomas Durward or Hostiarius, who had distinguished himself to Alexander and his father in part through his involvement in suppressing Gofraid Meic Uilleim's rebellion.[114] Alan became justiciar at around the same time he was given Alexander's daughter in marriage. The couple had two known daughters.

Marjorie's historical significance, beyond being the grandmother of Nicholas de Soulis, one of the Competitors in the Great Cause, lies in an unusual episode concerning her illegitimacy and an apparent attempt to manipulate the royal succession. Both surviving accounts of it place the events at around the time of the marriage of her half-brother, Alexander III, to Margaret, daughter of Henry III, which took place in December 1251.[115] The gist of these accounts is that there was an attempt to obtain a papal legitimation for Marjorie, so as to smooth the way for the crown to pass to someone in Durward's immediate family should Alexander III die before procreating an heir.[116] The king and his bride were aged ten and eleven respectively, and it would be ten years before they produced their first child.

No details of the content of the petition have survived. It was highly unlikely to have been a case of the pope being asked to rule on whether or not Marjorie's parents' union was a valid marriage and to effect her legitimation

1130–c. 1230)', *ODNB*, 27 March 2019.

112 *Chron. Lanercost*, 40–1.

113 Witte, *Sins of the Fathers*, 37–8, 40, 96.

114 For Alan Durward and his family, see M. W. Hammond, '*Hostarii Regis Scotie*: the Durward Family in the Thirteenth Century', in Boardman and Ross, *Exercise of Power in Medieval Scotland*, 118–38.

115 *Gesta Annalia I* in Skene, *Fordun*, i, 296; *Chron. Melrose*, 109–10; *ESSH*, ii, 571.

116 *Gesta Annalia I* says the legitimation sought was for Marjorie and the *Melrose Chronicle* version says it was for her daughters. Since the daughters were already legitimate what seems to have been meant is that Durward sought to provide the legal basis for their claim to the throne, through legitimisation (i.e. of their mother).

by this method. Innocent III had been asked to do this some fifty years earlier for the French king and had declared the 'marriage' null, but had granted the legitimation by special grace, and pronounced the French king's children capable of inheriting the throne. This same favour – legitimation by special grace, rather than by convalidation of marriage – was probably what was sought in Marjorie's case. The timing of Durward's petition is of note since it took place only a few years after the then pope, Innocent IV, had granted a similar *ex gratia* legitimation to a royal bastard. In 1246 the reigning Norwegian king, Hákon IV, obtained a papal legitimation.[117] He had succeeded to the throne despite his illegitimacy, but sought the regularisation of his status out of a recognition that legitimacy was, or was becoming, an important characteristic of European kingship.[118] These two precedents may have encouraged Durward to believe that if Marjorie were legitimated, she would be capable of transmitting the kingship to their children.

The *Melrose Chronicle* account says Durward sent gifts to the pope, apparently as inducements. It was not unusual for petitioners of any kind to send gifts to powerful figures in the hope of being looked on favourably, so if the mention of gifts was intended to portray Durward as wickedly offering bribes, the accusation could be applied equally to many others in similar situations. Indeed, until the second half of the thirteenth century, when the papacy introduced a schedule of tariffs for dispensations and other services, payment for these was expected to take the form of gifts and donations.[119] The same account makes it very clear that Durward's behaviour was far from innocuous, commenting, 'And if he had obtained this, none doubted that he would have turned traitor to the king and queen.'[120] The version in *Gesta Annalia* notes that the great seal of Scotland, which Durward had used to authorise the petition, was then broken up by the magnates 'in the people's sight'.[121]

It had been only a couple of generations since William the Lion's legitimate daughter Margaret, his heir according to law, had not been accepted as such by some of his magnates who cited the custom of brothers inheriting at the expense of daughters.[122] But there were important differences in the two situations. In William's case, his daughter Margaret was not the only possible candidate to replace him since he had a brother; Alexander in 1251 had no

117 *Diplomatarium Norvegicum*, i, 29 (letter dated 8 November 1246).

118 He also took steps to ensure only the offspring born of his marriage could succeed him, excluding his eldest but illegitimate son. Jochens, 'Politics of Reproduction', 346–8; C. Larrington, 'Queens and Bodies: The Norwegian Translated *lais* and Hákon IV's Kinswomen', *Journal of English and Germanic Philology* 108 (2009), 512.

119 Lunt, *Papal Revenues*, i, 81, 83.

120 *Chron. Melrose*, 110.

121 *Gesta Annalia I* in Skene, *Fordun*, i, 296.

122 *Chron. Howden*, iii, 299.

near male kin, nor any obvious heir presumptive.[123] The dispute over the inheritance of Galloway in 1234 forcefully established that legitimate daughters took precedence over other claimants in ordinary feus.[124] The kingdom was not such, but the possibility that kingship might be transmitted by a daughter was suggested by the accession of Donnchad I (d. 1040), grandson of Mael Coluim II via his daughter Bethóc.[125] A legitimated Marjorie, in the absence of alternatives, was a viable candidate. Given the assumption that should a woman inherit the throne, her husband would become the *de facto* ruler, this is probably what Durward hoped for. Duncan suggests that Marjorie died young and Durward was seeking a posthumous legitimation for her, so that her rights would pass to their eldest daughter.[126] The death of Alexander III without an heir of his body while Marjorie's daughter was a child could have enabled Durward to act as regent until his daughter was of age.

In his analysis of the *Melrose Chronicle* entry concerning the matter, Duncan argues that that the strong reaction to the legitimation attempt – Durward was removed from power and driven into exile – shows that, 'legitimation would make a difference'.[127] The political community's anger against Durward suggests that they understood papal legitimation of a king's offspring to be so fully effective for succession to the throne that it tied their hands should undesirable outcomes ensue from it. The upper nobility protested against Durward's actions because if he had accomplished his aim, his new standing would be a *fait accompli*. The fear that Durward 'would have turned traitor to the king and queen' could only have had as its basis that he would have benefited from so doing: that is, his position would have been transformed.[128]

Just a few years later, in 1255, Alan Durward would attempt to claim the earldom of Mar by alleging that ancestral illegitimacy invalidated the inheritance rights of the incumbent earl.[129] That both of these high-profile and controversial bids for advancement concerned legitimacy was no coincidence.

123 Duncan, *Kingship*, 155. Robert (V) Bruce, Competitor for the throne of Scotland in 1291–2, claimed that Alexander II had named him heir presumptive in 1238. E. L. G. Stones and G. G. Simpson, ed., *Edward I and the Throne of Scotland 1290–1296: an Edition of the Record Sources for the Great Cause* (Oxford, 1978), ii, 145, 170, 185–6. See also pp. 107 and 184.

124 Discussed at pp. 174–6.

125 John Balliol's and Robert I's right to the throne would both depend on their descent from daughters of David, earl of Huntingdon, grandson of David I. In England, Henry I's daughter Matilda was deemed able to transmit heirship of the English throne to her son, Henry II. In earlier centuries, transmission of the Scottish crown through a woman may have been unacceptable. Woolf, 'The Moray Question', 147, 155, 163 n.79.

126 Duncan, *Kingship*, 155. Marjorie was still alive on 4 July 1251; Alexander married in December that year.

127 Ibid. Hammond says a legitimation of Marjorie would 'potentially' have given Durward a place in the royal succession. Hammond, '*Hostarii Regis Scotie*', 132.

128 That is not to say he would have been unchallenged: it seems likely that Robert Bruce of Annandale would have asserted a claim.

129 See pp. 178–80.

Sometime between the late twelfth century and the middle of the thirteenth, it had become established in Scotland that a papal declaration of legitimacy made its recipient eligible for succession to estates. Legitimacy becoming a prerequisite for inheritance (in much, though not all, of Scotland), opened up another possibility, that of challenging the earl of Mar's right to the earldom on the basis that his forebears had succeeded according to the old rules and not the new.[130] Both of Durward's undertakings displayed a shrewd grasp of the opportunities presented by the changing legal climate around legitimacy, both were audacious, both failed.

Between the lifetimes of Donnchad II and Alan Durward, the meanings attached to illegitimacy changed. In the early years of the twelfth century, the subtle denigration of the line of Mael Coluim III's first wife, believed to be Ingibjǫrg, through the presentation of his second marriage, to Margaret, as his only legally valid union, was reinforced a generation later by a direct assertion of Donnchad II's illegitimacy, a designation heavily elaborated on in the thirteenth century and beyond. Initial suggestions that Donnchad was illegitimate were made by those close to his political rivals, Margaret's offspring. It is possible, though unprovable either way, that Donnchad was born of a marriage which was canonically faulty, but there is no evidence that this rendered him ineligible for the throne in his lifetime. If the marriage of Ingibjǫrg and Mael Coluim did not in fact comply with the Church model of lawful matrimony, this was not an issue until it became useful as a means of retroactively undermining the rights of Ingibjǫrg's son.

In the first half of the twelfth century, the bastardy of Mael Coluim, son of Alexander I, did not discourage at least some leading men in Scotland from supporting his bid for the crown. Similarly, from the death of David I in 1153 until the murder of the last, infant, Meic Uilleim in 1230, the ascription of bastardy to Donnchad remained inadequate, in the eyes of a significant section of the Scottish political community, as a means of disqualifying his descendants from kingship. It is possible that the allegation Donnchad was illegitimate was not believed, but at least equally possible it was considered irrelevant, or, at least, less important than other factors.

A century after the reign of Donnchad II, Robert of London was simply not considered a candidate for the throne. Their situations were very different: Robert was known to have been born of an extramarital relationship, rather than to parents who believed themselves married even if the Church disagreed; and, as Taylor suggests, there may additionally have been some value to William of the illegitimate Robert being conspicuously ineligible for the throne when it was, or had been, under threat from illegitimate claimants (Alexander I's son Mael Coluim) or the Meic Uilleim, descended from Donnchad II, described

[130] Ancestral illegitimacy in a royal context is discussed at pp. 83–93.

as illegitimate, via his grandson, who probably was illegitimate.[131] But even in Robert of London's time, the relationship between illegitimacy and throne-worthiness was not straightforward. The king-list which implies illegitimate succession is not as great an evil as succession by a brother may have arrived at this position through rhetorical exaggeration of its pro-primogeniture stance, but it does nonetheless suggest that illegitimacy was not uniformly regarded as an insurmountable barrier to kingship.

The timing of the king-list's production (1198x1214) is significant: it coincides with a period in which someone's illegitimacy became mutable. Legitimation *per subsequens matrimonium* had been known in legal circles from the time of the decretal *Tanta* in 1172, and so had been in circulation for at least twenty-six years, perhaps longer, by the time the king-list was drawn up; and a legitimation 'by special grace' of royal offspring whose parents were unequivocally not married to each other, expressly permitting the legitimated offspring to succeed to the French throne, took place for the first time in 1201. These showed that someone born a bastard may yet become legitimate, with the legal effects of bastardy expunged, making him or her fully able to inherit. This was the premise on which Alan Durward relied when he sought the legitimation of his wife Marjorie, Alexander II's illegitimate daughter, in 1251. Forty years later, the proceedings of the Great Cause would turn the spotlight once again on illegitimacy and inheritance of the throne.

131 Taylor, 'Robert de Londres', 109–10.

4

Illegitimacy and royal succession II: from the Great Cause to James I

I wald haue dred to mak ane wrangus are,
To put my realm and peopill in despair[1]

The Scottish succession crisis in the late thirteenth century appears to have put to the test the question of whether kingship and illegitimacy were compatible. Of the thirteen Competitors (fourteen if Edward I's claim is to be included), seven claimed descent from named royal offspring whose illegitimacy, actual or assumed, is not mentioned in their descendants' petitions (Tables 3 and 4).[2] None was successful.

Robert de Pinkeny asserted that he was a great-great-great-grandson of David I. According to his petition, Pinkeny's great-grandmother had been Marjorie, daughter of David I's son Henry.[3] Duncan describes the claim that Marjorie was a daughter of Henry as 'an impossibility' and says it is likely that she was an illegitimate daughter of David, earl of Huntingdon.[4] Only one illegitimate daughter of David is known with certainty: Ada, who married Mael Ísu, son of Earl Fer Téid of Strathearn.[5] Although the identities of Marjorie's parents is unknown, there is some evidence that she was an illegitimate royal daughter. Marjorie was granted lands at Elcho by Alexander II for the foundation of a priory, a remarkably generous gift to someone not within the royal kindred, but much less so if she was Alexander II's first cousin, or some other near relation.[6] Marjorie, as Pinkeny claimed, married David de Lindsay (d. bf. 1220), and some evidence suggestive of Marjorie's royal status

1 *King Alexander*, lines 179–80.

2 Stones and Simpson, *Throne of Scotland*, i, 14.

3 Stones and Simpson, *Throne of Scotland*, ii, 135–6.

4 Duncan, *Kingship*, 242 n.86. Barrow concurs, saying that he was 'almost certainly the great-grandson of a bastard daughter of Earl David of Huntingdon'. G. W. S. Barrow, 'Competitors for the Throne of Scotland (act. 1291–1292)', *ODNB*, 6 August 2018.

5 For Ada, see K. Stringer, *Earl David of Huntingdon 1152–1219* (Edinburgh, 1985), 41, 81–2, 87, 244–6, 270, 294 n.97; and *PoMS*, www.poms.ac.uk/record/person/1848/.

6 *Dunfermelyn Reg.*, no. 190. See also *PoMS*, www.poms.ac.uk/record/person/905/; and www.poms.ac.uk/record/person/4284/. Duncan offers the opinion that the land at

can be found in the activities of her Lindsay descendants. In 1233 Marjorie's grandson, David (III) Lindsay of Barnweill (d. ca. 1268) made a bequest of 20s annually, in perpetuity, to Balmerino Abbey for the welfare of Alexander II and himself, and for the soul of 'his lady', Ermengarde, the late queen of Scots.[7] The bequest, made in the immediate aftermath of Ermengarde's death, and to the abbey she herself founded, may be indicative of a family relationship.[8] So too may be evidence that in 1230 Marjorie's son, David (II) Lindsay (d. 1240x1), and another member of the Lindsay family, were overseas in the company of John 'the Scot', earl of Huntingdon (d. 1237), son of Earl David.[9] Alexander II's younger sister, Marjorie (d. 1244), gave the lands of 'Chirdene' in Tynedale to David Lindsay.[10] A relationship between the Scottish crown and the Pinkenys is further suggested by the fact that in 1255 Alexander III's queen, Margaret (d. 1275), appealed to her father, Henry III, to grant Pinkeny the favour of paying sums due to the royal exchequer in instalments.[11]

If Pinkeny was indeed descended from David I in some way, his declaration that his ancestor was a daughter of Prince Henry, rather than Henry's son David, may have been a genuine error, based on a mistake in memory or recording at some point, but it may equally have been a deliberate attempt by either the Competitor or an earlier member of his family to connect the illegitimate daughter more closely to former kings by making her a granddaughter of David I and sister of Mael Coluim IV and William the Lion, instead of their great-granddaughter and niece. If the misrepresentation was deliberate, this shows that the criterion of 'nearness of blood' was seen to be as relevant to illegitimate members of the family as to legitimate ones.[12]

Nicholas de Soulis was a great-grandson of Alexander II, being the son of Ermengarde, who was a daughter of Alexander's illegitimate daughter Marjorie.[13] One twentieth-century assessment judges him to have been 'by

Elcho formed part of the possessions of David, earl of Huntingdon, and that he gave them to Marjorie, his illegitimate daughter, as her tocher. Duncan, *Kingship*, 242 n.86.

7 *Liber Sancte Marie de Balmorinach*, ed. W. B. D. D. Turnbull (Abbotsford Club, Edinburgh, 1841), no. 19; *PoMS*, www.poms.ac.uk/record/person/4682/.

8 The gift was made between her death on 11 February, and 28 March, when the charter was confirmed by Alexander II.

9 *CDS*, i, no. 1089.

10 Ibid., i, no. 1981.

11 Ibid., i, no. 2032. An alternative source of the Pinkeny claim is suggested in *PoMS*: Marjorie's son, David (II) Lindsay was married to Christina Hose, whose second husband was Sir Robert de Pinkeny: www.poms.ac.uk/record/person/4284/. This is not mentioned in Pinkeny's petition; he claimed, truthfully, that Marjorie's daughter, Alicia, married Henry de Pinkeny. It is not impossible that the siblings Alicia and David (II) both married into the Pinkeny family, though the second to marry would very probably have needed to obtain a dispensation.

12 Illegitimate offspring were regarded as full members of the family, by the Church as much as by anyone else: the prohibited degrees affecting marriage applied identically to legitimate and illegitimate kin.

13 Stones and Simpson, *Throne of Scotland*, ii, 136.

far the nearest to the royal line' among the 1291–2 Competitors.[14] Nicholas de Soulis's grandson, Sir William de Soulis, would emerge later as a conspirator against Robert I, alongside Sir David de Brechin, also a descendant of a royal bastard.[15]

Two of the claimants, Patrick Galightly, a burgess of Perth, and Roger de Mandeville, of an Anglo-French family settled in Ulster, claimed descent from two otherwise unknown children of William the Lion – a son, Henry, and a daughter, Affrica, respectively.[16] Affrica was said to have married into the de Say family, but is not mentioned in any surviving records concerned with them; the number of generations between her and her alleged descendant Roger de Mandeville makes it implausible that she was born of William; and the Mandeville claim is accompanied by a fantastical tale alleging that Affrica had had two siblings, also the offspring of William the Lion, a brother having been murdered by his uncle (impossibly, William's brother Mael Coluim IV), and a sister having died subsequently.[17] While William the Lion's illegitimate son Robert of London frequently witnessed his father's charters, and he and his illegitimate half-sisters Isabella, Margaret and Ada are all found in other contemporary sources, no Henry or Affrica who were children of William the Lion appear in any charter or other record. Duncan and Taylor both contend that Affrica and Henry were invented by the 1291 claimants to provide grounds for their claims.[18]

This is possible, if unprovable. Whether the two claimants were descended from illegitimate royal offspring whose existence is now (and even then may have been) incapable of proof; whether they sincerely, but erroneously, believed themselves to be descended from suppositious illegitimate offspring of William, or whether they opportunistically fabricated the existence of Henry and Affrica, may never be known. Henry was the name of William's father, and the name given by William's brother David to three of his sons, while Affrica, a distinctively Gaelic name, is one that occurs in the relevant time period and in William the Lion's extended, but not in his immediate, family.[19]

14 T. McMichael, 'The Feudal Family of de Soulis', *TDGNHAS*, 3rd series 26 (1947–8), 184.

15 Brechin was a grandson of Henry of Brechin, an illegitimate son of David, earl of Huntingdon. Albin (no surname is recorded), bishop of Brechin (d. 1269), was rumoured to be an illegitimate son of Henry of Brechin. D. E. R. Watt, *A Biographical Dictionary of Scottish Graduates to A.D. 1410* (Oxford, 1977), 6.

16 Stones and Simpson, *Throne of Scotland*, ii, 135–7; Duncan, *Kingship*, 263. This is also discussed in Taylor, 'Robert de Londres', 102.

17 Duncan, *Kingship*, 263; Taylor, 'Robert de Londres', 102. It appears to be a reworking of story told by Orderic Vitalis, in which David I's young son was disembowelled by a 'certain wretched clerk'. Chibnall, *Orderic Vitalis*, iv, 275–7.

18 Duncan, *Kingship*, 263; Taylor, 'Robert de Londres', 102.

19 Fergus of Galloway (d. 1161) had a daughter of that name who married Óláfr (d. 1153), king of Man and the Isles; Óláfr's son, also probably Affrica's, Guðrǫðr (d. 1187), had a daughter called Affrica (d. in or after 1219), who married John de Courcy (d. 1219). Courcy was the son of Avice (or Amice) de Rumilly, whose sister, Alice de Rumilly, was

If the claimants invented their ancestry, the choice of Henry as the name of Galightly's forebear could have been based on common knowledge that this was a significant family name, but the selection of Affrica for Mandeville's ancestor seems an unusual choice: safer, surely, to have gone for a name more closely associated with William, such as Ada or Margaret.

Of the other Competitors, William de Vescy, William de Ros and Patrick Dunbar were the descendants of William's illegitimate daughters Margaret, Isabella and Ada respectively.[20] William de Ros, great-grandson of Isabella, appears to have made an attempt to show that Isabella had at some point been legitimated. Stones and Simpson, in their analysis of the record sources for the Great Cause, point out that during the process there seems to have been an inquest relating to Ros's petition: they suggest that this may be connected to the legitimation claim and that the lack of any further information 'illustrates the losses which must have occurred among the subsidiary documents'.[21] Perhaps so, but the possibility cannot be ruled out that Ros knowingly made a false claim that Isabella's legitimacy had been, or could be, confirmed. Clearly, the claim that Isabella had been legitimated was made in the expectation that if it had been accepted, it would have lifted William de Ros out of the category of those Duncan calls the 'no-hopers'.[22] The effectiveness of papal legitimation in relation to inheritance of the throne of Scotland would not be properly tested until the fourteenth century, but the reaction to Alan Durward's attempt, some forty years earlier, to obtain a legitimation for his wife Marjorie, Alexander II's illegitimate daughter, suggests that legitimated royal offspring were regarded as capable of inheritance by the middle of the thirteenth century.[23] If this was out of the question, there was little point in Ros's attempts to persuade the tribunal of Isabella's revised status. Presumably in the absence of documentation supporting his declaration, and perhaps with some inducement, Ros withdrew his claim days before Edward I ruled in favour of Balliol.[24]

If they stood no chance of being taken seriously, why then did these Competitors put themselves forward? Possibly some regarded their case as not entirely hopeless: that claimants from illegitimate, and purportedly illegitimate, royal lines in the twelfth and earlier thirteenth centuries had been able to muster support for their cause may have encouraged their ambitions. A

married to William fitz Duncan, son of Donnchad II, who in turn was a son of William the Lion's great-grandfather, Mael Coluim III.

20 Stones and Simpson, *Throne of Scotland*, ii, 134–5; Duncan, *Kingship*, 241–2. For these daughters, see pp. 124–6 and 196, and Table 3.

21 Stones and Simpson, *Throne of Scotland*, i, 190.

22 Duncan, *Kingship*, 242. Duncan notes, on the same page, that one group of Paris lawyers ruled out William de Ros because Isabella 'had been legitimated, not born legitimate', but since no evidence for her legitimation seems to have been brought forward, it is not clear how they formed the impression she was legitimated.

23 Durward's legitimation attempt is discussed at pp. 78–81.

24 Duncan, *Kingship*, 294.

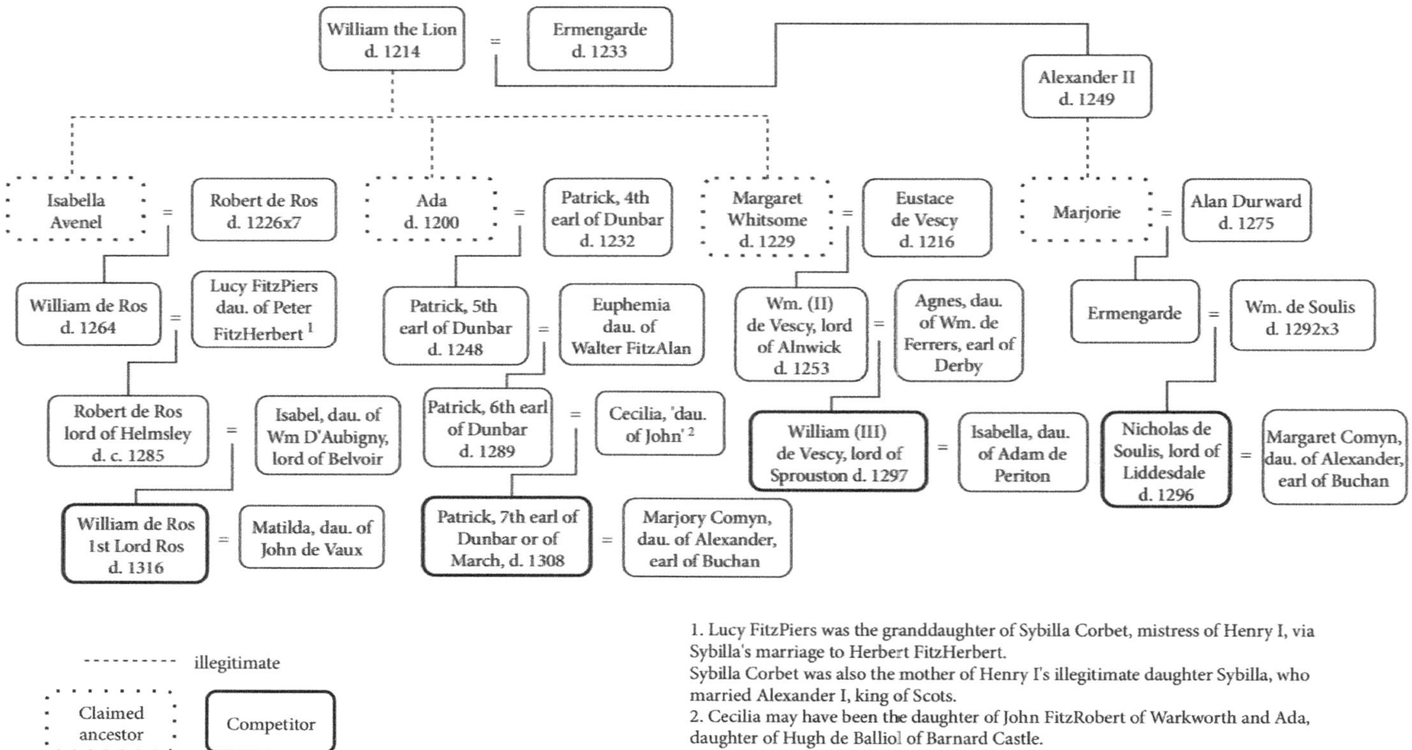

1. Lucy FitzPiers was the granddaughter of Sybilla Corbet, mistress of Henry I, via Sybilla's marriage to Herbert FitzHerbert.
Sybilla Corbet was also the mother of Henry I's illegitimate daughter Sybilla, who married Alexander I, king of Scots.
2. Cecilia may have been the daughter of John FitzRobert of Warkworth and Ada, daughter of Hugh de Balliol of Barnard Castle.
PoMS, https://www.poms.ac.uk/record/person/5875/

Table 3. Competitors descended from known illegitimates

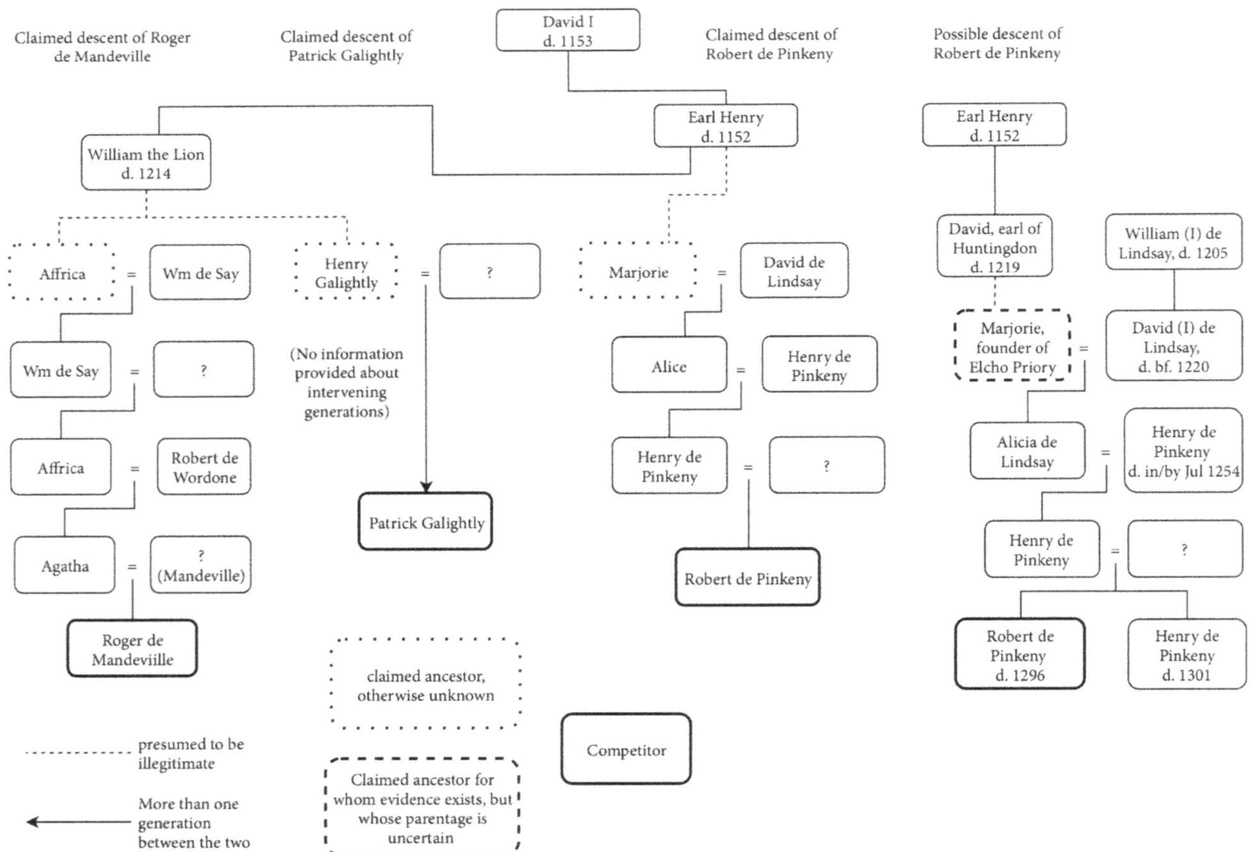

Table 4. Competitors descended from unknown, presumed illegitimates

bold claim to be of royal blood might just pay off. Even if it did not, advantage was to be had merely by advertising the connection. Understanding their chances to be slim, the Competitors might nonetheless succeed in elevating their reputations by gaining the status of an acknowledged royal claimant. In this context, we might interpret Pinkeney's possibly deliberate attempt to manipulate his 'nearness' ranking as intended to enhance further his prestige among contemporaries. Candidates from these lineages were proud of their ancestry: bloodline counted for a great deal. Social stigma was not the reason they remained silent on the illegitimacy of those ancestors through whom they were connected to the royal house: simply, they recognised the legal consequences of bastardy and so omitted the information which harmed their case in law.

They may have relied on uncertainty about the birth status of an ancestor keeping them in the race. As the Ros claim showed, someone's birth status could be changed legally; and inheritance disputes over the lands of Lennox and the earldom of Mar in the mid-thirteenth century highlight how difficult it could be to prove someone was illegitimate.[25] Chronicle accounts of the lineage of William the Lion's queen, Ermengarde, are an example of how someone's origins might be obscured, either inadvertently or by deliberate misrepresentation.[26] The level of scrutiny which was, or could be, applied to the claims may not have been consistent. It seems to have been simply accepted that Comyn's royal ancestor, on whom his bid for the throne relied, was a legitimate daughter of Domnall III Bán.[27] The status of Domnall's relationship with Bethóc's mother in the eleventh century is unknown to us now; the question is whether it was known to anyone in the late thirteenth century, or whether the auditors in the Great Cause took it on trust that she was the product of a lawful marriage – or, at least, of a union understood in its time to be a valid marriage.

This, in turn, presents us with an interesting question: at what point in a Competitor's lineage did the illegitimacy of a forebear count against him? After all, the throne had been held by Mael Coluim IV and William the Lion, whose grandmother, Maud de Senlis, wife of David I, was the granddaughter of Adelaide, illegitimate daughter of Robert, duke of Normandy.[28] William the Lion's son, Alexander II, was descended not only from Adelaide, but also, via Alexander's mother Ermengarde, from an illegitimate daughter of Henry I; and so the same applied to Alexander III. Ancestral illegitimacy was not a bar to the throne in their cases. None of the illegitimate forebears concerned were the product of a putative marriage, a union that was thought to be lawful marriage but was invalid because of an impediment. They were unambiguously

[25] See pp. 45 and 178–80.

[26] Discussed at p. 121; see also Table 8.

[27] She was of the same generation as her cousin Donnchad II, called illegitimate after his death by his political rivals.

[28] Maud's mother was Judith, niece of William the Bastard.

illegitimate, as products of sexual liaisons outwith marriage. The same applied to the illegitimate offspring on whom the claims of various Competitors rested. John Balliol, the eventually successful Competitor, had at least three illegitimate forebears: Adelaide of Normandy, great-great-great grandmother of Balliol's grandmother, Margaret of Huntingdon; Robert of Gloucester, the illegitimate son of Henry I who was Margaret's great-great-grandfather; and the unnamed daughter of Henry I who was great-grandmother of Alan of Galloway, Balliol's grandfather (Table 5).

The Church deemed a union out of conformity with its regulations to be a non-marriage, and, in the absence of a dispensation rectifying this, the children were illegitimate. Despite the apparent concern to eliminate from contention for the throne those descended from illegitimates, there is no surviving evidence that scrutiny was applied to the marriages from which each member of the generations between the royal ancestor and the Competitor was born, to ensure every candidate was born of lawful marriage.[29] There may well have been an impediment to the marriage of Margaret of Huntingdon, whose status as the eldest daughter of David, earl of Huntingdon, was – ostensibly – decisive in settling the kingdom on her grandson John Balliol. John's mother, Dervorguilla, was born of Margaret's marriage to Alan of Galloway, which took place in 1209. In 1222, judges-delegate were appointed to enquire into Alan's marriage which, it was alleged, breached canonical prohibitions in respect of both consanguinity and affinity.[30] Pope Honorius III (d. 1227) explained that 'very many' (*quamplures*) bishops of Scotland had written to him expressing disquiet about the marriage and that, due to nearness of degree, Alan and his wife could not have sexual relations without mortal sin. The wife is not named in the papal mandate. Alan was married at least three times, and Stringer has said the wife in question 'does not seem to have been Margaret', arguing that the investigation related to his third known wife, Rose de Lacy, daughter of the earl of Ulster, being a kinswoman of his first, a daughter of Roger de Lacy, constable of Chester (d. 1211).[31] The date of his second de Lacy marriage is given in the *Lanercost Chronicle* as 1229, but Stringer points out that this may not be reliable, and it could have taken place several years before, that is, in advance of the letter of 1222.[32]

Certainly, it is not clear why a marriage contracted in 1209 should become the subject of concern only some thirteen years later. But consideration of their ancestry suggests the marriage between Alan of Galloway and Margaret of

[29] The claim that Isabella Avenel, ancestor of William de Ros, had been legitimated was investigated, but any supplication for legitimation in Isabella's case presumably requested papal grace in the matter; the alternative, a request that her parents' relationship be accepted as a lawful marriage, seems out of the question.

[30] Theiner, *Vet. Mon.*, no. 48.

[31] K. Stringer, 'A New Wife for Alan of Galloway', *TDGNHAS* 49 (1972), 52.

[32] *Chron. Lanercost*, 40.

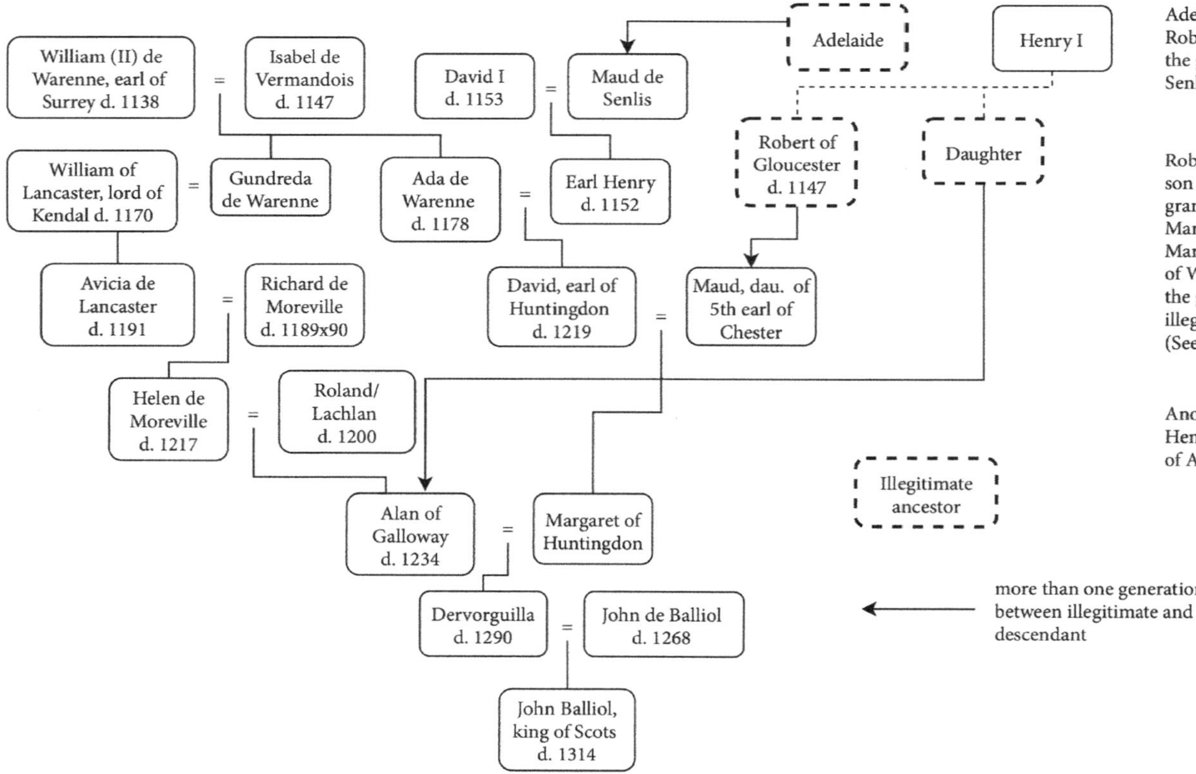

Adelaide, illegitimate daughter of Robert, duke of Normandy, was the grandmother of Maud de Senlis.

Robert of Gloucester, illegitimate son of Henry I, was the great-grandfather of Maud, mother of Margaret of Huntingdon. Margaret's father was the brother of William the Lion, who married the great-granddaughter of an illegitimate daughter of Henry I. (See Tables 8 and 9.)

Another illegitimate daughter of Henry I was the great-grandmother of Alan of Galloway.

Table 5. Illegitimates in the ancestry of John Balliol, king of Scots

Huntingdon may have been invalid. Alan's maternal grandmother was Avicia (or Avice), daughter of William of Lancaster, lord of Kendal (d. 1170).[33] William was married to Gundreda, daughter of William (II) de Warenne, earl of Surrey (d. 1138) and Isabel de Vermandois (d. 1147).[34] Gundreda's sister was Ada de Warenne (d. 1178), mother of David, earl of Huntingdon and grandmother of Margaret. If Avicia's mother was Gundreda, then Alan and Margaret were both descended from William (II) de Warenne, and Isabel of Vermandois and were related by consanguinity, but even if Avicia was a daughter of William of Lancaster with an earlier spouse, his marriage to Gundreda created an impediment of affinity between their descendants.[35]

Writing in the fifteenth century, Walter Bower claimed that Alan and Margaret's daughter, Dervorguilla, was 'a bastard who was born illegitimate' (*bastarda et illegitime nata*).[36] He says that 'according to some', the couple were related to each other within the forbidden degrees, and provides an erroneous genealogy in which Margaret's mother and Alan's grandmother are sisters.[37] Bower is motivated by the desire to show that Balliol, whose kingship he regards as disastrous, should never have become king; claiming that Dervorguilla was illegitimate removed her from any line through which the right to rule could be transmitted, thus disqualifying her descendants from the kingship. His claim is made in bad faith, and his genealogy of Dervorguilla is garbled, but he may well have been correct in alleging that ancestors of Alan and of Margaret were sisters.[38]

This was not the only possible impediment to the marriage of Alan and Margaret. Alan had previously been married to a daughter of Roger de Lacy. Her brother, John de Lacy, was married to Margaret de Quincy, whose aunt, Matilda or Maud (d. 1233), was the wife of David, earl of Huntingdon, and mother of Margaret, whom Alan later married.[39] Margaret of Huntingdon was therefore first cousin to Margaret de Quincy, the wife of Alan's former brother-in-law; the two Margarets shared a grandfather in Hugh, fifth earl of Chester (d. 1181). There may have been other connections still: Margaret's paternal grandmother, Ada de Warenne, had twelve siblings (four full siblings and eight half-siblings; Ada's mother had previously been married to the politically

[33] *PoMS*, www.poms.ac.uk/record/person/1220/.
[34] D. Crouch, 'Roger, Second Earl of Warwick (d. 1153), Magnate', *ODNB*, 20 May 2020. Warwick was Gundreda's first husband.
[35] Table 6.
[36] *Chron. Bower*, vii, 289.
[37] Ibid.
[38] He claims elsewhere that Margaret is a legitimate heir of Alan, in contradistinction to her illegitimate half-brother, Thomas. *Chron. Bower*, v, 147.
[39] Further intermarriages between the de Quincy kindred and the offspring of both David of Huntingdon and Alan of Galloway create a yet more complicated picture, but these marriages took place after the union of Alan and Margaret.

prominent Robert de Beaumont, count of Meulan and earl of Leicester). The marriages and remarriages of these siblings, their offspring and grandchildren, placed Ada and her descendants in a vast network of elite connections, creating enormous potential for unions between members of her own and succeeding generations to fall within the forbidden degrees.[40]

There does seem to be a case to answer, at least, in respect of Alan and Margaret's marriage. Was this unknown to Edward I and his co-adjudicators in the Great Cause, some seventy years later? Perhaps, and yet Bower seems to have had an inkling of it much later than that. In assessing the Competitors' claims, it is possible the tribunal drew a distinction between children born in what appeared to be a marriage (though the Church might disagree) and those born of clearly extramarital fornication, even though both categories of offspring were formally illegitimate. It may be that the outcome of the Great Cause, the selection of a compliant John Balliol, was a foregone conclusion, or, at least, that there was a deliberate effort to bend the proceedings towards that result.[41] In this case, it is possible that those involved chose not to look too closely at the marriages in John Balliol's direct line. Contrary to appearances, there may not have been any rigorously enforced policy regarding illegitimacy and inheritance of the throne. Legitimacy mattered, but perhaps not overwhelmingly so: a blind eye might be turned to some forms of illegitimacy in a lineage if doing so ensured a preferred candidate came out on top.

In the Great Cause, the birth order of the (legitimate) daughters of David of Huntingdon, through whom, the tribunal decided, the throne descended, was critical. John Balliol was the eldest surviving male of the line of Earl David's eldest daughter Margaret, and as such was awarded the kingship in preference to Robert, the son of David's younger daughter. Bruce's argument was that he was a grandson of Earl David, while John was a great-grandson, and so he was nearer to the relevant ancestor than Balliol; however, the tribunal ruled that primogeniture should apply, making Earl David's eldest daughter his lawful heir, and John Balliol king through the principle of representation.[42] The selection of John Balliol followed the principles of primogeniture, excluding all illegitimate offspring from inheritance and prioritising seniority over nearness of degree. This ignored the implications of a parliamentary act of tailzie in 1284, and also the 1281 treaty for the marriage of Alexander III's daughter to Eric of Norway, both of

[40] Connections in previous generations, such as that both Alan and Margaret were descended from Henry I via two of Henry's illegitimate daughters, were, by the thirteenth century, too distant to place them within the forbidden degrees.

[41] Duncan, *Kingship*, 238, 241, 275 and Chapter 13, esp. 290–4 and 304–11; M. Penman, '*Diffinicione successionis ad regnum Scottorum*: Royal Succession in Scotland in the Later Middle Ages', in F. Lachaud and M. Penman, ed., *Making and Breaking the Rules: Succession in Medieval Europe, c. 1000–c.1600/Établir et abolir les normes: la succession dans l'Europe médiévale, vers 1000–vers 1600* (Turnhout, 2008), 43–59.

[42] By which the lineal descendants of an heir who has died prior to succession assume his or her inheritance rights.

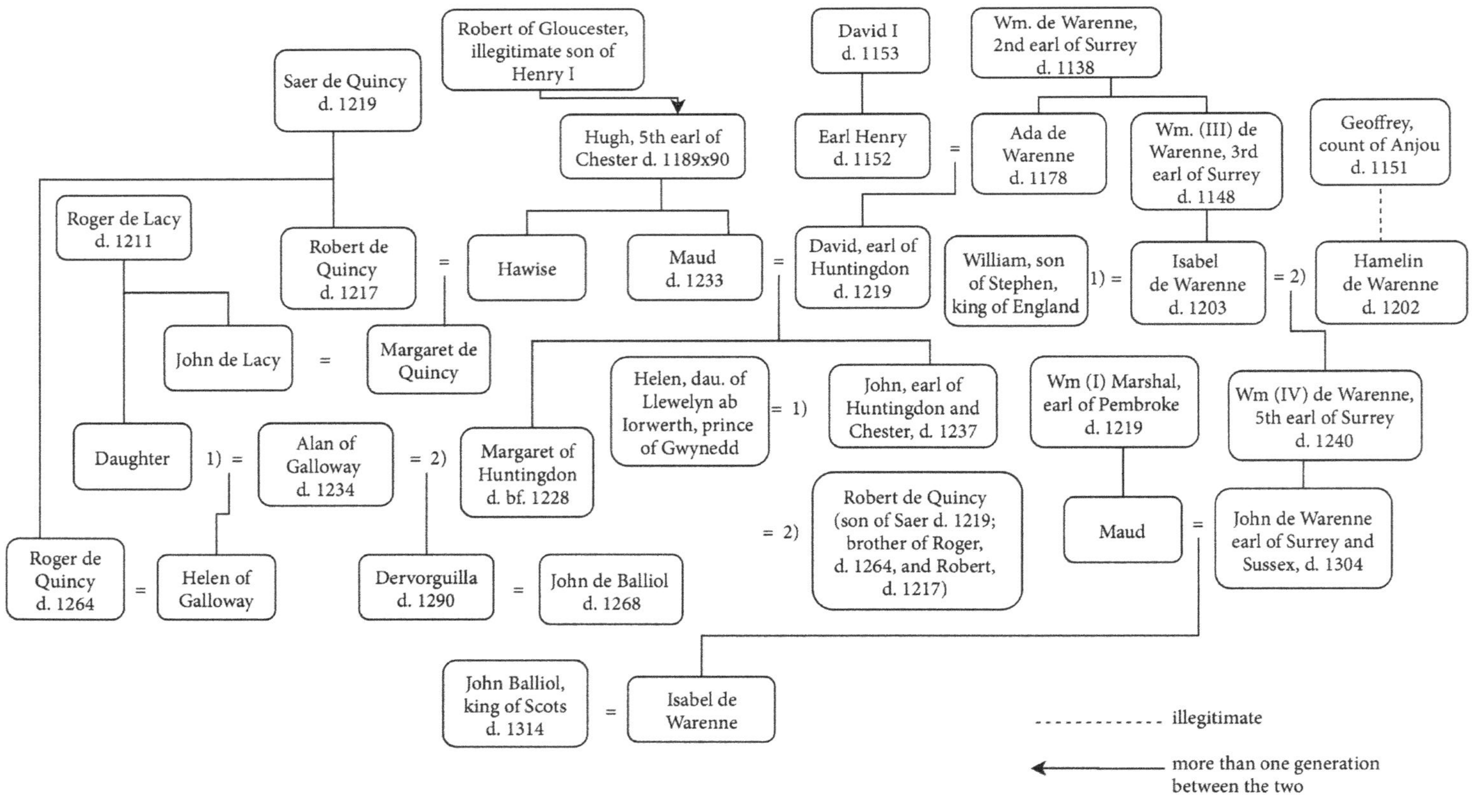

Table 6. Margaret of Huntingdon, Alan of Galloway and John Balliol

which made it clear that nearness of degree was preferred over seniority.[43] The 1284 legislation provided that any child, male or female, Alexander may have in future would succeed ahead of his eldest daughter Margaret or her line.[44] The decision in favour of Balliol also ignored legal advice that, in the absence of any fixed law or custom governing succession in Scotland, Roman Imperial law, favouring nearness of degree, should be adopted.[45]

Robert I (r. 1306–29)

The seizure of the throne by Robert the Bruce in 1306 fulfilled his grandfather's ambitions for his lineage. Robert I had married (ca. 1290) Isabel, daughter of Domnall, earl of Mar, by whom he had a daughter, Marjorie (d. 1317). His second wife, Elizabeth de Burgh, whom he married in 1302, was in English captivity between 1306 and 1314, and their only surviving legitimate son, the future David II, did not make an appearance until 1324. In 1315, the Scottish Parliament at Ayr recognised Robert's brother Edward Bruce, then aged around thirty-five, as heir, in preference to Marjorie; in the event of Edward's death without legitimate issue – he was already the father of at least one illegitimate son, Alexander Bruce – Marjorie and her line would inherit the throne, but only if she married according to the wishes of her father or, in the event of his death before her betrothal, to someone approved by the Scottish nobility.[46] This instrument prioritised a collateral over an heir of line, simultaneously acknowledging Marjorie's right (she is given as Robert's 'apparent heir') while denying it by subordinating it to an assumed right of Edward. The king's brother's right may have been dubious, but political considerations overruled all others. The fact that relegating Marjorie's place in the succession required a legal instrument shows that primogeniture could not be ignored, but that such a mechanism was deployed shows also that Robert (who was himself not king according to primogeniture) was unwilling to be bound by primogeniture to accept heirs he did not want, or who may be unacceptable to Scottish political society. Marjory's acceptability as an heir, already doubtful because of her sex (and all the more so because the country was at war with England), was further eroded by the fact that her father was regarded by some as a usurper, and by the existence of an alternative line: the deposed John Balliol had died the year before but his son, Edward, was alive and in his thirties. In that context a tailzie insisting on the throne passing to a militarily experienced brother, whom failing to a daughter only if married to someone with the right credentials to defend the Bruce inheritance, may have had as much to do with

43 Duncan, *Kingship*, 168–70.

44 *APS*, i, 422b, 424; *Foedera*, i, II, 638; Penman, '*Diffinicione successionis*', 44.

45 Penman, '*Diffinicione successionis*', 44, 49; Stones and Simpson, *Throne of Scotland*, ii, App. E.

46 *RPS*, 1315/1; 1318/30.

insecurity of the throne as it did with reluctance to have a female ruler. The general bias against queens regnant was compounded by a perceived need for a king experienced in warfare, given the state of Anglo-Scottish relations. The last time a king with living, legitimate offspring was succeeded by a brother was when Domnall III Bán replaced Mael Coluim III in 1093. There were indications in 1195, when William the Lion believed himself to be mortally ill, that a brother might be preferred to a female heir, but the matter had not been put to the test.[47]

Not long after the 1315 parliament Marjorie was given in marriage to Walter the Steward (d. 1327); their son, Robert, was born in 1316. In October 1318 Edward Bruce was killed. A tailzie of December 1318, by which time Marjorie was also dead, named young Robert heir to the throne in the event that Robert I should die without heirs of his body.[48] The political community had sworn, using 'bodily oaths', to observe the 1315 tailzie, on pain of 'all manner of ecclesiastical censures'; the tailzie of 1318 was also accompanied by lords and prelates swearing an oath of loyalty and of obedience to the tailzie, and by their sealing the document while touching the bible and saints' relics; while anyone who violated the 1318 ordinance was to be considered a traitor and guilty of lèse-majesté.[49] Robert's seizure of the throne in 1306 was regarded by some as unlawful, and the nominations of his brother and grandson as heirs to the throne were therefore not uncontroversial. The birth of David in 1324 (and probably the death in infancy of his twin brother) prompted a further tailzie in 1326, by which David was formally recognised as heir to Robert I ahead of the king's grandson, Robert Stewart. On the one hand, the tailzies were evidence that the succession was open to dispute, or at least not a foregone conclusion; on the other, the 1318 and 1326 instruments can be seen as simply formalising the largely uncontroversial propositions that a king's legitimate surviving heir of line should inherit the throne (1318), and that a king's legitimate son should succeed him in preference to all others (1326). The consequences of the Great Cause – a failed Scottish kingship, war with England, and internal strife – were so serious that agreeing the succession in advance was deemed essential, to prevent a similar occurrence in future.

Robert I's illegitimate children did not figure in plans for the succession. One of them was, as Robert of London had been, a leading figure in the realm. Robert Bruce of Liddesdale (d. 1332) was the king's eldest known child.[50] He was given the family name of Robert Bruce, was knighted in 1314 (just before

47 See pp. 72–6.
48 *RPS*, 1318/30.
49 Tanner argues that the production of these documents involved strong-arm tactics. R. J. Tanner, 'Cowing the Community? Coercion and Falsification in Robert Bruce's Parliaments, 1309–1318', in K. M. Brown and R. J. Tanner, ed., *Parliament and Politics in Scotland, 1235–1560* (Edinburgh, 2004), 64–73.
50 See also pp. 202–3.

Bannockburn) by his father the king, bore royal arms, and was granted very considerable estates and other privileges. He would certainly have made a prestigious match, but, unusually for a person of his rank, remained single and is not known to have had any children. At the time Liddesdale was of an age to marry (men could marry at fourteen), Robert I had no legitimate sons, and three of his four brothers had perished in service of his campaigns.[51] Robert's only surviving brother was still alive when Liddesdale was in his mid-teens to mid-twenties, but in addition to being highly active militarily (and so vulnerable to an early death), Edward had no legitimate sons of his own. Between 1318 and the death of Robert I in 1329, the recognised heirs to the kingdom, Robert the Steward and David Bruce (and, briefly, David's twin brother), were minors.

A royal letter of legitimation was issued in the reign of Robert I to an unknown recipient.[52] Its date is also unknown, since it survives only in a fifteenth-century copy. Duncan remarks that the recipient 'would surely be of prominence'.[53] It has been suggested that the letter was intended for Robert of Liddesdale, on the basis that the generous privileges enshrined in it were intended as compensation for his remaining single and childless, thereby not founding a lineage which might threaten that of his father.[54] If so, this would imply that illegitimate birth was still not seen as a definitive bar to royal succession, even in the first part of the fourteenth century. However, there is good reason to doubt that the brieve could have been intended for Liddesdale. Before turning to this, it is worth considering an aspect of the document which may have encouraged the belief it was produced for Robert I's illegitimate son. The letter grants the recipient the right to appoint an heir or heirs of his own choosing.[55] Illegitimate people could not have heirs other than those of their body legitimately procreated and so could not ordinarily dispone their property to collaterals or others, so granting an unmarried bastard this concession was a valuable privilege. It implies the granter believed that the

51 Neil was captured at Kildrummy in 1306, and on the orders of Edward I was drawn, hanged and beheaded at Berwick; Alexander and Thomas, taken prisoner at Galloway in the winter of 1306/7 and removed to Carlisle, were similarly executed by command of the English king, their heads displayed on one of the town gates (Alexander) and the castle keep (Thomas). *Gesta Annalia II* in Skene, *Fordun*, i, 342; *Flores Historiarum*, ed. H. R. Luard (London, 1890), iii, 135; *Scalacronica. The Reigns of Edward I, Edward II and Edward III as Recorded by Sir Thomas Gray*, transl. H. Maxwell (Glasgow, 1907), 34; *Chron. Lanercost*, 205–6; G. W. S. Barrow, *Robert Bruce and the Community of the Realm of Scotland* (Edinburgh, 1988), 161, 169, 170–1, 318–19, 361 n.25.

52 *Scottish Formularies*, ed. A. A. M. Duncan, Stair Society 58 (Edinburgh, 2011), 41–2, 78–9 (E56). The unknown recipient is given in the fifteenth-century copy of the brieve as 'P de E'.

53 Duncan, *Scottish Formularies*, 79.

54 I am grateful to the publisher's anonymous reader for suggesting this interpretation and identification.

55 Duncan, *Scottish Formularies*, 78–9.

illegitimate concerned would never marry, and so it is tempting to see it as a 'deal' between the king and the recipient to this effect.

If the letter had stopped there, we might accept that it could have been addressed to Liddesdale, but it goes much further. Announcing that the king wishes to show special grace to the recipient in the matter of his defect of birth, and to 'adorn him with the title of legitimacy'; he issues a dispensation and legitimation, making good this person's status.[56] If Liddesdale was the recipient, it would have complicated the succession, rather than the reverse, since it might be used to argue for his being formally legitimated by royal decree and so, as firstborn son of the king, having a better right to the throne than the existing heir presumptive.

A precedent for a ruler legitimating his own son had been set in the thirteenth century by Emperor Frederick II (1194–1250), who legitimated by rescript his son Enzo, conferring on him the right to inherit the throne.[57] If it was Robert I's intention to make Liddesdale his successor, we would expect the document to mention this, and Robert to have been given a place in the succession, probably with the creation of another tailzie. We might also expect to see this mentioned in other sources: a king legitimating his own bastard would surely have been the subject of widespread comment, in part because of its novelty (in Britain, at least), but mainly because of its wider implications. The creation of a rival heir to Edward Bruce and Robert the Steward and the king's son David (all of them born legitimate) could only have been disastrously divisive. In this, little had changed since the days of William the Lion and his son, Robert of London.

In the event of the failure of those heirs named in the tailzies of 1315 and 1318, a legitimated Liddesdale might still face opposition from the sons of Robert I's sisters.[58] Domnall, eighth earl of Mar (d. 1332) may have had some right, as nephew to Robert I twice over.[59] The recipient of the letter may have been prominent, as Duncan claims, but even this is not certain. Robert II issued a similar letter, but with even more generous terms, to a burgess of Dundee, Patrick of Inverpeffer, in 1375.[60] Patrick appears to have been important to Robert II (unless the letter was simply purchased) but seems not to have been especially prominent otherwise. The letter of Robert I surely cannot have been intended for a royal bastard. Illegitimates belonging to other estates could receive a legitimation without it having political ramifications

56 '... *super defectu natalium quem petitur graciam facere specialem ac ipsum legitimacionis titulo decorare cum ipso graciose de nostre regie potestatis plenitudine dispensamus ac ipsum habilitamus et legitimamus* ...'. Duncan, *Scottish Formularies*, 79.

57 McDougall, *Royal Bastards*, 233–5.

58 M. Penman, *Robert the Bruce: King of the Scots* (New Haven, CT, 2014), 161.

59 He was the son of Robert I's sister and of Gartnait, earl of Mar, who was the brother of Robert's first wife. F. Watson, 'Donald, Eighth Earl of Mar (1293–1332), Magnate', *ODNB*, 3 February 2018.

60 *RMS*, i, no. 629.

at the highest level, but this was not the case for the sons of kings. As far as we know, Liddesdale died unmarried and childless. Taken together with the similar experience of Robert of London, this gives the appearance of a deliberate policy of eldest bastard sons ensuring that they did not establish lineages that might later attempt to claim the throne. Had Alexander II or III, or John Balliol, had illegitimate sons, it might be possible to suggest whether or not such a policy existed, but attempting to draw this conclusion from what we know of these two men, especially Liddesdale, about whom only scant information survives, presents insurmountable difficulties.

Edward Bruce, heir presumptive from 1315 until his death in 1318, had a bastard son, Alexander, who died at Halidon Hill in 1333. Bower relates that when a man claiming to be Alexander Bruce turned up in Scotland in 1344, David II ordered him to be captured and tried as an imposter, and Robert the Steward attended his execution.[61] Bower says that many believed the pretender was the real Alexander Bruce and he had been executed after an improperly conducted trial, to protect the interests of those who had taken over Alexander's lands after his death.[62] This story has given rise to a theory that the real source of Robert's interest in this matter was a fear that the man presenting himself as Alexander might make a claim to the throne, based on the legislation of 1315 which gave the sons of Edward a place in the succession ahead of Robert.[63] The 1315 tailzie states that if Edward Bruce became king, the throne was to descend to Edward's 'heirs male legitimately begotten of his body', apparently ruling out Alexander, so the theory relies on the argument that Alexander was legitimated. While this cannot be disproved conclusively, neither is there any positive evidence for it. Further, the 1315 tailzie had, by the time of the impostor's appearance in 1344, been superseded by the legal instruments of 1318 and 1326. The 1326 tailzie is lost but the 1318 act made no mention of Alexander, and allowed for succession by 'the nearest male from a collateral line' should the king die without an heir of line. This did not rule out Alexander if legitimated, but he would have been in competition with men belonging to other collateral lines. These lines all descended from sisters of Robert I but this should not have disqualified them: the principle that women could transmit heirship was established, and had permitted Robert I's own kingship. Donald, eighth earl of Mar, was dead by 1344 but his son

61 *Chron. Bower*, vii, 159.

62 Initial grants of land were made to Alexander and his mother, but later grants were made to him in his own name. *RMS*, i, App. 2, nos 319, 320, 441 (repeated at 460), 622, 623, 624. In 1329, on his cousin David II's succession, Alexander was given the earldom of Carrick previously held by the heir to the throne.

63 M. Penman, *David II, 1329–71* (Edinburgh, 2004), 40–1, 114; Penman, '*Diffinicione successionis*', 54. Similarly, Sir Roger de Clarendon, illegitimate son of Edward the Black Prince, eldest son of Edward III, was hanged for treason in 1402. It was later thought that he was executed because he was seeking to claim the throne, though no contemporary sources suggest this. Given-Wilson and Curteis, *Royal Bastards*, 134–6.

Thomas was around fourteen years old; William, fifth earl of Ross (d. 1372), another nephew of Robert I, was both an adult and a prominent magnate. On balance, the evidence for a returning Alexander posing a meaningful threat to the dynastic ambitions of Robert Stewart is very slight. It is more likely that Stewart attended the execution simply because it was a major political and judicial event (important enough to be recorded by chroniclers) and also, perhaps, to see for himself whether the man being hanged was indeed his great-uncle's son. Alexander Bruce and Robert would surely have known each other, as they had been contemporaries and members of a family in which the rituals, benefits and obligations of kinship were extended to all its members, illegitimate or not.

Robert II (r. 1371–90)

That papal legitimation changed someone's status definitively was relied upon much later by Robert II. When he ascended the throne on 27 March 1371, he was fifty-five years old and had a number of legitimate and illegitimate children. The legitimation some twenty-four years earlier of several of his children with Elizabeth Mure (d. in/bf. 1355) was a politically motivated and hugely significant event for the future king.

Robert and Elizabeth began having children in the 1330s.[64] At that time Robert was lieutenant of Scotland and heir presumptive to his uncle David II, who had gone to France as a boy of ten in 1334. By the time David returned to Scotland to begin his personal rule in 1341, the twenty-five-year-old Robert already had three sons with Elizabeth as well as daughters, and would have a fourth son within the next few years. Despite this, Robert and Elizabeth remained unmarried in the eyes of the Church until at least 1347, and probably 1349.[65] Barrow points out that observance of traditional, non-canonical marriage customs in late medieval Scotland was 'one of the permanent legacies of the lost Gàidhealtachd' and that this 'surely' accounted for Robert and Elizabeth's long cohabitation, which he regards as an irregular marriage, prior to their formal matrimony.[66] Robert, he argues, was a west Highland magnate with lands in Cowal and Bute, and Elizabeth was descended from Gilla Críst Mór, 'one of the few substantial landowners in Cunningham by the mid-thirteenth century to belong to a native Gaelic-speaking family'.[67] The

64 In 1350 their daughter, Margaret, was old enough to marry. Theiner, *Vet. Mon.*, no. 588.

65 The couple received a papal dispensation to marry, issued in 1347 (see p. 102); *Gesta Annalia II* in Skene, *Fordun*, i, 317, our only source for the marriage, says it occurred in 1349.

66 G. W. S. Barrow, 'The Lost Gàidhealtachd of Medieval Scotland', in W. Gillies, ed., *Gaelic and Scotland: Alba agus a Gàidhlig* (Edinburgh, 1989), 72–3.

67 Barrow, 'Lost Gàidhealtachd', 73.

implication is that both parties, steeped in Gaelic culture, naturally abided by those traditional marriage practices that were not recognised by the Church.

But Robert was much more than an ordinary magnate, Gaelic or otherwise. The legislation of Robert I between 1315 and 1326 gave the younger Robert a prominent place in the succession. The status of his children was clearly significant: should David II, away in France during much of the 1330s, die before procreating heirs of his own or changing the tailzie, Robert would be king. It is unlikely that the Steward would have entered into the kind of secular, Gaelic marriage ceremony assumed by Barrow, knowing that such a ceremony did not conform to Church rules and rendered any children of the union illegitimate. Boardman suggests that, 'The confused situation in the mid-1330s, with David II in exile and the young Robert left as the senior representative of the Bruce–Stewart dynasty in Scotland, may well have encouraged a rapid marriage for the young heir to the throne and might have made the lengthy process of applying for a dispensation unattractive at that stage.'[68]

It cannot be assumed that the Steward's relationship with Elizabeth was always intended to be a marriage. The simplest, and likeliest, explanation for the delay in obtaining a marriage dispensation is that Robert did not initially plan to marry Elizabeth, and he decided only later to change the status of what had become a long-standing and presumably successful relationship. Our only contemporary account of Robert and Elizabeth's marriage contains no hint that traditional marriage practices or confused political situations accounted for their delaying a formal marriage, but rather implies that Robert simply embarked on a sexual relationship with someone he decided later to marry:

> This Robert had a sexual relationship with one of the daughters of Adam More, knight, and with her procreated sons and daughters out of wedlock. Later, having sought and obtained a dispensation from the Holy See, he married her lawfully, according to the forms of the Church; this was in the year 1349.[69]

It is surprising that someone of Robert's status should marry the daughter of a knight rather than someone of a higher social standing. As heir presumptive he was a prestigious catch. Elizabeth Mure was from a noble family, as were at least two of Robert's mistresses: Mariota Cardney was the mother of at least three of Robert's sons; and one of the reasons he needed a dispensation to marry Elizabeth was that he had earlier had an affair with her kinswoman, Isabella Boutellier.[70] But the social rank from which Robert took

68 S. I. Boardman, 'Robert II (1316–1390)', *ODNB*, 19 January 2018.

69 '*Ipse Robertus copulavit sibi de facto unam de filiabus Adæ More militis, de qua genuit filios et filias extra matrimonium; quam postea, impetrate dispensatione sedis apostolicæ et optenta, disponsavit canonice in forma ecclesiæ, anno scilicet Domini MCCCXLIX.*' *Gesta Annalia II* in Skene, *Fordun*, i, 317.

70 Theiner, *Vet. Mon.*, no. 577.

his mistresses, though respectable enough, is unlikely to have been the rank into which he intended to marry.[71]

It has been said that the battle at Neville's Cross in October 1346, in which David II was badly injured and captured, concentrated the Steward's mind on the matter of succession and acted as a prompt for him to seek legitimation of his children with Elizabeth Mure.[72] A dispensation permitting the marriage and retrospectively legitimating the offspring of the relationship was issued in late 1347.[73] A papal mandate of 1345, though, suggests the possibility that Robert had turned his mind in that direction well before David II had been removed to England. In January that year, Clement VI issued a mandate declaring null a marriage between one Hugh Giffard and an Elizabeth More, who 'were married by their friends when Hugh was in his ninth and Elizabeth in her eleventh year'.[74] According to the petition cited in the papal letter, the 'marriage' – the couple did exchange vows of present consent, but were not of the legal age to marry – was never consummated and they expressly renounced it once they were of age.[75] In law, then, the marriage had never properly existed and it might seem somewhat over-cautious of anyone to go to the trouble and expense of obtaining papal confirmation of this. But, just as couples who contracted a marriage which was unlawful due to a legal impediment (such as age) could seek a dispensation making their union valid, a papal declaration that the two were conclusively not married might have been felt to offer the best reassurance against future doubt in the matter. Dowden argues that there was something more behind the move to have this particular marriage declared non-existent.[76] He contends that the bride was the same Elizabeth who later married the future Robert II, and papal acknowledgement of the invalidity of the marriage was sought to prevent the possibility of her earlier contract being used to undermine the validity of her marriage to Robert – if the youthful union was held to be valid, with Giffard still living, Elizabeth's marriage to Robert would have been bigamous and therefore null.

71 Penman suggests that in the 1330s and early 1340s Robert may have been hoping to marry Isabella, the daughter of Donnchad (IV), earl of Fife, a theory loaned weight by English chronicler Thomas Gray's claim that a plan to sell Isabella to Robert the Steward in marriage was frustrated when she married her guardian. M. A. Penman, 'The Scots at the Battle of Neville's Cross', *SHR* 80 (2001), 169–70; *Scalacronica*, transl. Maxwell, 126. Robert's hopes in this regard cannot be known with certainty, but Isabella, whose mother was a granddaughter of Edward I, was of a rank more in keeping with a bride for someone of royal status. Isabella's second marriage, 1360x61, was to Walter, Robert's second son with Elizabeth Mure.

72 S. Boardman, *The Early Stewart Kings. Robert II and Robert III 1371–1406* (East Linton, 1996), 8; Nicholson, *Later Middle Ages*, 147.

73 Theiner, *Vet. Mon.*, no. 577.

74 Theiner, *Vet. Mon.*, no. 565; *CPL*, iii, 187.

75 Theiner, *Vet. Mon.*, no. 565.

76 Dowden, *The Medieval Church*, 264–5.

The papal mandate is dated 20 May 1345, some seventeen months before Neville's Cross, suggesting that succession issues may have been on Robert's mind even before David II, with whom Robert had an uneasy relationship, was taken captive by the English. This cannot be known with certainty, since it is also at least possible that the annulment was instigated by Hugh Giffard's family, the socially and politically prominent Giffards of Yester, or his prospective in-laws, the Douglases.[77] The date of Hugh Giffard's marriage to Joanna Douglas is not known, but is likely to have been in the mid-1340s.[78] Both families would have been concerned to ensure the marriage, and so the legitimacy of the resulting children, was not imperilled by a pre-contract between Hugh and Elizabeth.

If, instead, the annulment of 1345 was sought by Robert, then the initial impetus for him to regularise his relationship with Elizabeth could have sprung from the marriage of David II's sister Margaret Bruce (d. 1346x7) to William, fifth earl of Sutherland (d. 1370x1). They obtained a papal dispensation in December 1342, acknowledging that they were related in the fourth degree of consanguinity.[79] It is assumed that they married in the following year, though the date of their marriage is not known. Their only known child, John, was not born until early 1346, so it is possible that they did not in fact marry until 1345.[80] Between September and November 1345 the couple received from David II some thanages and a barony 'in free marriage', and the lands they held of the crown, and the earldom of Sutherland, were erected into a free regality.[81] At the time these grants were made, Margaret's pregnancy would have been known. A male Sutherland infant would be next in line to the throne after Robert, but since the boy would be a full nephew to the king and not, like Robert, a half-nephew, and since his parents were Bruce partisans rather than Stewart supporters, there was a real risk that David II might nominate him heir ahead of Robert. David's grants to William and Margaret in late 1345 were perhaps an intimation of his intentions towards their offspring: even if this child was a girl, there would almost certainly be others. Around the time of John's birth, David II gave his parents a grant of the stronghold of Dunottar, with permission to reinforce it.[82] Fifteenth-century chroniclers believed that David II was keen to name John as his heir even while John was in his infancy, and

77 The Giffards were also related to the royal dynasty in Scotland, though rather distantly by 1345: a papal judgement of 1250 describes Richard Giffard (d. 1176x82), ancestor of Hugh, as *consanguineus* of the Scottish king. Theiner, *Vet. Mon.*, no. 142.

78 Their eldest daughter, Joanna Giffard, married Sir Thomas Hay of Locherworth, who was born in 1340; Joanna (Douglas), lady of Yester, had at least one adult grandson (via a younger daughter) in 1400. J. W. Buchan, *A History of Peeblesshire* (Glasgow, 1925–7), ii, 296; *Yester Writs*, no. 43; *SP*, viii, 422.

79 Theiner, *Vet. Mon.*, no. 552 (1 December 1342).

80 He died in 1361, aged fourteen.

81 W. Fraser, ed., *The Sutherland Book* (Edinburgh, 1892), iii, 12–14.

82 Ibid., 15–16.

perhaps before.[83] If this is true it would explain why Robert may have started clearing the way for his children to be legitimated – by removing the possible obstacle of Elizabeth's pre-contract – around the time of Margaret's marriage to Sutherland.[84] As things stood, Robert's children were not candidates for heirship, and were therefore excluded from the succession. This may have been felt to weigh against him at a point when his position was already vulnerable.

If Robert had been behind the move to have the youthful Mure–Giffard union annulled in 1345, he appears to have done little in the short term to progress the matter of his own marriage. Neville's Cross may very well have provided Robert with a sharp reminder of his own mortality, and stirred him into deciding finally that the sons he had already with Elizabeth, rather than those that might come along in the future, once he had negotiated a marriage contract with someone else, would make perfectly acceptable heirs. Just as importantly, Neville's Cross ramped up the stakes for him to regularise the status of his relationship and his offspring. Robert's abandonment of David II on the field established definitively Robert's status as a rival for the kingship, and made an enemy of a king who had it in his power to establish an alternative heir presumptive – and who had already given indications that he was seeking to do so, in the person of his infant nephew John. By that time, it was beginning to look as though David might not produce an heir of his own body, without which the crown would fall to Robert unless an alternative heir of the king's own choice was accepted. David and his queen had been children in 1328 when they married; but in 1346 Joan was twenty-five years old and he was twenty-two, and they were still without issue.

Robert could hardly fail to realise that his own actions on the field of battle would result in David redoubling his efforts to nominate an alternative heir. Robert had little incentive to work towards the release of a king whose enmity he had earned, and a great deal of incentive to have his children legitimated before any such release had been effected by others. By marrying Elizabeth, Robert made himself a more attractive prospect for kingship: not only was he older and more experienced than David, physically present in, and guardian of, the country; now he had three or four male heirs as a marker, if not a

83 Ibid., 12–16; Boardman, *Early Stewart Kings*, 9. Bower claimed that John (whom he mistakenly calls earl) would have succeeded David under the terms of a tailzie, a claim copied in *Liber Pluscardensis*, while Boece suggested that David had Margaret's son formally recognised as his heir in 1357, again by virtue of a tailzie. *Chron. Bower*, vi, 377; *Liber Pluscardensis*, ed. F. J. H. Skene (London, 1877–80), i, 240; H. Boece, *The History and Chronicles of Scotland*, transl. J. Bellenden (Edinburgh, 1821), ii, 448. See also M. Penman, 'David II (1329–1371)', in M. Brown and R. Tanner, ed., *Scottish Kingship 1306–1542: Essays in Honour of Norman MacDougall* (Edinburgh, 2008), 56.

84 John was born in early 1346. The marriage of his parents was being actively considered from 1342 and took place sometime between December 1342 (the date of the dispensation) and summer 1345; the papal letter dissolving the union between Giffard and Mure is dated May 1345.

guarantee, of the stability of a royal line descended from him. These factors stood in stark contrast to the absent and childless David, who, within a year or so of Robert's marriage, was treating to make an English prince his heir presumptive, a proposal revisited in the early 1360s.[85] The decision to marry Elizabeth suggests a substantial degree of confidence that legitimation *per subsequens matrimonium* would be effective for royal succession. If he had entertained serious doubts that his sons with Elizabeth would be accepted as heirs, it would have made more sense for him to marry someone else instead, perhaps someone of higher rank, this time waiting until after the wedding to found a family.

Robert and Elizabeth were related by both consanguinity and affinity. Although dispensations from similar impediments were often granted, the high stakes involved in Robert's case encouraged him to ensure his supplication had prestigious sponsors. The use of David II's seal implied his support, while Philip VI of France loaned his name to the petition along with seven Scottish bishops – Williams Landel (St Andrews), Rae (Glasgow), and Deyn (Aberdeen), Richard Pilmuir (Dunkeld), Adam Murray (Brechin; himself illegitimate), Martin (Argyll) and Maurice (Dunblane).[86] The lining up of assorted 'big hitters' to back Robert's application indicates that he was highly concerned about the outcome, and determined the supplication should succeed. At the same time, he seems to have had a curiously cavalier attitude to fulfilling the terms of the dispensation. Pope Clement VI had stipulated that Robert found one or more chaplaincies, under the guidance of the bishop of Glasgow. But Robert did not meet his obligation in this regard until 1364, when the threat of an alternative heirship arrangement, by which a son of Edward III would replace Robert as heir presumptive, was proposed by David II.[87] Robert's tardiness in fulfilling the terms of the papal dispensation might suggest that he did not attach as much importance to the legitimation as is implied in his co-opting of seven Scottish bishops and the king of France to sponsor it. The same impression is gained by Robert and Elizabeth apparently not undergoing a marriage ceremony until 1349 (if the writer of *Gesta Annalia* is correct), despite the dispensation having been granted at the end of 1347.[88] The apparent time-lag between the dispensation and the marriage may also

[85] *CPP*, i, 203; *APS*, i, 492–5; Penman, *David II*, 153–5, 308–10; A. A. M. Duncan, 'A Question About the Succession', *Miscellany of the Scottish History Society* 12 (Edinburgh, 1994), 1–57, esp. 5–12.

[86] David II was at this time a hostage in England and his seal was used in his absence. The inclusion of Maurice of Dunblane indicates that the petition was sent to Rome some months, at least, before the date of the dispensation itself: Maurice died no later than the summer of 1347 and the dispensation is dated November of that year. J. Dowden, *The Bishops of Scotland* (Glasgow, 1912), 203. The illegitimate bishop of Brechin, Adam Murray (d. 1349), is discussed at pp. 160 and 164–5; Richard Pilmuir at p. 158.

[87] Boardman, *Early Stewart Kings*, 20.

[88] *Gesta Annalia II* in Skene, *Fordun*, i, 317.

lend weight to the hypothesis that Robert's impulse to marry Elizabeth was stimulated by intimations of mortality he experienced at Neville's Cross: 1349 was the year in which the Black Death came to Scotland.[89]

Following David's unexpected death in 1371, Robert succeeded; a royal declaration formally recognising his eldest son John, the first of Elizabeth Mure's sons and born before her marriage to Robert, as heir to the throne of Scotland was issued shortly after his coronation that year.[90] It was followed in 1373 by an Act of Parliament which tailzied the crown on John and his male heirs, whom failing on Robert II's other sons (and their male heirs) in order of seniority.[91] This tailzie, wherein the sons of Euphemia, David and Walter, were ranked below the three surviving sons of Robert and Elizabeth, set out that only if the lines of all three of their elder half-brothers failed would David and Walter be eligible for the throne. The legal instrument determining the succession followed on from those deployed by Robert I in 1315, 1318 and 1326; David II had also intended to use tailzies to make members of the English royal family his heirs, and may also have planned to do so in respect of his nephew John Sutherland.[92] Nothing could be guaranteed, however. Alexander III's tailzie of 1284 had been made long before the consequences of the Great Cause sharpened the need to lay down the succession in advance, and was made in anticipation of the very situation that eventuated: the death of the king without an heir whose right was so evident it could be said to precede rival claims. Its lack of a contingency heir in the event of the infant Maid of Norway's death rendered it redundant after 1290.[93]

Tailzies were a means of formalising an older tradition of kings designating their heirs. Mael Coluim III was said to have appointed his son Edward as his heir; whether this would have dissuaded Domnall III Bán or Donnchad II from pressing rival claims had Edward survived is open to speculation.[94] David I seems to have been designated by Alexander I as his successor.[95] David I unambiguously nominated his son Henry, who was styled *rex designatus*.[96] Despite David having no other son and no surviving brothers, it was apparently

89 K. Jillings, *Scotland's Black Death: the Foul Death of the English* (Stroud, 2003), 1, 59.

90 *RPS*, A1371/4.

91 *RPS*, 1373/3.

92 S. I. Boardman, 'Robert III', *ODNB*, 13 March 2019. See above, n.83, for Bower's belief that David made his nephew John Sutherland his heir by means of a tailzie.

93 Penman points out that designating as heir to the throne the Maid of Norway, the daughter of a daughter, created a problem in respect of designating an alternative, since it made it difficult to justify excluding the next nearest heir, Dervorguilla Balliol, also the daughter of a daughter. Penman, '*Diffinicione successionis*', 48.

94 Arnold, *Symeonis Monachi Opera Omnia*, ii, 222. Duncan points out that this is the only source for the claim. Duncan, *Kingship*, 54. Ross argues for its plausibility, since the sons of Margaret would have been seen as having 'a claim to the kingship of the Anglo-Saxons' which the sons of Ingibjǫrg did not. Ross, *Kings of Alba*, 160.

95 Chibnall, *Orderic Vitalis*, 275; *Chron. Picts-Scots*, 190.

96 Barrow, *Charters of David I*, nos 126, 129.

not a given that Henry would succeed his father without such measures being in place. After Henry's unexpected death, David designated Henry's son Mael Coluim as his successor instead, a rather harder sell, and perhaps effective only because the designation was so vigorously defended.[97] William the Lion sought, with only partial success, to designate his daughter Margaret as his heir. He had less difficulty in doing the same with his son but, despite the absence of obvious alternatives, Alexander's right seemingly was not absolute, and required the consent of the political community. Alexander II may have designated his cousin, Robert (V) de Bruce, his heir in 1238, before the future Alexander III was born.[98] When Alexander III's pregnant wife travelled to England in 1260, he and his magnates (and the English king) designated his unborn child heir to the throne; so much is implicit in the agreement that the baby would be taken to Scotland shortly after being born, whether or not its mother, or father, or both, had died in the meantime.[99] Later, Alexander used a tailzie to designate as his successor any child he might have with his second wife Yolande of Dreux (d. in/aft. 1324), before his granddaughter or any posthumous child of his son Alexander.

English kings, too, designated their heirs (or attempted to do so), and from the late thirteenth and fourteenth centuries similarly came to deploy written forms of these.[100] William the Bastard designated his second son, William, his successor to the throne of England.[101] In 1290, Edward I designated his last surviving son, Edward of Caernarvon (later Edward II), his heir, followed by any other sons the king might have in future, whom failing the king's daughters, and any subsequent daughters, in order of seniority.[102] This effectively relegated the king's brother Edmund (d. 1296) to the bottom of the heap in succession terms. Edward III drew up an entail in 1376–7 making his grandson Richard (later Richard II), the eldest surviving son of his eldest son, his heir; if Richard should die without a male heir, the crown passed to

97 For apparent hostility to Mael Coluim IV's accession, see pp. 68–9.

98 Stones and Simpson, *Throne of Scotland*, ii, 145, 170, 185–6, 318–19. There is plenty of room for scepticism about Bruce's claim. Duncan, *Kingship*, 123–6. Penman argues that it should not be dismissed, given the political context and lack of alternative heirs in 1238, drawing parallels with 1318. Penman, '*Diffinicione successionis*', 46–7. Oram suggests the designation may have been tacit rather than explicit. R. Oram, 'Overview of the Reign of Alexander', in Oram, *Reign of Alexander II*, 16. The claim is referred to indirectly in the 'Appeal of the seven earls of Scotland': *PoMS*, www.poms.ac.uk/record/source/7324/.

99 *CDS*, i, no. 2229. The baby was Margaret, later mother of the Maid of Norway.

100 C. Given-Wilson, 'Legitimation, Designation and Succession to the Throne in Fourteenth-century England', in A. Alfonso and others, ed., *Building Legitimacy: Political Discourses and Forms of Legitimacy in Medieval Societies* (Leiden, 2003), 89–105.

101 William of Malmesbury, *Gesta Regum*, 543.

102 *Foedera*, i, II, 742; Given-Wilson, 'Legitimation', 99–100.

Edward III's sons in order of seniority, but all daughters were excluded.[103] These were, however, largely private documents, not subject to ratification or approval by magnates. The English Parliament recognised Henry IV's son Henry as his heir in 1399 and again in 1404, but the first use of a parliamentary statute to regulate the succession in England was by Henry IV in 1406.[104] Given-Wilson argues that parliament's role – in this instance, at least – was to provide 'public confirmation of a private deed of conveyance which was already a *fait accompli*'.[105]

In September 1396 a papal marriage dispensation for John of Gaunt and Katherine Swynford had declared their children legitimate.[106] The dispensation was sought to make good the invalid marriage they had contracted earlier that year, when the eldest of their four children, who were given the name Beaufort, was in his mid-twenties. It required an Act of Parliament in February 1397 to make John and his siblings capable of heirship, since England had rejected over 150 years earlier the canon law doctrine that legitimation by subsequent marriage was effective for inheritance.[107] Neither of these legitimations were understood at the time to have established a place for the Beauforts in the royal succession. The four are not mentioned in the parliamentary proceedings of 1399 and 1404, nor are they included in either of the statutes of 1406 which set out intentions for the succession. But evidently Henry IV recognised the potential for John, Henry, Thomas and Joan, or their descendants, to be considered heirs to the throne on the basis of their legitimation. In 1407 he reiterated the secular legitimation of 1397 but had the record of it altered by the interpolation of a statement expressly excluding them from the royal succession.[108] None attained the throne themselves, but the Tudor king Henry VII (1457–1509) was descended from John Beaufort (d. 1410), marquess of Dorset and Somerset, eldest legitimated son of John of Gaunt and Katherine Swynford. So too were the queens of James I (Joan Beaufort) and James IV (Margaret Tudor).[109] James IV was descended from two legitimated bastards: his great-great-grandfathers Robert III and John Beaufort.[110]

[103] M. Bennett, 'Edward III's Entail and the Succession to the Crown, 1376–1471', *English Historical Review* 113 (1998), 580–609.

[104] *Rotuli Parliamentorum*, ed. Strachey, iii, 525 (1404), 574–6 (June 1406), 580–3 (December 1406).

[105] Given-Wilson, 'Legitimation', 104.

[106] *CPL*, iv, 545.

[107] *Calendar of Patent Rolls, Richard II*, vi, 86 (9 February 1397); *Rot. Parl.*, iii, 343.

[108] *Calendar of Patent Rolls, Henry IV*, iii, 284; *Excerpta Historica*, ed. S. Bentley (London, 1831), 152–4; C. Given-Wilson, *Henry IV* (London, 2016), 306.

[109] James V thereby had a 'double helping' of legitimated Beaufort blood since he was descended from the marquess twice over, through his mother (Margaret Tudor), and his great-great-grandmother (Joan Beaufort).

[110] Table 7.

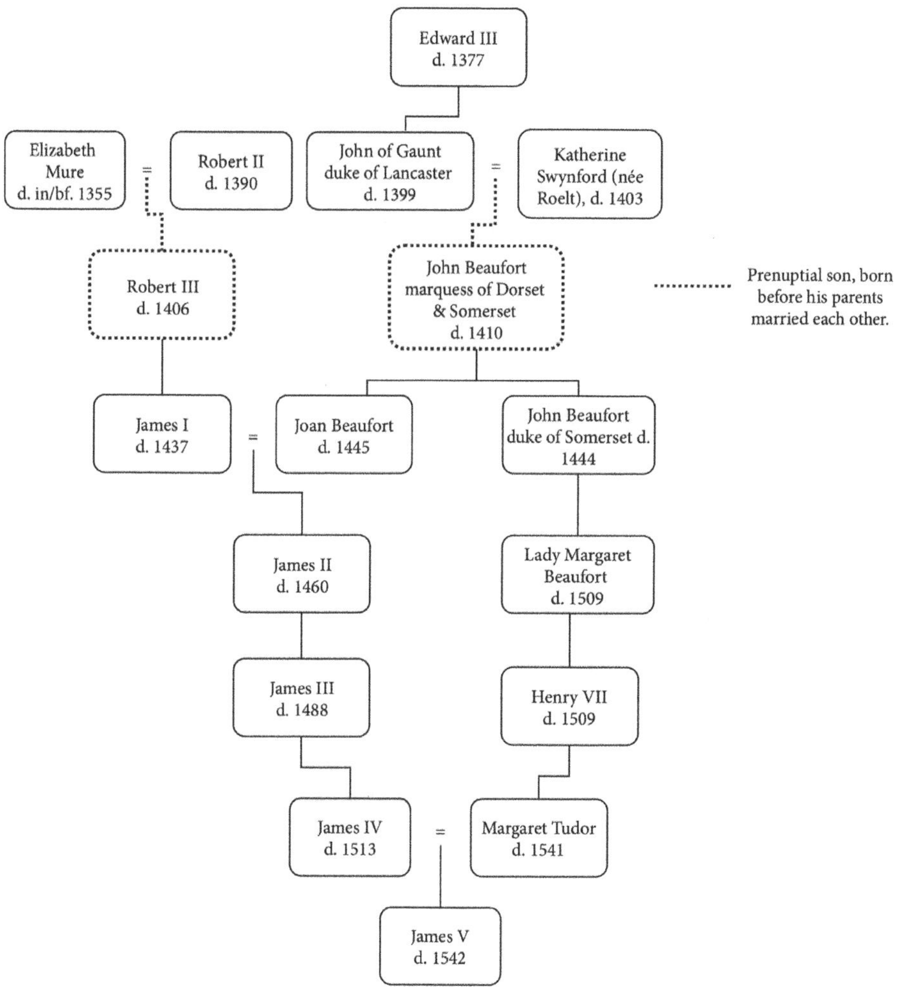

Table 7. Beauforts and Stewarts (simplified)

During Robert II's reign, while the kingdom was tailzied on the legitimated John of Carrick and his brothers, an unlegitimated bastard was reigning in Portugal. João I (d. 1453), illegitimate son of King Pedro I of Portugal (r. 1357–67), and half-brother of Pedro's successor, Fernando (d. 1383), became king of Portugal in 1385, in preference to Beatriz, the daughter and only heir of Fernando.[111] Beatriz was married to João I of Castile, a union agreed as part of a peace treaty following several years of war between the two countries. The prospect of Beatriz's accession in 1383 raised fears of Castilian dominance, leading to an interregnum as the Portugese resisted Castilian efforts to claim the throne in the name of Beatriz. In Froissart's account of this, Fernando had made the leading men of the kingdom swear to accept Beatriz as heir to the throne when she was five years old, but the Portugese were reluctant to accept her because she was born of a union they believed was adultery, not a valid marriage, and because they did not want to be ruled by a woman.[112] Froissart has a Portugese ambassador, supposedly addressing the soon-to-be-crowned João of Portugal, state the nub of the case: 'we want to make you our king, although you are a bastard. We say the lady Beatriz, your niece, and Queen of Castile, is more of a bastard than you ...'.[113] Froissart's version of events portrays a hierarchy of illegitimacy which spoke to the popular imagination as regards acceptable rulership.

Robert III (r. 1390–1406) and James I (r. 1406–37)

An implied hierarchy of legitimacy is discernible in some historiography concerning the assassination in 1437 of Robert II's grandson, James I. That Robert II's sons with Euphemia Ross, David and Walter, may have been seen – and seen themselves – as having a stronger right to the throne than their half-brother Robert III, on the grounds that they were legitimately born and Robert was not, has been linked to theories about James I's murder. James succeeded in 1406 as the third, but eldest surviving, son of Robert III.[114] Robert's half-brother Walter, earl of Atholl, was executed as a conspirator in the murder of James. Some historians, including Balfour-Melville in 1936, Nicholson in

[111] For a summary of the circumstances of his accession, see H. V. Livermore, *A New History of Portugal* (Cambridge, 1976), 100–2. Aviz married Philippa of Lancaster (d. 1415), (legitimate) daughter of John of Gaunt (and sister of Henry IV), with whom he had several children. His three illegitimate children included Beatrice, who married Thomas Fitzalan, fifth earl of Arundel (d. 1405), and later John Holland, duke of Exeter (d. 1447). Holland's father was half-brother to Richard II.

[112] *Oeuvre de Froissart*, ed. K. de Lettenhove (Brussels, 1867–77), xi, 275–8.

[113] '... *nous vous voulons faire roy de ce pays, jà soiés-vous bastart; mais nous disons que madame Biétrix, vostre cousine* [*nièce*], *la royne de Castille, est plus née en bastardie que vous ne estes* ...'. Ibid., xi, 278.

[114] Euphemia's eldest son, David, died before March 1389. The assassination of James I took place at the Dominican friary at Perth, on the night of 20–21 February 1437.

1974, and Grant in 2015, have argued that the murder of James was linked to his father's status as a legitimated bastard.[115] Balfour-Melville said that the inheritance rights of the children of Elizabeth Mure remained questionable after the papal dispensation, hence the need for the 1373 tailzie, and that Walter's involvement in the murder was directly related to his 'hereditary right to possess the throne usurped by the elder line'.[116] Grant elaborates on this, agreeing with Balfour-Melville that David and Walter had a stronger claim to the throne because they were born in marriage rather than born of fornication and subsequently legitimated. He suggests they were displaced from their rightful position in the line of succession because their father, Robert II, came under intense pressure to nominate John of Carrick (later Robert III) as his heir ahead of them.

Following David II's unexpected death in 1371, there was an armed demonstration in protest against the yet-to-be-crowned Robert II, led by William, earl of Douglas.[117] The reasons for it are obscure but it was serious enough to force Robert to make concessions to him. Grant argues that John of Carrick may have been commonly regarded as the most likely heir to David II after the death of David's nephew John Sutherland in 1361; that is, more likely than Robert II, who was older than David and might have been expected to die sooner than the king.[118] The challenge to Robert II's accession may have been prompted by supporters of John, resulting in a deal being struck between Robert and John to make the latter his heir at the expense of his sons with Euphemia, who (according to Grant) were the rightful heirs according to *Regiam Majestatem*, which expressly rejected legitimation *per subsequens matrimonium* and held that those born prior to their parents' intermarriage could not succeed to heritage.[119] In law, John 'could never become king', and the conspirators behind the assassination of James believed that if they

115 E. W. M. Balfour-Melville, *James I, King of Scots 1406–1437* (London, 1936), 4–5, 247; R. Nicholson, *Scotland: the Later Middle Ages* (Edinburgh, 1974), 185–6, 322–4; Grant, 'Royal and Magnate Bastards', 323–4. George Burnett held this view in the nineteenth century. *ER*, iv, clxii. Brown does not mention legitimacy issues in connection with the assassination: he attributes Atholl's role in it to political rivalries of the 1430s between him, the queen, and the earls of Angus and Douglas, which contrived to alienate Atholl and present a clear threat to his interests. M. Brown, *James I* (Edinburgh, 1994), 177–81. Elsewhere he points to James's 'aggressive royal lordship' which 'dangerously upset Scotland's political balance' as wider motivating factors. Brown, '"Vile times": Walter Bower's Last Book and the Minority of James II', *SHR* 79 (2000), 185. See also M. Brown, '"I have thus slain a tyrant": *The Dethe of the Kynge of Scotis* and the Right to Resist in Early Fifteenth-century Scotland', *IR* 47 (1996), 24–44.

116 Balfour-Melville, *James I*, 4.

117 Boardman, *Early Stewart Kings*, 39–49.

118 Grant, 'Royal and Magnate Bastards', 322. Brown suggests something similar, saying that, 'Carrick was the acceptable face of the Stewart dynasty.' Brown, *Black Douglases*, 69.

119 Grant, 'Royal and Magnate Bastards', 323; *RM*, ii, ch. 51.

managed to seize power, 'they could have had the 1371 declaration reversed' so as to install Walter.[120]

This line of analysis can be disputed. John had become king not only on the basis of the 1371 declaration but on the legislation of 1373, which named each of Robert II's sons, in order of birth, as heirs to the kingdom. Reversing this to deny the lawfulness of Robert III's kingship would also involve removing from the succession Robert and Elizabeth's other pre-nuptial sons, leaving only the sons of Robert and Euphemia. Even if Walter could neutralise the adverse reactions of the disinherited descendants of Elizabeth's sons, such a move would not necessarily make Walter king. Because the tailzie of 1373 had named the sons of Euphemia and their male heirs in birth order, Walter's older brother David, earl of Strathearn and Caithness (d. ?1386), and his male heirs, took precedence over Walter and his. David had a living grandson in Malise, earl of Menteith (1406x13–1490), so any contention that legitimately born sons had a superior right over pre-nuptial ones thereby established the rights of Malise. If Walter's intention was to take the throne, he needed to persuade his magnates not only that the sons of Elizabeth ought to be excluded, but that seniority of line should be set aside and nearness of degree should apply instead.[121]

The motivation of the 1437 conspirators was not to restore the 'rightful' royal line but to get rid of an unpopular king whose governance was perceived as a threat to the stability of political society and, more immediately, to the interests of Atholl and others.[122] This does not exclude the possibility that those who plotted his murder may have intended, after the deed was done, to present the case for Walter as his lawful successor, on the grounds that Robert III had been a usurper because he was a wrongful heir. But this would have been a desperate strategy. Sixty-six years had elapsed since Carrick was accepted by the estates as heir to the throne and forty-seven years since he had become king. Retroactively declaring Robert III a wrongful king because his legitimacy was the same as that of many sons of the nobility, and arguing that Walter's rights had been grievously abrogated some decades earlier, though he had done nothing to address this until he was well into his seventies, would have been difficult to do.

120 Grant, 'Royal and Magnate Bastards', 323–4.

121 An argument seeking to exclude Malise on the basis that the tailzie designated male heirs only and he was born of a daughter, rather than a son, of David's was unlikely to be successful as the capacity of women to transmit heirship of the throne was well-established.

122 The author of 'The Dethe of the Kynge of Scotis', a fifteenth-century account of the assassination, says that James I imposed unfair taxes on the people, was greedy and cruel, and killed his own kinsmen. 'The Dethe of the Kynge of Scotis', in L. M. Matheson, ed., *Death and Dissent. Two Fifteenth-Century Chronicles* (Woodbridge, 1999), 27–8, 31, 43–4. Bower hints that James's taxes and political policies were a source of tension. *Chron. Bower*, viii, 241, 245, 251–3; Brown, '"Vile times"', 168–9.

More significantly, the contention that the sons of Euphemia had a superior right to the throne depends to a large extent on an acceptance of the *Regiam Majestatem* provision cited by Grant as being one which was applied in Scotland. Balfour-Melville does not mention the law-book's rejection of legitimation *per subsequens matrimonium* in his discussion, though he may well have had it in mind; if not, he at least regards the papal legitimation as being ineffective for inheritance of the throne. This was clearly the case in England, and Balfour-Melville takes it to be true also of the Scottish situation. However, *Regiam Majestatem* is simply not reliable on this matter. There is strong evidence that both before and after the law-book was compiled, pre-nuptial children in Scotland were treated as heirs without qualification.[123]

The kingdom's magnates had embraced papal marriage dispensations and concomitant legitimation of their offspring as a means of ensuring their estates passed to their children, and they were in no position to oppose the principle that legitimation was fully effective for inheritance. If Robert II had rejected Carrick (and his brothers-german) in 1373 in favour of David and Walter, this may have set an unwelcome precedent if it thereby encouraged challenges to inheritance by younger sons of the nobility, born after their parents' marriage dispensations or, like David and Walter, from a second marriage which was lawful from the outset. The claim that the kingdom was a special case may not have been wholly persuasive. The 1318 tailzie, which explicitly stated that Scotland was not an ordinary fief, made no reference to the implications of this for retrospectively legitimated royal offspring. This is hardly surprising since the exigencies of Robert I's situation did not require it and the tailzie was intended only to deal with the particular circumstances obtaining at that time. The same might be said for all the tailzies pertaining to the succession: each one was specific to the circumstances which prompted its creation. Those of 1315 and 1318 in particular may very well have been seen as temporary measures, a Plan B in case the always-preferred option, the king having sons in marriage, did not materialise. This consideration was much less relevant in 1373, when Robert II already had numerous sons.

Balfour-Melville points out that *de facto* possession of the throne would have counted for a great deal. This is undoubtedly true: Robert I had shown that seizure of the throne in the right circumstances could be followed by parliamentary confirmation of 'right', helped by judicious patronage,

[123] Bower, writing not long after the assassination, is clear that legitimation by subsequent marriage was accepted for royal succession. *Chron. Bower*, vii, 447. The *Liber Pluscardensis*, based on Bower's *Scotichronicon*, explains that because John was legitimated by his parents' marriage he succeeded to the throne, and adds that Atholl was thought to be illegitimate (specifically, not the king's son but an adulterine bastard). *Chron. Pluscarden*, i, 329–30. Clearly this was intended to distance him from the royal lineage, and perhaps also to suggest that the inherent flaw in his character imparted by his mother's crime might account for his murderous actions.

suppression of dissenters, and propaganda.[124] But in Walter's case, the already challenging circumstances would have been compounded by additional practicalities. The rights of the earl of Menteith would have been only one consideration. The assassins would have had to slay the queen also (as seems to have been the intention, but she was merely injured), to prevent opposing support coalescing around her and the prince. But even if they had killed Joan, the problem of her son would have been a major sticking point. The argument that Walter was the correct heir necessarily disinherited young James, but the possibility was strong that his cause would be taken up by powerful defenders, not least the English crown and others associated with his mother's family, the Beauforts, as well as by at least some in Scotland. The enterprise risked plunging Scotland into another war with England, and perhaps a Scottish civil war. Doing away with the six-year-old James may have forced the Scots to accept Walter, as long as the latter was not discovered to be implicated in the regicide, assassination of the queen and the murder of a small child who was accepted as the kingdom's only prince. The pretext for all of this, that Walter was the true heir to the throne, needed to be founded on something a great deal stronger than a spurious legal contention that legitimated sons could not inherit, especially when, all around, legitimated sons were doing exactly that.

The advantage Walter hoped to gain from his nephew's assassination may well have been more than protecting his landed interests and halting what was seen as a destructive or tyrannous kingship. Perhaps, as Bower claimed, he hoped to be regent.[125] Perhaps he even hoped that his grandson Robert would succeed, should the young James meet with an unfortunate accident before he was of an age to marry and father an heir: a tailzie naming Robert as heir after James could have been produced during the regency. But the 1437 regicide was not linked to any credible claim that Walter had a superior claim to the throne on legitimacy grounds.

The historiography of medieval Scotland contains conflicting views on the effects of legitimation. The theory that an imposter claiming to be Alexander Bruce, illegitimate nephew of Robert I, aroused so much anxiety in royal circles that he was executed, depends on the hypothesis that Alexander was legitimated. The danger he posed is understood to relate directly to this assumed legitimation: without it, he was just another royal bastard, with no

124 Tanner, 'Cowing the Community?', 64–73.

125 *Chron. Bower*, viii, 301–3. Bower later says that Atholl 'planned that … he would be raised to the throne', on the basis that he believed a prediction to this effect made long before by a fortune-teller. Ibid., 331. 'The Dethe' also says, without further explanation, that Walter secretly wanted the crown for himself. Matheson, *Death and Dissent*, 32. But, for the reasons given here, this is not plausible. 'The "dynastic ambitions" of David and Walter would seem to have been exaggerated in order to provide a suitably dishonourable explanation of Walter's much later involvement in the assassination of his nephew James I in 1437.' S. I. Boardman, 'Stewart, David, First Earl of Strathearn and First Earl of Caithness (*b.* in or after 1357?, *d.* 1386?), Magnate', *ODNB*, 20 July 2019.

prospect of obtaining the kingship and so offering no threat to the ambitions of Robert II; a legitimated Alexander was an entirely different proposition. There are hints that in the 1360s David II considered Robert's son John a possible heir. David gave Annabella Drummond, the queen's niece, to John in marriage, and granted them and their heirs the dynastically significant earldom of Carrick.[126] This interpretation of David's actions is based on the unstated premise that for David II, the reigning king, John's legitimation was fully effective for inheritance of the throne. But for some historians, the acquisition of legitimacy by papal decree was a second-class type of legitimacy, with no validity for inheritance, or at least not inheritance of the crown. Accordingly, the enthronement of the legitimated Robert III was never fully accepted by the political community of Scotland, and was a factor in the assassination of his son James I. Belief that legitimation was not effective for inheritance of the throne also underlies the assumption that a king might provide full legitimation to his bastard son without this having significant consequences for the line of succession.

Alan Durward's attempt to obtain a legitimation for his wife in the middle of the thirteenth century strongly suggests that by then legitimation was understood to transform illegitimate people into heirs, capable of inheriting, and transmitting, heirship to the throne. In the Great Cause, the efforts of William de Ros to show that his ancestor, Isabella Avenel, was legitimated, provide further evidence of this. The ousting of every Competitor whose ancestor was not included among the known legitimate offspring of kings implies that illegitimacy was a non-negotiable barrier to the throne, but the reality was rather more complex. It is true that those who were descended from a demonstrably illegitimate forebear within the previous handful of generations – from Earl Henry onwards – did not reach the final round of consideration. The elimination of the descendants of Isabella, Margaret, Ada and Marjorie, all kings' daughters known to be illegitimate; of Henry and Affrica, and of Marjorie, none of whom could be accounted for among the ranks of legitimately-born royal offspring, makes it look very much as though illegitimacy was the decisive factor in their exclusion. But what gives the impression of being a firm policy, based on the principle that illegitimacy precluded inheritance or transmission of the throne, was not quite as fixed as it appears. For one thing, the illegitimacy of more distant ancestors seems not to have counted. For another, the principle of excluding candidates with an illegitimate ancestor in more proximate generations was not so vitally important as to prompt an investigation into the validity of each marriage in the direct ancestral line of each Competitor, to establish that each link-person in the chain of succession was incontestably legitimate. This is not to say that illegitimacy did not matter – it clearly did – but only to highlight that in

[126] 'The king's grant thus seemed to acknowledge John as the likely heir to the throne if David died childless.' Boardman, 'Robert III'.

the Great Cause, at least, what looks from one perspective like an inviolable principle in action may in fact have been a slightly messy compromise between law, custom and political expediency.

5

Wives, daughters, and sisters

> Quha was mare ioyfull na the ladie fare,
> That God hed send hir a son to be hir are[1]

Walter Bower in *Scotichronicon* offers a tale purporting to be an account of an exchange between a Scottish and English knight at a banquet following a Scottish victory at a tournament in England near the end of the fourteenth century.[2] An unnamed English knight says to a Scottish counterpart, Sir William de Dalzel, that the military prowess shown by Sir David Lindsay could be accounted for by the possibility that he was fathered by an Englishman:

> it will not have escaped your recollection that not long ago your unhappy province was carved up and conquered by Englishmen. At that time there were perhaps among you some fair and desirable young ladies with whom some noble Englishmen of high birth and brave spirit had sexual relations and fathered young branches growing from noble roots. Such a man is perhaps this David Lindsay of yours... he has conducted himself so robustly to the extent that, bearing in mind his origin, his distinction should by rights be ascribed to English blood.[3]

Dalzel retorts that the wives of the English knights, while their husbands were away in Scotland fathering illegitimate children on Scotswomen, were at home conceiving the illegitimate offspring of others, since these wives,

> being deprived too long of marital sexual relations and not having the strength to contain themselves any more but desiring new sexual partners, invited into their closest intimacy cooks and churls, villeins and serfs, and sometimes friars and confessors. From these unions there emerged (unless I am mistaken) men neither suited to warfare nor efficient at fighting battles. We rejoice therefore that we have arisen from your stock and that we are born as gentlemen while you from your stock have turned out degenerate.[4]

1 *King Alexander*, lines 17371–2.
2 *Chron. Bower*, viii, 13. Bower's source for the flyting tale is not known.
3 *Chron. Bower*, viii, 15.
4 *Chron. Bower*, viii, 17.

Clearly this is intended to be an amusing story, one that humorously turns the tables on the backhanded compliment from the English knight, a compliment that praised the Scots by denying their Scottishness and called them bastards into the bargain. But the resonances of the story were quite serious, since Scottish women of all ranks had in reality been subjected to capture and to being treated as war booty by English men during the Wars of Independence.[5]

Bower's underlying assumption here is that illegitimacy on its own is not enough to create a degenerate character; it is the nobility or otherwise of the father (they were 'of high birth and brave spirit'), and also, importantly, the character of the mother, that matters. In Bower's flyting story the English wives lack 'the strength to contain themselves' sexually, and, further, are not only prepared to debase themselves by sleeping with men of low birth and with friars and confessors, they in fact instigate such encounters (it was they who 'invited' the men to bed). The virtue of the Scottish women, in contrast, is not impugned. They are described simply as 'fair and desirable' and no mention is made of their willingness or otherwise to engage in sexual relationships with the occupying English knights. Bower thus invites the interpretation that the women concerned did not encourage the attentions of their English consorts but rather were, like Scotland itself, subject to an unwelcome invading force which they were obliged to endure.

The implication that some mothers of bastards were honourable while others were not doubtless accorded with social experience in medieval Scotland. Many families had illegitimates among their number; there is ample evidence that these children were loved and valued, and their mothers were unlikely to have been social pariahs. The women concerned may have been in stable though non-marital sexual relationships with the fathers, or their children may have been born from shorter-lived liaisons, but in either case the mothers of illegitimates were daughters and granddaughters, sisters and nieces, belonging to communities and families in which having an illegitimate child may have been recognised as 'wrong', but which may not have attracted significant opprobrium.[6] But Bower's division of women into the 'fair and desirable' mothers of valiant knights and the adulterous, '[lacking] the strength to contain themselves' mothers of degenerates reflects something of contemporary attitudes to both illegitimacy and women. There was a tension between the rules governing female conduct, especially in respect of

[5] G. Seabourne, *Imprisoning Medieval Women: The Non-Judicial Confinement and Abduction of Women in England, c. 1170–1509* (Farnham, 2011), 17–19, 37–9, 41, 44, 47; C. Neville, 'Widows of War: Edward I and the Women of Scotland during the War of Independence', in S. S. Walker, ed., *Wife and Widow in Medieval England* (Ann Arbor, MI, 1993), 109–39.

[6] Although sometimes it did: see the examples below of Margaret, sister of James III, and Isabella, sister of the earl of Strathbogie.

their marital and sexual lives, and the messier realities of human experience: illegitimacy was evidence of this.

Scottish queens and illegitimacy

Alexander I is the only Scottish king known to have married someone who was illegitimate. He wed Sybilla (d. 1122), one of Henry I's many illegitimate daughters.[7] Henry used these daughters to build international alliances through marriage into selected, high-ranking families along the Anglo-Norman periphery, as part of his efforts to create, as Hollister and Keefe termed it, 'an encircling ring of friendly princes' to protect his empire.[8] He would not have been able to do this unless prestige attached to these daughters as spouses in the international marriage economy.[9] William of Malmesbury, noting that Sybilla was illegitimate, claimed that 'she lacked correctness of manners and charm of person'.[10] His low opinion of Sybilla seems not to have been shared by Alexander; after her death he granted the island on Loch Tay, and some associated lands, to the canons of Scone in return for their prayers for her (and his own) soul.[11] She attested at least one of Alexander's charters and was active in ecclesiastical affairs.[12] Writing some two hundred years after her death, Wyntoun gave her as a daughter of William the Bastard, but whether this was genuine error or an attempt to obscure her status is unclear.[13] If the latter, this almost certainly reflected attitudes to illegitimacy in Wyntoun's own time, rather than in Alexander's.[14]

7 Her mother was probably Sybilla Corbet, daughter of a Shropshire landowner, who had at least one other child with Henry I. Alexander's queen did not produce heirs, or at least none that lived long enough to be recorded, which may account for why she is infrequently mentioned in contemporary Scottish sources. The *Melrose Chronicle* mentions her only in a very brief note of her death. *Chron. Melrose*, 32. See also J. Nelson, 'Sybilla (d. 1122), Queen of Scots and Consort of Alexander I', *ODNB*, 10 May 2020.

8 C. W. Hollister and T. K. Keefe, 'The Making of the Angevin Empire', *The Journal of British Studies* 12 (1973), 5; Oram, *Domination and Lordship*, 304–5. See Given-Wilson and Curteis, *Royal Bastards*, 60–74 for details of Henry I's illegitimate offspring. Another of his illegitimate daughters married Fergus, lord of Galloway; their daughter Affrica married Óláfr Guðrǫðarson (d. 1153), king of Man.

9 None, however, married as well as his legitimate daughter Matilda, though her marriageability was further enhanced by her being his sole surviving legitimate child.

10 William of Malmesbury, *Gesta Regum*, 727.

11 *Liber Ecclesie de Scon* (Bannatyne and Maitland Clubs, 1843), no. 2. Duncan says that 'the slight documentary evidence suggests they were a devoted couple'. Duncan, *Kingship*, 65 n.53

12 *Scon Lib.*, no. 1; *Dunfermelyn Reg.*, nos 1, 2; Lawrie, *Early Scottish Charters*, 294.

13 *Chron. Wyntoun*, ii, 174. See discussion of the representation of Ermengarde's lineage, p. 121.

14 For the acceptance of Sybilla as a royal bride, see Given-Wilson and Curteis, *Royal Bastards*, 64; E. Hamilton, *Mighty Subjects: the Dunbar Earls in Scotland, c.1072–1289* (Edinburgh, 2010), 100; D. Broun, *Scottish Independence and the Idea of Britain: From the Picts to Alexander III* (Edinburgh, 2007), 105–6; D. Messer, '*Filia Notha* or *Filia*

In later centuries, the prestige value of illegitimate royal daughters as brides declined. A king's illegitimate daughter may still have been prized by the nobility, but such a bride might be seen as an affront to the dignity of a king. In 1489 or 1490, the Spanish ambassador Roderigo de Puebla was tasked with dangling in front of James IV the prospect of marriage with a Spanish princess, to prevent Scotland entering into an alternative alliance that might work against Spain's interests. The ambassador discussed with his Scottish counterparts a marriage between James and Doña Juana, giving them to believe that she was King Ferdinand's legitimate daughter when in fact she was his illegitimate child.[15] Discovering this, Ferdinand and Isabella wrote to de Puebla and his fellow ambassador Diego de Guevara, urging the former to come clean. 'The consequences might be very serious. He must tell the Scotch ambassadors the truth before they leave, because it would be better that they should learn it from him than from strangers. ... If the king of Scots know [*sic*] this and nevertheless likes to marry her, her marriage portion might be doubled.'[16] What is of note here is that although offering Doña Juana was understood to be a possible cause of offence to James, at the same time it was thought he may just accept her. True, her dowry would have to be substantially increased to compensate for her illegitimacy, but as far as Ferdinand and Isabella were concerned, her birth status did not necessarily rule her out altogether. This may not have been very realistic of them, but it does highlight the liminal status of an illegitimate royal daughter: depending on the circumstances, she may be good enough for someone of very high rank.

Returning to the twelfth century, Alexander's grandnephew, William the Lion, also married – after some hesitation, we are told – a woman given to him by his contemporary on the English throne.[17] Ermengarde de Beaumont (d.

Regis?: Kinship and the Acquiescence of Royal Illegitimate Daughters (c. 1090–1440)', *Foundations* 1.1 (2003), 52; and D. Messer, 'Medieval Monarchs, Female Illegitimacy and Modern Genealogical Matters: Part I: Sybilla, Queen of Scotland, c.1090–1122', *Foundations* 1.2 (2003), 100.

15 Ferdinand did have a legitimate daughter with the same name, though it appears the deception did not involve pretending one was the other; de Puebla invented a clandestine marriage for Ferdinand to explain the provenance of the young woman on offer. *Calendar of Letters, Despatches, and State Papers, Relating to the Negotiations between England and Spain: Preserved in the Archives at Simancas and Elsewhere*, ed. G. A. Bergenroth and others (London, 1862), i, no. 41.

16 Ibid. (quote on p. 26).

17 Howden, *Gesta Regis Henrici*, i, 347, 351. They married in 1186. Ermengarde is described as a 'girl' (*puella*) in Howden, which has given rise to the belief that she was barely twelve at the time of her marriage. But Adeliza of Louvain is similarly given as *puella* in 1121 on her marriage to Henry I, when she was either seventeen or eighteen. *The Chronicle of John of Worcester 1118–1140: Being the Continuation of the 'Chronicon ex Chronicis' of Florence of Worcester*, ed. J. R. H. Weaver (Oxford, 1908), 16. Ermengarde may have been very young, but this cannot be assumed only from the use of *puella*. It may be the chroniclers in both cases were seeking to emphasise the discrepancy in age between the bride and groom: William was in his forties and Henry in his fifties.

1233) was legitimate, but descended from a bastard.[18] William's queen was a granddaughter of another of Henry I's illegitimate daughters, Constance, who married Roscelin of Beaumont, hereditary *vicomte* of Maine.[19] Their son Richard was the father of Ermengarde. The illegitimacy of Ermengarde's grandmother is obscured in the chronicle sources. Howden gives her as the daughter of Richard de Beaumont, a grandson of King Henry, without mentioning the grandson was born of Henry's illegitimate daughter.[20] The *Chronicle of Melrose* more seriously misrepresents her descent, making her 'the daughter of the count of Beaumont, who was the son of the daughter of the elder son of William the Bastard'.[21] The *Gesta Annalia* gives her the same forebears, naming Robert Curthose as the count of Beaumont's grandfather, and this is repeated by Wyntoun and by Bower.[22] The post-Howden accounts may have been based on error, or they may simply have been attempts to add lustre to her pedigree by making her descend from the eldest, rather than the youngest, son of William the Bastard. Alternatively, Ermengarde's fictional genealogy in these later chronicles may reflect a diminution after the twelfth century of the acceptability of illegitimacy in the direct lineages of royal figures. Curthose did have a daughter, but she too was illegitimate. If it was the Melrose chronicler's intention to hide the illegitimacy of Ermengarde's ancestor, the choice of Curthose as her great-grandfather was attractive for a reason other than his seniority: unlike Henry I, Robert Curthose spent almost all his life outside Britain, thus the legitimacy or otherwise of his offspring was less likely to be known with confidence.

Royal wives, whatever their own status, had little option but to tolerate their husbands' procreation of illegitimate offspring with mistresses. Their feelings about their husbands' bastards are not recorded. There is a slight hint in the reign of James IV that the matter might be a sensitive one. The treasurers' accounts note that his illegitimate offspring were temporarily removed from their residence at Stirling Castle, and lodged in the town of Stirling instead, when James took his new queen, Margaret Tudor, to the castle in 1504.[23]

18 Tables 8 and 9.

19 Given-Wilson and Curteis, *Royal Bastards*, 63, 70, 71; K. Hapgood Thompson, 'Dowry and Inheritance Patterns: Some Examples from the Descendants of King Henry I of England', *Medieval Prosopography* 17 (1996), 49–50.

20 Howden, *Gesta Regis Henrici*, i, 347.

21 *Chron. Melrose*, 45.

22 *Gesta Annalia I* in Skene, *Fordun*, i, 275; *Chron. Wyntoun*, ii, 215; *Chron. Bower*, iv, 369.

23 *TA*, ii, 445. They had married the year before.

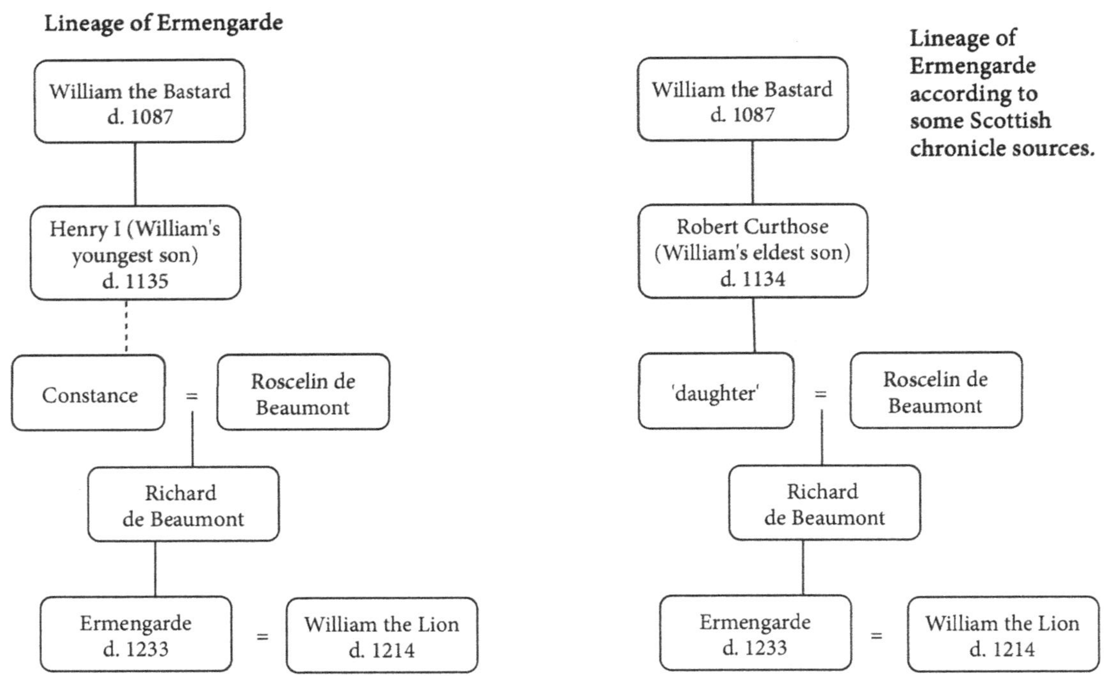

Table 8. Lineage of Ermengarde de Beaumont

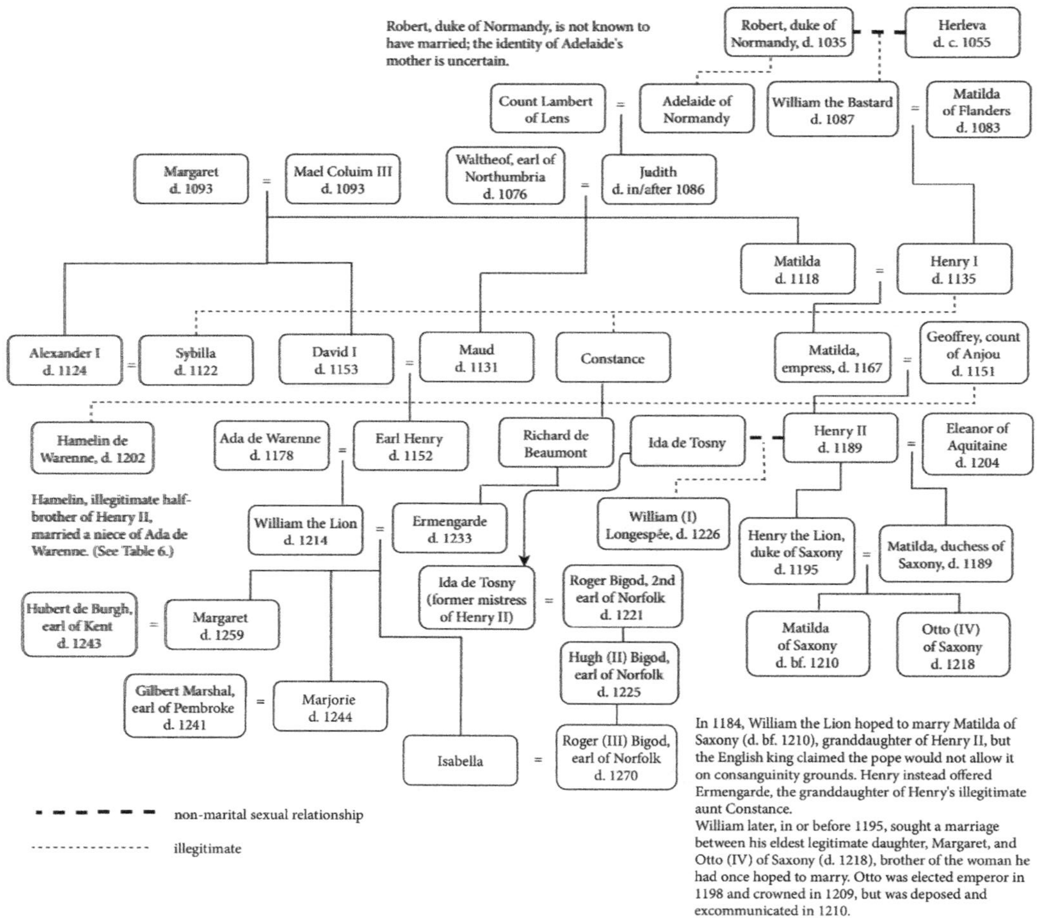

Table 9. William the Lion and Ermengarde

Illegitimate daughters of Scottish kings

Four Scottish kings between 1100 and ca. 1500 are known to have had illegitimate daughters. William the Lion, Robert I and James IV each had three illegitimate daughters who survived childhood and Alexander II had one such daughter. There is indirect evidence suggestive of Robert II having illegitimate daughters, and it would be remarkable if he had not: in a very active extramarital sexual career spanning over four decades he had at least nine illegitimate sons, and it is overwhelmingly likely his affairs produced daughters also.

One way of measuring the status of illegitimate royal daughters would be to compare their marriageability to that of their legitimate half-sisters. However, of the four kings whose illegitimate daughters are clearly identified as such, only two – William the Lion and Robert I – also had legitimate daughters who lived long enough to marry. In both cases, comparisons between their marital fortunes are complicated by the exigencies of their fathers' circumstances. In William's case, he was required to surrender his two eldest legitimate daughters to the English king and died before either they or his younger daughter with Ermengarde married. In Robert I's reign, war with England closed off some possibilities, and he died before he could arrange the marriages of two of his three legitimate daughters.

William the Lion is known to have had three illegitimate daughters.[24] At least two of his daughters were fathered on the daughters of border lairds, and it was to border magnates that William gave all three in marriage. The *Chronicle of Melrose* records that in 1183 William gave, 'in honourable manner', his daughter Isabella in marriage to Robert de Brus.[25] Her mother was a daughter of Robert Avenel.[26] In 1191 the same Isabella, now a widow, was given in marriage to Robert de Ros, at Haddington.[27] In 1184 William's daughter Ada (d. 1200; her mother is unknown) married Patrick, earl of Dunbar, and in 1193 his daughter Margaret was given in marriage at Roxburgh to Eustace de Vescy (a friend, political ally and neighbour of his new brother-in-law, Robert de Ros).[28] Margaret's mother was a daughter of Adam de Whitsome. William's role in their marriage careers was no different from that of any father of the time: he secured husbands for them, providing tochers (marriage-portions) in the form of lands.

24 All three had descendants who were Competitors in the Great Cause: see Table 3.

25 *Chron. Melrose*, 44.

26 For an account of this family, see R. C. Reid, 'The Scottish Avenels', *TDGNHAS* 37 (1958–9), 70–7.

27 *Chron. Melrose*, 48.

28 *Chron. Melrose*, 44, 48. For this family, see K. J. Stringer, 'Nobility and Identity in Medieval Britain and Ireland: the de Vescy family, c.1120–1314', in B. Smith, ed., *Britain and Ireland, 900–1300: Insular Responses to Medieval European Change* (Cambridge, 1999), 199–239.

was a descendant of the Angus-based de Lundin family. Alan's father, Thomas, had held the honorific post of king's *hostiarius*, or usher, by which the family had acquired the name Durward ('Doorward'). The match was a politically expedient, but not especially prestigious, one. As we have seen, Marjorie was the subject of an attempted legitimation which excited political hostility against her husband, and was the ancestor from whom a Competitor in the Great Cause claimed a right to the Scottish throne.[34]

Robert I had three illegitimate daughters: Margaret, Elizabeth and Christina (or Christian), and three legitimate daughters from two marriages. None of his illegitimate daughters married an earl, as his legitimate daughter Margaret did; nor were they considered marriageable to a prince (the same Margaret was the subject of negotiations to wed Edward II's son, Edward of Chester), but of the two whose marriages are known, neither married a mere squire, as was the husband of Robert's legitimate daughter Matilda.[35]

The illegitimate Margaret married Robert Glen. Robert was probably the son of John Glen, a Peebleshire landowner who in the 1290s had commanded the troops of Robert Wishart, bishop of Glasgow, against the English, and who had also fought at Bannockburn; his kinsman, Richard Glen, had had his family lands confiscated by Edward I in 1298.[36] John Glen, Robert I's sergeand, was in possession of Balmuto, Fife, before 29 January 1319.[37] Robert Glen and his wife, Margaret Bruce, the king's sister, were given lands at Nether Pittedye, neighbouring Balmuto, by David II.[38] The name of Christina or Christian of Carrick's husband, if she married, is not known.[39] She received a pension of £2 from Robert I in 1328 and again the following year.[40] She also obtained a charter from him.[41]

Elizabeth married, in 1364, Sir Walter Oliphant of Aberdalgie (d. in/aft. 1378), son and heir to Sir William Oliphant of Dupplin and Aberdalgie

34 Discussed at pp. 78–81 and p. 84; see also Table 3. Durward had an illegitimate son, Thomas.

35 *Gesta Annalia II* in Skene, *Fordun*, i, 369; *Chron. Pluscarden*, i, 240; Penman, *Robert the Bruce*, 253–4, 377 n.79. Matilda and her sister Margaret appear to have been still single in November 1343 (*CPP*, i, 27), suggesting they were children when their father died in 1329; Matilda died in 1353 in Aberdeen, and Margaret was dead before November 1347, when her husband remarried.

36 *Documents and Records illustrating the History of Scotland*, ed. F. Palgrave (London, 1837), 345; *PoMS*, www.poms.ac.uk/record/source/7407/. For the family, see T. A. Glenn, 'Genealogical Notes regarding the Family of Glen, or Glenn', *The Pennsylvania Magazine of History and Biography* 36 (1912), 480–99.

37 *RRS*, v, no. 144; *RMS*, i, App. 2, nos 633, 634.

38 *RMS*, i, App. 2, no. 1029.

39 Robert also had a sister of the same name. She married Sir Christopher Seton (d. 1306) and Sir Andrew Murray (d. 1338).

40 *ER*, i, cxxx, 114, 209.

41 *RMS*, i, App. 2, no. 565.

(d. 1329).[42] Sir William's service to Robert I had been rewarded with grants of land and the office of escheator.[43] His son was also a loyal Bruce supporter, and was given the governorship of Stirling Castle in 1368. Sir Walter resigned his various estates to David II in 1365 and the king regranted them to him and Elizabeth, on the same day that the king also granted Walter and Elizabeth a barony in Angus.[44] David II also gave his sister gifts of a cask of wine worth £7 6s 8d, and the escheat, valued at £3, of one William Clapham.[45] Elizabeth and Walter had three sons. Their grandson, Sir William Oliphant, the heir of their eldest son John, was numbered among those knights surrendered as hostages for the ransom of James I, and is believed to have died during his captivity.

There is a hint in the fourteenth century that legitimacy of a royal daughter might sometimes matter to the family of a prospective groom. William, first earl of Douglas (d. 1384), had opposed Robert II's succession to the throne in 1371. His opposition was bought off by Robert making a number of concessions to him, among which was that William's son and heir, James, should marry a daughter of Robert's. According to the *Chronicle of Wyntoun*:

> Swa tretyt thai, that his son suld wed
> This kingis Dochtyr off lawchful bed.[46]

The emphasis on the bride being 'of lawful bed' may indicate that an illegitimate daughter would not have been acceptable to the earl. On the other hand, as Burnett suggests, it may simply indicate widespread knowledge of Robert's illegitimate brood, or mean nothing more than that Wyntoun was looking for a rhyme for 'wed'.[47]

If Wyntoun did in fact intend in this line to draw a distinction between Robert's legitimate and illegitimate daughters, it is an interesting verse for another reason. Several illegitimate sons, but no daughters, are firmly identified as Robert's in record and narrative sources. Some indirect evidence hints at the existence of three such daughters. Robert had five daughters with his first wife, Elizabeth Mure; Boardman considers it probable that the king and his second wife, Euphemia Ross, had more daughters than the two (Egidia

[42] J. Anderson, ed., *The Oliphants in Scotland* (Edinburgh, 1879), 5–6; *SP*, vi, 537; *ER*, i, cxxx; ii, 222; E. Maxtone Graham, *The Oliphants of Gask. Records of a Jacobite Family* (London, 1910), 35; F. Watson, 'Oliphant [Olifard] Family (*per*. 1141–*c*. 1500), Nobility', *ODNB*, 24 April 2018.

[43] The king's escheator was a legal officer responsible for ensuring lands and property were restored to the king in cases where the holder died without heirs or where the property was forfeited by the crown because of an offence. *CDS*, ii, no. 857; *Documents Illustrative of the History of Scotland, 1286–1306*, ed. J. Stevenson (Edinburgh, 1870), i, no. 88.

[44] *RRS*, vi, nos 337–43. The final two are incomplete; in the first five, Elizabeth is given as 'our beloved sister'.

[45] *ER*, ii, 222.

[46] *Chron. Wyntoun*, iii, 8. Robert's daughter Isabella (d. ca. 1410) married Sir James Douglas (d. 1388) in 1371. Theiner, *Vet. Mon.*, no. 691 (she is mistakenly called Margaret in this).

[47] G. Burnett, preface to *ER*, iv, clxiv.

and Elizabeth) who are conventionally listed as their offspring.[48] Of the three putative daughters of Robert obliquely indicated in our sources, Katherine might possibly have been a legitimate child of Robert and Euphemia, but it is unlikely that the other two, Agnes and Mary, were legitimate.

Katherine Stewart, wife of Sir Robert Logan of Grougar and Restalrig (Admiral of Scotland from 1400), appears to have been a daughter of Robert II, on the strength of a 1394 charter in which Logan is described by Robert III as his 'beloved brother'.[49] A Lady Katherine Logan received payment from the king (James I) in 1434.[50] The lands of Grougar were in the barony of Cunningham, Ayr, and 'Grugere' had been given to Hugh of Cunningham by Robert I, probably in 1314.[51] Logan held them only temporarily, since they were later back in the hands of the Cunninghams, a kindred loyal to the crown and in its affinity for much of the later middle ages.

Hugh's descendant, Sir William Cunningham of Kilmaurs (d. 1413x5) married Margaret Danielston, of another important Ayrshire family with members in the king's household.[52] Margaret was not the mother of his son William Cunningham (d. 1426x7), vicar of Dundonald, papal chaplain, canon of Glasgow, and the king's chancellor.[53] The illegitimate cleric was born in the 1360s, apparently before Sir William was married, and his mother was called Agnes.[54] In petitions to the pope, William junior claimed kinship with Robert III, Robert, duke of Albany, and James I.[55] Watt suggests Agnes was, therefore, 'most likely an unknown daughter of Robert II'. In fact, previous generations of William's family were styled 'kinsman' of Scottish kings from Robert I onwards, and it is possible William was trading on these historic links.[56] On the other hand, if the only blood relationship between the crown and the Cunninghams dated from the early part of the fourteenth century, the connection would be a little thin by the time the cleric was ordained, in or before 1392, and during his subsequent career. Certainly, William received very favourable treatment from the papacy, on a par with that given to Robert II's own illegitimate sons.[57] A pre-existing kinship would not rule out a more recent connection, especially since no marriage was involved, and so it is plausible, if unprovable, that Agnes was a daughter of Robert II.

48 Boardman, 'Robert II'.

49 *RMS*, ii, no. 1411 (transumpt); *SP*, i, 16.

50 *ER*, iv, 592.

51 *RRS*, vi, no. 438; *PoMS*, www.poms.ac.uk/record/source/10414/.

52 Boardman, *Early Stewart Kings*, 44, 141, 183.

53 For his career, see Watt, *Graduates*, 137–8.

54 *Muniments of the Royal Burgh of Irvine* (Ayrshire and Galloway Archaeological Association, 1890–1), i, 125–7.

55 *CPP*, i, 636–7; *CSSR*, i, 167; Cameron, *Apostolic Camera*, 315.

56 *RRS*, v, no. 351, and vi, nos 437, 438; *RMS*, i, no. 113.

57 Among the favours granted to him was permission to hold a plurality of incompatible benefices and to remain silent on his illegitimacy in future petitions.

Sir William Cunningham's wife, Margaret, was the daughter of Sir Robert Danielston (d. 1397), son of Sir John Danielston. A dispensation for the marriage of Margaret's sister Elizabeth to Robert Maxwell says the union is sought by Robert, duke of Albany, and that Elizabeth's late father, Robert Danielston, was the duke's nephew.[58] The relationship could be explained by Albany having a sister who married Robert Danielston's father, John.[59] None of the duke's seven known sisters and half-sisters were married to Danielston, whose wife's name is given in a Church record as Mary.[60] Another dispensation, issued in 1409 to the same William Cunningham (father of the cleric), permitting marriage between William and Mary Stewart, daughter of Robert III, states that Mary stood in the second, as well as third, degree of consanguinity to William's first wife, Margaret Danielston.[61] Robert Danielston's mother being a daughter of Robert II (and so sister of Robert III) would make Margaret and Mary first cousins, that is, related in the second degree. The record naming Mary is from 1377, and shows that at least two of John and Mary's sons were then adults. Mary could not have been a daughter of Robert II's marriage to Euphemia, as she must have been old enough to marry at around the time of Euphemia's marriage in 1355, if not some years before. If she was a daughter of Robert II, she was among his illegitimate offspring.

The identification of Katherine, Agnes and Mary as daughters of Robert II rests on inference rather than anything substantive, especially as far as Mary and Agnes are concerned. The absence of any direct reference to non-marital daughters of Robert is difficult to explain. If the three were indeed his daughters then he arranged good marriages for them, but any other provision for them remains unknown.

The known illegitimate offspring of Robert III and James II are also sons. James I and his grandson James III are not known to have had any illegitimate children. In the case of James I, this could be attributable to uxoriousness: there is some evidence that his relationship with Joan included genuine affection or love, and he may not have sought female companionship outside his marriage.[62] Royal and elite marriages were primarily political matches; feelings of affection may or may not have followed. Mistresses were

58 McGurk, *Letters of Benedict XIII*, 270–1.

59 J. P. Ravilious, '"Nephew of the Duke": the Danielstons of that Ilk, and a Hitherto Unknown Daughter of Robert II, King of Scots', *The Scottish Genealogist* 54 (2007), 134–7. See also J. P. Ravilious, 'Maria Stewart, Illegitimate Daughter of Robert II, King of Scots', *The Scottish Genealogist* 56 (2009), 29–30.

60 *Glas. Reg.*, no. 315.

61 *CPP*, i, 639.

62 James I is generally accepted to be the author of *The Kingis Quair*, a poem which includes a section (stanzas 40–52) describing the love felt by the poet for a woman he meets while in captivity. *The Kingis Quair of James Stewart*, ed. M. P. McDiarmid (London, 1973). James was held in England between 1406 and 1424, where he was given Joan Beaufort as his queen. Brown notes James's 'personal delight' at the match. Brown, *James I*, 26.

probably chosen for more personal reasons to do with attraction, although political considerations may also have played a part. It is unlikely to have been coincidental that at least two of William the Lion's known mistresses were the daughters of border lairds: his children with them were used for marriages to men who were also border landholders, in pursuit of his ambition to regain his northern English patrimony.[63]

The next Scottish king known to have had illegitimate daughters is James IV. The mothers of these children were all women to whom James was related, though the kinship was not close.[64] Katherine was his daughter with Marion Boyd of Bonshaw (with whom he also had a son, Alexander), Margaret was born of his liaison with Margaret Drummond, and Janet was his daughter with Isabel or Agnes Stewart, who was herself illegitimate.[65] James's affair with Janet Kennedy resulted in three known children, but of the three only his son, James earl of Moray, seems to have survived. The sex of the other two is not known, but at least one, born in 1503, was probably a girl as although there is no mention of her death in James's lifetime, she did not receive any titles, nor does she appear by name in any public records, as did her brother James and half-brother Alexander. Neither are there any references to her being married, suggesting she died in childhood or early adulthood. James and Janet's other child, born in 1502, died before her or his first birthday: the treasurers' accounts include an entry for the cost (2s) of a winding sheet for the small body.[66]

From infancy onwards, all of James's known illegitimate children were provided with the necessaries of life by their father. He paid for their wet-nurses and carers, their clothing, food, education and travel. 'The bairns' whose expenses appear in the accounts comprised not only James's illegitimate offspring but also their child companions, and the sons and daughters of nobles who were taken into the king's household and were educated alongside James's children.[67] While his illegitimate sons Alexander and James were provided with university-educated tutors, little is recorded of his daughters' education.

Margaret Drummond's early death may have resulted in her daughter, Margaret Stewart, having a special place in her father's affections.[68] While

63 Discussed above at pp. 124–6.

64 Tables 10, 11 and 12.

65 She was a daughter of James Stewart earl of Buchan and his mistress, Margaret Murray. She is sometimes given as Isobel in the sources.

66 *TA*, ii, 394. A payment (5s) was also made to Thomas Fleming, who rode to Edinburgh to deliver the news to the king of 'the deing of ane of the barnis'.

67 M. Cowan and L. E. Walkling, 'A "gret cradil of stait": Growing Up with the Court of James IV', in J. Nugent and E. Ewan, ed., *Children and Youth in Premodern Scotland* (Woodbridge, 2015), 15–31. James IV had two legitimate daughters who both died in infancy, as did three of his four legitimate sons.

68 Margaret died in 1502 (after her liaison with James had ended) along with two of her sisters, apparently either deliberately or inadvertently poisoned by a meal taken at Drummond Castle.

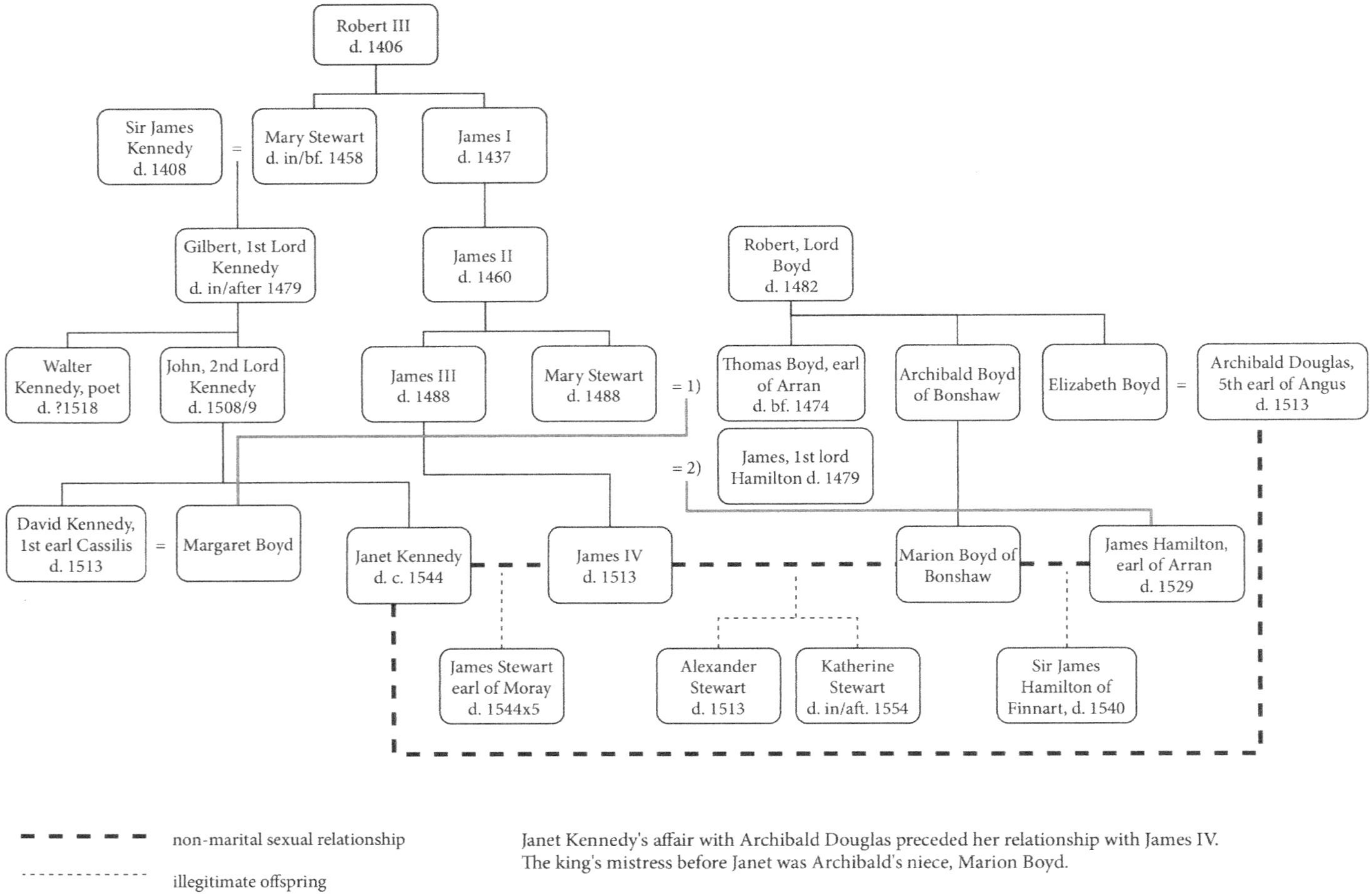

Janet Kennedy's affair with Archibald Douglas preceded her relationship with James IV.
The king's mistress before Janet was Archibald's niece, Marion Boyd.

Table 10. James IV, the Boyds and the Kennedys

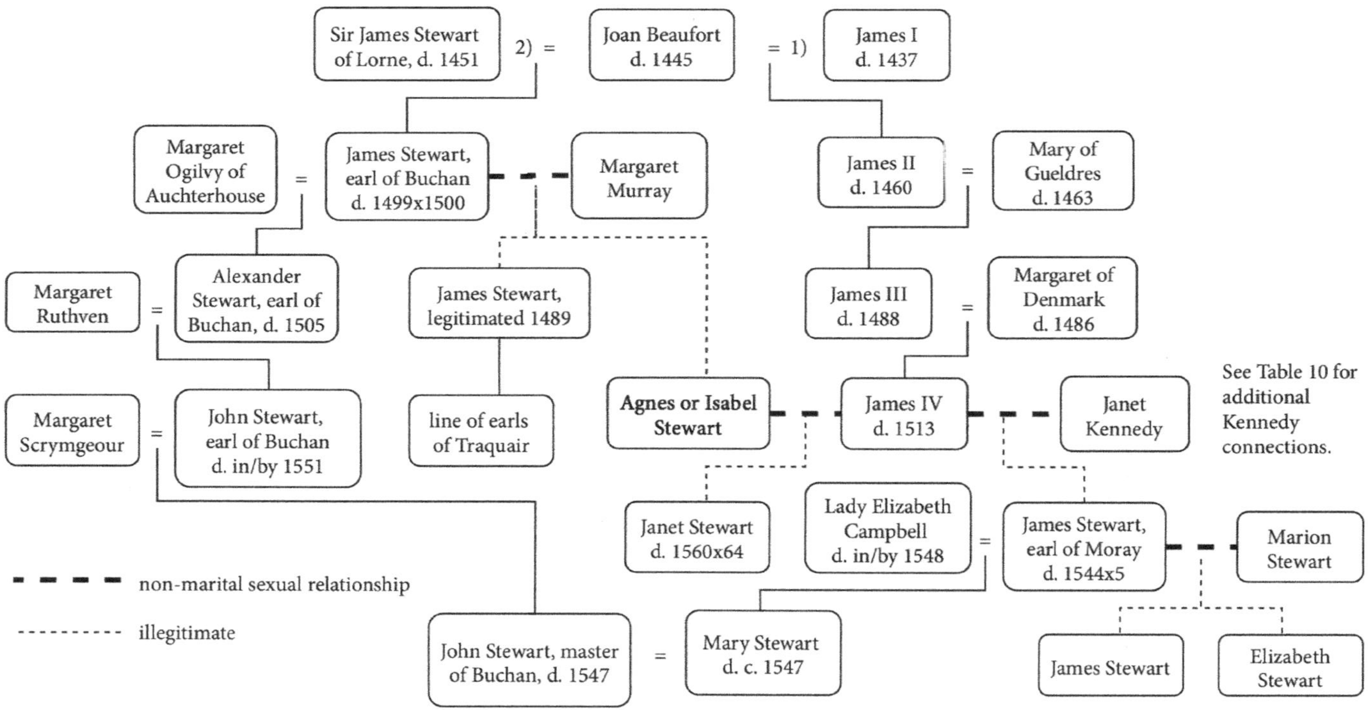

Table 11. Agnes or Isobel Stewart

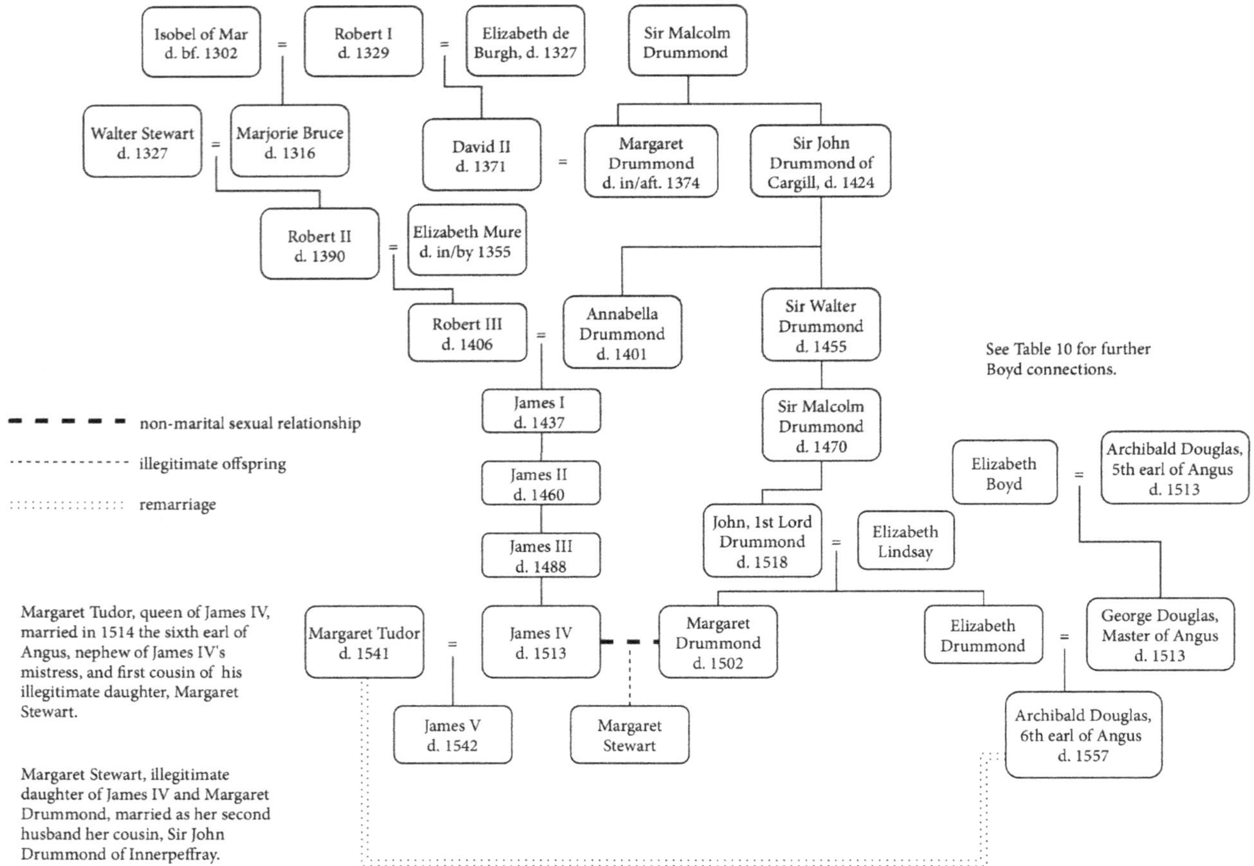

Margaret Tudor, queen of James IV, married in 1514 the sixth earl of Angus, nephew of James IV's mistress, and first cousin of his illegitimate daughter, Margaret Stewart.

Margaret Stewart, illegitimate daughter of James IV and Margaret Drummond, married as her second husband her cousin, Sir John Drummond of Innerpeffray.

Table 12. Drummonds and Stewarts

Katherine is never referred to by name in the treasurers' accounts, her half-sister is frequently found as 'Lady (later, Mistress) Margaret, the king's daughter'.[69] Her father provided her with companions in the form of two 'Moor lasses', the recorded expenses of whom are always associated with Margaret; a third child, Marjorie Lindsay, was also in Margaret's retinue. Possibly his other daughters had companions also, but Margaret's were evidently considered to be in a special category as no others are recorded as a separate expense. She also seems to be the only one who received dance lessons from one of the king's musicians.[70] Margaret's clothing was sumptuous: a single gown for the little girl in 1504 (when she was around seven years old), made of velvet, ermine and other furs, cost £28 11s in fabrics and dressmaking expenses.[71] Her companions were also provided with expensive clothing.

James lived long enough to find husbands for his two older daughters, Katherine and Margaret, but he died while his youngest surviving daughter, Janet, was still a child. All three married relatively young. Katherine, probably born in 1494, was married in or by December 1507 to James Douglas, heir to the earldom of Morton (and earl from 1511x5); her tocher was £547 2s 8d.[72] Douglas was considerably older than Katherine, and related to her: he was a great-grandson of James I (Katherine's great-great-grandfather) via his daughter Joan, who married James Douglas, first earl of Morton. Around the time of their marriage James IV gave Katherine and James the barony of Preston, in Kirkcudbright, resigned by the earl of Morton.[73] James V later gave his half-sister Katherine and her husband his own barony of Buthill, also in Kirkcudbright.[74]

Margaret, whose birth occurred in late 1496 or early 1497, wed John Gordon, the Master of Huntly, heir to that earldom, in or by April 1510. James gave them the lordship of Badenoch with the castle and manor house of Ruthven, and the lands of Fortingall in Perthshire with the fortress at Garth, resigned by John's father Alexander, earl of Huntly.[75] John died in 1517, predeceasing his father, and so Margaret's son George (1513–62), became the fourth earl of Huntly in 1524; another son, Alexander (ca. 1516–75), was archbishop of Athens, bishop-elect

69 *TA*, ii, 330, 478; iii, 93, 99, 101, 309; iv, 416, 417, 432, 433. She is also given as 'the king's daughter', without title or name: *TA*, ii, 376; iv, 409, or as 'Lady Margaret': *TA*, iii, 114, 117. Katherine is never recorded as anything other than one of 'the bairns'. Janet is not named either, but was only around three at the time of her father's death.

70 *TA*, iii, 129.

71 *TA*, ii, 330–1.

72 *RMS*, ii, no. 3160; *TA*, i, 101; *RSS*, i, nos 2835, 3733; *ER*, xiv, 106, 200.

73 *RMS*, ii, no. 3160.

74 *RSS*, i, nos 2835, 3733.

75 *RMS*, ii, no. 3452.

of Galloway, and commendator of Inchaffray.[76] Margaret's second marriage was to Sir John Drummond of Innerpeffry.[77]

Janet, perhaps born in 1510, married Malcolm Fleming, later the third Lord Fleming, around 1524. A marriage contract made by Janet's mother, Agnes Stewart, Lady Bothwell, and Malcolm Fleming in February of 1523 records that Agnes was to pay for a papal dispensation to overcome the known impediment between her daughter and Malcolm, but that if a second impediment should later come to light (as in fact it did), he would be responsible for the expense of a second dispensation enabling the couple to marry anew.[78] The couple had at least eight children and Janet's sons James (d. 1558) and John (d. 1572) were the fourth and fifth Lord Fleming respectively. Janet's husband lord Fleming died in 1547 and the following year she travelled to the French court as governess (as well as illegitimate aunt) to the five-year-old Mary Queen of Scots who was betrothed to the dauphin of France. Janet's daughter, Mary Fleming (d. 1600), was one of the 'Queen's Maries', child companions and maids of honour to the young queen. Another two of Janet's daughters were also in the Queen of Scots' retinue.

Janet Stewart, Lady Fleming, illegitimate daughter of a king, born of an illegitimate daughter of an earl, had an illegitimate royal son, Henry de Valois (1551–86), by King Henri II of France.[79] *Le Batard d'Angoulême*, as her son was known, was abbot of Chaise-Dieu from around the age of eleven. Legitimated and made duke of Angoulême, 'Harry' became a military commander, Grand Prior of France, Governor of Provence and Admiral of the Levantine Sea before being killed in a duel in his mid-thirties.

None of James's legitimate daughters survived infancy. His two surviving illegitimate daughters who married in his lifetime were given heirs to earldoms as their husbands. Had he lived, it is likely that Janet too would have been matched with a prospective earl. Nonethelesss, her status as a sister of James V (who had no surviving legitimate siblings) helped to ensure she enjoyed special privileges in respect of his heir, which in turn resulted in her becoming the mother of a child believed to be the French king's favourite bastard.

76 Dowden, *Bishops*, 374–5; D. Shaw, 'Gordon, Alexander (c. 1516–1575), Bishop of Galloway', *ODNB*, 22 March 2019.

77 *SP*, i, 22.

78 *Analecta Scotica: Collections Illustrative of the Civil, Ecclesiastical and Literary History of Scotland*, ed. J. Maidment (Edinburgh, 1834–7), ii, 50–2; *RMS*, iii, no. 1119.

79 *The Warrender Papers*, ed. A. Cameron (STS, 1931–2), i, 85–6; *Calendar of the State Papers Relating to Scotland and Mary Queen of Scots*, ed. J. Bain and others (Edinburgh, 1898–1969), i, no. 889; *SP*, viii, 540.

Sisters

Royal mistresses and their families could usually expect valuable preferment or protection from the king and this royal patronage helped to ensure there were relatively few adverse reactions to daughters having affairs with royal figures.[80] But although many Scottish kings and their male kin fathered illegitimate children with apparent impunity, not every male relative of a royal mistress was prepared to accept such conduct. The circumstances surrounding the birth of Alexander Bruce, illegitimate son of Robert I's brother Edward, were held by Barbour, writing around 1375, to be behind a notorious incident on the eve of Bannockburn when David of Strathbogie, earl of Atholl and nephew of Robert I, defected to the English.[81] Atholl was also descended from an illegitimate daughter of King John of England and recognised by the English royal family as a kinsman, and so had loyalties to both crowns, and landed interests in both countries.[82] His murder of Sir William Airth and his sacking of the Scottish army's stores, which supplies he then provided to the English, was said to have been a response to the fact that Edward Bruce had impregnated Atholl's sister Isabel and refused to marry her.[83]

That Isabel's illegitimate pregnancy would cause her brother to exact revenge in this way has been questioned on the grounds that Barbour's work is a romance, so inclined to portray the earl's actions as a chivalric response to a wronged sister, and that the earl was actually motivated by being excluded from taking a commanding role in the battle and by an unwillingness, also demonstrated in other contexts, to take up arms against a fellow Plantagenet.[84] In arguing against Isabel's illegitimate pregnancy being of any great significance, Ross claims that Isabel's decision to remain in Scotland is evidence that she was not 'particularly disconcerted' by her situation.[85] This latter point implies that if she had been unhappy about her predicament she could have voted with her feet, but in reality this would have meant abandoning her son. Alexander would have been regarded as the property of the Scottish royal house, and neither Edward nor any other member of it would have permitted him to be

80 'There seems no doubt that the Earl of Angus owed much of his advancement, possibly even his Chancellorship, to his Boyd niece's long association with the king'; '[James IV's] long-standing affair with Marion [Boyd] probably served as protection for her Boyd kinsmen and their Ayrshire friends…'. Macdougall, *James IV*, 98, 107. See also *Cal. State Papers (Spain)*, i, no. 210 (in which the Spanish ambassador claims that James IV's womanising was encouraged by men who made their female kin available to him in the hope of political advantage).

81 J. Barbour, *The Bruce*, ed. A. A. M. Duncan (Edinburgh, 1997), 504–7.

82 A. Ross, 'Men for All Seasons? The Strathbogie Earls of Atholl and the Wars of Independence, c. 1290–1335', *Northern Scotland* 20 (2000), 2–6.

83 Barbour has it that Isabel of Atholl was married to Edward, who repudiated her in favour of another woman, but Edward and Isabel did not marry.

84 Ross, 'Men for All Seasons?', 12–13, 17, 20.

85 Ibid., 17.

removed to England, especially given the state of Anglo-Scottish relations at the time. The fact that he was illegitimate did not make him worthless to his father or his paternal kin, and it is difficult to come to any judgement about Isabel's thoughts on the matter based on her continuing residence in the same place as her child.

Barbour may indeed have been writing according to the conventions of chivalric romance literature, but that does not mean that we should discount his version of these events as pure fiction. Some circumstantial evidence supporting the view that Isabel's pregnancy caused real outrage in her family is offered by Duncan. He says that in 1314–15 Henry, bishop of Aberdeen, in some obscure way offended the king, resulting in the seizure of his temporalities, which were restored to him soon after the death of Edward Bruce.[86] Duncan conjectures that Henry had sided with the Atholls and censured Edward, who had reacted strongly against the cleric; because of this it was only once Edward died that Henry was able to regain his possessions. It is quite possible that Atholl had more than one reason for his defection, and to allow that he was responding to unfavourable treatment by Robert I, and his sense of kinship with the English throne, does not exclude the strong likelihood that his sister's illegitimate pregnancy was a very important, and perhaps a deciding, factor. If anything, these other motives strengthen the argument for the pregnancy being the grounds for his actions, as the first two speak to a very well-developed sense of honour and pride in his personal and family reputation. The same sense of honour and pride is completely compatible with a reaction of outraged affront to his sister's rejection by her erstwhile suitor and the damage done to her marriage prospects (she seems never to have married). That reputational injury caused by reneging on a promise to marry a near kinswoman might provoke defection to the enemy, even without the woman concerned being deflowered and impregnated, is demonstrated by the case of George, ninth earl of Dunbar or of March. He defected to the English in 1400 when his daughter Elizabeth was repudiated by David, duke of Rothesay, the heir to the throne.[87]

It was usual for noble men to be the guardians of the chastity of their unmarried female kin, since a noble woman's virginity was highly important to her value as a bride. The difference between Edward Bruce and at least some other royal men who had mistresses seems to be that Edward had failed to obtain Atholl's acquiescence in the affair. The case of Isabel of Atholl highlights the role of male kin of royal mistresses: if it was their right to determine who

86 *RRS*, v, 416–17.

87 A. J. Macdonald, 'Kings of the Wild Frontier? The Earls of Dunbar or March, c. 1070–1435', in Boardman and Ross, *Exercise of Power*, 158. Macdonald highlights the 'injured pride' and 'outrage' evident in Dunbar's letter to Henry IV regarding the matter. Elizabeth did not marry again but entered a nunnery. See also English reaction to the collapse of plans for the marriage of the future James IV and Cecilia, daughter of Edward IV, below, p. 143; and James III's treatment of William Crichton at pp. 144–5.

their daughters or sisters should marry, it was equally their right to permit or deny sexual liaisons that would affect not only the marriageability of the women in question, but also the status and prosperity of her kin. Whether Edward had been refused Isabel but proceeded anyway, or whether he had never sought permission but thought the earl would accept the situation, or could be bought off if he did object, it was a serious miscalculation on his part. Atholl's defection on the eve of Bannockburn was an event of major political significance. It was enormously embarrassing for Robert I that no less a figure than the constable of Scotland should abandon the cause hours before a crucial battle, and the message it sent – that Robert could not count on the loyalty of his upper nobility – had the potential to be highly destabilising.[88] Atholl's seizure of the Scottish host's supplies was also an act which could have had grave consequences for the Scots. In November 1314 he became the first Scottish earl since the twelfth century to be forfeited. Illegitimacy in this instance, in which a well-born woman bore an illegitimate child, had political ramifications for Scotland as well as personal and political consequences for Atholl's family.

The consequences of Isabel of Atholl's pregnancy illustrate attitudes to female virginity and sexual conduct. The Church held that both men and women should be chaste, engaging in sexual intercourse only in marriage, and even then within limits: various prohibitions applied to the timing of sexual encounters (during pregnancy, Lent, on Sundays, and so on) and also to their frequency and purpose (spouses should not be too enamoured of the act and should perform it primarily for the sake of procreation, though it was also regarded as important to prevent sexual sin outside the marriage and to strengthen the marital bond).[89] In noble society, unmarried women were expected to be virgins when they were given in marriage and once married to be faithful to their husbands, strictures that were not applied to men with nearly the same vigour.[90] For noble daughters, virginity composed a large element of their value on the marriage market.[91] 'Deflowering' was a canonical offence, attracting a fine or requiring the offender to compensate his victim, that

88 M. Brown, *Bannockburn: The Scottish Wars and the British Isles, 1307–1323* (Edinburgh, 2008), 124.

89 P. Payer, *The Bridling of Desire: Ideas of Sex in the Later Middle Ages* (Toronto, 1993), 84–131.

90 There is also Scottish evidence that some husbands or families tried to ensure that a widow did not remarry or live with another man. Sanctions included loss of her home, income and/or children. *Protocol Book of James Young*, nos 253, 778, 807.

91 J. H. Arnold, *Belief and Unbelief in Medieval Europe* (London, 2005), 159; J. A. Brundage, 'Carnal Delight: Canonistic Theories of Sexuality', in S. Kuttner and K. Pennington, ed., *Proceedings of the Fifth International Congress of Medieval Canon Law* (Vatican City, 1980), 375.

reflected the social and economic value of virginity.[92] Male promiscuity before marriage and infidelity afterwards was generally tolerated, providing men did not transgress in ways that caused offence to their male peers. Noble women did not always behave chastely, but the consequences for their reputation tended to be more severe than they were for men. The high-born mother of an illegitimate child, whether she was unmarried or whether she had conceived the child in adultery, was by definition a woman who had violated established norms of behaviour.[93] Lack of chastity in women undermined confidence in the paternity of her children. A woman who failed to keep herself pure before marriage had shown herself to be unable to control her sexual appetite and could not be trusted to be faithful to her husband. Sexually incontinent women created an unacceptable risk of a family's patrimony ending up in the hands of a false heir and their behaviour could be a source of humiliation or offence to their near male kin.

In royal circles, the stakes were even higher as the patrimony in question was more exalted. The sexual conduct of queens and princesses was expected to be exemplary. The paucity of known examples of royal women in medieval Scotland having illegitimate children, compared to that of their male counterparts, is an indication of how much more unacceptable it was for royal women to participate in extramarital sexual relationships. James III's sister, Margaret Stewart (ca. 1460–ca. 1503), is a rare example of a Scottish royal who was the mother of an illegitimate child (Table 13).

An infant in 1460 when her father James II died, Margaret spent most of her childhood in the Cistercian convent at Haddington.[94] In the mid-1470s the amount spent on her dresses and accessories indicate that she was the subject of dynastic marriage considerations, required to be presented and displayed as a potential royal bride.[95] She made occasional visits to court before joining it properly in 1477 or 1478.[96] At the end of 1478 James III and Edward IV agreed Margaret should marry Edward's brother-in-law, Anthony Wydeville, the second earl Rivers.[97] The match was one sought by James, who was eager to foster closer links with the English crown: his own son and heir, James, was

92 C. Donahue Jr, *Law, Marriage and Society in the Middle Ages: Arguments About Marriage in Five Courts* (Cambridge, 2007), contains instances (none Scottish) too numerous to list, including at 349, 351–4, 466–7, 469–72, 477–9, 481–2; K. Salonen, 'Nine Marriage Disputes in the Consistorial Court of Freising in the Late Middle Ages', in M. Korpiola, ed., *Regional Variations in Matrimonial Law and Custom in Europe 1150–1600* (Leiden, 2011), 190–2, 194–6.

93 For example, petitions for marriage dispensations from couples who had children sometimes asked for the dispensation to be granted 'that [the mother of the children] may not remain defamed'. *CSSR*, ii, 181–2, 213–14.

94 *TA*, i, cclxxxv–vi; *ER*, vii, 583; viii, 310.

95 *TA*, i, 72–4 (expenditure on clothing for Margaret in 1473–4 of £138 13s 3d).

96 *TA*, i, cclxxxvi–vii; *ER*, viii, 541–2.

97 *Foedera*, xii, 162, 171–2.

betrothed to Edward's daughter Cecilia. A contract for the Rivers/Margaret marriage was drawn up by the end of the year and the details confirmed in January 1479, when a safe-conduct for her travel to England was issued.[98] She was to make the journey by 16 May 1479; when she failed to do so, a second safe-conduct was issued in August that year.[99] The marriage was to take place at Nottingham in October 1479, with Edward in attendance.

Margaret's second safe-conduct expired on 1 November 1479, unused.[100] It is possible, though uncertain, that her pregnancy by William, third Lord Crichton, had been discovered by this point. The collapse of diplomatic relations between James and Edward at around this time, the principal manifestation of which was Edward IV's threat to wage war against Scotland unless various unreasonable demands – including that James III's heir was handed over to him and Berwick returned to the English – were met, has been linked by some Scottish historians to Margaret's pregnancy.[101] Nicholson says that it was 'doubtless' around late November 1479 that Margaret's condition was discovered, and that not long afterwards James was 'probably… smarting under Edward's recriminations over the Lady Margaret'.[102] Croft Dickinson notes that James's inability to fulfil the agreement that Margaret should marry Rivers, because 'she took a Scottish lover and became pregnant' contributed to the breakdown of relations with England.[103] Grant makes a related point (though he does not claim Margaret's pregnancy was a factor), arguing that by 1480 it was not only Edward who had lost patience with the Scots, but also the Wydevilles, since the Scots were reneging on earl Rivers's royal marriage.[104]

If this was in fact the cause of Edward's hostility, the ultimatum threatening invasion makes no mention of it.[105] The insult to the English royal house was not negligible, but hardly justified the expense and trouble of a war. It may just possibly have served as a pretext for an invasion that was sought for

98 *CDS*, iv, 295; N. Macdougall, *James III* (Edinburgh, 2009), 143–4.

99 *Rot. Scot.*, ii, 457.

100 Ibid.; MacDougall, *James III*, 172.

101 *CDS*, iv, 412–14. The original of this document has been checked and corresponds to the wording provided by Bain. See also Nicholson, *Later Middle Ages*, 489–90; Macdougall, *James III*, 172, 174.

102 Nicholson, *Later Middle Ages*, 489–90. He is not the earliest Scottish historian to link the collapse of the marriage plans, if not the declaration of war, to Margaret's pregnancy. George Burnett in *ER*, viii (published in 1885) remarked that the espousals were 'very probably' broken off because of her pregnancy and 'rumours to the prejudice of the princess reaching England' (p. lxiii); Thomas Dickson, writing in 1877, said that the proposed marriage of Margaret and Rivers 'came to nothing, possibly in consequence of rumours getting abroad unfavourable to the character of the princess'. *TA*, i, cclxxxvii.

103 W. Croft Dickinson, *Scotland from the Earliest Times to 1603*, 3rd edn., ed. A. A. M. Duncan (Oxford, 1977), 238–9.

104 A. Grant, 'Richard III and Scotland', in A. J. Pollard, ed., *The North of England in the Age of Richard III* (Stroud, 1996), 121.

105 *CDS*, iv, 412–14; Macdougall, *James III*, 174.

other reasons, but if this was the case then it would surely have been stated as a grievance: it could not have been used as a pretext for war without being declared as a genuine offence against the English crown. It is true, however, that James did not seek to use Margaret for a marriage alliance after 1479. Her absence from the marriage market after the cessation of hostilities is significant, and it seems certain that her daughter, also Margaret, was born between 1479 and 1484. If the princess had not been pregnant or mother of an illegitimate child at the end of the conflict, James would very likely have wished to use her for a marriage with a member of the English royal affinity.[106] No match was then possible with Rivers, who died in 1483. Margaret's intended groom had evidently given up on the proposed marriage quite quickly; the wedding not having materialised in 1479, he married ca. 1480 Mary Lewis, a descendant of John of Gaunt and Katherine Swynford.[107]

While a number of Scottish historians of the period consider Margaret's pregnancy significant enough to mention as possibly being of relevance, even crucial relevance, alongside other factors that are generally agreed to have played a part, English historians do not mention it at all.[108] A partial exception may be made for Cora Scofield, who in her 1923 work claims that the proposed marriage between Margaret and Rivers was abandoned after Edward withdrew Cecilia from her betrothal to the Scottish prince and demanded the return of the sums he had paid towards her dowry.[109] Scofield adds darkly that, 'there were other good reasons' why it could not proceed: 'Margaret's character, it had now been learned, was by no means above reproach'.[110] A footnote refers readers to an *Exchequer Rolls* volume wherein Margaret's illegitimate pregnancy is noted, but Scofield does not mention it directly herself.[111] This coy, moralistic approach is common to historiography of Scofield's era when it comes to Margaret: the princess is elsewhere described as having 'a reputation

[106] James's response to Edward IV's ultimatum was highly conciliatory; its tone suggests he hoped to maintain cordial relations with the English king. *CDS*, iv, 414. Tanner highlights James's 'dogged pursuit of alliance after alliance with England come rain or shine', in the 1470s and 1480s. R. Tanner, 'James III (1460–1488)', in Brown and Tanner, *Scottish Kingship*, 222.

[107] M. Hicks, 'Woodville, Anthony, Second Earl Rivers (*c.* 1440–1483)', *ODNB*, 6 November 2018. Rivers had no legitimate children and his only surviving issue was an illegitimate daughter, Margaret.

[108] C. Ross, *Edward IV* (London, 1974), 278; M. Hicks, *Edward IV* (London, 2004), 145–6 (and Hicks's *ODNB* entry for Anthony Wydeville cites 'differences with Scotland' as the reason the marriage did not go ahead); K. Dockray, *Edward IV: A Sourcebook* (Stroud, 1999), 111–12; K. Dockray, *Richard III: a Source Book* (Stroud, 1997), 31; A. J. Pollard, *Late Medieval England 1399–1509* (New York, 2000), 316–18.

[109] C. L. Scofield, *The Life and Reign of Edward IV* (London, 1923), ii, 353. Scofield erroneously dates the resiling from the marriage contract to 1482, and seems to think the second safe-conduct of 1479 actually belonged to 1482, though elsewhere (ii, 251) she notes that it belonged to 1479 and was wrongly placed under 1482.

[110] Scofield, *Edward IV*, 353.

[111] The reference is to *ER*, viii, lxii–iii.

that was more than loose', and a character 'which, if we may trust Buchanan, was not stainless'.[112]

In looking at this division between Scottish and English historiographical treatments of the events of 1479–80, it is worth noting that the Crowland chronicler, giving a contemporary English view, implicates the non-fulfilment of the marriage contract between Cecilia and the future James IV in the causes for war: he accuses Louis XI of France of interfering in Anglo-Scottish relations, inducing the Scots not just to break the truce, but 'to spurn the offer of our Cecily in marriage'.[113] He claims that it was a direct result of these offences that Edward IV 'proclaimed a terrible and destructive war against the Scots'.[114] Cecilia and her fiancé were both under the canonical age of marriage in 1480 and it was not very unusual for marriage agreements concerning young children to be revoked as the political fortunes of their families changed, but evidently the chronicler felt that claiming James had reneged on the agreement was an effective way of declaring that the Scots had brought the war on themselves. He was exaggerating, but the one-sided breach, or threatened breach, of any marriage contract was indeed seen as an insult and a source of grievance. It is therefore understandable that Scottish historians have given some consideration to the possibility that the breakdown of the other marriage agreement, between Anthony Wydeville and Margaret Stewart, was a factor in Edward's 'well-orchestrated diplomatic fury'.[115]

Margaret's illegitimate pregnancy, whenever it occurred (if not 1479, then possibly in 1482, when James was in captivity), was a flagrant breach of protocol for a princess and a public humiliation for James III. Margaret's condition usurped his right to arrange the marriage of his sister and denied him the political benefits of such a marriage, and demonstrated his inability to exert any control at all over the behaviour of his nearest female kin. The king was not only unable to win the confidence of the Scottish nobility, he was also incapable of ensuring members of his own family conducted themselves in ways that supported, rather than worked against, him.[116] James had courted unpopularity by providing very generous royal patronage to illegitimates such as Andrew, lord Avondale, and William Scheves, at the expense of those who felt they had a better claim to the king's favour, and had further politicised

[112] *SP*, iii (1906), 66; *TA*, i (1877), cclxxxvii. The mention of Buchanan is a reference to the sixteenth-century historian's rather startling claim that Margaret Stewart had had an incestuous sexual relationship with her brother James III. G. Buchanan, *The History of Scotland*, transl. J. Aikman (Edinburgh and Glasgow, 1827–9), ii, 213. He does not suggest her daughter was James's.

[113] N. Pronay and J. Cox, *The Crowland Chronicle Continuations, 1459–1486* (London, 1986), 147.

[114] Ibid., 147.

[115] Macdougall, *James III*, 172.

[116] Tanner, 'James III', 226–8; L. O. Fradenburg, *City, Marriage, Tournament: Arts of Rule in Late Medieval Scotland* (Madison, WI, 1991), 35–6.

bastardy by making it treasonous for anyone other than himself to issue secular legitimations.[117] Now his sister's pregnancy brought illegitimacy into political life in a way he did not anticipate and could not control.

The effects of Margaret's illegitimate pregnancy can be traced in her life and in the life of Crichton. In the early 1480s Crichton allied himself to the duke of Albany in rebellion against the crown and was among the core conspirators who sought to replace James III on the throne with his brother. Their efforts failed, and in March 1483 an indenture was drawn up between James and Albany, among the provisions of which was that Crichton be banished from Scotland and England for three years.[118] Only Crichton, James Stewart, earl of Buchan, and James Liddale of Halkerston were condemned to exile for their parts in the Albany rebellion. Each had played a significant part in it, but Crichton's role was in some ways less prominent than the others. Buchan was among those who had arrested and imprisoned James III in July 1482 and had attempted to repeat the deed with his brother Albany in January 1483, but Crichton was not a participant in either event.[119] Liddale was Albany's steward and right-hand man, among the handful of rebels who were with him in the days immediately before the abortive coup of 2 January 1483. Again, Crichton was not among them, though he was with the duke at Dunbar Castle the following month.[120] Crichton, along with Liddale and Buchan, had joined Albany in entering into bonds of allegiance with Edward IV – but then so had Archibald, earl of Angus and Andrew, lord Gray, neither of whom was banished. The inclusion of Crichton among those to be exiled for their participation in the rebellion does not appear to be wholly explicable except, as Macdougall suggests, as an act of revenge by James for his sister's pregnancy.[121] Later charged with treasonable fortifying of Crichton Castle against the king, Crichton was forfeited in 1484, as were his two brothers. James III's death in 1488 did not result in the restoration of his lands and title, prompting him to join the rebels against James IV in

[117] See pp. 186–7.

[118] *APS*, xii, 31–3.

[119] Macdougall, *James III*, 196–7, 223. Buchan was the father of Agnes (sometimes given as Isobel) Stewart, who would later become the mistress of James IV and mother of the king's illegitimate daughter Janet. The earl was married to Margaret Ogilvy, daughter and heir of Sir Alexander Ogilvy of Auchterhouse, hereditary sheriff of Angus, but had several children in a relationship with a Margaret Murray. In February 1489 one of these children, James, who became the ancestor of the earls of Traquair, received a royal legitimation from James IV. He was later given a remainder in a tailzie charter to his legitimate brother, in which James is described as 'son of the late James Stewart earl of Buchan with Margaret Murray and made lawful by the king'. *RSS*, i, no. 340.

[120] Macdougall, *James III*, 220. Liddale would be executed in 1485.

[121] Ibid., 231. Macdougall holds (p. 172) that Margaret's pregnancy provoked Edward's ultimatum to James, but, even if this was not the case, the pregnancy would still have given James plenty of reason to treat Crichton more punitively than he did other conspirators.

1489.[122] In July of that year he was denounced, along with a handful of others, and a reward offered for his capture.[123] He died sometime before October 1493, the only one of the 1489 rebels not to have had his forfeiture cancelled.[124]

Margaret Stewart, like Isabel of Atholl, never married, instead retiring around 1490 to the Cistercian nunnery at Elcho.[125] Crown payments made to her there continued until February 1502–03, when she moved to Hamilton, perhaps living with her nephew James, second Lord Hamilton.[126] She seems to have died there, perhaps in 1503, as there are no records of payments after that year. The arrival of her daughter appears to have been the defining event of her life. Her illegitimate pregnancy curtailed any chance of the right kind of marriage: the few fragmentary references to her in the royal accounts provide our only knowledge of her.[127]

In the early years of the twelfth century, a Scottish king married the illegitimate daughter of his English counterpart. In the fifteenth century, the suggested pairing of a Scottish king with an illegitimate daughter of the king of Spain was considered a possible insult. Attitudes to illegitimacy had changed, but the principle that royal daughters, illegitimate or not, were of value in furthering the political aims of their fathers through marriage, had not. Illegitimate daughters of Scottish kings were given in marriage to families with which the king wished to forge or cement alliances, or to men whom he wished to reward for service. None married into another royal family, as some legitimate daughters of Scotland did, but their husbands were drawn from the nobility rather than from lower ranks in society.

The one example we have of a royal woman having an illegitimate child indicates the situation of royal women differed from that of their male counterparts. In the late fifteenth century, Margaret Stewart's marriage prospects were effectively ruined by her extramarital pregnancy, while her nephew, James IV, fathered a number of illegitimate children without this having any effect on the plans, later realised, to marry him to the eldest daughter of the English king. Although there was no comparable censure of kings, royal sons and brothers, or other elite men who fathered illegitimate offspring, the example of Edward Bruce and Isabel of Atholl suggests that a royal male would have had to negotiate a 'price' with the male guardian of a well-born mistress, to ensure the affair was not politically disruptive. In the case of kings, there may have been a tacit understanding that the family would be advantaged,

[122] N. Macdougall, *James IV* (Edinburgh, 1989), 66.

[123] *APS*, 1489/7/13; Macdougall, *James IV*, 68.

[124] Ibid., 66, 165.

[125] *ER*, x, 202, 256, 315, 449, 483.

[126] *TA*, i, cclxxxix.

[127] Lesley (himself illegitimate) says only that '[she] disseased unmaried', while Boece claims that she married Crichton, 'and of her come litill successioun worthy to have memory'. J. Lesley, *The History of Scotland from the Death of King James I in the Year 1486 to the Year 1561* (Bannatyne Club, 1830), 32; Boece, *History and Chronicles*, ii, 267.

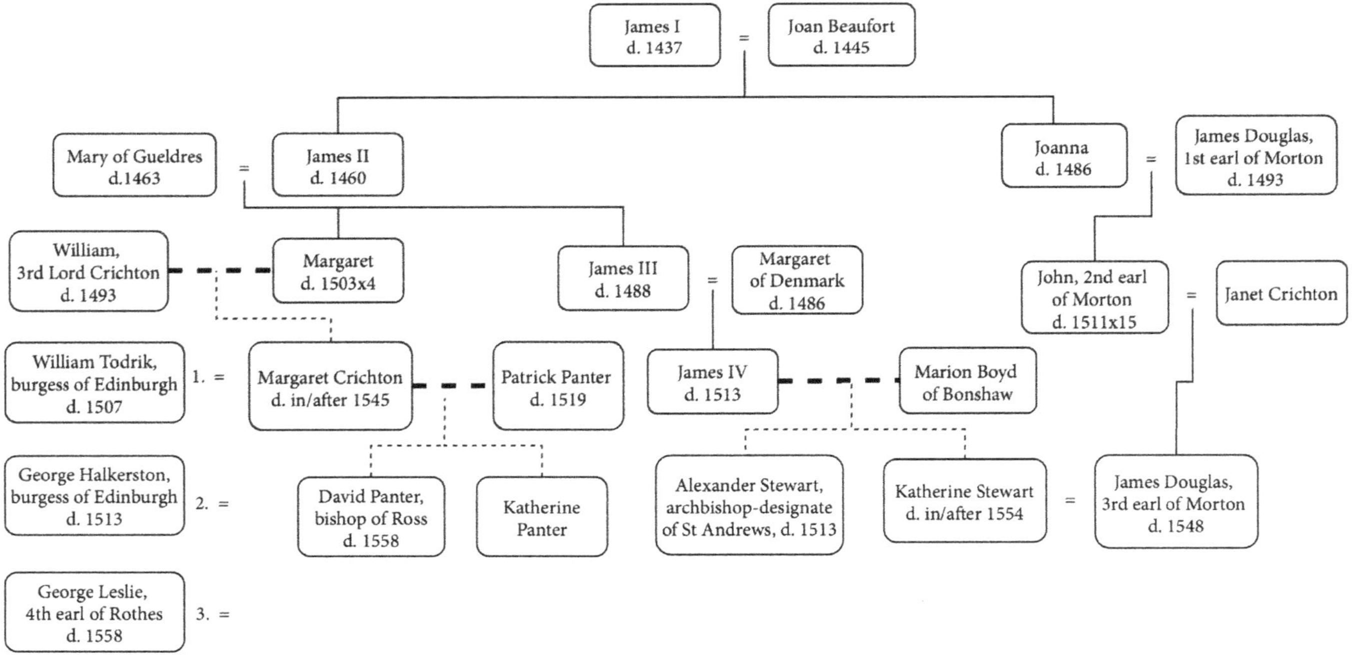

Margaret's marriage to Leslie was annulled on grounds of consanguinity. Their four children were deemed legitimate on the claim that one or both parties to the marriage was or were ignorant of the impediment.

Patrick Panter was secretary to James IV and tutor to his illegitimate sons, Alexander and James.
His children with Margaret Crichton, Katherine and David, obtained royal letters of legitimation in 1513 from James IV, their mother's first cousin.

Table 13. Margaret Crichton and the Stewarts

materially or reputationally or both, by their association with him. That the sexual conduct of elite women reflected on the honour of their male guardians applied equally to royal households as to those of earls and lords. Margaret Stewart's was not the only reputation affected by her pregnancy: her brother, James III (their father had died long before) was exposed as a king unable to rule his own family.

The picture this paints of women's roles and behaviours is not the whole story: clearly, some women engaged in non-marital sexual relationships without this occasioning significant disruption to the social order. The widowed Countess of Angus, who had an illegitimate son with her sister-in-law's husband, and was an important political player in her own right, appears to have been largely indifferent to conventions concerning female sexual conduct.[128] She was not a lone case. Perhaps the most prolific source we have for the non-marital sexual activity of women is papal records of dispensations given to illegitimate clergy, each of which provides some scant information about the supplicant's parents. Some of those seeking dispensation from defect of birth say they are of noble birth on both sides. The mothers, noble or otherwise, are often single, sometimes married, and, very occasionally, nuns. The experience of their offspring, the illegitimate men and women in the medieval Scottish Church, tells us something of ecclesiastical ideology concerning illegitimacy, and what being illegitimate meant in practical terms for those in religious life.

[128] See p. 182 and Table 16.

6

Church careers and sacrilegious bastards

Quha suld me wyte alsua, sen I na ma
Change my birth, nor put my weird away?[1]

From the eleventh century, illegitimacy began to be seen as an 'irregularity' in respect of holy orders, and during the twelfth it became an impediment to ordination and to the exercise of sacred ministries.[2] Irregularities to ecclesiastical orders fell into two categories: those 'by delict' debarred the subject from ordination because of a personal fault, such as commission of a crime, making the person unworthy to be ordained, while those excluded 'by defect' may have committed no wrong but were in a condition held to be incongruous with the exercise of the sacred ministry. Illegitimacy – *defectus natalium* ('defect of birth') – was in this latter category. Irregularities of either kind could be remedied by means of a dispensation issued by a competent authority, but these were always discretionary. Illegitimates embarking on a clerical career were required to obtain a dispensation *de* (or *ex*) *defectu natalium* prior to ordination, while those who were ordained and sought to hold multiple benefices or to progress to a higher office in the Church needed a *de uberiori* ('more abundant') dispensation permitting this. The third type of dispensation specifically for illegitimates was the *ubi pater* ('where the father is'), which enabled an illegitimate person to minister in the same clerical institution as their parent had served or was serving. The majority of illegitimate people in monastic life, rather than in the secular clergy, had no need of a dispensation, which was required only if a monk or a nun sought a position of authority in the convent.[3]

1 *King Alexander*, lines 2129–30.

2 Genestal, *Histoire de la Légitimation*, 10–30.

3 Some orders, such as the Dominicans, refused entry to illegitimate women, though this was technically a breach of canon law. J. R. McDonald, 'The Papal Penitentiary and Ecclesiastical Careers: the Requests of Scottish Clergy in the Registers of the *Sacra Apostolica Penitenzieria*, 1449–1542' (unpublished PhD thesis, University of Aberdeen, 2005), 48; L. Schmugge, 'Female Petitioners in the Papal Penitentiary', *Gender and History* 12 (2000), 687. Women refused entry to an order sometimes obtained dispensations

The requirement for illegitimates seeking a Church career to be dispensed *ex defectu natalium* seems not to have been known in the early Church. In 845–6 the Council of Meaux-Paris denied all illegitimates the right to hold Church offices, but this was a provincial synod and its canons were not binding on the whole Church.[4] The purity of the ordained clergy may have been the Church's primary concern, but part of the impetus for the later creation of *defectus natalium* came from a desire to stem the tide of priests' offspring claiming rights of inheritance over clerical offices or property.[5] As the Church moved from regarding marriage as unsuitable for those administering the eucharist and other sacraments, to making it legally incompatible with ordination, the position of clerical offspring altered.[6]

Church reforms beginning in the tenth century, and gathering pace in the eleventh and twelfth, sought to draw a much sharper distinction between the sphere of the Church and that of the lay world. Sacerdotal celibacy was deemed essential to ensure bodily purity, deemed a vital component of spiritual authority, and signified the Church's distinctiveness, setting its personnel apart from the worldly concerns which necessarily arose from the bonds and obligations surrounding marriage and children. In this schema, clerical offspring were an aberration. Provincial and ecumenical Councils alike expressed concern about *filii presbyterorum*. The Council of Bourges in 1031 drew a parallel between illegitimates and sons of priests. It stated that the sons of higher clerics (subdeacons and above) could not be raised to the priesthood

overturning their rejection. Schmugge, 'Female Petitioners', 688. Entering monastic life acted as an automatic dispensation from illegitimacy according to canon law, but the effects of this were evidently very limited as formal dispensation was still required for any promoted office. However, there seems to have been room for confusion on this front, since there is at least one example of a monk mistakenly believing his regular status to have acted as a dispensation for promotion. *CPL*, xiv, 186 (diocese of Clogher, Ireland, in 1485).

4 C. 64 of the Council of Meaux-Paris. *Die Konzilien der Karolingischen Teilreiche 843–859*, ed. W. Hartmann (Hannover, 1984), 115.

5 In 1139, the Church abolished claims to Church office made on hereditary grounds, at the same time as it outlawed sexual activity by those in holy orders. Second Lateran Council, cc. 6–8, 16. Tanner, *Decrees*, i, 198, 201. See also Wertheimer, 'Children of Disorder', 382–407.

6 From at least the fourth century, the Church held that those administering the eucharist and other sacraments should refrain from sexual activity for reasons of purity. This did not mean they could not be married, only that if married, they ought to practise continence. A renewed and strengthened emphasis on bodily purity, and a concomitant prohibition on contact with women, emerged from the so-called Gregorian Reform, beginning rather before Pope Gregory VII's papacy (1073–85) and continuing throughout the twelfth century. There is a wealth of scholarship on the history of clerical celibacy: see, for example, H. Parish, *Clerical Celibacy in the West: c. 1100–1700* (Aldershot, 2010), and M. Frassetto, ed., *Medieval Purity and Piety. Essays on Medieval Clerical Celibacy and Religious Reform* (New York, 1998).

themselves, and though it did not proclaim such sons illegitimate, it found that they were on a par, legally speaking, with people born illegitimate, and thus debarred from both parental inheritance and acting as a witness.[7] The 1089 Council of Melfi decreed that the offspring of priests should be removed from ministries of the sacred altar, unless living in monasteries or canonries. This canon entered Church law through its inclusion among the decrees of the Second Lateran Council (1139).[8] Gratian's *Decretum* (ca. 1140) includes this canon, but he added that it should be understood as applying only to those offspring who copied their fathers' lack of sexual continence, whereas those who lived honourably and in accordance with the law should be able to hold even high offices in the Church.[9] This came to be applied as a general rule to most illegitimates, not just the offspring of clergy, and remained a test of suitability throughout the middle ages. Innocent III ruled in 1206 that illegitimate sons could be dispensed for holy orders providing they had not shown themselves to be following in their fathers' immoral footsteps, and dispensations sometimes sounded a cautionary note in this regard.[10] A typical example is the papal dispensation of 1375 permitting Thomas Stewart, illegitimate son of Robert II, to hold clerical office, 'if the said Thomas should otherwise be suitable, not an imitator of his father's incontinence, but of good life and conduct'.[11]

Gratian's remarks notwithstanding, the Third Lateran Council (1179) stipulated that bishops must be born in lawful wedlock.[12] Two dispensations issued by Pope Alexander III (1159–81), permitting illegitimates of sufficiently good character to hold sees, made it clear that each was a special case and should not be considered a precedent.[13] Some regions of Christendom took

7 Council of Bourges, c.8. *Mansi*, xix, col. 504. The Ninth Council of Toledo in 655, another provincial synod, imposed a penalty on sexually incontinent priests in the ranks of subdeacons to bishops (c. 10): their offspring were to be slaves of the Church. Mansi, x, col. 29.

8 Second Lateran Council, c. 21. Tanner, *Decrees*, i, 202.

9 '*Sed hoc intelligendum est de illis, qui paterne incontinentie imitatores fuerint. Verum si morum honestas eos commendabiles fecerit, exemplis et auctoritate non solum sacerdotes, sed etiam summi sacerdotes fieri possunt.*' Gratian, D. 56. c.1, d.c.p.1.

10 Gratian, 3 Comp. 1.8.4 (= X 1.9.10) § 6; P. D. Clarke, 'Innocent III, Canon Law and the Punishment of the Guiltless', in Moore, *Pope Innocent III*, 279–80. Clarke points out that Innocent III had no objection in principle to offspring being penalised for their parents' offences and was more punitive in this regard than some other popes, as evidenced by his much greater willingness to impose blanket penalties on the descendants of heretics and of those who resisted ecclesiastical authority.

11 '*... si dictus Thomas alias sit ydoneus, nec sit paterne incontinentie imitator, sed bone conversationis ac vite ...*'. Theiner, *Vet. Mon.*, no. 709.

12 Third Lateran Council, c. 3. Tanner, *Decrees*, i, 212. The other criteria were that a bishop should be aged at least thirty, and should be able to show by his life and education that he was worthy of the office.

13 *Audito laudabili* and *Dignum est*, discussed by C. Duggan and A. Duggan, 'Ralph de Diceto, Henry II and Becket with an Appendix on Decretal Letters', in B. Tierney and P.

this injunction more seriously than others. No medieval bishops of Norway are known to have been illegitimate, whereas numerous Scottish bishops certainly were.[14]

In principle, the ease with which illegitimate people could obtain dispensations for Church careers stood in inverse proportion to the gravity of the sexual offence that had resulted in their birth. Explaining this, Aquinas pointed out that 'a man's good name is bedimmed by sinful origin' and dispensations were therefore 'the more difficult to obtain, according as their origin is the more discreditable'.[15] In consequence, illegitimates seeking dispensations for careers in the Church were required to provide details of their parents' status so that judgement could be made as to the granting of the dispensation. Various permutations of status are found in the records, from the relatively innocuous 'an unmarried man and an unmarried woman' – though this term sometimes concealed that the father was actually a cleric – to the more disgraceful, such as 'a married man and a nun'.[16] Although the medieval Church's requirement of illegitimates that they obtain dispensations to hold any office that included cure of souls or authority over others was never relaxed, the practice of granting dispensations for illegitimacy apparently became routine.[17] That said, popes retained the right to refuse requests or to restrict the careers of certain categories of illegitimate. In 1245, Pope Innocent IV allowed that the monks of Dunfermline may have as their abbot a brother who was of illegitimate birth, 'provided that he may not be from adultery or incest'.[18]

The question of who – bishops, archbishops or the pope – had the right to dispense illegitimates for clerical careers was initially a contested one, and not resolved until 1200, when Pope Innocent III enacted that the right to dispense for bastardy belonged exclusively to the pope.[19] The majority of dispensations were sought by means of supplications to the pope, but papal legates, nuncios and senior Churchmen were sometimes empowered to provide dispensations

Linehan, ed., *Authority and Power: Studies on Medieval Law and Government Presented to Walter Ullman on his Seventieth Birthday* (Cambridge, 1980), 76–7, 80; C. Duggan, *Decretals and the Creation of 'New Law' in the Twelfth Century: Judges, Judgements, Equity and Law* (Aldershot, 1998), 79.

14 This is discussed further below.

15 Aquinas, *Summa Theologica*, Supplement, Q. 39 art.5.

16 McGurk, *Letters of Benedict XIII*, 325–6.

17 L. Schmugge, 'Cleansing on Consciences: Some Observations Regarding the Fifteenth-Century Registers of the Papal Penitentiary', *Viator* 29 (1998), 347.

18 *Dunfermelyn Reg.*, no. 282. The abbot in question was Robert Kenleith, later abbot of Melrose and chancellor of the kingdom (d. 1273). He was an ally of Alan Durward and was implicated in an attempt to use the Great Seal in furtherance of Durward's plan to have his wife, Marjorie, illegitimate daughter of Alexander II, legitimated: see pp. 78–81.

19 C. R. Cheney, *Pope Innocent III and England* (Stuttgart, 1976), 60–1.

in particular localities, at their own discretion. This discretion was limited by the papal mandates imposing restrictions on both the number of persons to be dispensed, and the type of person or office eligible for dispensation. In 1383 Duncan Petit, provost of St Andrews, was given faculty to dispense twelve people, whatever their parents' status (that is, clerical or lay, single or married), to be ordained and to hold benefices, including those with cure of souls.[20] In 1431, John de Obizis, papal nuncio to Scotland, England and Ireland, was granted faculty to dispense fifteen illegitimate men providing they were sons of 'an unmarried man and an unmarried woman, or of a priest and an unmarried woman, or of an unmarried man and a married woman', allowing them 'to be promoted to all, even holy orders and hold a benefice even with cure'.[21] Restrictions on the faculty to dispense ensured the papacy maintained a tight grip on the use of this power. In 1419, Henry Wardlaw, bishop of St Andrews, supplicated for the authority to dispense from defect of birth a hundred Scots, men or women, 'by any unlawful union, even of married religious or by other unions in whatsoever degrees of affinity and consanguinity, even of sons of prelates', to hold any Church office, including dignities.[22] The papacy responded by permitting him faculty to dispense twenty-five persons to hold only simple benefices, or cures that were not dignities.

The absence of medieval episcopal registers for Scotland means that we cannot know whether, or how, these twenty-five dispensations were used, but we do know that the papacy sought (not always successfully) to exercise oversight of dispensations, by whomever awarded, to ensure that the limits of a dispensation were not exceeded. Albin, the son of an unmarried man and an unmarried woman, was dispensed by the papal legate Cardinal Otto Ubaldini (d. 1273) in 1245 to hold the precentorship of Brechin.[23] But the dispensation was not valid for possession of a see, and so when he was later postulated to the bishopric, the pope ordered an enquiry to be made by the bishops of St Andrews, Glasgow and Dunkeld, who were to extend the dispensation and consecrate him on two conditions: that they found the postulation to be canonical, and that they were satisfied Albin possessed 'the character and learning befitting the government of the church of Brechin'.[24]

[20] Burns, *Letters of Clement VII*, 89.

[21] Theiner, *Vet. Mon.*, no. 743. John, bishop of Moray, was empowered in 1329 to dispense from defect of birth five clerics who were born of unmarried men and unmarried women. Ibid., no. 491.

[22] *CSSR*, i, 107.

[23] *PoMS*, www.poms.ac.uk/record/person/407/; Theiner, *Vet. Mon.*, no. 116; *CPL*, i, 227; Ferguson, *Medieval Papal Representatives*, 96. His father may have been Henry of Brechin, the illegitimate son of Earl David of Huntingdon, brother of Mael Coluim IV and William the Lion.

[24] Theiner, *Vet. Mon.*, no. 116; *CPL*, i, 227.

Dispensations could be obtained from a number of sources in the Church: the apostolic penitentiary, the chancery, and, from the fifteenth century, the datary. The latter two had the facility to offer dispensations in conjunction with expectative graces or collations to specific benefices and so were the preferred source of dispensations for many, but the higher fees they charged for this enhanced service discouraged requests from those lower down the social scale.[25] A study of Scottish supplications between 1449 and 1552 shows that 1,104 Scots were dispensed from illegitimacy so that they could embark on, or progress in, a clerical career.[26] In the same period, the total number of Scottish dispensations issued for all impediments to clerical careers was 1,622, making illegitimacy, at 68 per cent of the total, overwhelmingly the single most common reason for Scottish clerics to seek a dispensation.[27]

We do not know the frequency with which illegitimate people seeking a career in the Church simply decided not to draw attention to their status by seeking a dispensation. On the one hand, it seems likely there was quite a strong confessional imperative involved, aided no doubt by the Church's general willingness to provide dispensations to those who met the criteria for a Church career. On the other, we know that the requirement for applicants to mention their illegitimacy each time they sought a benefice was sometimes done away with.[28] That this exemption was regarded as a special grace suggests some stigma or difficulty, actual or potential, attached to being illegitimate in the Church.[29] The requirement to mention birth status each and every time they supplicated the pope for a new benefice or higher office suggests a perceived need to scrutinise the character or performance of illegitimates to a greater extent than of legitimately born office-holders. This may have discouraged some from disclosing their illegitimacy. Concealment carried risks, as clerics who did so and who were discovered were subject to excommunication and required absolution as well as dispensation to continue in their careers.[30]

Illegitimates could not be ordained without a dispensation disclosing their birth status and so one way of concealing illegitimacy was to evade ordination. Complaints that the current or previous holder of a benefice did so illegally

25 J. R. McDonald, 'The Requests of Scottish Clergy in the Registers of the *Sacra Apostolica Penitenzieria*, 1449–1542', *RSCHS* 37 (2007), 11.

26 McDonald, 'Requests of Scottish Clergy', 48. Ninety-eight of these were for *de uberiori* dispensations.

27 McDonald, 'Requests of Scottish Clergy', 48.

28 Thomas Stewart, archdeacon of St Andrews, and his brother Alexander, both illegitimate sons of Robert II, were recipients of this grace. Burns, *Letters of Clement VII*, 63, 114–15.

29 Macfarlane notes that William Elphinstone's illegitimate state was 'a handicap' that the future bishop 'was not lightly to overcome'. Macfarlane, *William Elphinstone*, 16.

30 P. Clarke, 'New Sources for the History of the Religious Life: the Registers of the Apostolic Penitentiary', *Monastic Research Bulletin* 11 (2005), 9–10; Schmugge, 'Cleansing on Consciences', 346.

because he was practising as a priest without having been ordained were more common in Scotland than in England.[31] Illegitimacy may not have been the only reason behind lack of ordination, but, as Barrell suggests, it 'points to a rather casual attitude towards the niceties of canon law'.[32] Ecclesiastical regulations did not always accord with local conventions. Medieval Scotland was not homogeneous in respect of its social structures and cultural traditions, and these could influence the development of clerical careers. A study of illegitimacy dispensations for Argyll has shown that between 1449 and 1542, the proportion of men in the dioceses of Argyll and Sodor already active in the Church before obtaining a dispensation from defect of birth far outstripped those of the rest of Scotland, and of Europe.[33] Ordinarily, it was much more common for men seeking dispensations to describe themselves as *scholari* (men who had yet to enter even minor orders) rather than as *clerici* (men in minor orders). In Scotland, 56 per cent of supplicants were *scholari* and only 23 per cent *clerici*; in Europe *scholari* made up 62 per cent of supplicants and *clerici* 33 per cent. In Argyll and Sodor these proportions were more or less reversed: 65 per cent of petitioners from Argyll, and 77 per cent from Sodor, defined themselves as *clerici*. As far as Argyll is concerned, MacDonald notes a higher incidence of clerical sons among petitioners calling themselves *clerici*, and suggests that, in defiance of canon law, Church authorities in late medieval Argyll 'may have given *de facto* approval for illegitimate sons of priests to remain in their fathers' homes and train for the priesthood'.[34]

For illegitimates embarking on a clerical career the lack of a dispensation *ex defectu natalium* rendered their ordination invalid, and failure to declare illegitimacy when supplicating for a new benefice or higher office imperilled possession of the benefice so obtained.[35] Competition for benefices was such that someone in this position was vulnerable to challenge by a validly ordained candidate. David Crach, minister of the Trinitarian house at Berwick and rector of the parish church of Kettins, obtained these offices without obtaining the proper dispensation from illegitimacy; in 1456 a rival claimant, Robert

31 A. D. M. Barrell, *Medieval Scotland* (Cambridge, 2000), 64.

32 Ibid. There were other barriers to ordination, such as lack of a suitable education, having a physical or sensory disability and being too young. These also required dispensations.

33 Macdonald, *Clerics and Clansmen*, 168. The statistics which follow are from the same page.

34 Ibid., 168. Sarah Thomas's study of 211 clergy in fourteenth- and fifteenth-century Sodor found that sixty-seven of them declared themselves to be illegitimate, with fifty of the sixty-seven saying they were sons of priests, monks or clerks, but some of the remaining 144 may also have been clerical offspring, or at least illegitimate. S. Thomas, 'Clerical Illegitimacy in the Diocese of Sodor – Exception or Rule in the Late Medieval Church?', in A. P. Roach and J. R. Simpson, ed., *Heresy and the Making of European Culture: Medieval and Modern Perspectives* (Farnham, 2013), 320–1.

35 Schmugge, *Kirche, Kinder, Karrieren*, 155–6; J. R. McDonald, 'The Papal Penitentiary, Illegitimacy and Clerical Careers in the Peripheries: a Case Study of the Provinces of Nidaros and Scotland, 1449–1542', *Northern Scotland* 3 (2012), 33.

Clogstown, successfully petitioned the pope to replace him.[36] However, as is suggested by the preponderance of *clerici* in Argyll, family relationships and local connections could be as important as canon law. The system of patronage by which elite families did much to maintain their local church or monastic house, and were influential on the appointment of office-holders in them, could protect the clerics concerned, especially if the local priest belonged to the patrons' kindred, or to an allied kin-group.[37] In some parts of Scotland, non-royal lay patronage was in decline by the middle of the fourteenth century.[38] In others, lay patronage remained an important feature of ecclesiastical life. The earls of Douglas, for example, held the patronage of numerous religious foundations in their earldom and other lordships.[39] In 1391, Archibald the Grim, third earl of Douglas, petitioned successfully for his illegitimate kinsman, John de Douglas, to obtain the deanery of Moray, a region with a notable Douglas presence, and largely dominated by Douglas kinsmen, the Murrays.[40] John was already rector of the parish church of Newlands, Glasgow (the patronage of which was formally passed to Dunfermline in 1317 but which in practical terms was held by the Douglas of Dalkeith branch of the Douglas kindred) at the time of the petition.[41] He was granted leave to hold the rectorship simultaneously with the deanship, the latter being 'the greatest dignity of the cathedral after that of the bishop'. John had been dispensed in 1381 from defect of birth and also of age (he was born ca. 1362), and in 1388 was dispensed to hold any Church dignity, including an archbishopric.[42] In papal correspondence he is given as a kinsman of the third earl of Douglas,

36 *CPL*, xi, 47–8.

37 Macdonald, *Clerics and Clansmen*, 180; M. MacGregor, 'Church and Culture in the Late Medieval Highlands', in J. Kirk, ed., *The Church in the Highlands* (Edinburgh, 1998), 5, 19, 27; A. Macquarrie, 'Kings, Lords and Abbots: Power and Patronage at the Medieval Monastery of Iona', *TGSI* 54 (1984–6), 355; S. Thomas, 'Bishops, Priests, Monks and Their Patrons: the Lords of the Isles and the Church', in R. Oram, ed., *The Lordship of the Isles* (Leiden, 2014), 134. This was not only a Scottish phenomenon. Ecumenical councils of the Church legislated to restrict the influence of lay patrons repeatedly in the twelfth and thirteenth centuries. Tanner, *Decrees*, 199, 220, 254, 325–7.

38 D. Ditchburn, *Scotland and Europe. The Medieval Kingdom and Its Contacts with Christendom 1214–1560* (East Linton, 2000), 84.

39 Examples can be found at Burns, *Letters of Clement VII*, 34, 145, 153, 158; McGurk, *Letters of Benedict XIII*, 59, 80, 83, 93, 199, 221, 327–8; *Origines Parochiales Scotiae* (Bannatyne Club, 1851–5), i, 62, 109, 153, 517. See also M. Brown, *Black Douglases. War and Lordship in Late Medieval Scotland 1300–1455* (East Linton, 1998), Chapter 9, esp. 190–4.

40 *CPP*, i, 575; Burns, *Letters of Clement VII*, 160; MacKay and Ditchburn, *Atlas of Medieval Europe*, 180; Brown, *Black Douglases*, 183–4, 234.

41 I. Cowan, *Parishes of Medieval Scotland* (SRS, 1967), 156; Watt, *Graduates*, 154. Brown discusses numerous examples of the Douglases using their rights of patronage to further the careers of clerics in their service, but says that 'by contrast with other magnate families, patronage was not used by the Douglases to advance their own family in the church'. Brown, *Black Douglases*, 193. John de Douglas seems to be an exception.

42 Watt, *Graduates*, 154 (he notes that the dispensation was probably extended in 1384); *CPP*, i, 570.

of Robert, king of Scots, and of queen Annabella of Scotland.[43] Annabella's brother, Sir Malcolm Drummond, was married to Isabella Douglas, daughter of William, first earl of Douglas; the cleric John de Douglas may have been an illegitimate son of this William.[44]

A cleric did not have to be a family member to benefit from lay patronage. John de Merton, it was alleged in 1420, held illegally the provostship of Bothwell and the parish church of Kirkmaho, Glasgow, as he had not declared his defect of birth when supplicating to be collated to them.[45] Bothwell was in the patronage of the Douglases, and Merton one of the clerics in their service.[46] Failure to mention his illegitimacy was not Merton's only crime, but it was included in a petition by John Elwald, who sought to use Merton's omission as a means to oust him and take his place.[47] Merton held a prebend of Glasgow as well, but he must have declared his status in that supplication, since Elwald had to deploy a different allegation against him in respect of that benefice. Although Elwald was successful, the terms of his complaint indicate that Merton had managed to avoid the consequences of his failure to declare his illegitimacy, and of his other offence, for over a year. According to canon law he ought to have been excommunicated, but having an influential patron may have offered him some protection.

On a more modest scale, landholders large and small might have rights of patronage over one or more of the churches, monastic houses or dependent chapels in their area, at any of which Church livings might be had.[48] Although only the papacy had formal authority to appoint clerics, in many cases they acceded to the recommendation of the local patron. In the Hebrides and parts of Argyll the lords of the Isles maintained their patronage across a large proportion of the Church estate in the middle ages.[49] It has been argued that

43 *CPP*, i, 575; McGurk, *Letters of Benedict XIII*, 77–8; Burns, *Letters of Clement VII*, 185.

44 Watt, *Graduates*, 154. One of Robert III's sisters-german, and one of his half-sisters, also married into the Douglas family, and three of Annabella and Robert's daughters married Douglases (their fourth daughter died unmarried).

45 CSSR, i, 154–5.

46 Watt, *Graduates*, 392; Brown, *Black Douglases*, 193, 194, 196; W. Fraser, ed., *The Douglas Book* (Edinburgh, 1885), iii, nos 342, 344; *CDS*, iv, no. 664.

47 Merton had previously occupied two offices simultaneously, in breach of the 1317 constitution *Execrabilis*, which barred clerics from holding two or more benefices with cure of souls without first obtaining papal license, and revoked all permissions given by John XXII's predecessor popes. In the absence of papal habilitation, he ought to have been disqualified from obtaining any others, even though he had demitted the first two. See also *CSSR*, i, 144. At around the same time, Elwald challenged the right of another incumbent he said had been appointed in breach of canon law, similarly asking to replace him: ibid., 149–50.

48 Examples at Burns, *Letters of Clement VII*, 49–50, 74–5, 161, 165, 179; McGurk, *Letters of Benedict XIII*, 12, 187, 194, 198, 203, 213–14, 240; *Orig. Par. Scot.*, i, 94, 99, 322, 390; ii, Pt. 1, 200; ii, Pt. 2, 460, 840; *CSSR*, i, 103, 112–13, 115, 149, 158, 179–80, 187, 218, 220, 221, 239, 251, 305.

49 Thomas, 'Bishops, Priests, Monks', 123, 131.

the fluctuating fortunes of those members of the MacKinnon kindred who were monks on Iona in the fourteenth and fifteenth centuries depended on whether the MacKinnons were in or out of favour with the MacDonald lords of the Isles.[50] Finguine MacKinnon was said in 1359 to have kept concubines and diverted the wealth of the abbey to support the resulting illegitimate offspring; one of these offspring, also Finguine (d. ca. 1425), sought the abbacy in 1421 but did not obtain it because, argues Macquarrie, at that point it suited the MacDonalds to have Dominic MacKenzie, a member of the kindred which had recently allied with them, as abbot instead.[51] The second Finguine MacKinnon's son, grandson of the former abbot, became abbot himself, despite strenuous objections by McKenzie.[52] But later accusations that MacKinnon's mistresses included the prioress of the nearby convent, and one of her daughters, and that he had fathered children with both, were used by the MacDonalds in 1444 to have him replaced.[53] Evidently, MacDonald patrons were prepared to present robust – and successful – challenges to anyone who tried to unseat their own choice of abbot, and to be just as ruthless when they sought to depose him.

Lay influence might protect an illegitimate candidate who obtained a position in breach of canonical rules, but social bonds and ties of kinship were no less present among Scottish Churchmen. William Lamberton, bishop of St Andrews, appointed Robert Moyne to the church at Kineff, despite Moyne being underage and not ordained.[54] In 1345, 'after many years' in this position, Moyne resigned the post, and married. The original appointment was surely made by Lamberton because of some personal connection with Moyne or his family. The obligations of kinship or friendship might protect clerics installed in breach of canon law, but they could also be used to opposite effect. William de Angus was evicted from his offices as prebendary and canon in Rattray, Dunkeld diocese, in 1345 because he had not obtained a dispensation for his illegitimacy.[55] The bishop of Dunkeld, Richard Pilmuir, was within his rights to declare the offices void on this account, but his motives may not have been entirely to do with enforcing Church discipline: he petitioned the pope to have his nephew, Thomas Pilmuir, installed in Angus's place.

Illegitimacy and the Scottish episcopate

Research into the differences between Scotland and parts of Scandinavia in respect of illegitimate clergy between 1449 and 1542 has revealed a dramatic

50 Macquarrie, 'Kings, Lords and Abbots', 362–7.
51 *Highland Papers*, iv, 156–8; *CSSR*, i, 272; Macquarrie, 'Kings, Lords and Abbots', 362–4.
52 *CSSR*, ii, 139; Macquarrie, 'Kings, Lords and Abbots', 365.
53 *CSSR*, iv, 239; *CPL*, ix, 407–9; Macquarrie, 'Kings, Lords and Abbots', 366.
54 *CPP*, i, 85–6.
55 *CPL*, iii, 149; Watt, *Graduates*, 13.

difference in their career prospects.[56] In the provinces of Uppsala and Nidaros (taking in parts of Norway, Sweden and Finland), illegitimate clergy seem to have been severely restricted in their opportunities for advancement, with no known illegitimate bishops in the middle ages.[57] McDonald says that, 'In stark contrast to Norway, illegitimacy was not a bar to promotion within the Scottish Church.'[58] While this is true for the period she examines, looking at the prevalence of illegitimate bishops across the thirteenth, fourteenth and fifteenth centuries tells a slightly different story.

It is not always straightforward to determine which bishops in Scotland between 1200 and 1500 were legitimate. We know to be illegitimate those for whom a record of papal dispensation for defect of birth, or of royal legitimation, survived. There are occasionally oblique clues that a Scottish bishop for whom there is no record of a dispensation may not in fact have been legitimate: George Lauder, bishop of Argyll (d. in/bf. 1275), survived his father but the family lands were inherited by his sister.[59] Did he renounce them, or was he never entitled to them?[60] The same question applies to the thirteenth-century bishop of Aberdeen, Hugh de Bennum (d. 1281x2).[61] Appellations denoting kinship in respect of a cleric were sometimes used to obscure the fact that the person so described was a son. Robert Wishart, bishop of Glasgow (d. 1316) is given as *nepos* (nephew) of William Wishart, bishop of St Andrews, but may in fact have been his son.[62] A royal legitimation issued by James IV in 1497 made lawful one 'Henry Fantoch, cousing to the bischop of Orkney'.[63] In reality, Henry (Phankouth) was not the cousin but the son of the bishop, Andrew Pictoris.[64]

Scottish bishops appointed in the thirteenth century, for whom we have better evidence of illegitimacy were:

56 McDonald, 'Illegitimacy and Clerical Careers in the Peripheries', 39–41.

57 Ibid., 39–40. Nidaros included five sees on the Norwegian mainland.

58 Ibid., 40.

59 *ER*, ix, 663.

60 Gilbert Fleming, an apparently legitimate heir, renounced his inheritance in favour of his younger brother David in 1346. Watt, *Graduates*, 190–1.

61 Watt, *Graduates*, 39.

62 A. A. M. Duncan, 'Wishart, Robert (*c.* 1240–1316)', *ODNB*, 23 March 2019; Watt, *Graduates*, 585. *Nepos* could also mean grandson, but for obvious reasons this was no better than son. That '*nepos*' often or usually masked a father–son relationship has been challenged by Barrow, who says clerics did not routinely try to conceal the fact of their offspring, and those who did commonly used other kinship terms. J. Barrow, *The Clergy in the Medieval World: Secular Clerics, Their Families and Careers in North-Western Europe, c.800–c.1200* (Cambridge, 2015), 125.

63 *RSS*, i, no. 135.

64 *CPL*, xvi, 350; B. Smith, 'In the Tracks of Bishop Andrew Pictoris of Orkney, and Henry Phankouth, Archdeacon of Shetland', *IR* 40 (1989), 92. The use of 'cousin' here bears out Barrow's contention that kinship terms other than '*nepos*' might be deployed to disguise relationships. Royal legitimations of Churchmen are evidence that papal dispensations, even to hold bishoprics, did not have civil effects.

Table 14. Illegitimate bishops in Scotland in the thirteenth century

Name	See	Year of appointment
Abraham (d. bf. 1226)	Dunblane	1210 or later
Hugh (d. 1218)	Brechin	by 1214
? Adam (d. 1222)[65]	Caithness	1214
Geoffrey de Liberatione (d. 1249)	Dunkeld	1236
Albin (d. 1269)	Brechin	1246
Peter de Ramsey (d. 1256)	Aberdeen	1247
Henry (d. 1269)[66]	Orkney	1248
Abel (d. 1254)	St Andrews	1254
Gamelin (d. 1271)	St Andrews	1255

A comparative list for the fourteenth century must be even more tentative, in part because the bishops whose origins are obscure are even more numerous in that century – but it can hardly be called a list at all, as the only Scottish bishop of the fourteenth century who was certainly illegitimate seems to have been Adam Murray ('de Moravia') (d. 1349x50), bishop of Brechin from 1328 until his death.[67]

The fourteenth century appears to have been unusual in this respect, as illegitimate bishops became much more numerous in the fifteenth century. Eleven individuals of known illegitimate birth (i.e. those who obtained dispensations) attained bishoprics, with a further three who were elected, nominated or postulated to bishoprics but who for various reasons did not take them up. The illegitimate bishops were:

65 The *Orkneyinga saga* claims he was a foundling. Canonists were divided between those holding that foundlings must benefit from the general presumption of legitimacy, since their parentage is not known, and those who held that the fact of their being abandoned creates a strong presumption that they were illegitimate. In the end, the former position became law.

66 *CPL*, i, 241.

67 *CPL*, ii, 283, 284; Theiner, *Vet. Mon.*, no. 364; Dowden, *Bishops*, 180–1; Watt, *Graduates*, 405–7.

Table 15. Illegitimate bishops in Scotland in the fifteenth century

Name	**See**	**Year of appointment**
Angus (d. ?1441)	The Isles	1426
Michael Ochiltree (d. 1445x7)	Dunblane	1430x1
Thomas Livingston (d. 1460)[68]	Dunkeld (titular)	1440
Ingram de Lindsay (d. 1458)[69]	Aberdeen	1440
John Ralston (d. 1451x2)	Dunkeld	1447
Thomas Lauder (d. 1481)[70]	Dunkeld	1452
William Scheves (d. 1496x7)	St Andrews[71]	1479
John Campbell (d. 1510)	The Isles	1487
William Elphinstone (d. 1514)[72]	Aberdeen	1488
David Hamilton (d. bf. 1524)	Argyll	1497
John Fraser (d. 1507)	Ross	1497

The illegitimate candidates who did not progress to consecration were Thomas Stewart, archdeacon of St Andrews, who was elected to the bishopric of St Andrews in 1402 but was replaced by Walter Danielston; Andrew de Munroy, archdeacon of Ross, whose postulation by the chapter to the see of Ross in 1440 was disallowed by the pope (Eugenius IV); and Donald Macnachtan, elected bishop of Dunkeld in 1437, but who died before his appointment could be confirmed.[73]

68 Livingston, provided to the see by Pope Felix V, never had effective episcopal possession of Dunkeld but as 'bishop of the universal church' was confessor and counsellor to James II. J. H. Burns, 'Livingston, Thomas (1390/91–1460), Titular Bishop of Dunkeld and Diplomat', *ODNB*, 22 February 2019.

69 Dowden, *Bishops*, 124. He was 'the son of a baron unmarried and an unmarried woman'; there is some evidence suggestive of his father being David de Lindsay, third earl of Crawford. Ingram had a brother, Alexander, also illegitimate and also a cleric.

70 Preceptor of James II; legitimated by royal rescript in February 1472–3. *RMS*, ii, no. 1107. He resigned the bishopric in 1475. Dowden, *Bishops*, 75–7.

71 Archbishopric.

72 Elphinstone's seals as bishop of Aberdeen both incorporated a depiction of St Kentigern, probably because Elphinstone was brought up in Glasgow and for a time was the official general of that city, but it may be significant that both surviving *vitae* of Kentigern have him born out of wedlock. On Kentigern's illegitimacy, see S. Marshall, 'Illegitimacy and Sanctity in the Twelfth-Century Lives of St. Kentigern', in *Jocelin of Furness: Essays from the 2011 Conference*, ed. C. Downham (Donington, 2013), 67–90.

73 For Thomas Stewart, see pp. 197 and 205–6. Andrew de Munroy and Donald Macnachtan (Macnaughton): Dowden, *Bishops*, 218 and 71–2 respectively. Macnachtan was a nephew of Robert de Cardney, presumed brother of Mariota, mother of at least three, perhaps

What we are left with is an apparent gap in the appointment of illegitimate men to the bishoprics of Scotland from 1255 until 1426, with the single exception of the appointment of Adam Murray in 1328. We may expect to find a somewhat smaller number of illegitimate bishops in the fourteenth century simply because there were fewer bishops elected to Scottish sees compared to neighbouring centuries, but this does not account for the number of illegitimates being so much smaller. In the thirteenth century, taking legitimate and illegitimate candidates together, there were a total of eighty-six appointments (and fifteen nominated candidates who were not appointed) and in the fifteenth, seventy-nine (and fourteen), whereas in the fourteenth century there were only sixty-seven (and seven or eight). If we ignore the nominees, we find that in the thirteenth century, over 10 per cent of Scottish bishops (nine out of eighty-six) were illegitimate (or 9.3 per cent if we allow the legitimacy of alleged foundling Adam of Caithness); in the fifteenth century the figure is closer to 14 per cent (eleven out of seventy-nine). This difference is not statistically significant, being within the boundaries of normal sampling variation.[74] The fourteenth century had just under 1.5 per cent (one out of sixty-seven) of its bishops as illegitimate: in statistical terms, this is highly significant.

Various factors may have influenced the virtual disappearance of illegitimate bishops from the Scottish scene in the fourteenth century. Before then, appointments to bishoprics in Scotland were usually made with the involvement (and not infrequently at the direction) of the king and, not unusually, of magnates who had rights of patronage in the see; bishops so selected would have their appointments ratified by the pope, in many cases as a matter of course. From around 1300, the papacy became much more inclined to cancel such elections or nominations in favour of a papal bull of provision, by which the pope would impose a bishop of his own choosing for which the diocese would be charged a fee.[75] Sometimes the bishop-elect would be the same man subsequently provided by the pope, albeit after his election was declared void; but in other instances the local choice, even when his candidature was supported by the Scottish king, would be rejected by the papacy.[76] The paucity of illegitimate bishops in the fourteenth century may

four, of Robert II's illegitimate sons. Watt, *Graduates*, 368, 80. Macnachtan may also have been a son of Mariota's, by Alexander Macnachtan. *Highland Papers*, i, 111.

74 I am grateful to Irene Angus of the University of Aberdeen's Institute of Mathematics (School of Natural and Computing Sciences) for analysing the data on bishops.

75 J. H. Cockburn, *The Medieval Bishops of Dunblane and their Church* (London, 1959), 148; D. E. R. Watt, 'The Papacy and Scotland in the Fifteenth Century', in B. Dobson, ed., *The Church, Politics and Patronage in the Fifteenth Century* (Gloucester, 1984), 127; A. D. M. Barrell, *The Papacy, Scotland and Northern England, 1342–1378* (Cambridge, 1995), 79–124, 184, 197, 199–201; Watt, *Graduates*, 28; Y. Renouard, transl. by D. Bethell, *The Avignon Papacy 1305–1403* (Hamden, 1970), 92.

76 Barrell, *The Papacy*, 197, 199; Dowden, *Bishops*, 112, 181 and Theiner, *Vet. Mon.*, no. 364 (examples of men being elected, their elections being declared null, then the same men

be related to a belief that, to minimise the risk of a candidate preferred by the Scottish crown and prelates being summarily replaced, it was safer to field only those men whose backgrounds could give no cause for objection.

Any such conservatism was likely to have been intensified by tensions, then war, with England. In 1265 the papal legate for England, Wales and Ireland was given powers in Scotland, a decision apparently made without the Scottish king (Alexander III) being consulted.[77] The following year, and again in 1268 and 1269, there were attempts to use a papal legate in Scotland to collect revenues which were to be diverted to the English king, an initiative with which the Scots refused to comply.[78] The papal appointment in 1259 of an English cleric to the see of Glasgow, which drew protests (to no avail) from the Scottish king, was an early example of English interference in Scottish Church appointments, which would escalate during the fourteenth century.[79] In 1318, for example, the chapter of Glasgow elected John de Lindsay to the bishopric, but at the request of Edward II, Pope John XXII instead consecrated John de Egglescliffe, an English friar.[80] The attempts of successive English kings from Edward I to exert control over Scotland included concerted efforts to 'Anglicise' monastic houses and other ecclesiastical institutions in the Scottish Borders, and to extend English royal involvement in diocesan appointments, administration of temporalities and other matters pertaining to the regulation and control of bishoprics.[81] It also sought to strengthen English crown influence in the papal curia.[82] One relatively minor example of this occurred in the reign of Edward II, when two cardinals sent by Pope John XXII as nuncios to England were given additional powers to provide benefices, or canonries and prebends, in other parts of Britain, including St Andrews, Whithorn, Dunkeld, Dunblane, Brechin, Aberdeen, Moray, Ross, Caithness and Argyll.[83] One of the cardinals,

---

being provided); 309–10.

77 D. E. R. Watt, *Medieval Church Councils in Scotland* (Edinburgh, 2000), 90–1.

78 Ibid., 92–3.

79 Dowden, *Bishops*, 304–5. The pope quashed the election of Nicholas de Moffat and provided instead the Englishman John de Cheyam, sending letters to this effect not to the Scottish king or prelates but to the bishops of Lincoln and Bath.

80 Dowden, *Bishops*, 309–10. Appointed during intense hostilities between England and Scotland, four years after Bannockburn and three months after Scotland had recaptured Berwick, Egglescliffe met some resistance to his authority.

81 R. D. Oram, 'Dividing the Spoils: War, Schism and Religious Patronage on the Anglo-Scottish Border, *c.* 1332–*c.* 1400', in A. King and M. A. Penman, ed., *England and Scotland in the Fourteenth Century: New Perspectives* (Woodbridge, 2007), 136–56; Barrow, *Kingdom of the Scots*, 215–17; K. Harvey, *Episcopal Appointments in England, c.1214–1344* (Farnham, 2014), 215–16. Dowden, *Bishops*, has further examples of English interference in ecclesiastical appointments at 23 n.1, 25, 60, 61, 62, 63, 64 n.1, 201, 213, 214, 238–9, 241, 280, 308, 360, 382.

82 B. Bombi, 'The English Crown and the Election of Pope John XXII', *Journal of Ecclesiastical History* 68 (2017), 278–9; J. R. Wright, *The Church and the English Crown 1305–1334* (Toronto, 1980), 114–18.

83 *CPL*, ii, 128.

Luca Fieschi, appears to have been a kinsman of Edward II, and received a number of gifts from him and from English prelates.[84] Bids to extend English power in Scotland by influencing Church appointments did not always meet with success, but concern about it may have been reason enough for Scottish kings, diocesan chapters and others to promote candidates whose birth status was less likely to provide grounds for opposition, particularly if it was felt – rightly or wrongly – that decisions being taken in the papacy might be subject to English influence.[85]

During the fourteenth century, some conflict between interpretations of canon law concerning the power of dispensations for defect of birth, hinted at in the records of petitions, might also have encouraged caution. Joan, queen of Scotland, supplicated in 1345 for her chaplain, John de Marr, to retain the church at Crimond, Aberdeen.[86] The petition was needed because 'although doctors [i.e. canonists] hold that an illegitimate person having a papal dispensation to be ordained and hold a benefice can obtain successive benefices with cure of souls, the style of the papal chancery is contrary to this opinion'. Other examples of the chancery contesting the extent and power of previously granted dispensations from illegitimacy occurred the previous year, in relation to Irish clerics.[87] The chancery could and did refuse to grant petitions which did not conform to its rules, and not just in respect of the law: wording that did not conform to regulation could see a petition thrown out.[88]

The one certainly illegitimate bishop of the fourteenth century, Adam Murray, was appointed to the see of Brechin by papal provision in October 1328, shortly after having arrived there as bishop-elect.[89] A graduate, Murray had been a procurator at Avignon for Robert I, and was among those responsible for securing a two-year relaxation of the interdict on Scotland and obtaining absolution for Robert, undertaking to ensure payment of 20,000 florins to the papacy.[90] He was provided to Brechin a matter of days thereafter, and granted a dispensation from defect of birth to hold a bishopric.[91] In the reign of Robert

84 Wright, *Church and Crown*, 121, 290. Gifts were also made a few years later to another two cardinals dealing with Scottish affairs. Ibid., 121–2.

85 S. Layfield, 'The Pope, the Scots, and their "Self-Styled" King: John XXII's Anglo-Scottish Policy, 1316–1334', in King and Penman, *England and Scotland*, 157–71.

86 *CPP*, i, 87.

87 *CPP*, i, 39, 40.

88 One of its objections in relation to John de Marr was that the original petition had used 'a phrase which the chancery does not allow'. In 1363 the chancery refused to expedite a letter providing John de Berkyngg, priest, to a canonry at St Paul's, London, because 'the name of the saint was omitted from the petition', so that Berkyngg lost out on the appointment. *CPP*, i, 87, 425. See also P. N. R. Zutshi, 'Proctors Acting for English Petitioners in the Chancery of the Avignon Popes (1305–1378)', *Journal of Ecclesiastical History* 35 (1984), 16.

89 Theiner, *Vet. Mon.*, no. 475.

90 Theiner, *Vet. Mon.*, no. 474; *ER*, i, clxxxiii–iv; Watt, *Graduates*, 406.

91 *CPL*, ii, 283.

I, Murray was one of the envoys sent to treat with the king of France, and in that of David II he was a royal advisor, ambassador and chancellor of the realm.[92] Pope Clement VI (1342–52), made particular use of Murray – more than any other Scottish bishop of that time – to execute provisions in Scotland. Thirty-one mandates addressed to Murray between 1342 and 1349 gave him authority to enact papal will in respect of Church appointments.[93] He was evidently a highly skilled negotiator and administrator, with a reputation for sound judgement and trustworthiness. It may be that his personal abilities were exceptional enough to outweigh his illegitimacy, at a time when illegitimacy and appointment to a see appear to have been very uneasy bedfellows.

The later fifteenth century saw a resurgence of illegitimate bishops in Scotland. Among them was William Scheves, who found preferment in the court of James III. Scheves's father was probably John Scheves, a clergyman who was not from a baronial family and who was official of St Andrews during the reign of James II.[94] William Scheves enjoyed a very rapid elevation from his position in the 1470s as a rather lowly court physician who also had some responsibilities in respect of the king's wardrobe, to archbishop of St Andrews and the king's heavily relied-upon 'fixer' by 1479.[95] He may have been a highly competent administrator who displayed enduring loyalty to James III, but the king's decision to reward the loyalty of a man who had no theological training by placing him at the pinnacle of the Church hierarchy in Scotland unsurprisingly occasioned considerable resentment.[96]

Religious lifestyles and illegitimate offspring

In Scotland, as elsewhere, Church patronage was a common means of obtaining professional qualifications. Men who wanted to attend university were frequently obliged to enter minor orders to do so, but the legal incompatibility of holy orders and lawful marriage meant that they could not marry either before or afterwards, and any children they had were by definition illegitimate.[97] Many Churchmen were not graduates (and no female religious was) but, whether they had embarked on Church careers out of a sincere religious vocation or from some other motive, there is ample evidence that significant numbers found themselves unable to comply with the Church's requirement that they remain celibate. The surviving statutes of the Scottish

92 Dowden, *Bishops*, 180–1; Watt, *Graduates*, 405–7; *PoMS*, www.poms.ac.uk/record/person/23120/; Penman, *David II*, 38, 53, 78, 80, 85, 86 n.31, 147, 152, 156, 163, 169.

93 Barrell, *The Papacy*, 208.

94 L. J. Macfarlane, 'The Primacy of the Scottish Church, 1472–1521', *IR* 20 (1969), 115.

95 Macdougall, *James III*, 146–8.

96 Macfarlane, 'Primacy of the Scottish Church', 116–17; Macdougall, *James III*, 146–7, 164.

97 Macfarlane, *William Elphinstone*, 16. That this was widespread across the Latin west is suggested by the Second Lateran Council (c. 9) railing against clerics who practised as civil lawyers or doctors. Tanner, *Decrees*, 198.

Church's provincial councils, beginning in 1225, speak to a commitment to the wider programme of ecclesiastical and moral reform, with calls for the elimination of clerical concubinage and of the transfer of church offices from father to son.[98] The fact that they had to be repeated suggests a persistent strand of nonconformity to these rules, and the evidence of the papal registers bears this out.

McDonald's analysis of Scottish illegitimacy dispensations from 1449 to 1542 found that well over half the supplicants had a parent who was in clerical orders.[99] As far as nuns were concerned, the evidence is scant. Sons such as John Gray (d. ca. 1451), a cleric whose mother was a nun, would presumably have been given to a family member either at birth or in childhood, while daughters may have stayed longer, or permanently, in their mothers' monastic houses.[100]

It was usual for supplicants to state whether each of their parents was in the clergy or the laity and, if the latter (as most of the mothers were; few of those seeking dispensations were offspring of nuns), if they were single, married or widowed. They were not, however, expected to give the names of their parents, although some petitioners or their sponsors did, and others claimed connection to a relative or associate of high rank, in the expectation that this would help their applications.[101] Very few *ubi pater* dispensations were issued by the penitentiary in the later middle ages, suggesting that the Church was quite strict about not letting the many sons of clergy become priests in their fathers' churches.[102] One example of its occurrence is the case of John Masterton ('Marstretoun'), who in 1424 took over the benefice previously held by his father, William, at Ballingry, near Loch Leven.[103] Another may have been Thomas Kininmund. He held the canonry and prebend of Belhelvie in the

98 Patrick, *Statutes*, lxxxviii, 14, 37, 44, 55, 59–60 (all pre-1500; later statutes indicate the problems continued).

99 McDonald, 'Papal Penitentiary and Clerical Careers', 241.

100 *CPP*, i, 592.

101 J. R. McDonald, 'Illegitimate Scots in the Registers of Supplications and the Registers of the Apostolic Penitentiary during the Pontificate of Sixtus IV (1471–1484)', in G. Jaritz and others, ed., *... et usque ad ultimum terrae: The Apostolic Penitentiary in Local Contexts* (Budapest, 2007), 33–42, 37–9. One example was James, a sub-deacon and 'kinsman of David earl of Crawford'. McGurk, *Letters of Benedict XIII*, 111. In supplications by Walter, earl of Atholl and Caithness (d. 1437) on behalf of his illegitimate son Alan, Walter describes himself as 'son of the erstwhile Robert King of Scotland and uncle of James, present King, and of Murdach, Duke of Albany, Governor'. *CSSR*, ii, 14, 37–8.

102 K. Salonen, *The Penitentiary as a Well of Grace in the Late Middle Ages: The Example of the Province of Uppsala, 1448–1527* (Saarijärvi, 2001), 194; McDonald, 'Illegitimate Scots in the Registers', 36. The Fourth Lateran Council, c. 31, forbade sons of canons from becoming canons in the same churches as their fathers. Tanner, *Decrees*, 249. Unsuccessful petitions were not preserved, so it is very difficult to know whether the small number reflects few requests or many refusals.

103 *CSSR*, ii, 69. The supplication mentions that this was being requested 'notwithstanding the rule of chancery which forbids anyone to succeed to the benefice of their father'.

diocese of Aberdeen, but in January 1345 his possession of them was declared void because he had not stated that his father also had a canonry and prebend 'of Aberdeen', which perhaps suggests that neighbouring churches were off-limits as well.[104] Thomas was allowed to remain in his posts, or rather to be reinstated to them, at the request of Joan, queen of Scotland.[105] It is possible that sons of priests sometimes quietly joined their fathers without drawing attention to this by seeking an *ubi pater* dispensation which was likely to be refused. The lack of names or other identifying data on parents obscures the picture in respect of this sort of arrangement, and masks the extent to which dynasties of clerics may have flourished in some parts of medieval Scotland. Clerical dynasties were not unusual in various parts of Europe in the centuries before Gregorian reform – the hereditary priests of Hexham are well-known – and there is some evidence that they prevailed in various regions, including Gaeldom, for a considerable time afterwards.[106]

Papal records concerning requests for dispensations from women, such as those by Christina (no surname is given), and by Janet or Johanna Wardlaw, who in 1403 sought a dispensation from illegitimacy and later became a prioress at Haddington, are more infrequent.[107] Studies of the post-1449 records of the papal penitentiary note that women appear in them much less often than men. The comparatively small number of women seeking dispensations from illegitimacy probably reflects the fact that far fewer women, illegitimate or otherwise, entered religious life, of which a necessarily smaller number aspired to hold positions of authority in their monastic houses for which they needed to be dispensed if they were illegitimate. McDonald, who looked at Scottish supplications between 1449 and 1542, found that out of the 600 dispensations

104 *CPL*, iii, 149; *CPP*, i, 83. His father was Malise Kininmund, nephew of Alexander Kininmund (d. 1380), bishop of Aberdeen. Watt, *Graduates*, 301–3 (Alexander); 305 (Malise and Thomas).

105 *CPL*, iii, 149. See also *CSSR*, ii, 149–50 for the case of Thomas Edname of Aberdeen, whose supplication to hold a benefice in the same church as his father fell foul of the rule against this practice, even though his father had been dead for over twenty years.

106 W. M. Aird, *St Cuthbert and the Normans. The Church of Durham, 1071–1153* (Woodbridge, 1998), 116–41; J. W. Fawcett, 'The Hereditary Priests of Hexham', *Hexham Parish Magazine*, May 1903, 37–8; Barrow, *The Clergy*, 143–6; S. Thomas, 'Bishops, Priests, Monks', 140; MacGregor, 'Church and Culture', 19. A study of illegitimacy dispensations issued to Irish clerics between 1449 and 1533 suggests Church careers were simply incorporated into the Gaelic tradition of professions as hereditary castes. M. J. Haren, 'Social Structures of the Irish Church: A New Source in Papal Penitentiary Dispensations for Illegitimacy', in L. Schmugge and B. Wiggenhauser, ed., *Illegitimität im Spätmittelalter* (München, 1994), 207–26. Dunlop notes that the Gaelic west is disproportionately represented in illegitimacy dispensations sought by sons of priests in the fifteenth century. *CSSR*, ii, xxvii n.3, xxviii–ix.

107 McGurk, *Letters of Benedict XIII*, 110; D. E. R. Watt and N. F. Shead, *The Heads of Religious Houses in Scotland from Twelfth to Sixteenth Centuries* (Edinburgh, 2001), 90–1, 116.

she analysed, only two (0.3%) were from women, both being nuns who sought dispensation from defect of birth.[108] The issue may be one of sources, though it is also likely that Scotland had proportionately fewer, and smaller, nunneries than did other parts of western Christendom.[109]

Like their male counterparts, women religious might also be parents of illegitimate children. Once a woman had entered holy orders, any child she had subsequently was by definition illegitimate since she could not legally marry. Some medieval women did leave their religious communities to live secular lives and have children, a few of whom obtained papal grace absolving them from excommunication (the automatic penalty for *apostasia a religione*, or leaving a monastery without permission), but the extent to which this occurred in Scotland is not known.[110] The incidence of former nuns having illegitimate children is necessarily very hard to determine, as only absconders who sought absolution might appear in the records, and there may have been no requirement for them to mention whether or not they had children (and they may in any case have had them later). Neither the penitentiary registers nor the register of supplications for the period after 1449 contain requests from Scottish nuns concerning apostasy.[111] Perhaps any late medieval Scottish nuns who renounced their vows to rejoin the world did not trouble the papacy with requests for absolution.

Traffic in the other direction may have been a problem for some nunneries. In 1375, a community of nuns at North Berwick sought permission for perpetual claustration in an effort to protect themselves from 'being much molested by the neighbourhood and visits of nobles and other secular persons'.[112] The disruption and expense of providing the expected hospitality to noble visitors, whether pilgrims or other travellers whose business took them across the Forth, probably accounted for this request, but such visitors may have included men who saw the women there as easy sexual prey. Such

[108] McDonald, 'Papal Penitentiary and Ecclesiastical Careers', 56–7, 236. Only one belonged to the pre-1500 period.

[109] Between 1140 and 1240, significantly fewer monastic houses were founded for women than for men in Scotland, and the number was also far smaller than for women in other regions of Britain; further, the communities of nuns were smaller in Scotland, and the documentary evidence for them is also poorer. R. A. McDonald, 'The Foundation and Patronage of Nunneries by Native Elites in Twelfth- and Early Thirteenth-Century Scotland', in E. Ewan, and M. M. Meikle, ed., *Women in Scotland c.1100–c.1750* (East Linton, 1999), 3.

[110] Schmugge, 'Female Petitioners', 690–1, discusses cases from German-speaking regions. All the Scottish cases of *apostasia a religione* discussed in McDonald's thesis concern men; all left their monasteries citing friction with fellow monks or their superior. McDonald, 'Papal Penitentiary and Ecclesiastical Careers', 170.

[111] McDonald, 'Papal Penitentiary and Ecclesiastical Careers', 176–7.

[112] Theiner, *Vet. Mon.*, no. 713; *CPL*, iv, 212; A. D. M. Barrell, 'The Papacy and the Regular Clergy in Scotland in the Fourteenth Century', *RSCHS* 24 (1991), 108.

occurrences are occasionally noted in papal records.[113] Accounts of this phenomenon appear much more frequently in narrative sources in the middle ages, from self-consciously literary works such as Boccaccio's *Decameron*, to hagiography, and reports of English diocesan visitations to nunneries.[114]

A claim that nuns in a Scottish religious community had borne illegitimate children is recorded in a papal letter of 1389.[115] Pope Clement VII wrote to the bishop of Glasgow, in response to a petition from Archibald, third earl of Douglas and lord of Galloway, about the convent of Lincluden. The priory had been founded by the earl's predecessor lords of Galloway and was now under his patronage.[116] Archibald alleged that the nuns, who by that time had been reduced to four in number, had 'taken to living dissolute and scandalous lives', allowing the building to fall into disrepair, 'while they dress their daughters, born in incest, in sumptuous clothes with gold ornaments and pearls'.[117] Archibald's use of the term 'incest' was not necessarily based on a belief that the nuns had been sexually active with their relatives: sexual intercourse with a professed nun was always regarded as incest because female religious were 'married' to God, the Father of all.[118] It did not hurt his cause that the medieval Church had a particular horror of incest, which may explain why he twice refers to the women as having committed the sin.[119]

The earl was seeking to have the nuns ejected and for Lincluden to be refounded as a college of priests and united with the hospital at Holyrood.[120] This does not mean that he invented the existence of the nuns' children. Although Archibald may have stood to gain in various ways (political and social) by his patronage, a false allegation on his part regarding the nuns would not, if discovered, have endeared him to the Church authorities whose cooperation he

113 Schmugge, 'Female Petitioners', 689–90. He cites an instance of a fifteenth-century Italian nun who had a child and afterwards sought absolution, but her case was untypical as she is said to have murdered and buried the newborn. The case of John Gray, mentioned above at p. 166, is a Scottish example of someone born of a married man and a nun.

114 G. Boccaccio, *The Decameron*, transl. G. H. McWilliam (Harmondsworth, 1972), 234–41 (Third Day/First Story); *Visitations of Religious Houses in the Diocese of Lincoln*, ed. A. Hamilton Thompson and others (Lincoln, 1914–29), i, 69–71; iii, 352, 355–6. See also G. S. Daichman, 'Misconduct in the Medieval Nunnery: Fact, Not Fiction', in L. L. Coon and others, ed., *That Gentle Strength: Historical Perspectives on Women in Christianity* (London, 1990), 103–4, 106, 107–8; Brundage, *Law, Sex, and Christian Society*, 151; T. Dean, 'Fornicating with Nuns in Fifteenth-Century Bologna', *JMH* 34 (2008), 374–82.

115 Burns, *Letters of Clement VII*, 145.

116 D. E. Easson, *Medieval Religious Houses: Scotland* (London, 1976), 120; Brown, *Black Douglases*, 192.

117 Burns, *Letters of Clement VII*, 145.

118 Brundage, *Law, Sex, and Christian Society*, 252. Another example of this usage is found in an official record instructing an enquiry into the case of a Lincolnshire nun who had a child, which referred to her having 'committed incest' and her infant being the result of 'incestuous embraces'. Hamilton Thompson, *Visitations*, i, 69–71.

119 See pp. 14–16.

120 Burns, *Letters of Clement VII*, 145.

was trying to secure. If the advantage he sought was also spiritual, then he was even less likely to have lied about so serious a matter. Whatever the strength of the allegations, however, he could expect a sympathetic hearing from the head of the see. The bishop of Glasgow in 1389 was Matthew Glendinning, the son of a family that was in the third earl's affinity and whose own career in the Church was based on his service to the earls of Douglas in the 1370s and 80s.[121] He had especially strong links with Archibald the Grim from 1388, the year after Glendinning became bishop and the year before the papal letter was issued that instructed the removal of the nuns from Lincluden.[122]

Archibald was himself illegitimate and the father of an illegitimate son, yet he had no hesitation in censuring the nuns for sexual conduct that in some ways mirrored his own and that of his parents. It is very unlikely he would have seen this as hypocritical or unfair. In contrast to the inhabitants of Lincluden, Archibald had not taken a solemn vow of celibacy in pursuit of a contemplative life in the cloister. Nonetheless, he was as subject to the laws of the Church as anyone else, and fathering illegitimate children was incompatible with these laws. His request to refound the priory was framed as an expression of piety and was one of a number of significant benefactions he made to the Church.[123] Oram has argued that religious devotion, not simply self-aggrandisement and political advantage, motivated his investment in Lincluden and in Bothwell, his other collegiate foundation.[124] Douglas was pragmatically exploiting the double standard in operation regarding his own and the nuns' parentage of illegitimate offspring. This was not simply a matter of him belonging to the laity whereas they had taken vows of religion. The double standard was applied on the basis of gender, as well as on the religious status of the mothers and fathers.

Some male secular clergy who had illegitimate offspring went on to hold advanced offices in the Church, including bishoprics. They included the thirteenth-century bishop of Dunkeld, Geoffrey de Liberatione, who had two known sons.[125] Himself illegitimate, Geoffrey was a former royal clerk who was closely associated with William the Lion's illegitimate son Robert of London. William Wishart (d. 1279), bishop of St Andrews, had at least one son.[126] Robert Cardney (d. 1436), bishop of Dunkeld and kinsman of Robert II's mistress

121 Dowden, *Bishops*, 316–17; Brown, *Black Douglases*, 48, 83–4, 193–5.

122 Brown, *Black Douglases*, 194.

123 Brown, *Black Douglases*, 191–4.

124 R. D. Oram, 'Lay Religiosity, Piety, and Devotion in Scotland c. 1300 to c. 1450', *Florilegium* 25 (2008), 107–13. A more sceptical view is taken by W. McDowall, *Chronicles of Lincluden as an Abbey and as a College* (Edinburgh, 1886), 42–8.

125 *Scon Lib.*, no. 97; *Charters, Bulls and other Documents relating to the Abbey of Inchaffray* (SHS, 1908), no. 69 (containing references to Geoffrey's two sons, Henry and David).

126 Watt, *Graduates*, 590. The nature of the complaints about his character were said to have startled the pope. Dowden, *Bishops*, 19.

Mariota, had two sons in clerical careers.[127] The illegitimate bishop Angus of the Isles (d. ca. 1441) had a son, Angus, a priest.[128] Henry Wardlaw (d. 1440), bishop of St Andrews and founder of its university, was the father of at least two sons, one of whom became a priest.[129] Henry Lychton (d. 1440) who held the sees of Moray and of Aberdeen, had a daughter, Janet; Henry Cockburne (d. 1476x7), bishop of Ross, was the father of a son, John; William Tulloch (d. 1482), bishop of Orkney and of Moray, was the father of Richard, and bishop of Orkney Andrew Pictoris's son, Henry Phankouth, was archdeacon of Shetland.[130] In these instances, at least, fathering an illegitimate child was no hindrance to promotion.

Centuries after the Church began insisting on a celibate clergy, Scottish priests, monks, nuns and others were continuing to fall short of the standards expected of them, as the existence of their offspring testifies. The frequency with which sons of clerics themselves pursued clerical careers strongly suggests that, in many cases, the children were brought up in households alongside their father, and acquired familiarity with the profession, and at least some of the requisite skills and knowledge, from him.[131] This in turn implies that some clerics maintained stable relationships with the mothers of their children, an impression confirmed by the Statutes of the Scottish Church not only warning clerics repeatedly against concubinage, but also prohibiting the practice of these clergy purchasing houses or other lay property for their concubines and children, and forbidding clergy from making wills leaving money or goods to these women.

Some illegitimate people in ecclesiastical life were born of relationships between people who could not marry for other reasons, such as being too closely related to each other according to canon law, or because one was married to someone else (or both were). There are glimpses in the records of these categories, the incestuous and adulterine bastards, being seen as especially tainted by the circumstances of their conception. Although concern about their fitness for clerical careers is not consistently visible, the hints we do get are enough to show that theories about gradations of sexual sin having

[127] *CSSR*, ii, 69; *CPL*, viii, 322; Watt, *Graduates*, 80.

[128] *CSSR*, v, 461.

[129] *CSSR*, ii, xxix, 198.

[130] Watt, *Graduates*, 360; *CPL*, viii, 447 (relating that Janet and her husband, Andrew de Glaster, required a dispensation to marry anew, since it had come to light that Janet's father was the bishop who had bestowed the sacrament of confirmation on Andrew, thus creating an impediment of spiritual affinity between the couple; the mandate for the dispensation was sent to the bishop of Ross instead of to the couple's own bishop (Lychton), since 'for certain causes the Bishop of Aberdeen is not to be written to in the matter'); Dowden, *Bishops*, 220; *CSSR*, v, nos 639, 643; *CPL*, xvi, 350; Smith, 'Bishop Andrew Pictoris', 92. Cockburne's son John was legitimated in 1507. *RSS*, i, no. 1552.

[131] Salonen and Schmugge, *A Sip from the "Well of Grace"*, 56–7.

concomitant effects on the moral characters of the resulting children had real force for at least some Churchmen. These theories formed the underlying rationale for illegitimate men having to declare their birth circumstances prior to ordination, and then at every step in their subsequent careers, and for illegitimate women having to do so when they sought any position of authority in their monastic houses. Legitimate people in ecclesiastical careers required episcopal or papal permission be promoted or to take on more benefices than the number they were already permitted to hold, but could be ordained without dispensation as long as they met the appropriate criteria. They did not have to declare, then or at any other stage of their career, that their parents had committed fornication, adultery, incest, or some other sexual crime in begetting them. The strictness of this requirement is indicative of the dim view taken by the institutional Church of sex outwith marriage, but its 'tough on illegitimacy, tough on the causes of illegitimacy' stance was not always reflected in the conduct of its own clergy.

Breaches of canon law in respect of clerical celibacy and hereditary possession of offices could be either ignored or used to remove a cleric, sometimes depending on political exigencies rather than papal policy. Lay patrons of religious foundations may have cared more about whether the appointment of candidates to benefices had social or political benefits than whether the flaw imparted by parental sin had been remedied by papal grace. Failure to obtain appropriate dispensations, however, might allow sharp-elbowed rivals to demand the removal of an incumbent. The theology and doctrine which gave rise to the creation of dispensations for defect of birth cast doubt on an illegitimate person's innate capacity for moral and spiritual excellence, but lived experience surely taught their fellow ecclesiasts, monks and nuns that they were no less capable of virtue, nor any more given to vice, than anyone else.

7

Illegitimacy in political life

Now am I sicker þairof for þow art he
To myne are succeid suld efter me.[1]

In the late twelfth century Ness, son of William of Leuchars, had two sons, Caustantín and Patrick, but it was his daughter Orabilis who inherited his extensive lands in Lothian.[2] The brothers are acknowledged as sons of Ness, but Orabilis is given in charters as Ness's heir.[3] It seems that she alone of the three was legitimate. Her father was evidently committed to the principle of legitimacy as a prerequisite for inheritance, since female inheritance was often avoided where possible. Orabilis's own great-granddaughter, grandchild of her son Saer de Quincy, was the heir of line to the earldom of Winchester, but the earldom was diverted instead to Saer's second son rather than to a female heir.[4]

The spread of legitimate primogeniture displaced some who might have expected to inherit, whether as collaterals or as children of unions not recognised as marriages under canon law. In 1213, William the Lion and his son Alexander presided over arbitration to settle a dispute between two brothers, both called Maurice, over the earldom of Menteith.[5] The older Maurice was in possession of the earldom but the younger claimed it by hereditary right. Although the source of his claim is not recorded, Barrow points out the likeliest explanation is that the younger son was legitimate while the elder was not.[6] If

1 *King Alexander*, lines 655–6.

2 *Liber Cartarum Prioratus Sancti Andree in Scotia* (Bannatyne Club, 1841), 290–1; G. W. S. Barrow, *Scotland and its Neighbours in the Middle Ages* (London, 1992), 80.

3 *PoMS*, www.poms.ac.uk/record/person/6664/. Orabilis married three times: to Robert de Quincy (d. 1197), constable of Scotland; to Adam, son of Donnchad, earl of Fife, and to Earl Gilla Críst of Mar.

4 R. D. Oram, 'Quincy, Saer de, Earl of Winchester (d. 1219), Magnate', *ODNB*, 20 March 2019.

5 *Calendar of Patent Rolls, Henry III*, v (London, 1910), 175, 176; W. Fraser, *The Red Book of Menteith* (Edinburgh, 1880–1), i, 7–8; *RRS*, ii, no. 519; *SP*, vi, 125–6; Fryde, *British Chronology*, 514.

6 Barrow, *Scotland and its Neighbours*, 80. Fraser and Paul suggest the same. Fraser, *Menteith*, i, 7; *SP*, vi, 125.

this was the case, William was enforcing law that insisted on legitimacy as a qualification for inheritance, even though a traditional succession practice allowing the illegitimate son to gain control of the property had already been implemented. In the event, the elder Maurice resigned the earldom to the king, who granted it to the younger brother. Maurice senior was permitted to hold some of the lands of the earldom by bailliary of the king, on the understanding that these lands would revert back to the rightful earl on the death of the elder Maurice; and the latter was also granted additional lands to use as marriage-portions for his daughters. By this agreement the former earl was able to continue to derive an income from the earldom, and to preserve family honour by dowering his daughters with land in the way expected of a man of his social standing. In an era when traditional inheritance practices were being replaced by those requiring legitimacy as a qualification for heirship, settlements which afforded some economic security and guarded against loss of face were likely to have been important. Increasing acceptance of succession practices that excluded illegitimates is the likeliest explanation for the growth in thirteenth-century Scotland of applications for marriage dispensations, as couples who had married irregularly or not at all sought to ensure their offspring would not be excluded from inheritances.[7]

The best-known example in the thirteenth century of a Scottish king intervening to prevent illegitimate succession concerns the lordship of Galloway and female inheritance. Alan, lord of Galloway, died in 1234 leaving three daughters born in marriage (two of whom were the daughters of Margaret of Huntingdon, the reigning king Alexander II's first cousin), and an illegitimate son, Thomas. Galloway as a lordship had an ambiguous relationship to the crown; an atypically loose arrangement of overlordship was in place, giving Galloway a greater degree of autonomy than some other parts of the kingdom, reflected in the region's maintaining its own laws.[8] The leading men of the lordship wanted Alan's illegitimate son to inherit. Alexander II insisted that the rights of the legitimate heirs be upheld, entailing partition of the lordship between the three daughters, and that Thomas be excluded as heir. That the men of Galloway were willing to defend, militarily and at the cost of lives, the illegitimate Thomas's claim to succeed his father was probably not something that Alan of Galloway himself had intended. If he expected Thomas to inherit Galloway he would not have identified a specific portion of land within Galloway to give him.[9] The fact that he ensured Thomas married

7 Ferguson, *Medieval Papal Representatives*, 10.

8 *APS*, i, 403; H. L. MacQueen, 'The Laws of Galloway: a Preliminary Survey', in R. D. Oram and G. P. Stell, ed., *Galloway: Land and Lordship* (Edinburgh, 1991), 131–43. At 137: 'There is some evidence for the existence and late survival in Galloway of customs relating to marriage, status and the rearing of children, which were at variance with the norms of the Church as expressed in the canon law.'

9 R. D. Oram, *The Lordship of Galloway* (Edinburgh, 2000), 141.

the daughter of king Rögnvaldr of Man (d. 1229) suggests that he hoped his illegitimate son might succeed to the kingdom of Man, rather than become lord of Galloway.[10] Thomas's illegitimacy seems not to have been regarded by Rögnvaldr, who was himself illegitimate and who had become king despite his legitimate brother being designated heir by their father, as a barrier to marrying into the Manx royal line.[11]

Notably, contemporary sources suggest that lordship by Thomas was proposed by the men of Galloway not as their first choice but as the least worst of the available options, since their primary goal seems to have been to prevent partition of the lordship. The *Melrose Chronicle* says that the Galwegians, 'preferring to have one lord rather than many' initially asked the king to assume the lordship in place of the sisters, and on his refusal they became 'angry beyond measure'.[12] This is echoed in the *Annals of Dunstable*, which attribute the ensuing 'great slaughter' to the fact that 'the people of the land refused to permit a division of the fief'.[13] Matthew Paris's account notes that the men of Galloway wanted the lordship to go to Alan's illegitimate son ('*filio Alani … notho*') or to any other family member, suggesting that it didn't much matter who, as long, presumably, as a single heir obtained it.[14] *Scotichronicon* records the reason for the rebellion as the Galwegians being 'extremely angry because they could not get the lord king to agree that Alan's … legitimate heirs should be disinherited and Thomas his natural son become the heir and their lord'.[15]

While protection of native tradition in respect of succession may not have been the main principle at stake, the willingness of the men of Galloway to move the dispute onto a military footing does demonstrate that they did not see illegitimacy as a barrier to inheritance. Possibly what the Galwegians sought was the right to choose between long-standing local tradition and recently introduced practices, depending on which offered the more desirable outcome

10 *Chron. Melrose*, 83; K. J. Stringer, 'Periphery and Core in Thirteenth-Century Scotland: Alan Son of Roland, Lord of Galloway and Constable of Scotland', in A. Grant and K. J. Stringer, ed., *Medieval Scotland: Crown, Lordship and Community: Essays Presented to G. W. S. Barrow* (Edinburgh, 1998), 96; Oram, *Lordship of Galloway*, 126–7.

11 In the event, Rögnvaldr was succeeded not by Thomas but by his own son, Gǫðreðr Donn (d. 1231).

12 '*Sed indigene illius terre, malentes habere unum dominum quam plures, ad dominum regem accesserunt, postulantes quatenus heredibus heredatis super se dominium acciperet, quod pius rex minime curavit. Quapropter Galuuethienses supra modum intumescentes …*'. *Chron. Melrose*, 83.

13 '*Sed quia populus terrae noluit divisionem fendi admittere, facta fuit strages magna*.' *Annales Monastici*, ed. H. R. Luard (London, 1864–9), iii, 143.

14 *Matthæi Parisiensis, monachi Sancti Albani, Chronica Majora*, ed. H. R. Luard (London, 1872–83), iii, 364.

15 '*Quod indigene non equo animo ferentes irati sunt valde quia a domino rege impetrare nequerant quod Thomas filius naturalis dicti Alani ex heredatis tribus filiabus suis heredibus legitimis fieret heres et eorum dominus …*'. *Chron. Bower*, v, 146–8.

in a given situation. The *Lanercost Chronicle*'s account ties the Galwegians' rejection of Alan's daughters to the men's wish to be rid of royal authority over the region and to have instead Thomas 'as their lord and virtual king', a version of events reflecting resentment at the men's more general loss of autonomy following Alan's death, exemplified and intensified by the imposition of partible inheritance by female heirs.[16]

It has been suggested that in all of this Thomas of Galloway was a passive figure, used by the men of Galloway as a means of furthering the political end of keeping the lordship whole.[17] That he was a figurehead, whatever his own ambitions may have been, was recognised by the Scottish crown. Thomas was kept in custody for some sixty years following the suppression of the uprising in support of his claim. The possibility that he might be able to muster support from Galwegians and others (the 1234 rebellion had included Irish and Manx contingents) to claim his 'heritage', or that forces inimical to the Scottish crown could use a compliant Thomas in this regard as a pretext for another rebellion, appears to have been sufficient to keep him in confinement. According to the *Lanercost Chronicle*, John Balliol, son of Thomas's half-sister Dervorguilla, sought his release in 1286 at a meeting of the king's council.[18] If this is accurate, the Balliols themselves seem not to have viewed their kinsman as a threat to their interests – unsurprisingly, given the length of time that had passed. No action resulted from the meeting, the king dying unexpectedly that same night.

That Thomas's assumed inheritance rights might still present a threat to the stability of the kingdom was also recognised further afield. In early March 1296 Edward I, on the brink of war with Scotland and attempting to bring to heel the Scottish king John Balliol, seems to have considered using the now extremely aged Thomas to undermine Balliol authority in Galloway, based on Thomas's supposed right to the lordship or, at least, a belief in his continuing ability to command support from Galwegians. A letter was prepared for Thomas prior to a planned release of the captive, who would then be sent into Galloway.[19] The letter claimed that the English king was restoring to the people of Galloway 'all their liberties and customs, as they and their ancestors held these in the time of King David and of Alan the said Thomas's father', with a further offer to consider remission of rents 'of such an amount… as will content them'.[20] It seems a fairly forlorn strategy since, as Oram points

16 '*cujus aspera gens ad mala prompta, post obitum domini non per duos annos manus a malo continentes, et a subjectione regis Scottorum recedere volentes, filium ipsius Alani illegitimum, Thomam nomime, filias abhorrendo, sibi dominum et quasi regem constituerunt*.' *Chron. Lanercost*, 42. This contradicts the *Melrose Chronicle*'s claim that they petitioned Alexander II to be their lord.

17 Oram, *Lordship of Galloway*, 141.

18 *Chron. Lanercost*, 116.

19 *CDS*, ii, no. 728 (on which it is noted this is a duplicate; *CDS*, v, p. 57 ['References and Corrections'], advises this document was 'Cut for cancellation').

20 *CDS*, ii, no. 728.

out, Thomas's influence could hardly have been significant after sixty years in custody, and in the meantime the Balliols had become firmly established as the region's ruling family.[21] It is not clear that this letter was ever used. It is dated 6 March, but a second document produced by Edward's chancery the following day instructed the sheriff of Westmorland to receive Thomas of Galloway and convey him to the constable of Carlisle Castle, where he was to be kept in safe custody.[22] By the end of August that same year he was free and on his way back to Galloway, but this time with the authority only to reclaim the lands given to him by his father.[23]

The expectation of Galwegians in 1234–5 that they should be allowed to settle the lordship on the person of their own choice is not surprising. Galloway had, after all, always maintained a certain level of independence from the Scottish crown. But the latter years of Alan of Galloway's rule had shown that this freedom could have dire consequences for the wider realm.[24] The death of Alan of Galloway without a legitimate male heir was undoubtedly useful to Alexander II, and for more than one reason. Stringer argues persuasively that Alexander II's decision to intervene in the succession was 'an act of royal domination' intended to bring to an end Galloway's customary level of self-governance.[25] It facilitated Galloway's transition from a 'kingdom within a kingdom' to a lordship that was more securely integrated into the realm. It also sent a clear message that a political unit which failed to prioritise crown interests over other concerns would be punished by having its long-established freedoms removed. For Alexander II, Thomas's illegitimacy could be used as a means of increasing royal power. The letter prepared for Edward I indicates that he too considered exploiting Thomas's birth status to the same ends, counting on the Galwegians continuing to recognise the inheritance rights of illegitimate sons: this is implied in his letter promising to restore to them their ancient 'liberties and customs'. The Galloway conflict highlights that illegitimate succession was not considered unacceptable in at least some parts of Scotland in the second quarter of the thirteenth century. The royal responses to Galwegian attempts to recognise an illegitimate son as an heir then and later indicate just how firmly attitudes to it were entrenched: Alexander II was forced to settle the dispute by violent means rather than negotiation, and Edward I hoped that Thomas's assumed rights might be relevant to the local population several decades afterwards. Thomas's illegitimacy had a political

[21] Oram, *Lordship of Galloway*, 145.

[22] *CDS*, ii, no. 729 (it is calendared next to the letter which was cut for cancellation); *Calendar of the Close Rolls preserved in the Public Record Office. Edward I* (London, 1900–8), iii, 475.

[23] *CDS*, v, no. 162; *Rot. Scot.*, i, 23.

[24] Alan of Galloway's involvement in the conflict for the kingdom of Man and the Isles left Scotland vulnerable to attack from the Meic Uilleim, claimants to the throne.

[25] Stringer, 'Periphery and Core', 97.

significance of some magnitude and this was recognised by both kings, who each tried to use it to serve their own purposes.

Another effect of the changing legal environment of the thirteenth century was that it opened up the possibility of challenging the succession not only of those who were illegitimate, but of legitimately born landholders who had inherited the property from someone whose legitimacy could be questioned. Alan Durward, who had sought, ca. 1251, to further his political ambitions by obtaining a papal legitimation for his wife Marjory, illegitimate daughter of Alexander II, was one who seized on the chance to manipulate legitimacy laws in pursuit of another type of advancement.[26] Towards the end of 1255 he launched a bid to obtain the earldom of Mar, in which he held some lands, by alleging that the current holder, William, was in illegal possession of the earldom because his father Donnchad (d. 1242x4) and grandfather Morcunn (d. 1182x3) had both been illegitimate.[27] This being a legitimacy issue, it fell under jurisdiction of canon law, and Durward obtained a mandate for the case to be heard by the bishop of Brechin and the dean of Dunkeld.[28] The terms of the mandate were that they should look into the matter and send the outcome of their deliberations to the pope.

In March 1257 William of Mar obtained a second mandate, issued by Pope Alexander IV and addressed to the abbot of Jedburgh and archdeacons of Teviotdale and Dunblane, which suggested that the original mandate may have been a forgery and instructed the Scottish Churchmen to investigate.[29] The matter was then remitted to Cardinal Otto Ubaldini, cardinal-deacon of St Mary in Via Lata. Durward's legal representative in Rome was unable to produce a copy of the original mandate – the allegedly forged document – for inspection by Ubaldani, since, he claimed, it was in Scotland.[30] Ubaldini accordingly anulled the whole action to date, but gave the parties licence to obtain further papal letters in connection with the dispute. The case then took an ominous turn, from Mar's point of view, when the pope charged the bishop-elect of Aberdeen and the prior of the Aberdeen Friars Preachers to look into the legitimacy of Morcunn, with the decision as to who should have the earldom being reserved to the king.[31] This neatly demonstrates the division between ecclesiastical and secular law in cases where inheritance was disputed

26 See pp. 78–81.

27 The letters initiating the legal proceedings were addressed to Albin, bishop of Brechin, and Robert de Stuteville, dean of Dunkeld. Hammond, '*Hostiarii Regis Scotie*', 132.

28 This mandate does not survive but a papal letter recorded refers to it. Theiner, *Vet. Mon.*, no. 196; *CPL*, i, 349; Ferguson, *Medieval Papal Representatives*, 159, 258–9. A spurious charter purporting to describe an inquest by William the Lion in 1171, which found Morcunn to be the lawful heir of Mar, has been dated to ca. 1290. *RRS*, ii, no. 119; Duncan, *Making of the Kingdom*, 359 n.19.

29 *CPL*, i, 349; Theiner, *Vet. Mon.*, no. 196.

30 *CPL*, i, 351; Theiner, *Vet. Mon.*, no. 203.

31 Theiner, *Vet. Mon.*, no. 203.

on bastardy grounds: the Church had jurisdiction over determining legitimacy but awarding inheritance was a secular legal process over which, in this case, the king presided.[32] Just a few weeks later, in late October 1257, William participated in a *coup d'état* that saw Durward toppled from government. The pressing need to protect his earldom may have acted as an additional spur to William, whose opposition to the Durward government was already well-established.[33]

Duncan considers the original mandate to have been genuine and notes that William 'consumed two years' challenging it.[34] Given that the earldom – his inheritance and his legacy, the source of his wealth and status – was at stake, this is hardly surprising. It is worth noting that Morcunn was born in the first half of the twelfth century and became earl of Mar in or before 1150, and succeeded according to the inheritance practices of the time.[35] It is very probable that he was able to do so without his parents' relationship conforming to the canonical rules of marriage, which were, in any case, still being worked out by the Church at the presumed time of their marriage. Any written outcome explaining how the case was resolved has not survived, but Durward clearly failed to obtain the earldom since William of Mar continued as earl until his death in or before 1281, when his son Domnall succeeded him.

Durward's pursuit of the earldom implied his rejection of a settlement made some thirty years before between his father, Thomas, and William of Mar's father, Donnchad, by which Thomas and his heirs received a large accession of land in the region while Donnchad and his descendants kept the earldom itself.[36] Despite this, the legitimacy action clearly did alarm William, enough for him to contest it quite robustly. Whatever deal was struck in the 1220s was, in one sense, beside the point. A successful challenge to the legitimacy of one of his forebears could see William evicted from the lands – even if Durward was not recognised as the rightful heir to them, someone else might be. It appears that Durward was responding to changes in the legal climate of the thirteenth century. Legitimacy was more readily defined through the Church having a settled definition of lawful marriage, articulated in the *Liber Extra* (1234) and through conciliar canons such as those of the Fourth Lateran Council (1215). The Church's increasingly professionalised court system and developments in royal justice in Scotland, including the increased use of brieves from the 1230s,

[32] See p. 29. Litigants may not always have relied on Church courts: see pp. 44–5.

[33] R. Oram, 'Continuity, Adaptation and Integration: the Earls and Earldom of Mar, *c.* 1150–*c.* 1300' in Boardman and Ross, *Exercise of Power*, 62.

[34] Duncan, *Making of the Kingdom*, 569 n.19.

[35] He is styled earl of Mar in 1150. Fryde, *British Chronology*, 513.

[36] Oram, 'Continuity, Adaptation and Integration', 55–6; Hammond, '*Hostarii Regis Scotie*', 124–6. The fact that Durward did not pursue the action after he was ousted in October 1257 is cited by Duncan as evidence that his claim was weak and was taken seriously only because of his political status. Duncan, *Making of the Kingdom*, 569.

further helped to establish a culture in which challenges to succession could be more readily pursued.[37] These challenges and resulting judgements endorsed and advertised the prohibition of illegitimate succession.[38] That men such as Durward would take advantage of these developments is not surprising.

If the suit had been concluded in favour of Durward, it could have had interesting repercussions, since there would surely have been other territories passed down noble lines which at some point in the past included title-holders of dubious legitimacy. None of the papal representatives in the Durward–Mar case appears to have rejected the principle that Morcunn's legitimacy should be taken into consideration in deciding who now should possess the earldom, so it was apparently quite possible that ancestral illegitimacy could undermine the rights of current property-holders.

The fourteenth century

While the thirteenth century saw inheritance of estates disputed on grounds of bastardy (alleged and actual), and the foregrounding of legitimacy as a requirement for kingship, the fourteenth century saw major estates, including earldoms, being held by illegitimates. Archibald the Grim (d. 1400), the illegitimate son of Sir James Douglas (d. 1330), became third earl of Douglas in 1389.[39] His inheritance of the earldom was made possible by a tailzie drawn up in 1342 which restricted inheritance to the male line and included Archibald as ultimate named heir to some significant lands within it.[40] The inheritance was disputed and the eventual award of it to Douglas was the result partly of his exploitation of contemporary political tensions, but owed as much, if not more, to his reputation for military prowess and chivalric honour.[41]

He was the only surviving son of 'the Good' Sir James, whose achievements in the Wars of Independence were renowned. Archibald's own military and diplomatic activities between the 1360s and 1380s, combined with the magnitude of his landed possessions, ensured he became a central figure in the government. His illegitimacy was less important than his personal abilities. Among the stories in circulation about him is one related in the fifteenth-

37 See pp. 41–5.

38 'The exclusion of bastards was not imposed upon an unwilling population by popes and canon lawyers. It emerged from inheritance disputes, with lay litigants asking for papal adjudication.' McDougall, *Royal Bastards*, 174.

39 His life and career are summarised in Brown, *Black Douglases*, 53–94, and M. Brown, 'Douglas, Archibald, Lord of Galloway and Third Earl of Douglas (*c*. 1320–1400)', *ODNB*, 17 March 2018. The earldom fell vacant on the death of Sir James Douglas, the second earl, in 1388.

40 *RRS*, vi, no. 51; Brown, *Black Douglases*, 82.

41 For discussions of the political circumstances surrounding the third earl's gaining of the earldom, see Boardman, *Early Stewart Kings*, 147–53; Brown, *Black Douglases*, 76–86; Grant, 'Royal and Magnate Bastards', 330–5.

century *Liber Pluscardensis*. It claims that in 1398 Robert III sought to elevate Archibald to ducal status – at that time a title bestowed only on members of the royal family.[42] Archibald's disdainful refusal is presented as an indication of his superiority even to princes of the blood: his scorn for showy titles stands in contrast to the dukes of Rothesay and Albany, whose acceptance of ducal status the writer has just described.[43] The originator of the story was primarily concerned with explaining the earl's lack of a dukedom in a way that turned it from a possible snub into a badge of honour. But it also conveys a belief that Archibald was on a par with royalty, and the only reason he was not a duke alongside the princes was that he had chosen freely not to be one. The account corresponds to medieval ideas about true nobility being an innate characteristic which manifests itself in courageous and virtuous behaviour.

Nobility's capacity to transcend birth circumstances, eradicating the stain of bastardy, was demonstrated not only in Archibald but in his son. In 1387, before Archibald had succeeded in winning the Douglas earldom, his illegitimate son William of Nithsdale (ca. 1360–91), was given Egidia, Robert II's daughter, in marriage. According to fifteenth-century chronicles, she was exceptionally attractive. The *Liber Pluscardensis* says she was known as Egidia the Beautiful, and when word of the combination of her physical appeal and her virtue reached the king of France, he had a likeness of her made and sent to him.[44] The French king, the story continues, wished to marry her, but she was already spoken for: she, and the lordship of Nithsdale, had been given to William 'because of his [military] prowess'.[45] Whatever the truth of the claim that she was sought as a bride by the king of France, there may well be some truth in the stories of Egidia's beauty.[46] Her being given to an illegitimate son of an illegitimate magnate shows that illegitimacy mattered less than character and accomplishments. No marriage at this level was inseparable from high politics, and there were undoubtedly pragmatic factors at work in the decision to forge an alliance between the king and his most powerful and probably wealthiest magnate. But although Archibald had two legitimate sons in 1387, at least one of whom (Archibald, b. ca. 1369) was old enough to marry, it was the illegitimate William, like his father a courageous and skilful border warrior,

42 *Chron. Pluscarden*, i, 331; ii, 254.

43 The writer says that Archibald turned it down saying that 'the domain was not worth taking the name of duke for', and mocking those who acclaimed him using the title he refused.

44 *Chron. Pluscarden*, i, 324. '*Ipsa enim Egidia Pulcra nominata est*.' The entry in *Pluscarden* makes no mention of the illegitimacy of either Archibald or William; the latter is described simply as a son of the former.

45 *Chron. Pluscarden*, i, 324–5; ii, 248.

46 Wyntoun does not have the story of the King of France's interest in her, but describes Egidia as 'the fairest of fassown and off face,/ That men mycht fynd that day lyẅand,/ Thoucht thai had soucht oure all Scotland.' *Chron. Wyntoun*, iii, 31.

who was given the princess.[47] Nithsdale was understood to be the heir to his father's inborn nobility, again irrespective of the fact he too resulted from a forbidden liaison, and so may have been seen to 'deserve' a renowned beauty at the very top of the social tree.[48]

Factional politics of the late fourteenth century resulted in an earldom being awarded to another illegitimate member of the nobility. George Douglas (1378x80–?1403) was the illegitimate son of the widowed Margaret Stewart, countess of Angus (d. in/by 1418), and William, first earl of Douglas (d. 1384), who was married to Margaret's sister-in-law at the time George was conceived. In the 1380s, an intense political rivalry developed between John of Carrick (later Robert III) and Robert, earl of Fife (later duke of Albany), two of the legitimated sons of Robert II and Elizabeth Mure. Margaret, an adept political operator, commanded the loyalty of a faction of influential men whose support was sought by Fife. The price Margaret negotiated for her men backing Fife was her illegitimate son, George, the product of both adultery and canonical incest, being made earl of Angus (Table 16).[49]

The case of Archibald Douglas and that of his son William of Nithsdale illustrates the relationship between martial prowess and entitlement to political power, a connection that existed independently of any relationship between legitimate birth and such an entitlement. Its foundation lay in the tradition by which 'worth' played a significant role in matters of inheritance, especially of the kingship. Before primogeniture, the decision as to which of the sons, brothers and other male kindred of the royal house should succeed the king might depend on the attributes and abilities of each: 'worth' – personal excellence and the expression of this through honourable conduct – lifted one candidate above the others. Wyntoun, who claimed that Mael Coluim III was illegitimate, said that although Mael Coluim was 'noucht of lauchfull bed', he was deemed worthy of the kingship because of his 'stark hart and stowtnes'.[50] In Wyntoun's time, the law may have insisted that heirship depended on legitimate birth, but long traditions of political and social organisation recognised that exceptional accomplishment carried its own authority. The idea sometimes found expression in the use of the term 'true heir', a phrase denoting a lawful heir when used in legal documents, but which in some contexts conveyed something more, or other, than legal right. The term 'true' was often used to suggest something was genuine, especially where

47 Macdonald, *Border Bloodshed*, 92, 93, 105, 122–3, 183.

48 Following their marriage, Egidia and William received an annuity of £300 from the crown: *ER*, iii, 149, 172, 207, 239, 281, 687, 691, 699. William was killed in Königsberg in 1391, having become involved in a brawl with English knights who were, like him, northern crusaders. Macdonald, *Border Bloodshed*, 191.

49 For an account of how Margaret exploited the political tensions between the earl of Fife and John of Carrick to achieve this, see Boardman, *Early Stewart Kings*, 160–4.

50 *Chron. Wyntoun*, ii, 135. 'Stark' and 'stowt' were both terms of approval denoting firm resolve and superior martial capabilities.

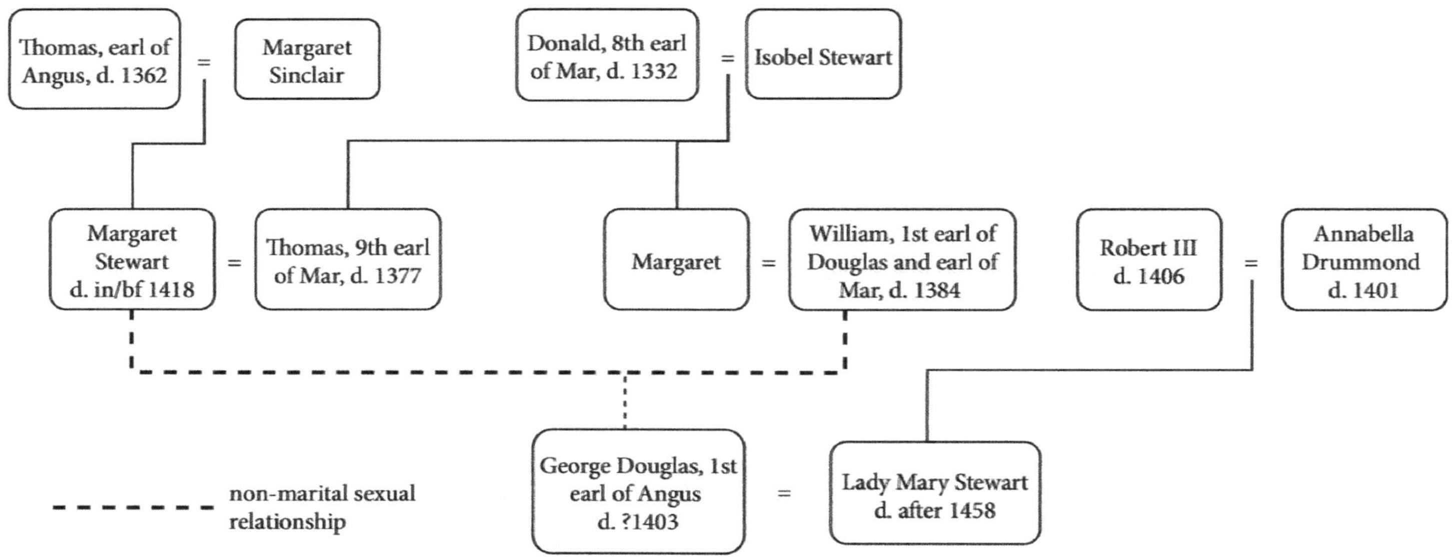

Table 16. George Douglas, first earl of Angus

its authenticity was not clear or might be doubted. In relation to heirship, 'true' could be used to claim that someone was the correct person to receive an inheritance, even though they may not be the obvious, or only, heir. In 1290 or 1291, Robert (V) Bruce had proclaimed that he was the 'legitimate and true heir designate' to the throne.[51] He was in the royal kindred, but so were others; Bruce's deployment of the term 'true heir' was intended to communicate his supposed right to the kingdom as the one most worthy of it.

A bastard, it was well-known, was a 'false heir'. The statutes of the Scottish Church condemned those who 'substitute false heirs' and doing so was an excommunicable offence.[52] Although 'bastard' is often found in Scottish legal texts as a neutral term denoting the simple fact of illegitimacy, its use to suggest a tainted, corrupt or dishonoured status, or as something false or counterfeit, was well known. 'But if ye be without chastisement, whereof all are partakers, then are ye bastards, and not sons,' advised the Old Testament.[53] Medieval culture recognised a dichotomy between sons and bastards.[54] According to Bernard of Parma (d. 1263), an illegitimate son was not a 'true' son, he merely had the appearance of one: *nothus … videtur verus filius, sed non est*.[55] Peter Damian (1007–72) described sexually active priests as 'bastard clerics' in contradistinction to their celibate counterparts. The latter were the 'legitimate sons of Abraham' who were heirs to the Promised Land, while the former would be excluded from the inheritance.[56] For these writers, sons and bastards are not only distinct categories but oppositional ones – although, biologically speaking, they are nothing of the kind – and these categories related to their status as heirs and non-heirs. The division also illustrates something of how the concept of bastardy could be played with to draw distinctions between authenticity and an empty imitation of it masquerading as the real thing. The rebellion against Henry II by his legitimate sons contrasted with the loyalty of his illegitimate son Geoffrey, whose successful campaign against the forces of William the Lion resulted in the capture of the Scottish king at Alnwick. According to Gerald of Wales, when the English king met with Geoffrey

51 *Anglo-Scottish Relations 1174–1328*, ed. E. L. G. Stones (London, 1970), no. 14. The use of 'designate' related to his claim that several decades before, Alexander II had made him his heir presumptive. See p. 107.

52 Patrick, *Statutes*, 75. The Church's ire may have been directed primarily at adulterous wives passing off their lovers' children as their husbands' heirs.

53 Hebrews, 12:8.

54 James V referred to his eldest legitimate brother as his father's 'fyrst begotten sone', despite James IV having had two older sons, born before marriage, one of whom was well known to James V. *RMS*, ii, no. 3204.

55 X 1.9.10, *Decretales D. Gregorii Papae IX. suae integritati una cum glossis restitutae*, in *Corpus Iuris Canonici* (Rome, 1582), at http://digital.library.ucla.edu/canonlaw/index.html (quote on p. 236). In the same gloss, Bernard of Parma defines *nothus* as one born of adultery.

56 *The Fathers of the Church. Mediaeval Continuation 7: Letters of Peter Damian 151–180*, transl. O. J. Blum and I. M. Resnick (Washington, DC, 1974), 150.

at Lincoln shortly afterwards, Henry declared, 'My other sons are the real bastards. He alone has proved himself legitimate and true.'[57] That character was transmitted through the bloodline raised suspicions of illegitimate sons inheriting their father's proclivity to sexual misconduct, but by the same token they might inherit their fathers' virtues, redeeming their status: bastards and non-heirs in law, true heirs in terms of their inheritance of noble character and so possessed of a special form of legitimacy that could transcend legal considerations.[58]

The fifteenth century

In the fifteenth century, the few illegitimates who came to have rights over an earldom were all members of the royal kindred. The first was Alexander Stewart (d. 1435), a grandson of Robert II via his son Alexander, earl of Buchan (d. 1405). The younger Alexander became earl of Mar in right of his wife, Isabella, countess of Mar (d. 1408) during the reign of his uncle, Robert III.[59] Opposition to the marriage from Buchan's brother, the duke of Albany, resulted in a marriage settlement stipulating that in the absence of any children of the marriage the earldom should revert to Isabella's heirs (not, as the initial contract had specified, Stewart heirs), but awarding Alexander life-rent.[60] Despite this, in 1427 Alexander managed to have his illegitimate son, Thomas, formally recognised as his successor to the earldom.[61] In the event Thomas predeceased his father and, since heirship status had not been extended to any of Alexander's other illegitimate sons, on Alexander's death the earldom escheated to the crown.

Another Stewart who obtained rights in an earldom, though not the title of earl, was Andrew Stewart, Lord Avondale (ca. 1420–88), an illegitimate great-great-grandson of Robert II.[62] Avondale obtained life-rent of the earldom of Lennox in 1471.[63] Although a great-grandson of Donnchad, earl of Lennox, through whose daughter Isabella the earldom passed to Avondale's paternal line, he was not the lawful heir; the life-rent was a gift of James III rather than

57 '*Alii filii mei se revera bastardos, iste vero solus se legitimum et verum esse probavit.*' *Giraldi Cambrensis Opera*, ed. J. S. Brewer (London, 1861–91), iv, 368.

58 For the belief that illegitimate offspring inherited a tendency to sexual incontinence, see p. 151.

59 S. Boardman, 'Lordship in the North-East: The Badenoch Stewarts I, Alexander Stewart, Earl of Buchan, Lord of Badenoch', *Northern Scotland* 16 (1996), 20–1.

60 *RMS*, ii, no. 1239; *Illustrations of the Topography and Antiquities of the Shires of Aberdeen and Banff*, ed. J. Robertson (Aberdeen, Spalding Club, 1847–69), iv, 167–8, 169–70.

61 *RMS*, ii, no. 53.

62 He was the son of Walter Stewart, son of Muiredach, second duke of Albany. Walter and Muiredach were both executed by James I in 1425.

63 *RMS*, ii, no. 1018; Macdougall, *James III*, 138–40.

something to which Avondale had a legal entitlement.[64] Avondale, along with his brothers Arthur and Walter, also obtained letters of legitimation from James III, in 1472 and 1479, both legitimations coming after, rather than before, his grant of the Lennox estates.[65] The king did not go so far as to give Avondale the title of earl, which designation was conferred on John Stewart, Lord Darnley, some two and a half years later, then transferred to John Haldane of Gleneagles three years after that, but Avondale continued to have liferent of the earldom even while others held the title.[66] The legitimations of 1479 made Arthur and Walter heirs to their brother Avondale, who was then in his late fifties. They could not, however, expect to obtain Lennox, as the grant to Avondale had not included heritable rights in the earldom.

No such scruples affected the king's successor: James IV simply granted an earldom to his illegitimate baby boy, James (b. 1500) in 1501.[67] The award of Moray to Janet Kennedy's son was the first of its kind – before then, the circumstances in which earldoms were granted to bastards were such that patronage of this kind could be understood as a matter of political expediency or a form of reward for service. James IV's grant is strikingly novel in the context of illegitimate babies born to the mistresses of kings, but perhaps less surprising in light of the fact that from James II onwards, kings' legitimate male children were given earldoms in babyhood. Extending the practice to non-marital children speaks to its normalisation in subsequent generations, but also to something else. The granting of an earldom to the infant James is illustrative of the way that the later fifteenth-century kings of Scotland, particularly James III and IV, conceived of their kingship as imperial in nature. James III's 1469 legislation enshrining the political philosophy that 'the king is emperor in his own realm' had direct implications for illegitimates, since it outlawed the activities of those notaries-public who derived their authority from the Holy Roman Emperor, unless they had first obtained permission to practise under the authority of the Scottish king.[68] These notaries-public could, it seems, provide written instruments of legitimation issued under imperial power, and so the legislation restricted one avenue by which people could obtain these. Although decisions and pronouncements previously made by such notaries would be allowed to stand, thenceforward their acts had no legal force, unless the notary concerned had previously subjected himself to examination the chief legal officer of his local bishop. The official forming a

64 J. Wormald, *Court, Kirk and Community: Scotland 1470–1625* (Edinburgh, 1981), 11.

65 *RMS*, ii, nos 1066–8 and 1425.

66 Macdougall, *James III*, 139.

67 *RMS*, i, no. 2586.

68 *RPS*, 1469/20. There are numerous instances of Scottish clerks and priests in the fourteenth and fifteenth centuries designing themselves 'by imperial authority notary-public', or 'notary-public by apostolic and imperial authority'. Examples include Patrick, *Statutes*, 237; *RPS*, 1391/5, 1416/1, A1440/2/1, A1450/1/1, 1445/9.

favourable opinion of the notary's character and professional expertise was not enough, however, as his recommendation then had to be approved by the king:

> sen oure soverane lord has ful jurisdictione and fre impire within his realme, that his hienes may mak notaris and tabellionis, quhais instrumentis sal have ful faith in all contractis civile within the realme. And in tyme cummyn that na notaris maid nor to be maid be the imperouris autorite have faith in contractis civile within the realme les than he be examinyt be the ordinare and apprevit be the kingis hienes.[69]

The right to decide who could overturn the legal disability of illegitimacy was something that James III evidently saw as intrinsic to his exercise of imperial authority. In April 1478, Alexander Rait, a notary, was indicted for 'tresonable usurpaciouune uppone his his [*sic*] hienes in the pretendit legittinacioune of James Egir, bastarde, in the name and autorite of the emperoure, contrare to oure souverain lordis croune and majeste riale ...'.[70] Rait having failed to compear in the king's court, the case was continued until June. No record of it appears in the June or subsequent parliaments, suggesting the matter was dropped. Tanner argues that this may have been because the accused was very unlikely to travel from his residence in Rome back to Scotland for the purpose of being tried for treason. He also notes that the language used by James, that Rait had committed treason by usurpation of royal authority, had only one previous documented use, in connection with the summoning of the lord of the Isles in 1476 to answer for his rebellion against the crown, and describes the indictment as 'a major over-reaction to as everyday a matter as the legitimisation of a bastard'.[71] Far from regarding it as an 'everyday matter', James III was seeking to make a public statement about who had the right to legitimate bastards, and about the possible consequences to those who commandeered such a right in defiance of royal decree. As far as James III was concerned, the secular prerogative to legitimate belonged strictly to the king, and to sidestep his authority in the matter of would be construed as treason. Rait did not have to appear in person, nor the case be brought to a conclusion, for that message to be transmitted and understood.

In the final years of William the Lion's reign, a son who had inherited the earldom of Menteith on the death of his father was required by the king to surrender it to a younger brother. While we do not know the full details of

69 *RPS* 1469/20. Tabellion = a subordinate notary.

70 *RPS*, 1478/4/4. Tanner discusses the case in 'James III (1460–1488)' in Brown and Tanner, *Scottish Kingship*, 214, 217–18. He suggests the charge against Rait may have been brought because of machinations by Archibald Whitelaw, ecclesiastical magnate and royal secretary, who had been in a dispute with Rait in the three years beforehand. For Alexander Rait generally, see E. Williamson, 'Alexander Rait, Familiar of the Pope, d. 1479', *IR* 52 (2001), 29–41.

71 *APS*, ii, 108; Tanner, 'James III', 214, 217.

the case, the overwhelmingly likely explanation is that the younger brother was the only legitimate one of the two. But the right of the younger was not, it seems, unequivocal at this time; arbitration by no less a figure than the king himself was required to settle what was evidently a dispute with rights on both sides. Some twenty years later, the men of Galloway wanted that lordship to be inherited by an illegitimate son, taking up arms against Alexander II over the matter. Another twenty years on, and a thirteenth-century earl of Mar who had inherited his earldom lawfully found his tenure of it threatened by the alleged bastardy of his forebears. These events were not the only legitimacy-related controversies in the politics of thirteenth-century Scotland. John of Kinross and Ailwin of Lennox spent five years disputing ownership of the earldom of Lennox on the premise that Ailwin was not lawfully born.[72] The last members of the Meic Uilleim line, whose progenitor, Donnchad II, was described as illegitimate, were executed for their attempts to claim the throne. Alan Durward, son of one of the magnates who helped to suppress the Meic Uilleim rebellion, sought (unsuccessfully) to have his wife, Alexander II's illegitimate daughter Marjorie, legitimated in an effort to make her and their children heirs to the kingdom. Descendants of royal illegitimates, including of Marjorie, presented themselves as Competitors for the Scottish throne in the last decade of the century. Evidence of wider shifts in inheritance practices are seen in the thirteenth century. Neil, earl of Carrick (d. 1256), having only daughters, separated the headship of the kindred from possession of the title and lands of Carrick: the headship passed by charter to his nephew Lachlann, while the earldom was inherited by his eldest daughter, Marjorie.[73] MacQueen, pointing to hints in Welsh and Irish texts suggestive of heads of kindred being elected, says it is possible the separation had nothing to do with 'conscious avoidance' of the requirements of primogeniture and was simply a case of Lachlann being designated head of the kindred.[74] Nonetheless, it does suggest that the kindred preferred male leadership, and it was felt important that this preference be given legal recognition in a charter.

The experience of war in fourteenth-century Scotland provided opportunities for men to distinguish themselves on the battlefield. A stellar reputation for martial prowess could, it seems, eclipse the disadvantage, where such existed, of illegitimate birth. An illegitimate man could become an earl, and his illegitimate son could marry a princess. The third earl of

[72] See p. 45.

[73] *RMS*, i, nos 508–9; J. Bannerman, 'Macduff of Fife', in Grant and Stringer, *Medieval Scotland*, 33–4.

[74] H. L. MacQueen, 'The Kin of Kennedy, "Kenkynnol" and the Common Law', in *Medieval Scotland*, ed. Grant and Stringer, 281. He adds, 'Perhaps, as John Bannerman has suggested above [a reference to Bannerman's essay in the same volume], it should be seen as an instance of the accommodations between two systems of which there are other examples at this period [...].'

Douglas obtained his earldom only partially through his military success and the warlike qualities which had propelled his career: he owed much to the fact that, decades previously, a kinsman had included him as a remainder in a tailzie of some important estates within the earldom. The use of tailzies, which became very extensive in the fourteenth century, allowed landholders to recognise illegitimate family members, ordinarily non-heirs, as lawful recipients of family lands, though usually only if – as happened in the third earl of Douglas's case – a legitimate line failed.[75]

It was the third earl's political clout that enabled him to gain the hand of the king's (legitimate) daughter for his illegitimate son; similarly, the Countess of Angus's political strength and influence was deployed to obtain an earldom for her illegitimate son. Royal connections and the king's favour were responsible for rights in earldoms being granted to other prominent illegitimates in the fifteenth century. The relationship between illegitimacy and royal power took on a different complexion in the reign of James III, with his issue of a royal edict forbidding public notaries from involving themselves in legitimations, which were now the exclusive prerogative of the king. Failure to recognise this was treason. In one sense, this was extraordinary; in another, it was merely the logical conclusion of three centuries in which royal power was routinely exerted to control and manage the access to lands, wealth and power available to illegitimates.

75 See pp. 47–8.

Conclusion

Before the thirteenth century, the expectation of a medieval Scot that he (and sometimes she) might succeed to heritage was not necessarily linked to confidence that his parents' union was a marriage conforming to the canon law definition of the term. Evidence from the twelfth century, though patchy, suggests that some fathers were concerned to ensure only legitimate children were recognised as heirs, while others understood heirship rights to inhere in other factors, to do with the perceived competence of sons or brothers to manage the estates.

The thirteenth century was a turning point. The Church's development of settled definitions of lawful marriage, legitimacy and illegitimacy, and its dissemination of the compilation of decretals known as the *Liber Extra*, occurred at around the same time as the enlargement in Scotland of the range of legal instruments and processes in royal law intended to ensure estates came into the possession of lawful heirs. Together these created a legal environment in which succession to estates was more widely understood to be the sole prerogative of the legitimate, and inheritances could be more readily challenged on grounds of a claimant's illegitimacy.

A series of high-profile political events and disputes in thirteenth-century Scotland centring on illegitimate succession, in relation to the earldoms of Menteith, Galloway, Mar and Lennox, and in relation to the kingdom itself – the killing of the last Meic Uilleim, the attempted legitimation of Alexander II's daughter Marjorie, and the Great Cause – drove home the message that illegitimacy and heirship were incompatible.

Arriving at this position was not a straightforward process. Some indication of its complexity can be seen at the national level, in the matter of inheritance of the throne. Donnchad II (d. 1094) is the first king of Scots to be called illegitimate in our sources. Writing between six and thirteen years after Donnchad's death, Turgot implies Donnchad's illegitimacy by saying that, of Mael Coluim III's sons, only the sons of Margaret were born of a legal marriage. Turgot's claim goes further than saying Mael Coluim was not lawfully married to Donnchad's mother: he says that there were no legal marriages in Scotland before that of Margaret and Mael Coluim. The obvious implication of Turgot's assertion is that Mael Coluim III was illegitimate, but there is no hint in Turgot's writing that Margaret was married to someone who should not have been king. Around 1126, another source close to the English throne baldly describes Donnchad as *nothus*. The same chronicle calling him a bastard makes no suggestion he was a wrongful king. However the imputation of illegitimacy to Donnchad came to be used later, there was no clear-cut relationship in eleventh-century Scotland between canonical legitimacy and rights to the throne. Donnchad's throne-worthiness depended far more on the fact that he was a son of Mael Coluim III, and descended from a venerable Scottish royal line, than on whether or not his parents' union conformed to the contemporary canon law definition of a legally valid marriage.

Neither was the relationship between birth status and eligibility for the throne uncomplicated in the twelfth century. Mael Coluim, son of Alexander I, did not consider his illegitimacy to be a fatal impediment to kingship, and neither did his supporters. Mael Coluim was, like Donnchad, the son of a king of Scots in a long line of the same, and also, by virtue of his paternal grandmother Margaret, a scion of the West Saxon royal line. He and his followers perhaps saw his birth circumstances as trivial when set against those lineages. The only surviving grandson of Donnchad II to descend through Donnchad's male line also considered himself to be throne-worthy, and gained powerful supporters who appear to have agreed with this assessment. Domnall Bán mac Uilleim was very probably illegitimate, although this cannot be known with certainty. Scotland had only legitimately born kings in the twelfth century, but this was in part the result of their good fortune in being able to defeat these challenges; had an illegitimate rival been militarily successful, it seems highly unlikely he would have been rejected as king on the grounds that his parents' union did not meet the criteria for lawful marriage.

The thirteenth century saw the extinction of the Meic Uilleim threat. Well before the end of that century, it was widely accepted that illegitimacy was incompatible with kingship, or with heirship more generally. But even in the 1290s, it was not so vitally important a qualification for a prospective king that marriages in previous generations were examined to ensure the resulting offspring, through whom a right to the throne descended, were lawfully born. The principle that illegitimacy of an antecedent made present tenure of an estate insecure had been established some decades earlier, but it seems to have been selectively applied in the Great Cause.

By this time, it had been established that not everyone born illegitimate need remain so. One consequence of this in the fourteenth century was that a bastard-born royal son became king of Scots. Historians have disagreed over the effectiveness of legitimation for inheritance, especially of the throne. The sticking-point has been a provision in *Regiam Majestatem* which flatly denies the inheritance rights of those legitimated by their parents' later intermarriage. Careful examination of our sources, however, reveals that the evidence points in the other direction: that legitimation was fully effective for inheritance in

Scotland from at least the middle of the thirteenth century, and very possibly from the latter part of the twelfth.

This was germane to all families, not just the royal line. The legal disability excluded illegitimate people from inheritance but even in matters of heirship, where it should matter most, illegitimacy was not always the most undesirable quality in an heir. In the late twelfth or early thirteenth century, there is a hint that royal succession by an illegitimate son is understood to be unlawful, but that fraternal succession is overtly wrongful. In the fourteenth, the use of tailzies shows that for some, an illegitimate male successor was better than a legitimate female one.

The formulation of laws by which children born outside marriage were denied heirship rights was part of a wider effort to reform society. Scots accepted the rules but demanded means of circumventing them. Families took advantage of mechanisms in both canon law and common law to render their offspring legitimate, or, if this was not possible, to ensure they received some share of the family's wealth. Some parents could regularise their children's status by marrying, and if there was no legal impediment to their union then they could do so without incurring the cost of a dispensation; without a dispensation they do not appear in our records. Our evidence, therefore, is necessarily skewed towards those families who had lands or property to begin with, and sufficient means to pay for a marriage dispensation, or the fee for a notarial instrument, or some other expense associated with ensuring offspring were provided for. At the heart of this activity was an unwillingness to write off children whose birth circumstances denied them an advantage enjoyed by their legitimate peers but whose value to the family was measured by other criteria.

Illegitimacy was a deeply personal matter for individuals, touching on their most intimate relationships, and on the composition and organisation of their families. Over the course of the middle ages, illegitimacy as a personal concern increasingly came to overlap with legal, political, social, economic and religious developments. This book investigates how it did so in Scotland. As a case study of illegitimacy within a geographical boundary, it seeks to contribute to wider discussions about the medieval family in Britain, Europe and beyond. The scope for direct comparison with other societies is limited by, among other things, variations in the survival (and creation in the first place) of relevant records or narrative sources. We know a good deal about aspects of illegitimacy in late medieval Italy, and Florence in particular, thanks to the preservation of a significant body of legal and financial material associated with widespread, institutionalised slave ownership. Much of it was generated by the need to determine the status and rights of children fathered on slave women by freeborn men, and by a taxation system which collected information on illegitimate people alongside others in households and institutions.[1] Fathering children on women of unfree status surely went on in Scotland as everywhere else, but since there was no systematised collection of data related to it, we know very little about the Scottish incidence of this.

Among those of sufficient wealth to leave traces in our records, the experiences of some are harder to recover than others. The low visibility of women in our sources presents challenges. Our knowledge of the mothers of Scottish royal bastards before the 1490s is very slight, and there are important figures whose birth status is unknown to us, because we have no knowledge of their mothers' identity or their relationship to the fathers concerned. Domnall Bán mac Uilleim made a concerted bid for the throne as the son of William fitz Duncan. Does Dommall's mother not appear in our sources because her relationship with Domnall's father was a non-marital liaison, or because any evidence of their marriage that may once have existed has been lost? Our inclination is to assume the former, but we hesitate to do so because it is not all that unusual for us to know nothing, or next to nothing, about the wives of even high-profile men.[2]

Although the bureaucracy of the Church was prodigious, Scottish survivals are relatively few, and questions about the careers of Scottish illegitimate clerics remain to be answered. Why, for example, did Scotland consecrate only one bishop known to be illegitimate after 1255 and before 1426? I have tentatively suggested that English interference in Scottish ecclesiastical affairs from the late 1250s, combined with the political climate resulting from war in much of the fourteenth century, may have had something to do with it. The matter requires further investigation, to establish whether other factors also had a role to play.

Studies of illegitimacy in medieval France suggest that from the late fourteenth century, and especially in the fifteenth, the most important royal and Church offices increasingly came to be held by the illegitimate sons of the upper nobility.[3] The example set by French kings and upper nobility

1 T. Kuehn, *Illegitimacy in Renaissance Florence* (Ann Arbor, MI, 2002); T. Kuehn, *Emancipation in Late Medieval Florence* (New Brunswick, NJ, 1982); see also A. Molho, *Marriage Alliance in Late Medieval Florence* (London, 1994); R. M. Karras, *Unmarriages: Women, Men and Sexual Unions in the Middle Ages* (Philadelphia, PA, 2012), 80–108. Karras includes Iceland in her analysis. Other works by Kuehn shed further light on late Florentine bastardy: see, in particular, 'Reading between the Patrilines: Leon Battista Alberti's *Della Famiglia* in Light of His Illegitimacy', in *Law, Family, and Women: Toward a Legal Anthropology of Renaissance Italy*, ed. T. Kuehn (Chicago, IL, 1991), 157–75; and '"As if Conceived Within a Legitimate Marriage": A Dispute Concerning Legitimation in *Quattrocento* Florence', *The American Journal of Legal History* 29 (1985), 275–300.

2 For example, we do not know the identity of the wives of Earl Cospatric (I) of Lothian (d. 1138) or renowned warrior Sir James Douglas (d. 1330); we have only a first name (Eleanor) for the second wife of Robert (VI) Bruce (d. 1304), father of Robert I.

3 M. Harsgor, '*L'essor des bâtards nobles au XVe siècle*', *Revue Historique* 253 (1975), 337–40, 342–3. See also F. Autrand, '*Naissance illégitime et service de l'Etat: les enfants naturels*

in displaying and fêting their illegitimate offspring, it has been suggested, encouraged lesser nobles to do the same. This raises intriguing possibilities for the effect that Robert II's many bastard sons being known in public life may have had on attitudes to illegitimacy among the Scottish nobility, especially when viewed in conjunction with the high status of certain illegitimate men, such as Archibald the Grim Douglas and his son William of Nithsdale, and with the granting of an earldom to George Douglas.

While looking at areas for future exploration, we also need to reassess our treatment of the subject to date. Our understanding of illegitimacy in medieval Scotland has lacked nuance, being too often generalised, influenced by Anglo-centric or Church-centric interpretations, and by the imposition of later readings onto earlier experiences. This book has sought to offer a corrective, and to demonstrate not only that illegitimacy was more important to Scottish society in the middle ages than has hitherto been appreciated, but that a fuller comprehension of it is essential to our understanding of relations between public and private life in medieval Scotland.

dans le milieu de robe parisien, XIVe–XVe siècle', *Revue Historique* 267 (1982), 289–303; T. R. Davies, 'The Glory of Being a Bastard?', *Coat of Arms* 3.108 (1979), 94–9. Both Harsgor and Davies discuss the late medieval French construction of high-born illegitimates as superior to their legitimate siblings.

Appendix I

Scottish kings and their illegitimate offspring

A brief outline of each of the sons is provided below this table.[1]

Alexander I r. 1107–24	**Mael Coluim** fl. 1124–56
William the Lion r. 1165–1214	**Isabella** (Avenel), m. i) 1183 Robert (III) de Brus; ii) 1191 Robert de Ros. Great-grandmother of William de Ros, Competitor.[2]
	Ada (d. in/by 1200) m. 1184 Earl Patrick of Dunbar. Great-grandmother of Earl Patrick of Dunbar or March, Competitor.
	Margaret (Whitsome) m. 1193 Eustace de Vescy. Grandmother of William de Vescy, Competitor.
	Robert of London ca. 1170–1225
Alexander II r. 1214–49	**Marjorie** m. Alan Durward. Grandmother of Nicholas de Soulis, Competitor.
Robert I r. 1306–29	**Sir Robert Bruce of Liddesdale** (d. 1332)
	Margaret m. Robert Glen
	Elizabeth m. 1364 Sir Walter Oliphant of Gask
	Christian or Christina of Carrick fl. 1328–9
	Nigel of Carrick? (d. 1332)

[1] For daughters, see pp. 124–36.
[2] 'Competitor' = Competitor for the Scottish throne in 1291–2.

Robert II	**James Stewart of Kinfauns** fl. 1372–1405
r. 1371–90	**Sir John Stewart of Cardney** fl. 1372–1425
	Alexander Stewart of Inverlunan fl. 1378–84
	Sir John Stewart of Dundonald (d. 1425) m. in/aft. 1408 Elizabeth Graham, daughter of Sir William Graham
	John Stewart (d. in/bf. 1449), heritable sheriff of Bute, m. in/by 1419 Jonet Sympill, daughter of John Sympill of Eliotstown
	Thomas Stewart (1360–1430), archdeacon of St Andrews
	James Stewart (d. in/bf 1379), canon of Glasgow and prebendary of Stobo
	Alexander Stewart (ca. 1374–in/aft. 1407), canon of Glasgow and prebendary of Barlanark
	Walter Stewart (d. 1433x4), dean of Moray, treasurer of Scotland
	Katherine? m. Sir John Logan
	Agnes? Mother of William Cunningham, vicar of Dundonald (the latter d. 1426x7)
	Mary? m. Sir John Danielston
	Sir Walter Stewart of Burleigh? (d. in/bf. 1454)
Robert III	**James Stewart of Kilbride** fl. 1395–1421
r. 1390–1406	**Sir John Stewart of Auchengowan, Blackhall and Ardgowan** fl. 1390–1423
James II	**Sir John Stewart of Sticks?**
r. 1437–60	

James IV r. 1488–1513	**Alexander Stewart** (ca. 1493–1513), archbishop-designate of St Andrews and administrator **Katherine Stewart** (ca. 1494–1543x50) m. in or by December 1507, James Douglas, later third earl of Morton and lord of Dalkeith **James Stewart**, Earl of Moray, Lord Abernethy, sheriff of Elgin and Forres (1500–1544x5), m. Lady Elizabeth Campbell (d. in/bf. 1548), daughter of Colin Campbell, third earl of Argyll **Margaret Stewart** (1496x7–in/aft. 1562) m. i) in or by April 1510, John Gordon, Master of Huntly (d. 1517); ii) ca. 1530, Sir John Drummond of Innerpeffry **Janet Stewart** (ca. 1510–62), m. ca. 1523 Malcolm Fleming, later third Lord Fleming (d. 1547); mistress of King Henri II of France

Appendix II

Illegitimate sons of Scottish kings

It is probable that some illegitimate royal children of medieval Scotland are unknown to us, either because of poor record survival, or because arrangements made for them were never recorded in the first place. Among the publicly acknowledged offspring, for the most part we know only about those who survived to adulthood, but surely some illegitimate children, like their legitimate counterparts, died before gaining maturity.[1] Before those of James IV, illegitimate daughters appear in our records mainly in relation to their marriages. References to illegitimate sons, while also appearing in connection with grants of land, or payments from the royal coffers, are additionally visible as participants in their fathers' military campaigns, or occupying roles associated with royal government, or pursuing careers in the Church.

The birth of any child provided reassurance of paternal fecundity, but the arrival of sons tended to be especially welcome, as signifiers of masculinity and God's favour. Those born before their fathers' marriages may have been viewed as a highly promising sign that male heirs would follow. William the Lion's son, Robert of London, was born around sixteen years before William's marriage and perhaps twenty-eight years before his heir, Alexander, made an appearance.[2] The year in which Robert of Liddesdale, illegitimate son of Robert I, was born is not known with certainty: it may have been just before the birth of his daughter in marriage, or it may have been a few years after this event, but it was certainly over twenty years (and perhaps around thirty years) before the king's legitimate son and heir was born.[3] Both of James IV's illegitimate sons, Alexander and James, had been born before he married

1 The birth, and death in infancy, of one of James IV's illegitimate children are known only from terse entries in the Treasurers' Accounts, as is the birth of another who later disappears from the record. *TA*, ii, 45–7, 298, 358, 393–4, 407, 408; iii, 344, 311.

2 He was probably born around 1170. William married in 1286 and Alexander II was born in 1198.

3 Watson puts Liddesdale's birth between ca. 1293 and ca. 1300; Penman suggests 1296. F. Watson, 'Bruce, Sir Robert, Lord of Liddesdale (c. 1293–1332), Royal Bastard', *ODNB*, 26 March 2019; Penman, *Robert the Bruce*, 49. David II was born in 1324.

Margaret Tudor; their first son, who died in infancy, arrived some fourteen years after Alexander's birth.[4]

These four illegitimate sons were treated particularly well by their fathers. As far as the overall picture is concerned, paternal support and generosity was variable. The reasons why some sons fared better than others are hard to discern, suggesting that at least some of the factors were personal to the individuals and relationships concerned. Robert II appears to have done more to promote the Church career of his son Thomas than he did the careers of his other clerical sons, but whether this was born of a particular fondness he had for Thomas (or Thomas's mother), or some other reason concerning Thomas's own talents and aptitudes, or some anticipated political advantage, may not be knowable. None of these reasons are incompatible with each other, nor with other possible motives for the king's preferment of this son. It may be noted that Robert II did not treat all his legitimate sons equally either: his youngest, Walter, received more modest estates than his brother and half-brothers, obtaining an earldom only in his forties.

Robert of Liddesdale was part of his father's household, living alongside not only his legitimate half-brother David, but also his illegitimate cousins, Alexander and Thomas Bruce, sons of Robert I's brother Edward, who were educated alongside the future king.[5] The education of illegitimate royal offspring alongside their legitimate kin and other children at court was by no means unique to the Bruces: it was also a feature of James IV's court, and may have been quite usual. Such arrangements encouraged bonds between illegitimate children and other members of the king's family, and account at least in part for some illegitimate royal offspring, after their fathers' deaths, continuing to receive support, gifts or recognition from their legitimate royal kin. Alexander II included his half-brother Robert of London in the business of government: Robert was a witness to Alexander's charters, as he had been to their father's. Robert III granted his illegitimate half-brother John Stewart the lands of Cardney in 1399, several years after the death of their father. The same John Stewart was knighted, along with another of Robert II's illegitimate sons, also called John Stewart, on the occasion of their nephew James I's coronation. James IV provided tochers for the first two marriages of his illegitimate cousin Margaret Crichton.[6] These are among many similar examples offering persuasive evidence that illegitimate royal sons and daughters formed an integral part of the royal family.

4 Alexander Stewart was probably born in 1493; his brother James in 1500. James IV married Margaret Tudor in 1503 when she was only thirteen and it was 1507 before their first son, James (1507–8) was born. James IV's only surviving legitimate son, James V, would later refer to this short-lived brother as his father's 'fyrst begotten sone'. *RMS*, ii, no. 3204. He clearly was not; James V's comments should be viewed in the context of 'sons' and 'bastards' belonging to conceptually distinct categories: see pp. 184–5.

5 Penman, *David II*, 39.

6 *ER*, xii, 465, 564–5; *RSS*, i, nos 1219, 2089. James died before Margaret married a third time. Her second husband perished with James, his son Alexander, and many others, at Flodden.

Known illegitimate sons of Scottish kings

Alexander I

Alexander I's illegitimate son Mael Coluim (fl. 1124–56) is known only through chronicle entries detailing his rebellions against the kingship of his uncle David, successor to Alexander.[7] He had at least one son with a woman from the family of Sumarliði (d. 1164), king of the Hebrides and ruler of Argyll and Kintyre; she seems to have been either Sumarliði's sister or his daughter, since Mael Coluim's sons are given as Sumarliði's *nepotes* (nephews or grandsons). Mael Coluim was captured and imprisoned in 1134 and was still alive in 1156, when his son Domnall joined him in prison following his involvement in an uprising against David's grandson, Mael Coluim IV. Their eventual fates are not recorded.

William the Lion

William the Lion's son Robert of London (ca. 1170–1225) had 'strikingly close associations with his father', and was active in political life from his mid-teens, usually within the king's immediate circle.[8] His natal family was the 'of Londons' who held lands in Lessudden (St Boswells) in Roxburghshire. Robert received from William the old royal centres of Cadzow (Clydesdale), Aberdour, and Kellie (both Fife), as well as a toft in every royal burgh.[9] He was a frequent witness to his father's charters, often styled 'my son', and in the earliest extant example of the future Alexander II witnessing one of his father's charters, both Alexander and Robert are described identically as 'son of the lord King'.[10] Robert was in service to the English crown for a time during the second decade of the thirteenth century.[11] The nature and purpose of this service are obscure but may have related to the pact entered into by William the Lion and King John of England in 1212, when John provided Brabantine mercenaries to help the Scottish king defeat the Meic Uilleim.[12]

7 See pp. 57–9.

8 Taylor, 'Robert de Londres', 106. Taylor's essay on Robert provides the fullest account of him. Stringer describes Robert as 'William I's favourite bastard'. K. Stringer, 'The War of 1215–17', in Oram, *Reign of Alexander II*, 108. Robert is also briefly discussed by G. W. S. Barrow in *The Anglo-Norman Era in Scottish History* (Oxford, 1980), 63–4, 101–2, 183–4. See also *PoMS*, www.poms.ac.uk/record/person/307/.

9 Taylor, 'Robert de Londres', 107–8, 112.

10 In *RRS*, ii, no. 493, Alexander is in first place among the witnesses, Robert in third. See p. 70 n.72 for examples of Robert being styled the king's son, without reference to his illegitimacy.

11 *CDS*, i, no. 746; *Royal and Other Historical Letters Illustrative of the Reign of Henry III*, ed. W. W. Shirley (London, 1862–6), i, 163–4; Taylor, 'Robert de Londres', 110–18.

12 Taylor, 'Robert de Londres', 113–14. Taylor argues that Robert was among a faction at the Scottish court opposed to Alexander II's war with John.

After Robert of London's death in 1225 (or just possibly in the early weeks of 1226), we know of no more illegitimate sons born to Scottish kings until the closing years of that century.

Robert I

Robert I's eldest known son, Robert of Liddesdale (d. 1332), similarly occupied a privileged position in his father's family.[13] Knighted by his father on the eve of Bannockburn, Robert was given various grants of land including, in 1321, Sprouston, which was to be held by him as it had been held by the de Vescy family, as a regality.[14] Sprouston had been brought into the de Vescy holdings by Margaret, illegitimate daughter of William the Lion, as her tocher when she married Eustace de Vescy in 1193.[15] Prior to coming into Robert I's hands, Liddesdale had been held by Nicholas de Soulis, the Competitor who was grandson of Alexander II's illegitimate daughter Marjorie. It was forfeited by his son, Sir William, following discovery of his part in the so-called Soulis Conspiracy against Robert I in 1320. Robert of Liddesdale also had lands in Angus, though he later lost them when they were restored to Henry Percy by the terms of the Anglo-Scottish peace of 1328.[16] That same year, Liddesdale received the first instalment of a 500-merk grant from his father.[17] He was killed at the battle of Dupplin Moor in 1332.[18]

Nigel of Carrick may possibly have been another illegitimate son of Robert I. He had an annuity of £20 between 1328 and 1331.[19] His being called 'of Carrick' in some sources may be suggestive of him being Robert's son, but does not make it certain; John of Carrick (d. 1380x1), canon of Glasgow and

13 *RRS*, v, no. 172 and 23–4; *RMS*, i, App. 1, no. 53; Ibid., App. 2, nos 283, 291, 356, 458, 462, 548; *ER*, i, 115, 212, 287; Stevenson, *Documents*, ii, 464. Liddesdale was a witness to several of his father's charters. *RRS*, v, nos 244, 267, 293, 294, 309, 310, 312, 329, 353, 354; *RMS*, i, App. 1, 19.

14 *RRS*, v, no. 172; *RMS*, i, App. 2, nos 283, 291; A. Grant, 'Franchises North of the Border: Baronies and Regalities in Medieval Scotland', in M. Prestwich, ed., *Liberties and Identities in the Medieval British Isles* (Woodbridge, 2008), 167.

15 J. Morton, ed., *The Monastic Annals of Teviotdale* (Edinburgh, 1832), 115; *Orig. Par. Scot.*, i, 440. Sprouston again came into the hands of a high-ranking illegitimate in the early 1360s, when it was held by Archibald the Grim, third earl of Douglas. Brown, *Black Douglases*, 166, 170, 192.

16 *RMS*, i, App. 1, no. 53 and App. 2, nos 355 (Liddesdale) and 458 (Angus); Penman, *David II*, 27, 31. He was given lands of the heirs of Alexander of Abernethy, who was forfeited in 1315; hostilage in the town of Scone, and the lands and hostilage of the late Roger Mowbray. *RMS*, i, App. 2, nos 356, 462, 548, 485.

17 *ER*, i, 115, 212, 287.

18 *Scalacronica*, transl. Maxwell, 91; *Chron. Wyntoun*, ii, 388; T. Walsingham, *Historia Anglicana*, ed. H. T. Riley (London, 1863), i, 194; *Chronicon Henrici Knighton, vel Cnitthon, Monachi Leycestrensis*, ed. J. R. Lumby (London, 1889–95), i, 463.

19 *ER*, i, cxxix–xxx, 114, 208, 339, 367, 400.

chancellor from 1370 to 1377, was not the king's son.[20] Notably less is known of Nigel than of Liddesdale. Contemporary sources do not call him a son of the king and he is not known to have received lands or charters. Walsingham gives him as '*Nigellus Brus*', whereas in his preceding sentence, Liddesdale is '*Robertus Brus Nothus*'.[21] In modern historiography, Nigel is very frequently said to have died at Neville's Cross, perhaps because Burnett says this, and therefore so did Dunbar (citing Burnett); one or both may have influenced Paul.[22] Burnett claims Walsingham and Knighton as authorities for Nigel's death at Durham, but both chroniclers place his death at Dupplin Moor in 1332.[23] There are no payments to him recorded after 1331.

Robert II

Of the nine known illegitimate sons of Robert II, at least three – James, Alexander and John Stewart – were the result of his relationship with Mariota de Cardney. They may have had a fourth son, Walter. In 1372 James Stewart, 'beloved son' of the king, was given a lifetime annuity of £16 sterling from the barony of Abernethy; should James not have legitimate heirs, the annuity was heritable by his uterine brother, John.[24] In January 1379, Alexander was given Inverlunan in Forfar, lands which were among those resigned to the king by Richard Mowat, canon and chancellor of Brechin Cathedral.[25] Richard may have done so in exchange for the £20 sterling annuity he received from the customs of Dundee for the remainder of his life, and also perhaps – though this came some months later – for the king regranting to Richard his barony of Kinblethmont in Angus on the basis that Richard's illegitimate son ('*filio suo bastardo*') would be heir to that estate.[26] Five years later Alexander was given the neighbouring land of Lunan, and at the same time he received Pitfour in Aberdeenshire.[27]

This second grant, in January 1384, was made on the same day that Robert II gave Perthshire lands to his other two sons with Mariota. John was given

20 Burnett says that Nigel 'is shown almost certainly to have been a son of the king' because one entry in *ER* styles him 'of Carrick'. *ER*, i, cxxix–xxx. See Watt, *Graduates*, 89–92 for examples of men styled 'of Carrick' who were not sons of kings.

21 Walsingham, *Historia Anglicana*, i, 194.

22 *ER*, i, xxx; Dunbar, *Scottish Kings*, 142; *SP*, i, 8 (Paul gives no reference for his statement that Nigel was killed at Durham in 1346); G. W. S Barrow, 'Robert I [Robert Bruce] (1274–1329), King of Scots', *ODNB*, 26 March 2019.

23 Walsingham, *Historia Anglicana*, i, 194; *Chron. Knighton*, i, 463.

24 *RMS*, i, no. 519. See also a crown annuity to him of £10, paid between 1391 and 1405. *ER*, iii, 276, 388, 414, 441, 475, 521, 540, 570, 629.

25 *RMS*, i, no. 669.

26 *RMS*, i, nos 670, 671; A. Jervise, *The History and Traditions of the Land of the Lindsays in Angus and Mearns, with Notices of Alyth and Meigle* (Edinburgh, 1882), 228. Richard had previously (in 1377) resigned his barony of Fern in favour of William. *RMS*, i, no. 663.

27 *RMS*, i, no. 731.

lands in the thanage of Kinclaven, while James was granted the east half of Kinfauns, along with Rate and the mill of Forteviot.[28] Each of the charters makes it clear that the recipient is a son of the king by Mariota de Cardney, and for each grant the heirs are to be the recipient's own legitimate issue, whom failing, his uterine brothers in turn. Another charter issued the same day shows why such precision was required: in it, the king gives other lands within the thanage of Kinclaven to another illegitimate son of his, also called John Stewart, whose mother is not Mariota but a woman called Mor.[29] The two Johns who share the thanage between them are unambiguously different men, as Mariota's son John is included as a remainder, along with his brothers James and Alexander, in this charter.

James of Kinfauns studied at St Andrews in the mid-1380s, and was keeper of Edinburgh Castle for a time in the 1390s, receiving expenses for this in 1398.[30] Mariota's son John studied in France in the mid-1390s, and was given Cardney in 1399 by his half-brother Robert III, who also gave him a pension and other monies.[31] John of Cardney and his illegitimate half-brother John Stewart of Dundonald were knighted at the coronation of their nephew James I, and were among those arrested and briefly detained by the king later that year.[32] Dundonald had been clerk of audit between 1402 and 1408, after which he continued to receive annuities from the customs of Edinburgh, Linlithgow and Perth.[33] In or after 1408 he married Elizabeth Graham, daughter of Sir William Graham.[34] He appears in the exchequer rolls intermittently until 1416, when, as John Stewart of Dundonald, 'natural brother of the late king', he was in receipt of an annual £20 pension from the customs of Edinburgh.[35] He was among those killed defending Dumbarton Castle in a rebellion led by his kinsman James Stewart, son of Muiredach, second duke of Albany, in 1425.[36]

28 *RMS*, i, nos 729, 730. Wyntoun claims Mael Coluim III was born out of wedlock, from a night his father spent with the daughter of a miller in Forteviot. *Chron. Wyntoun*, ii, 120–2. See p. 66 n.52 and p. 182.

29 *RMS*, i, no. 745. Mor as a woman's forename occurs rarely but is also found in a papal marriage dispensation of 1393, where Mor is a daughter of Colin Campbell of Argyll. Burns, *Letters of Clement VII*, 188–9.

30 *ER*, iii, 121, 138, 439.

31 *ER*, iii, 276, 347; *RMS*, i, App. 2, nos 1893 (Cardney), 1779 (£41 from the customs of Edinburgh and Linlithgow). He may have been the John Stewart who, as 'brother of the king' (Robert III) received 20 merks of the customs of Inverkeithing, but equally this could have been one of the king's other two illegitimate half-brothers called John. *RMS*, i, App. 2, no. 1954.

32 *Extracta e variis cronicis scocie*, ed. W. B. Turnbull (Edinburgh, 1842), 227; *ER*, iv, cx.

33 *ER*, iii, 568, 576, 633; iv, 1, 35, 40, 64, 89 (as clerk of audit); 2, 52, 75, 111, 167, 192, 243, 269, 295, 318, 342, 343, 364 (all Linlithgow); 11, 55, 89, 110, 174, 202, 222, 254, 274, 301, 345 (from customs of Perth in exchange for previous annuity from customs of Edinburgh); *RMS*, ii, nos 379, 403.

34 McGurk, *Letters of Benedict XIII*, 170; *ER*, iv, 254.

35 *ER*, iv, 254.

36 *Chron. Bower*, viii, 243, 245; Brown, *James I*, 65.

Duncan Stewart's eighteenth-century genealogy of the Stewarts claims the 1399 charter giving Cardney to Mariota's son John Stewart included a remainder to a younger brother, Walter.[37] He is not mentioned in the earlier grants to Mariota's sons, so if the genealogy is correct, he was almost certainly born after these were made, making him still a child when Robert II died in 1390. Two possibilities present themselves as to the identity of this Walter. One is that he was the Walter given as brother of the duke of Albany in papal letters concerning his career in the Church.[38] The other is that he was Walter Stewart of Burleigh (d. in or before 1454), who was certainly connected with Mariota and her other sons, though the exact relationship is unclear.[39]

A third John Stewart was sheriff of Bute and keeper of Rothesay Castle.[40] He also received the fermes of Ormidale in Argyll, and in the reign of his brother, Robert III, John (as his half-brother James had done previously) derived an income of 20 merks from the barony of Abernethy.[41] John and his wife Jonet, daughter of John Sympill of Eliotstoun, resigned their lands of Finnock (Renfrew) in favour of their son William in January 1444.[42] John died in or before 1449, when an instruction was issued that the payments due to him were to be made instead to his eldest son, James, who continued as keeper of Rothesay castle and sheriff of Bute.[43]

Four illegitimate sons of Robert went into the Church: Thomas, James, Alexander and Walter. Thomas benefited most from his father's influence,

[37] According to this, the lands were granted to John and his heirs, whom failing to his younger brother Walter and his heirs, with a reversion to the king. D. Stewart, *A Short Historical and Genealogical Account of the Royal Family of Scotland* (Edinburgh, 1739), 59, 213.

[38] See p. 207.

[39] Burleigh in Kinross had been given to Mariota by Robert II and was heritable by their offspring. *RMS*, i, no. 413. Walter of Burleigh also ended up in possession of lands given by Robert to Alexander, a son with Mariota. *Illustrations of Aberdeen and Banff*, iv, 44–5; W. Fraser, *History of the Carnegies, Earls of Southesk, and of Their Kindred* (Edinburgh, 1867), ii, no. 74. But it was John of Dundonald, a son of Robert with someone else, who was styled '*alias Burlie, patruum regis*' in a chronicle account referring to the year 1425. *Extracta e variis cronicis scocie*, ed. Turnbull, 228. If this Walter was both Robert's son and born after the early 1380s, he would have been a young child when his father died and this may explain why his identity is now uncertain. On the obscurity of illegitimate royal children born late in their fathers' lifetimes, see comments about Morgan, provost of Beverley, probable bastard of Henry II, by Given-Wilson and Curteis in *Royal Bastards*, 99. It is also possible this Walter was a grandson of Robert, perhaps via one of Mariota's sons or John of Dundonald.

[40] *ER*, iii, 686; v, 88, 163, 166, 209, 250, 251, 288, 332, 364.

[41] *ER*, iii, 458 (£10 13s 4d); *RMS*, i, App. 2, no. 1881.

[42] *RMS*, ii, no. 285.

[43] *ER*, v, 364; 410, 453, 574, 664. The line of this John Stewart has survived, continuously associated with the lands given to their progenitor, and is now represented by the Crichton-Stuarts, marquesses of Bute.

becoming archdeacon of St Andrews.[44] Robert was assiduous in promoting Thomas's career, arranging for Charles VI of France to petition the pope in 1375 to dispense Thomas Stewart, scholar of the diocese of Glasgow, for a clerical career.[45] Thomas is described as 'the illegitimate son of a married man and an unmarried woman', but the dispensation states that the French king 'asserts that Thomas is the son of Robert king of Scotland'.

Another dispensation was provided the same day for a James Stewart who, like Thomas, was a 'scholar of the diocese of Glasgow'. This was surely another illegitimate son of Robert's, the same one whose death is mentioned in papal letters of 1379 and 1380, the latter providing Thomas to a canonry of Glasgow and the prebend of Stobo, 'vacant by the death of his brother James Senescalli; at the petition of king Robert, who is his natural father'.[46] This James Stewart could not have been the James who was born of Robert and Mariota, as that James was still alive in January 1384 to receive a charter of Kinfauns and Rate from his father. Thomas was provided to his late brother's benefices on the same day that he was made archdeacon of St Andrews, again by Robert's petition.[47]

After Robert II died, Robert III continued to ensure that Thomas was supported.[48] Preferential treatment could be subordinated to political expediency, however: in 1402 Thomas was elected to the see of St Andrews, but stepped (or was pushed) aside to allow Walter Danielston to be appointed, a move that appears to have been engineered by Thomas's half-brother and governor of the kingdom, Robert, duke of Albany, as a *quid pro quo* for Danielston surrendering the strategically important castle of Dumbarton.[49] Albany made it up to Thomas to some extent in 1413, by successfully petitioning the pope to grant him an indult to visit churches and obtain procuration dues.[50]

Alexander Stewart was dispensed in 1386 from the twin defects of age (being in his twelfth year) and of birth as 'the king's natural son by an unmarried woman'.[51] The dispensation allows his promotion to all grades of holy orders and to accept multiple benefices, as long as they are not major or principal dignities, and provided that they are compatible. Like his brother Thomas,

44 Thomas's career is outlined in Watt, *Graduates*, 513–15 and he is also discussed briefly in Dowden, *Bishops*, 28–9. The considerable extent to which his father personally, or through his influence with notable figures such as the king of France, ensured Thomas's rapid career progression is not highlighted in these works.

45 *CPL*, iv, 215.

46 Burns, *Letters of Clement VII*, 38, 41.

47 Further interventions by Robert in support of Thomas: ibid., 62, 63, 148, 149.

48 McGurk, *Letters of Benedict XIII*, 108; *ER*, iii, 524, 551; *Rot. Scot.*, ii, 130 (safe-conduct for Thomas to travel to England).

49 D. E. R. Watt, *Fasti Ecclesiae Scoticanae Medii Aevi ad annum 1638* (Edinburgh, 1969), 294–5; Boardman, *Early Stewart Kings*, 256–7. Albany and Thomas may have been near kinsmen of Walter Danielston: see p. 130.

50 Burns, *Letters of Clement VII*, 149.

51 Burns, *Letters of Clement VII*, 114–15. He is of the diocese of Dunblane.

Alexander was exempted from mentioning his illegitimacy in petitions for future graces.[52] He became a canon of Glasgow and in 1407 witnessed a charter of Robert II's legitimate son, Robert duke of Albany, in which both he and John Stewart of Dundonald are given as Albany's brothers.[53]

Walter Stewart is given as 'son ('*natum*') of Robert King of Scotland' in documentation concerning a dispute over benefices in 1421.[54] Three years earlier he had obtained the deanery of Glasgow, worth £100 Scots, along with a canonry and prebend of the same diocese, and dispensation to hold an additional two benefices.[55] The two papal letters for these both describe him as brother of Robert duke of Albany, and as a bachelor of canon law and student of the same at Avignon. He was rector of Tannadice; briefly treasurer of Dunkeld before exchanging this for the deanship of Moray, and treasurer of Scotland 1432–3.[56] He may have been the Walter said to be mentioned as a younger brother of John Stewart of Cardney in the lost charter of 1399.

Robert III

Robert III had two illegitimate sons. Within a few weeks of Robert becoming king, he granted his son John the Renfrewshire lands of Auchengowan; Blackhall was given to John in 1396, and the lands of Ardgowan followed in 1403.[57] John Stewart witnessed a royal charter in 1402, in which he is given as '*filio nostro naturali*'.[58] He resigned some lands in Cowal to his father in 1404, which Robert granted to Colin Campbell of Lochawe, whose son Duncan would later (in or after 1423) marry John's daughter Margaret.[59] In 1405, the king gave John the lands 'called Tenpennyland' on the island of Arran.[60] John is mentioned in a charter giving his illegitimate brother James Stewart an annuity from the customs of Edinburgh.[61] This James Stewart received the barony of Kilbride, erected into a regality, from his father, and a crown annuity.[62] Following the death of Sir William Danielston, Robert III gave James the ward of Danielston's heir, with payments of the associated annuity

52 Burns, *Letters of Clement VII*, 63, 114–15.

53 *RMS*, i, no. 900.

54 *CSSR*, i, 244–5. He is sometimes confused with Walter Stewart, illegitimate son of Alexander, earl of Mar (also illegitimate), with whom his *floruit* overlapped.

55 McGurk, *Letters of Benedict XIII*, 378–9, *CPP*, i, 610, 612.

56 *CSSR*, ii, 235; Fryde, *British Chronology*, 187.

57 *Hist. MSS Comm., Fourth Report*, 528; *RMS*, i, App. 2. no. 1798. Robert became king on 19 April 1390; John was given Auchengowan on 20 May that year.

58 *RMS*, i, Addenda (p. 651), no. 1.

59 *Hist. MSS Comm., Fourth Report*, 478 (no. 76); *RMS*, i, App. 2. no. 1822; *CPL*, vii, 259; S. Boardman, *The Campbells 1250–1513* (Edinburgh, 2006), 107, 121. Duncan had previously been married to John's cousin, Marjory Stewart, daughter of Robert, duke of Albany.

60 *Orig. Par. Scot.*, ii, Pt. 1, 249.

61 *RMS*, i, App. 2., no. 1857.

62 *RMS*, i, App. 2, no. 1775; *ER*, iii, 489 (1400).

between 1395 and 1400.[63] James may have abused his position as the king's son to obtain monies unlawfully. In 1388 he was accused of deforcing the sheriff of Lanark of the castle-ward of Kilbride, and in 1400 he was apparently suspected of fraud or sharp practice, since an instruction was issued refusing him further payments from the customs of Edinburgh unless he produced the documentation showing his right to it.[64]

James II

James II may have had an illegitimate son, John Stewart of Sticks, progenitor of the Stewarts of Ballechin and Sticks. A nineteenth-century source asserts the existence of three charters, now apparently lost, one concerning the purchase by John of estates at Sticks in Glenquaich from Patrick Cardney (kinsman to Robert II's mistress); and another two, of 1486 and 1494, in which John is described as '*frater bastardus*' of James III.[65] This John Stewart's non-appearance in surviving contemporary sources may indicate that the royal credentials of John Stewart of Sticks were an invention by descendants seeking to burnish their standing in Perthshire society, but if John was indeed a son of James II, his obscurity may be explicable by the death of his father (James died at the age of twenty-nine in 1460) when John was still a minor.[66] Most medieval Scottish kings who had illegitimate children lived long enough to provide them with material support as adults, as well as to foster relationships between these offspring and other members of the family.

James IV

The same obscurity did not befall James Stewart (ca. 1500–1544x5), the younger illegitimate son of James IV, who was only thirteen when his father died. Given the earldom of Moray and the lordship of Abernethy not long after his first birthday, in adult life James became lieutenant-general of Scotland and a leading political and military figure in the reign of his brother James V, and in the first two years of the minority of Mary Queen of Scots.[67] He married Elizabeth, a daughter of Colin Campbell, third earl of Argyll. In his father's lifetime, James

63 *ER*, iii, 350, 384, 385, 465–6, 499. Sir William may have been a cousin of James Stewart of Kilbride: see p. 130.

64 *ER*, iii, 164, 489.

65 J. Burke, *A Genealogical and Heraldic History of the Commoners of Great Britain and Ireland* (London, 1835), ii, 149. He gives no authority for these charters.

66 See also Walter of Burleigh (above, p. 205). John and Alexander Stewart, illegitimate grandsons of the first John Stewart, were legitimated by Stewart rulers in 1540 and 1555 respectively. *RSS*, ii, no. 3443; *RMS*, iii, no. 2119, and iv, no. 1004. Burke says their father, having no legitimately born issue, settled the estate on them in 1543 and 1550.

67 *RMS*, ii, nos 2586, 2587; A. Thomas, 'Stewart, James, Earl of Moray (1500–1544/5), Nobleman', *ODNB*, 27 May 2019. Moray had two illegitimate children, James and Elizabeth. *Hist. MSS Comm. Sixth Report* (London, 1877), 671. His legitimate half-brother, James V, is known to have had nine illegitimate children (by nine mothers). P.

received an education befitting a prince, as did his older illegitimate brother, Alexander (ca. 1493–1513).[68] James IV set out to ensure an illustrious career for his eldest son. At the king's request, Alexander was dispensed from defect of birth by Pope Julius II in 1497, at the age of three or four.[69] His dispensation was even more extensive than that given to Robert II's son Thomas, permitting Alexander to hold any office, including archiepiscopal, and any number of offices simultaneously, with a range of other privileges. He was archdeacon of St Andrews by September 1502 (the position at one time held by Thomas Stewart), and archbishop-designate from 1504.[70] He was also chancellor of the kingdom when in his early teens.[71] Clearly these appointments were the result of his father's interventions, but he did receive one of the best educations available in Europe: his tutors included leading humanist scholars Raphael Regius and Desiderius Erasmus (who was also illegitimate).[72] Erasmus said of Alexander that 'none was more worthy to be the son of a king, and the son of King James IV'.[73] There is no suggestion that James entertained hopes that Alexander would succeed him; if nothing else, James's organisation of a career in the Church for him is evidence that the king did not count Alexander as a possible successor. Rather, Alexander embodied the same humanist and renaissance values of educational attainment and artistic sensibilities that James also cultivated as a feature of his own kingship. An indication of James IV's wholehearted acknowledgement of Alexander can be found on one of three external buttresses at the front of King's College in Aberdeen. The central buttress is carved with the armorials of James IV, while one flanking buttress bears those of his queen, Margaret Tudor. The remaining structure displays the armorials of Alexander.

D. Anderson, 'James V, Mistresses and Children of (Act. c. 1529–1592)', *ODNB*, 27 May 2019.

68 The two had different mothers. James was the son of Janet Kennedy while Alexander was born to Marion Boyd, who also had a daughter, Katherine, with the king. Like their sisters, the two boys were very finely outfitted; numerous entries in the treasurers' accounts testify to the considerable expenditure laid out on their clothing and accoutrements.

69 *CPL*, xvi, no. 813. Alexander's year of birth is not known with certainty but was probably 1493. MacDougall, *James IV*, 110 n.96. Erasmus said Alexander was 'about 20' when he died at Flodden. J. Herkless and R. K. Hannay, *The Archbishops of St Andrews* (Edinburgh, 1907), i, 262.

70 *TA*, ii, 430; *The Letters of James the Fourth 1505–1513, Calendared by R. K. Hannay*, ed. R. L. Mackie (Edinburgh, 1953), nos 20, 21, 24.

71 Fryde, *British Chronology*, 183. A letter from Patrick Panter, secretary of James IV and one of Alexander's tutors, to his former charge who was studying abroad, urged him to 'concentrate upon becoming a man and a scholar, and come back as soon as possible to be the father of his country and the ruler of his see.' Mackie, *Letters of James the Fourth*, no. 145. Panter had an affair with the king's illegitimate cousin, Margaret Crichton, resulting in two illegitimate children: see Table 13.

72 A panegyric to Alexander by his erstwhile tutor, Erasmus, is reproduced in Herkless and Hannay, *Archbishops*, i, 262–4.

73 Herkless and Hannay, *Archbishops*, i, 263.

Timeline of key events

1094	Donnchad II dies
1100x1107	Turgot's *Life of St Margaret, Queen of Scotland* claims her marriage to Mael Coluim III was the first legal marriage in Scotland
1114 or later	Alexander I marries Sybilla, illegitimate daughter of Henry I of England
1124	Alexander I dies; his illegitimate son Mael Coluim attempts to claim the throne
1126 (ca.)	William of Malmesbury, in *Gesta Regum Anglorum*, describes Donnchad II as illegitimate
1130	Rebellion by Mael Coluim, son of Alexander I, and supporters
1134	Mael Coluim, son of Alexander I, captured and imprisoned
1140 (ca.)	Production of the canon law collection known as *Decretum Gratiani*
1153	David I dies; rebellion against his successor, Mael Coluim IV, by sons of Mael Coluim, son of Alexander I, and their kinsmen (kin of Sumarliði of Argyll)
1156	Domnall, son of Mael Coluim, son of Alexander I, rebels against the crown; is captured and joins his father in prison
1172	Production of the decretal *Tanta*, declaring children are legitimated in canon law by the subsequent intermarriage of their parents
1179	Third Lateran Council decrees that bishops must be legitimately born
1179	Domnall Bán mac Uilleim, grandson of Donnchad II, attempts to seize the throne
1181	Further attack by Domnall Bán mac Uilleim
1186	Adam, 'the king's outlaw' (perhaps a grandson of Mael Coluim, son of Alexander I) is captured and imprisoned

1187	Domnall Bán mac Uilleim launches a further bid for the throne which ends with his death
1198x1214	Production of a king-list attacking fraternal succession, implying illegitimate succession is less undesirable
1201	Pope declares legitimate, and capable of heirship to the French throne, the children of Philip II Augustus, and Agnès of Meran, and confirms their parents' union is not a marriage
1211	Gofraid, son of Domnall Bán mac Uilleim, pursues the campaign begun by his father
1212	Gofraid is captured and killed
1213	Maurice of Menteith is required by William the Lion and his son Alexander to surrender his earldom to a younger brother
1214	William the Lion dies; Alexander II succeeds him
1215	Fourth Lateran Council reduces the number of forbidden degrees from six to four
1215	Domnall Bán Meic Uilleim attempts to seize the kingdom; is captured and killed
1229	Gillescop Meic Uilleim and his sons, who have continued to campaign for the kingship, are captured and killed
1230	Infant Meic Uilleim girl is publicly executed
1234	Production of the compilation of canon law known as *Liber Extra*
1234	Alan of Galloway dies; the men of Galloway want his illegitimate son to inherit the lordship
1236	English barons reject legitimation *per subsequens matrimonium* as effective for inheritance
1249	Alexander II dies and is succeeded by his seven-year-old son, Alexander III
1251	Alan Durward tries to have his wife Marjorie, the illegitimate daughter of Alexander II, legitimated
1252	Conclusion of five-year dispute between Ailwin of Callendar and John of Kinross over the earldom of Lennox; John had alleged Ailwin was illegitimate
1255	Alan Durward tries to claim the earldom of Mar by alleging the incumbent's right to it is undermined by the illegitimacy of his forebears

1291–2	The Great Cause, in which around half the Competitors for the throne of Scotland claimed descent from known or presumed illegitimate ancestors
1293	Alexander of Abernethy, a pre-nuptial son, is heir to his late father's lands
1349	Robert the Steward (later Robert II) marries Elizabeth Mure, thereby legitimating his children with her
1367–8	Two inheritance disputes concerning James Douglas, neither of which turn on, or mention, his status as a prenuptial son
1371	Robert II becomes king; declares his legitimated son John of Carrick heir to the throne
1373	Throne of Scotland is tailzied on John of Carrick, his legitimated brothers, and his half-brothers, in order of seniority
1387	William of Nithsdale, illegitimate son of the illegitimate Archibald the Grim Douglas, marries Egidia, legitimate daughter of Robert II
1389	Archibald the Grim, illegitimate son of Sir James Douglas, becomes third earl of Douglas
1390	Robert II dies; the legitimated John of Carrick succeeds as Robert III
1397	George Douglas, illegitimate son of the Countess of Angus and William Douglas, first earl of Douglas, is given the earldom of Angus
1427	Thomas Stewart, illegitimate son of Alexander Stewart, earl of Mar, formally recognised as heir to the earldom
1437	James I assassinated
1469	James III makes it treasonable for public notaries to issue legitimations
1471	James III grants liferent of the earldom of Lennox to illegitimate Andrew Avondale, royal favourite and kinsman
1478	Alexander Rait, notary-public, indicted for treason for his legitimation of James Egir
1497	James IV's illegitimate son, Alexander Stewart, aged ca. four, is granted a dispensation from defect of birth to pursue a clerical career
1501	James IV grants the earldom of Moray to his illegitimate son, James Stewart, aged one

Bibliography

Primary

Abstract of Protocol Book of the Burgh of Stirling, A.D. 1469–1484, ed. A. W. C. Hallen (Edinburgh, 1896)

Acts of the Lords of the Isles 1336–1493, ed. J. Munro and R. W. Munro, SHS 22 (Edinburgh, 1986)

Adomnán of Iona. The Life of St Columba, ed. and transl. R. Sharpe (London, 1991)

The Life of Ailred of Rievaulx by Walter Daniels, ed. F. M. Powicke (London, 1950)

Alcuin, The Bishop, Kings and Saints of York, ed. P. Godman (Oxford, 1982)

The Letters of St Ambrose, Bishop of Milan, translated, with indices (Devonport Society; Oxford, 1881)

Analecta Scotica: Collections Illustrative of the Civil, Ecclesiastical and Literary History of Scotland, ed. J. Maidment, 2 vols (Edinburgh, 1834–7)

Ancient Lives of the Scottish Saints, transl. W. M. Metcalfe (Paisley, 1895)

Andreae, J., *Novella in Sextum* (Graz, 1963)

The Anglo-Saxon Chronicle, ed. G. N. Garmonsway (London, 1972)

Anglo-Scottish Relations 1174–1328, ed. E. L. G. Stones (London, 1970)

Annales Monastici, ed. H. R. Luard, 5 vols (London, 1864–9)

Annals of the Reigns of Malcolm and William, Kings of Scotland, ed. A. C. Lawrie (Glasgow, 1910)

Annals of Ulster (to AD 1131), ed. and transl. S. Mac Airt and G. Mac Niocaill (Dublin, 1983)

The Apostolic Camera and Scottish Benefices 1418–1488, ed. A. I. Cameron (Oxford, 1934)

Aquinas, T., *Summa Theologica*, Christian Classics Ethereal Library [www.ccel.org/ccel/aquinas/summa.toc.html]

Augustine, *Concerning the City of God against the Pagans*, transl. H. Bettenson with an introduction by D. Knowles (Harmondsworth, 1972)

Barbour, J., *The Bruce*, ed. A. A. M. Duncan (Edinburgh, 1997)

The Complete Works of the Venerable Bede, ed. J. A. Giles, 12 vols (London, 1843–4)

The Biographical Writings and Letters of Venerable Bede, ed. J. A. Giles (London, 1845)

Boccaccio, G., *The Decameron*, transl. and intro. G. H. McWilliam (Harmondsworth, 1972)

Boece, H., *The History and Chronicles of Scotland*, transl. J. Bellenden, 2 vols (Edinburgh, 1821)

Buchanan, G., *The History of Scotland*, transl. J. Aikman, 6 vols (Edinburgh and Glasgow, 1827–9)

The Buik of King Alexander the Conquerour by Gilbert Hay, ed. J. Cartwright, 2 vols, STS 4th series, 16, 18 (Edinburgh, 1986 and Aberdeen, 1990)

Calendar of the Close Rolls preserved in the Public Record Office. Edward I, 5 vols (London, 1900–08)

Calendar of Patent Rolls, Henry III, Vol. 5: 1258–1266 (London, 1910)

Calendar of the State Papers Relating to Scotland and Mary Queen of Scots, ed. J. Bain and others, 13 vols (Edinburgh, 1898–1969)

Calendar of letters, despatches, and state papers, relating to the negotiations between England and Spain: preserved in the archives at Simancas and elsewhere, ed. G. A. Bergenroth and others, 13 vols (London, 1862–1954)

Calendar of Papal Letters to Scotland of Benedict XIII, 1394–1419, ed. F. McGurk (SHS, 1976)

Calendar of Papal Letters to Scotland of Clement VII of Avignon, 1378–1394, ed. C. Burns (SHS, 1976)

Calendar of Writs preserved at Yester House 1166–1503, ed. C. C. H. Harvey and J. Macleod (SRS, 1930)

The Book of the Thanes of Cawdor: A series of papers selected from the charter room at Cawdor 1236–1742 (Spalding Club, 1859)

Charters, Bulls and other Documents relating to the Abbey of Inchaffray (SHS, 1908)

The Charters of King David I, ed. G. W. S. Barrow (Woodbridge, 1999)

Chartulary of the Abbey of Lindores (SHS, 1903)

Charters of the Abbey of Inchcolm, ed. D. E. Easson and A. Macdonald (Edinburgh, 1938)

The Chronicle of Florence of Worcester, ed. B. Thorpe (London, 1849)

The Chronicle of John of Worcester 1118–1140: Being the Continuation of the 'Chronicon ex Chronicis' of Florence of Worcester, ed. J. R. H. Weaver (Oxford, 1908)

Chronicon Henrici Knighton, vel Cnitthon, Monachi Leycestrensis, ed. J. R. Lumby, 2 vols (London, 1889–95)

Chronicles of the Picts: Chronicles of the Scots, and other early memorials of Scottish History, ed. W. F. Skene (London, 1867)

Chronicles of the Reigns of Stephen, Henry II, and Richard I, ed. R. Howlett, 4 vols (London, 1884–9)

Matthæi Parisiensis, monachi Sancti Albani, Chronica Majora, ed. H. R. Luard, 7 vols (London, 1872–83)

Councils and Ecclesiastical Documents, ed. A. W. Haddan and W. Stubbs, 3 vols (Oxford, 1869–78)

The Crowland Chronicle Continuations, 1459–1486, ed. N. Pronay and J. Cox (London, 1986)

Decrees of the Ecumenical Councils, ed. N. P. Tanner, 2 vols (Washington, DC, 1990)

Decretales D. Gregorii Papae IX. suae integritati una cum glossis restitutae, in *Corpus iuris canonici* (Rome, 1582)

'The Dethe of the Kynge of Scotis', in *Death and Dissent. Two Fifteenth-Century Chronicles*, ed. L. M. Matheson (Woodbridge, 1999)

Diplomatarium Norvegicum, ed. C. C. A. Lange and others, 21 vols (Christiana and Oslo, 1849–1995)

Dockray, K., *Edward IV: A Sourcebook* (Stroud, 1999)

Dockray, K., *Richard III: A Sourcebook* (Stroud, 1999)

Documents and Records illustrating the History of Scotland, ed. F. Palgrave (London, 1837)

Documents Illustrative of the History of Scotland, 1286–1306, ed. J. Stevenson (Edinburgh, 1870)

The ecclesiastical history of Orderic Vitalis, ed. and transl. M. Chibnall, 6 vols (Oxford, 1969–1980)

Edward I and the Throne of Scotland 1290–1296: an edition of the record sources for the Great Cause, ed. E. L. G. Stones and G. G. Simpson, 2 vols (Oxford, 1978)

English Historical Documents, ed. H. Rothwell (London, 1975)

Excerpta Historica, or, Illustrations of English History, ed. S. Bentley (London, 1831)

Extracta e variis cronicis scocie, ed. W. B. Turnbull (Edinburgh, 1842)

Fagrskinna, a Catalogue of the Kings of Norway: a Translation with Introduction and Notes, ed. and transl. A. Finlay (Leiden, 2004)

Fasti Ecclesiae Scoticanae Medii Aevi ad annum 1638, ed. D. E. R. Watt (Edinburgh, 1969)

The Fathers of the Church. Mediaeval Continuation 7: Letters of Peter Damian 151–180, transl. O. J. Blum and I. M. Resnick (Washington, DC, 1974)

Flores Historiarum, ed. H. R. Luard, 3 vols (London, 1890)

Fraser, W., *The Red Book of Menteith*, 2 vols (Edinburgh, 1880–1)

—— *History of the Carnegies, Earls of Southesk, and of Their Kindred*, 2 vols (Edinburgh, 1867)

—— *The Douglas Book*, 4 vols (Edinburgh, 1885)

—— *The Sutherland Book*, 3 vols (Edinburgh, 1892)

Oeuvre de Froissart, ed. K. de Lettenhove, 28 vols (Brussels, 1867–77)

Gesta Stephani, ed. and transl. K. R. Potter, with introduction and notes by R. H. C. Davis (Oxford, 1976)

Giraldi Cambrensis opera, ed. J. S. Brewer, J. F. Dimock and G. F. Warner, 8 vols (1861–91)

Handbook of British Chronology, 3rd edn., ed. E. B. Fryde and others (London, 1986)

William Hay, *Lectures on Marriage*, transl. J. C. Barry (Edinburgh, 1967)

Highland Papers, ed. J. R. N. MacPhail, 3 vols (Edinburgh, 1914–20)

Hostiensis (Henricus de Segusio), *Summa Aurea* (Venice, 1570)

Howden, *Gesta regis Henrici secondi Benedicti Abbatis*, ed. W. Stubbs, 2 vols, Rolls series 49 (1867)

Chronica magistri Rogeri de Hovedene, ed. W. Stubbs, 4 vols, Rolls Series 51 (1868–71)

I Commentari di Enea Silvio Piccolomini, ed. G. Bernetti, 2 vols (Milan, 1981)

Illustrations of the topography and antiquities of the shires of Aberdeen and Banff, 4 vols (Spalding Club, 1847–69)

Instrumenta Publica sive Processus super Fidelitatibus et Homagiis Scotorum Domino Regi Angliae Factis 1291–96, ed. T. Thomson (Bannatyne Club, 1834)

The Kingis Quair of James Stewart, ed. M. P. McDiarmid (London, 1973)

Die Konzilien der Karolingischen Teilreiche 843–859, ed. W. Hartmann (Hannover, 1984)

The Laws of the Kings of England from Edmund to Henry I, ed. and transl. A. J. Robertson (Cambridge, 1925)

Lesley, J., *The History of Scotland from the Death of King James I in the Year 1436 to the Year 1561* (Bannatyne Club, 1830)

The Letters of James the Fourth 1505–1513, ed. R. K. Hannay and R. L. Mackie (SHS, 1953)

The Letters of Lanfranc Archbishop of Canterbury, ed. H. Clover and M. Gibson (Oxford, 1979)

The Letters of Robert Grosseteste, Bishop of Lincoln, ed. F. A. C. Mantello and J. Goering (Toronto, 2010)

Liber Cartarum Prioratus Sancti Andree in Scotia (Bannatyne Club, 1841)

Liber Ecclesie de Scon (Bannatyne and Maitland Clubs, 1843)

Liber Pluscardensis, ed. F. J. H. Skene, 2 vols (Edinburgh, 1877–80)

Liber Sancte Marie de Balmorinach, ed. W. B. D. D. Turnbull (Abbotsford Club, Edinburgh, 1841)

Liber Vitae Ecclesiae Dunelmensis (Surtees Society, 1841)

Lovelich, H., *The History of the Holy Grail*, ed. J. F. Furnivall (London, 1877)

Memoriale Fratris Walteri de Coventria, ed. W. Stubbs, 2 vols (London, 1872–3)

Memorials of St Edmund's Abbey, ed. T. Arnold, 3 vols (London, 1890–6)

The Monastic Annals of Teviotdale, ed. J. Morton (Edinburgh, 1832)

Muniments of the Royal Burgh of Irvine, 2 vols (Ayrshire and Galloway Archaeological Association, 1890–1)

The Oliphants in Scotland. With a selection of original documents from the Charter Chest at Gask, ed. J. Anderson (Edinburgh, 1879)

Origines Parochiales Scotiae, 2 vols (Bannatyne Club, 1851–5)

Orkneyinga saga. The History of the Earls of Orkney, ed. and transl. H. Pálsson and P. Edwards (London, 1978)

Pontificia Hibernica: Medieval Papal Chancery Documents Concerning Ireland, 640–1261, ed. M. Sheehy, 2 vols (Dublin, 1962–5)

Records of the Priory of the Isle of May, ed. J. Stuart (Edinburgh, 1868)

Reject Aeneas, Accept Pius: Selected Letters of Aeneas Sylvius Piccolomini (Pope Pius II), ed. T. Izbicki, G. Christianson and P. Krey (Washington, DC, 2006)

Royal and Other Historical Letters Illustrative of the Reign of Henry III, ed. W. W. Shirley, 2 vols (London, 1862–6)

Protocol Book of James Young 1485–1515, ed. G. Donaldson (SRS, 1952)

The Register of the Priory of St Bees (Durham, 1915)

Registrum de Dunfermelyn (Bannatyne Club, 1842)

Registrum Episcopatus Glasguensis (Bannatyne and Maitland Clubs, 1843)

Registrum Honoris de Morton, ed. T. Thomson, A. Macdonald and C. Innes, 2 vols (Bannatyne Club, 1853)

Reports of cases decided in the House of Lords, upon appeal from Scotland, from 1726 to 1822, ed. J. Stewart, J. S. Craigie and T. S. Paton (Edinburgh, 1849–56)

Rotuli Parliamentorum; ut et Petitiones, et Placita in Parliamento, ed. J. Strachey and others, 6 vols (London, 1767–77)

Scalacronica. The Reigns of Edward I, Edward II and Edward III as recorded by Sir Thomas Gray, transl. H. Maxwell (Glasgow, 1907)

Scottish Formularies, ed. A. A. M. Duncan, Stair Society 58 (Edinburgh, 2011)

Select Scottish Cases of the Thirteenth Century, ed. Lord Cooper (Edinburgh and London, 1944)

Short Scottish Prose Chronicles, ed. D. Embree, E. D. Kennedy and K. Daly (Woodbridge, 2012)

Statutes of the Scottish Church 1225–1559, ed. D. Patrick (SHS, 1907)

'The Taill of the Sone and Air of the foirsaid Foxe, callit Father wer: Alswa the Parliament of Fourfuttit Beistis, haldin be the Lyoun', in *Robert Henryson: The Poems*, ed. D. Fox (Oxford, 1987)

Three Chronicles of the Reign of Edward IV, intro. K. Dockray (Gloucester, 1988)

The treatise on the laws and customs of the realm of England commonly called Glanvill, ed. and transl. G. D. G. Hall (London, 1965)

Turgot, 'Life of Margaret', in *Ancient Lives of the Scottish Saints*, transl. W. M. Metcalfe (Paisley, 1895)

Vetera Monumenta Hibernorum et Scotorum Historiam Illustrantia, ed. A. Theiner (Rome, 1864)

Visitations of Religious Houses in the Diocese of Lincoln, ed. A. Hamilton Thompson and others, 3 vols (Lincoln, 1914–29)

Walsingham, T., *Historia Anglicana*, ed. H. T. Riley, 2 vols (London, 1863)

The Warrender Papers, ed. A. I. Cameron, 2 vols (SHS, 1931–2)

William of Malmesbury, *Gesta Regum Anglorum*, ed. and transl. R. A. B. Mynors, R. M. Thomson and M. Winterbottom, 2 vols (Oxford, 1998)

Unpublished thesis

McDonald, J. R., 'The Papal Penitentiary and Ecclesiastical Careers: The Requests of Scottish Clergy in the Registers of the *Sacra Apostolica Penitenzieria*, 1449–1542' (unpublished PhD thesis, University of Aberdeen, 2005)

Secondary

Aird, W. M., *St Cuthbert and the Normans. The Church of Durham, 1071–1153* (Woodbridge, 1998)

Anderson, J., *The Oliphants in Scotland* (Edinburgh, 1879)

Anderson, M. O., *Kings and Kingship in Early Scotland* (Edinburgh, 1980)

Anton, A. E., '"Handfasting" in Scotland', *SHR* 37 (1958)

—— 'Parent and Child', in *An Introduction to Scottish Legal History*, ed. G. C. H. Paton and others, Stair Society 20 (Edinburgh, 1958), 116–24

Archibald, E., '"The appalling dangers of family life": Incest in Medieval Literature', in *Medieval Family Roles: A Book of Essays*, ed. C. J. Itnyre (New York, 2000), 157–71

Archibald, E., *Incest and the Medieval Imagination* (Oxford, 2001)

Armstrong, J. W., 'The "Fyre of Ire Kyndild" in the Fifteenth-Century Scottish Marches', in *Vengeance in the Middle Ages*, ed. S. A. Throop and P. R. Hyams (Farnham, 2010), 51–84

Arnold, J. H., *Belief and Unbelief in Medieval Europe* (London, 2005)

Autrand, F., '*Naissance illégitime et service de l'Etat: les enfants naturels dans le milieu de robe parisien, XIVe–XVe siècle*', *Revue Historique* 267 (1982), 289–303

Bain, J., 'Notes on a Dispensation for the Marriage of Johanna Beaufort with the Black Knight of Lorn', *PSAS* 16 (1881–2), 169–75

Balfour-Melville, E. W. M., *James I, King of Scots, 1406–1437* (London, 1936)

Bannerman, J., 'MacDuff of Fife', in *Medieval Scotland: Crown, Lordship and Community. Essays Presented to G. W. S. Barrow*, ed. A. Grant and K. J. Stringer (Edinburgh, 1998), 20–38

Barrell, A. D. M., *Medieval Scotland* (Cambridge, 2000)

—— 'The Papacy and the Regular Clergy in Scotland in the Fourteenth Century', *RSCHS* 24 (1991), 103–21

—— *The Papacy, Scotland and Northern England, 1342–1378* (Cambridge, 1995)

Barrow, G. W. S., *The Anglo-Norman Era in Scottish History* (Oxford, 1980)

—— 'King David, Earl Henry and Cumbria', *TCWAAS*, Second Series 99 (1999), 117–27

—— *The Kingdom of the Scots: Government, Church and Society from the Eleventh to the Fourteenth Century* (Edinburgh, 2003)

—— *Kingship and Unity: Scotland 1000–1306* (Edinburgh, 1981)

—— 'The Lost Gàidhealtachd of Medieval Scotland', in *Gaelic and Scotland: Alba agus a Gàidhlig*, ed. W. Gillies (Edinburgh, 1989), 67–88

—— *Robert Bruce & the Community of the Realm of Scotland* (Edinburgh, 1988)

—— *Scotland and its Neighbours in the Middle Ages* (London, 1992)

Barrow, J., *The Clergy in the Medieval World: Secular Clerics, Their Families and Careers in North-Western Europe, c.800–c.1200* (Cambridge, 2015)

Beam, A. G., *The Balliol Dynasty 1210–1364* (Edinburgh, 2008)

Bennett, M., 'Edward III's Entail and the Succession to the Crown, 1376–1471', *English Historical Review* 113 (1998), 580–609

Boardman, S., *The Campbells, 1250–1513* (Edinburgh, 2006)

—— *The Early Stewart Kings. Robert II and Robert III 1371–1406* (East Linton, 1996)

—— 'Lordship in the North-east: The Badenoch Stewarts I. Alexander Stewart, Earl of Buchan, Lord of Badenoch', *Northern Scotland* 16 (1996), 1–29

Bombi, B., 'The English Crown and the Election of Pope John XXII', *Journal of Ecclesiastical History* 68 (2017), 260–84

Bossy, J., 'Blood and Baptism: Kinship, Community and Christianity in Western Europe from the Fourteenth to the Seventeenth Centuries', in *Sanctity and Secularity: the Church and the World. Papers Read at the Eleventh Summer Meeting and the Twelfth Winter Meeting of the Ecclesiastical History Society. Studies in Church History* 10, ed. D. Baker (Oxford, 1973), 129–43

Broun, D., 'The Adoption of Brieves in Scotland', in *Charters and Charter Scholarship in Britain and Ireland*, ed. M. T. Flanagan and J. A. Green (Basingstoke, 2005), 164–83

—— 'Contemporary Perspectives on Alexander II's Succession: The Evidence of King-lists', in *The Reign of Alexander II, 1214–49*, ed. R. D. Oram (Leiden, 2005), 78–97

—— *The Irish Identity of the Kingdom of the Scots in the Twelfth and Thirteenth Centuries* (Woodbridge, 1999)

—— *Scottish Independence and the Idea of Britain: From the Picts to Alexander III* (Edinburgh, 2007)

Brown, J. M., 'The Exercise of Power', in *Scottish Society in the Fifteenth Century*, ed. J. M. Brown (London, 1977), 33–65

Brown, M., 'Aristocratic Politics and the Crisis of Scottish Kingship, 1286–96', *SHR* 90 (2011), 1–26

—— *Bannockburn: The Scottish Wars and the British Isles, 1307–1323* (Edinburgh, 2008)

—— *The Black Douglases: War and Lordship in Medieval Scotland 1300–1455* (East Linton, 1998)

—— '"I have thus slain a tyrant": *The Dethe of the Kynge of Scotis* and the Right to Resist in Early Fifteenth-Century Scotland', *IR* 47 (1996), 24–44

—— *James I* (Edinburgh, 1994)

—— '"Vile Times': Walter Bower's Last Book and the Minority of James II', *SHR* 79 (2000), 165–88

—— *The Wars of Scotland, 1214–1371* (Edinburgh, 2012)

Brundage, J. A., 'Carnal Delight: Canonistic Theories of Sexuality', in *Proceedings of the Fifth International Congress of Medieval Canon Law*, ed. S. Kuttner and K. Pennington (Vatican City, 1980), 361–85

—— *Law, Sex, and Christian Society in Medieval Europe* (Chicago, IL, 1990)

Buchan, J. W., *A History of Peeblesshire*, 3 vols (Glasgow, 1925–7)

Burke, J., *A Genealogical and Heraldic History of the Commoners of Great Britain and Ireland*, 4 vols (London, 1833–8)

Byrne, F. J., 'The Trembling Sod: Ireland in 1169', in *A New History of Ireland. II. Medieval Ireland*, ed. A. Cosgrove (Oxford, 1987), 1–42

Chaney, W. A., *The Cult of Kingship in Anglo-Saxon England* (Manchester, 1970)

Cheney, C. R., *Pope Innocent III and England* (Stuttgart, 1976)

Clarke, P. D., 'Innocent III, Canon Law and the Punishment of the Guiltless', in *Pope Innocent III and His World*, ed. J. C. Moore (Aldershot, 1999), 271–85

—— 'New Sources for the History of the Religious Life: The Registers of the Apostolic Penitentiary', *Monastic Research Bulletin* 11 (2005), 1–21

Cockburn, J. H., *The Medieval Bishops of Dunblane and their Church* (London, 1959)

Courtney-Batson, D., '*Per venerabilem*: From Practical Necessity to Judicial Supremacy', in *Pope Innocent III and His World*, ed. J. C. Moore (Aldershot, 1999), 287–303

Cowan, I. B., *Parishes of Medieval Scotland* (SRS, 1967)

Cowan, I. B. and Kirk, J., eds, *The Medieval Church in Scotland* (Edinburgh, 1995)

Cowan, M. and Walkling, L. E., 'A "gret cradil of stait": Growing Up with the Court of James IV', in *Children and Youth in Premodern Scotland*, ed. J. Nugent and E. Ewan (Woodbridge, 2015), 15–31

Croft Dickinson, W., *Scotland from the Earliest Times to 1603*, 3rd edn, revd. and ed. A. A. M. Duncan (Oxford, 1977)

Crouch, D., *The Reign of Stephen 1135–1154* (Harlow, 2000)

—— 'Robert of Gloucester's Mother and Sexual Politics in Norman Oxfordshire', *Bulletin of the Institute of Historical Research* 72 (1999), 323–33

Davies, T. R., 'The Glory of Being a Bastard?', *Coat of Arms* 3.108 (1979), 94–9

D'Avray, D. L., *Dissolving Royal Marriages. A Documentary History, 860–1600* (Cambridge, 2014)

Daichman, G. S., 'Misconduct in the Medieval Nunnery: Fact, Not Fiction', in *That Gentle Strength: Historical Perspectives on Women in Christianity*, ed. L. L. Coon, K. J. Haldane and E. W. Sommer (London, 1990), 97–117

Dalton, P., *Conquest, Anarchy and Lordship: Yorkshire 1066–1154* (Cambridge, 1994)

Dean, T., 'Fornicating with Nuns in Fifteenth-Century Bologna', *JMH* 34 (2008), 374–82

Ditchburn, D., *Scotland and Europe: the Medieval Kingdom and its Contacts with Christendom, 1214–1560. Volume 1: Religion, Culture and Commerce* (East Linton, 2001)

Dodgshon, R. A., *Land and Society in Early Scotland* (Oxford, 1981)

Dolezalek, G., 'The Court of Session as a *Ius Commune* Court – Witnessed by "Sinclair's Practicks", 1540–1549', in *Miscellany IV*, ed. H. L. MacQueen, Stair Society 49 (Edinburgh, 2002), 51–84

Donahue Jr, C., *Law, Marriage and Society* in *the Middle Ages: Arguments About Marriage in Five Courts* (Cambridge, 2007)

Donaldson, G., *Scottish Church History* (Edinburgh, 1985)

Dowden, J., *The Bishops of Scotland* (Glasgow, 1912)

—— *The Medieval Church in Scotland: Its Constitution, Organisation and Law* (Glasgow, 1910)

Duggan, C. and Duggan, A., 'Ralph de Diceto, Henry II and Becket with an Appendix on Decretal Letters', in *Authority and Power: Studies on Medieval Law and Government Presented to Walter Ullman on his Seventieth Birthday*, ed. B. Tierney and P. Linehan (Cambridge, 1980), 59–81

Duggan, C., 'Equity and Compassion in Papal Marriage Decretals to England', in *Decretals and the Creation of 'New Law' in the Twelfth Century: Judges, Judgements, Equity and Law*, ed. C. Duggan (Aldershot, 1998), 59–87

Dumville, D. N., 'The Chronicle of the Kings of Alba', in *Kings, Clerics and Chronicles in Scotland, 500–1297: Essays in Honour of Marjorie Ogilvie Anderson on the Occasion of Her Ninetieth Birthday*, ed. S. Taylor (Dublin, 2000), 73–86

Dunbar, A. H., *Scottish Kings: A Revised Chronology of Scottish History 1005–1625* (Edinburgh, 1899)

Duncan, A. A. M., 'John King of England and the Kings of Scots', in *King John: New Interpretations*, ed. S. D. Church (Woodbridge, 1999), 247–71

—— *The Kingship of the Scots 842–1292: Succession and Independence* (Edinburgh, 2002)

—— 'A Question About the Succession', *Miscellany of the Scottish History Society* 12 (Edinburgh, 1994), 1–57

—— *Scotland: The Making of the Kingdom* (Edinburgh, 2000)

—— 'Yes, the Earliest Scottish Charters', *SHR* 78 (1999), 1–38

Easson, D. E., *Medieval Religious Houses: Scotland* (London, 1976)

Esmein, A., *Le Mariage en Droit Canonique*, 2 vols (Paris, 1929–35)

Evans Grubbs, J., *Law and Family in Late Antiquity: The Emperor Constantine's Marriage Legislation* (Oxford, 1999)

—— *Women and the Law in the Roman Empire* (London, 2002)

Ferguson, P. C., *Medieval Papal Representatives in Scotland: Legates, Nuncios, and Judges-Delegate, 1125–1286* (Edinburgh, 1997)

Fradenburg, O., *City, Marriage, Tournament: Arts of Rule in Late Medieval Scotland* (Madison, WI, 1991)

Frassetto, M., ed., *Medieval Purity and Piety. Essays on Medieval Clerical Celibacy and Religious Reform* (New York, 1998)

Lynch, J. H., 'Spiritual Kinship and Sexual Prohibition in Early Medieval Europe', in *Proceedings of the Sixth International Congress of Medieval Canon Law*, ed. S. Kuttner and K. Pennington (Vatican City, 1985), 271–88

McDiarmid, M. P., 'The Kingship of the Scots in their Writers', *SLJ* 6 (1979), 5–18

Macdonald, A. J., 'Kings of the Wild Frontier? The Earls of Dunbar or March, c. 1070–1435', in *The Exercise of Power in Medieval Scotland c. 1200–1500*, ed. S. Boardman and A. Ross (Dublin, 2005), 139–58

—— *Border Bloodshed: Scotland, England and France at War, 1369–1403* (East Linton, 2000)

MacDonald, I. G., *Clerics and Clansmen. The Diocese of Argyll between the Twelfth and Sixteenth Centuries* (Leiden, 2013)

McDonald, J. R., 'The Career Paths of Illegitimate Scottish Clergy: The Evidence of the Registers of the Apostolic Penitentiary, the Registers of Supplications and Lateran Registers', *Florilegium* 25 (2008), 151–73

—— 'Illegitimate Scots in the Registers of Supplications and the Registers of the Apostolic Penitentiary during the Pontificate of Sixtus IV (1471–1484)', in *... et usque ad ultimum terrae: The Apostolic Penitentiary in Local Contexts*, ed. G. Jaritz, T. Jørgensen and K. Salonen (Budapest, 2007), 33–42

—— 'The Papal Penitentiary, Illegitimacy and Clerical Careers in the Peripheries: A Case Study of the Provinces of Nidaros and Scotland, 1449–1542', *Northern Scotland* 3 (2012), 32–44

—— 'The Requests of Scottish Clergy in the Registers of the *Sacra Apostolica Penitenzieria*, 1449–1542', *RSCHS* 37 (2007), 5–53

McDonald, R. A., 'The Foundation and Patronage of Nunneries by Native Elites in Twelfth- and Early Thirteenth-Century Scotland', in *Women in Scotland c. 1100–c. 1750*, ed. E. Ewan and M. M. Meikle (East Linton, 1999), 3–15

—— 'Old and New in the Far North: Ferchar Maccintsacairt and the Early Earls of Ross, c. 1200–1274', in *The Exercise of Power in Medieval Scotland c. 1200–1500*, ed. S. Boardman and A. Ross (Dublin, 2005), 23–45

—— *Outlaws of Medieval Scotland: Challenges to the Canmore Kings 1058–1266* (East Linton, 2003)

Macdougall, N., *James III* (Edinburgh, 2009)

—— *James III: A Political Study* (Edinburgh, 1982)

—— *James IV* (Edinburgh, 1989)

McDougall, S., *Royal Bastards: the Birth of Illegitimacy, 800–1230* (Oxford, 2016)

McDowall, W., *Chronicles of Lincluden as an Abbey and as a College* (Edinburgh, 1886)

Macfarlane, L. J., 'The Primacy of the Scottish Church, 1472–1521', *IR* 20 (1969), 111–29

—— *William Elphinstone and the Kingdom of Scotland 1431–1514: The Struggle for Order* (Aberdeen, 1995)

M. MacGregor, 'Church and Culture in the Late Medieval Highlands', in J. Kirk, ed., *The Church in the Highlands* (Edinburgh, 1998), 1–36

Mackay, A., with Ditchburn, D., *Atlas of Medieval Europe* (London, 1997)

Dodgshon, R. A., *Land and Society in Early Scotland* (Oxford, 1981)

Dolezalek, G., 'The Court of Session as a *Ius Commune* Court – Witnessed by "Sinclair's Practicks", 1540–1549', in *Miscellany IV*, ed. H. L. MacQueen, Stair Society 49 (Edinburgh, 2002), 51–84

Donahue Jr, C., *Law, Marriage and Society* in *the Middle Ages: Arguments About Marriage in Five Courts* (Cambridge, 2007)

Donaldson, G., *Scottish Church History* (Edinburgh, 1985)

Dowden, J., *The Bishops of Scotland* (Glasgow, 1912)

—— *The Medieval Church in Scotland: Its Constitution, Organisation and Law* (Glasgow, 1910)

Duggan, C. and Duggan, A., 'Ralph de Diceto, Henry II and Becket with an Appendix on Decretal Letters', in *Authority and Power: Studies on Medieval Law and Government Presented to Walter Ullman on his Seventieth Birthday*, ed. B. Tierney and P. Linehan (Cambridge, 1980), 59–81

Duggan, C., 'Equity and Compassion in Papal Marriage Decretals to England', in *Decretals and the Creation of 'New Law' in the Twelfth Century: Judges, Judgements, Equity and Law*, ed. C. Duggan (Aldershot, 1998), 59–87

Dumville, D. N., 'The Chronicle of the Kings of Alba', in *Kings, Clerics and Chronicles in Scotland, 500–1297: Essays in Honour of Marjorie Ogilvie Anderson on the Occasion of Her Ninetieth Birthday*, ed. S. Taylor (Dublin, 2000), 73–86

Dunbar, A. H., *Scottish Kings: A Revised Chronology of Scottish History 1005–1625* (Edinburgh, 1899)

Duncan, A. A. M., 'John King of England and the Kings of Scots', in *King John: New Interpretations*, ed. S. D. Church (Woodbridge, 1999), 247–71

—— *The Kingship of the Scots 842–1292: Succession and Independence* (Edinburgh, 2002)

—— 'A Question About the Succession', *Miscellany of the Scottish History Society* 12 (Edinburgh, 1994), 1–57

—— *Scotland: The Making of the Kingdom* (Edinburgh, 2000)

—— 'Yes, the Earliest Scottish Charters', *SHR* 78 (1999), 1–38

Easson, D. E., *Medieval Religious Houses: Scotland* (London, 1976)

Esmein, A., *Le Mariage en Droit Canonique*, 2 vols (Paris, 1929–35)

Evans Grubbs, J., *Law and Family in Late Antiquity: The Emperor Constantine's Marriage Legislation* (Oxford, 1999)

—— *Women and the Law in the Roman Empire* (London, 2002)

Ferguson, P. C., *Medieval Papal Representatives in Scotland: Legates, Nuncios, and Judges-Delegate, 1125–1286* (Edinburgh, 1997)

Fradenburg, O., *City, Marriage, Tournament: Arts of Rule in Late Medieval Scotland* (Madison, WI, 1991)

Frassetto, M., ed., *Medieval Purity and Piety. Essays on Medieval Clerical Celibacy and Religious Reform* (New York, 1998)

Gelting, M., 'Marriage, Peace and the Canonical Incest Prohibitions: Making Sense of an Absurdity?', in *Nordic Perspectives on Medieval Canon Law*, ed. M. Korpiola (Saarijärvi, 1999), 93–124

Gemmill, E. and Mayhew, N., *Changing Values in Medieval Scotland: A Study of Prices, Money, and Weights and Measures* (New York, 1995)

Génestal, R., *Histoire de la Légitimation des Enfants Naturels en Droit Canonique* (Paris, 1905)

Given-Wilson, C. and Curteis, A., *The Royal Bastards of Medieval England* (London, 1984)

Given-Wilson, C., *Henry IV* (London, 2016)

—— 'Legitimation, Designation and Succession to the Throne in Fourteenth-Century England', in *Building Legitimacy: Political Discourses and Forms of Legitimacy in Medieval Societies*, ed. I. Alfonso, H. Kennedy and J. Escalona (Leiden, 2003), 89–105

Glenn, T. A., 'Genealogical Notes Regarding the Family of Glen, or Glenn', *The Pennsylvania Magazine of History and Biography* 36 (1912), 480–99

Goody, J., *The Development of the Family and Marriage in Europe* (Cambridge, 1983)

Grant, A., 'Acts of Lordship: The Records of Archibald, Fourth Earl of Douglas', in *Freedom and Authority. Scotland* c. *1050*–c. *1650*, ed. T. Brotherstone and D. Ditchburn (East Linton, 2000), 235–74

—— 'Crown and Nobility in Late Medieval Britain', in *Scotland and England 1286–1815*, ed. R. A. Mason (Edinburgh, 1987), 34–59

—— 'Franchises North of the Border: Baronies and Regalities in Medieval Scotland', in *Liberties and Identities in the Medieval British Isles*, ed. M. Prestwich (Woodbridge, 2008), 155–99

—— 'Richard III and Scotland', in *The North of England in the Age of Richard III*, ed. A. J. Pollard (Stroud, 1996), 115–48

—— 'Royal and Magnate Bastards in the Later Middle Ages: The View from Scotland', in *La Bâtardise et L'Exercice du Pouvoir en Europe du XIIIe au Debut du XVIe Siècle. Revue du Nord. Hors Série. Collection Histoire No 31*, dir. É. Bousmar, A. Marchandisse, C. Masson and B. Schnerb (Lille, 2015), 313–67

—— 'The St Bees Lord and Lady, and their Lineage', in *North-West England from the Romans to the Tudors. Essays in Memory of John McNair Todd*, ed. K. J. Stringer (CWAAS Extra Series no. 41, 2014), 171–200

Hamilton, E., *Mighty Subjects: the Dunbar Earls in Scotland, c. 1072–1289* (Edinburgh, 2010)

Hammond, M. H., '*Hostarii Regis Scotie*: the Durward Family in the Thirteenth Century', in *The Exercise of Power in Medieval Scotland c. 1200–1500*, ed. S. Boardman and A. Ross (Dublin, 2005), 118–37

Hapgood Thompson, K., 'Dowry and Inheritance Patterns: Some Examples from the Descendants of King Henry I of England', *Medieval Prosopography* 17 (1996), 45–61

Haren, M. J., 'Social Structures of the Irish Church: A New Source in Papal Penitentiary Dispensations for Illegitimacy', in *Illegitimität im Spätmittelalter*, ed. L. Schmugge and B. Wiggenhauser (München, 1994), 207–26

Harsgor, M., '*L'essor des bâtards nobles au XVe siècle*', *Revue Historique* 253 (1975), 319–54

Harvey, K., *Episcopal Appointments in England, c. 1214–1344* (Farnham, 2014)

Herkless, J. and Hannay, R. K., *The Archbishops of St Andrews*, 5 vols (Edinburgh, 1907)

Hicks, M., *Edward IV* (London, 2004)

Hollister, C. W., 'The Anglo-Norman Succession Debate of 1126: Prelude to Stephen's Anarchy', *JMH* 1 (1975), 19–41

—— *Henry I*, ed. A. C. Frost (New Haven, CT, 2001)

Hollister, C. W. and Keefe, T. K., 'The Making of the Angevin Empire', *The Journal of British Studies* 12 (1973), 1–25

Holt, J. C., 'King John and Arthur of Brittany', *Nottingham Medieval Studies* 44 (2000), 82–103

Hudson, J., 'Emotions in the Early Common Law (*c.* 1166–1215)', *The Journal of Legal History* 38 (2017), 130–54

Hudson, J., *Land, Law, and Lordship in Anglo-Norman England* (Oxford, 1994)

Jervise, A., *The History and Traditions of the Land of the Lindsays in Angus and Mearns, with Notices of Alyth and Meigle* (Edinburgh, 1882)

Jillings, K., *Scotland's Black Death: The Foul Death of the English* (Stroud, 2003)

Jochens, J. M., 'The Politics of Reproduction: Medieval Norwegian Kingship', *The American Historical Review* 92 (1987), 327–49

Karras, R. M., *Unmarriages: Women, Men and Sexual Unions in the Middle Ages* (Philadelphia, PA, 2012)

Keene, C., *Saint Margaret, Queen of Scots. A Life in Perspective* (New York, 2013)

Kelly, F., *A Guide to Early Irish Law* (Dublin, 1988)

Kuehn, T., '"As if Conceived Within a Legitimate Marriage": A Dispute Concerning Legitimation in *Quattrocento* Florence', *The American Journal of Legal History* 29 (1985), 275–300

—— *Emancipation in Late Medieval Florence* (New Brunswick, NJ, 1982)

—— *Illegitimacy in Renaissance Florence* (Ann Arbor, MI, 2002)

—— 'Reading between the Patrilines: Leon Battista Alberti's *Della Famiglia* in Light of His Illegitimacy', in *Law, Family, and Women: Toward a Legal Anthropology of Renaissance Italy*, ed. T. Kuehn (Chicago, IL, 1991), 157–75

Larrington, C., 'Queens and Bodies: The Norwegian Translated *lais* and Hákon IV's Kinswomen', *Journal of English and Germanic Philology* 108 (2009), 506–27

Layfield, S., 'The Pope, the Scots, and their "Self-Styled" King: John XXII's Anglo-Scottish Policy, 1316–1334', in *England and Scotland in the Fourteenth Century*, ed. A. King and M. A. Penman (Woodbridge, 2007)

Livermore, H. V., *A New History of Portugal* (Cambridge, 1976)

Lunt, W. E., *Papal Revenues in the Middle Ages*, 2 vols (New York, 1934)

Lynch, J. H., 'Spiritual Kinship and Sexual Prohibition in Early Medieval Europe', in *Proceedings of the Sixth International Congress of Medieval Canon Law*, ed. S. Kuttner and K. Pennington (Vatican City, 1985), 271–88

McDiarmid, M. P., 'The Kingship of the Scots in their Writers', *SLJ* 6 (1979), 5–18

Macdonald, A. J., 'Kings of the Wild Frontier? The Earls of Dunbar or March, c. 1070–1435', in *The Exercise of Power in Medieval Scotland c. 1200–1500*, ed. S. Boardman and A. Ross (Dublin, 2005), 139–58

—— *Border Bloodshed: Scotland, England and France at War, 1369–1403* (East Linton, 2000)

MacDonald, I. G., *Clerics and Clansmen. The Diocese of Argyll between the Twelfth and Sixteenth Centuries* (Leiden, 2013)

McDonald, J. R., 'The Career Paths of Illegitimate Scottish Clergy: The Evidence of the Registers of the Apostolic Penitentiary, the Registers of Supplications and Lateran Registers', *Florilegium* 25 (2008), 151–73

—— 'Illegitimate Scots in the Registers of Supplications and the Registers of the Apostolic Penitentiary during the Pontificate of Sixtus IV (1471–1484)', in *... et usque ad ultimum terrae: The Apostolic Penitentiary in Local Contexts*, ed. G. Jaritz, T. Jørgensen and K. Salonen (Budapest, 2007), 33–42

—— 'The Papal Penitentiary, Illegitimacy and Clerical Careers in the Peripheries: A Case Study of the Provinces of Nidaros and Scotland, 1449–1542', *Northern Scotland* 3 (2012), 32–44

—— 'The Requests of Scottish Clergy in the Registers of the *Sacra Apostolica Penitenzieria*, 1449–1542', *RSCHS* 37 (2007), 5–53

McDonald, R. A., 'The Foundation and Patronage of Nunneries by Native Elites in Twelfth- and Early Thirteenth-Century Scotland', in *Women in Scotland c. 1100–c. 1750*, ed. E. Ewan and M. M. Meikle (East Linton, 1999), 3–15

—— 'Old and New in the Far North: Ferchar Maccintsacairt and the Early Earls of Ross, c. 1200–1274', in *The Exercise of Power in Medieval Scotland c. 1200–1500*, ed. S. Boardman and A. Ross (Dublin, 2005), 23–45

—— *Outlaws of Medieval Scotland: Challenges to the Canmore Kings 1058–1266* (East Linton, 2003)

Macdougall, N., *James III* (Edinburgh, 2009)

—— *James III: A Political Study* (Edinburgh, 1982)

—— *James IV* (Edinburgh, 1989)

McDougall, S., *Royal Bastards: the Birth of Illegitimacy, 800–1230* (Oxford, 2016)

McDowall, W., *Chronicles of Lincluden as an Abbey and as a College* (Edinburgh, 1886)

Macfarlane, L. J., 'The Primacy of the Scottish Church, 1472–1521', *IR* 20 (1969), 111–29

—— *William Elphinstone and the Kingdom of Scotland 1431–1514: The Struggle for Order* (Aberdeen, 1995)

M. MacGregor, 'Church and Culture in the Late Medieval Highlands', in J. Kirk, ed., *The Church in the Highlands* (Edinburgh, 1998), 1–36

Mackay, A., with Ditchburn, D., *Atlas of Medieval Europe* (London, 1997)

McKechnie, H., *Judicial Process upon Brieves, 1219–1532* (Glasgow, 1956)

McMichael, T., 'The Feudal Family of de Soulis', *TDGNHAS* third series 26 (1947–8), 163–93

Macquarrie, A., 'Kings, Lords and Abbots: Power and Patronage at the Medieval Monastery of Iona', *TGSI* 54 (1984–6), 355–75

MacQueen, H. L., 'The Brieve of Right in Scots Law', *The Journal of Legal History* 3 (1982), 52–70

—— 'Canon Law, Custom and Legislation in the Reign of Alexander II', in *The Reign of Alexander II, 1214–49*, ed. R. D. Oram (Leiden, 2005), 221–51

—— *Common Law & Feudal Society in Medieval Scotland* (Edinburgh, 1993)

—— 'Dissasine and Mortancestor in Scots Law', *Journal of Legal History* 4 (1983), 21–49

—— 'Expectations of the Law in 12th and 13th Century Scotland', *Tijdschrift voor Rechtsgeschiedenis* 70 (2002), 279–90

—— 'The Kin of Kennedy, "Kenkynnol" and the Common Law', in *Medieval Scotland: Crown, Lordship and Community. Essays Presented to G. W. S. Barrow*, ed. A. Grant and K. J. Stringer (Edinburgh, 1998), 274–96

—— 'The Laws of Galloway: A Preliminary Survey', in *Galloway: Land and Lordship*, ed. R. D. Oram and G. P. Stell (Edinburgh, 1991), 131–43

—— 'Pleadable Brieves, Pleading, and the Development of Scots Law', *Law and History Review* 4 (1986), 403–22

—— '*Regiam Majestatem*, Scots Law and National Identity', *SHR* 74 (1995), 1–25

Marshall, S., 'Illegitimacy and Sanctity in the Twelfth-Century Lives of St. Kentigern', in *Jocelin of Furness: Essays from the 2011 Conference*, ed. C. Downham (Donington, 2013), 67–90

Martels, Z. von, 'The Fruit of Love: Aeneas Silvius Piccolomini About his Illegitimate Child', in *Pius II 'El Più Expeditivo Pontefice': Selected Studies on Aeneas Silvius Piccolomini (1405–1464)*, ed. Z. von Martels and A. Vanderjagt (Leiden, 2003), 229–48

Martindale, J., 'Succession and Politics in the Romance-speaking World, c. 1000–1140', in *England and Her Neighbours, 1066–1453*, ed. M. Jones and M. Vale (London, 1989), 19–41

Maxtone Graham, E., *The Oliphants of Gask. Records of a Jacobite Family* (London, 1910)

Mayali, L., 'Legitimization by Subsequent Marriage from Alexander III to Innocent III', in *The Two Laws: Studies in Medieval Legal History Dedicated to Stephan Kuttner*, ed. L. Mayali and S. A. J. Tibbetts (Washington, DC, 1990), 55–75

Messer, D., '*Filia Notha* or *Filia Regis*?: Kinship and the Acquiescence of Royal Illegitimate Daughters (c. 1090–1440)', *Foundations: Newsletter of the Foundation for Medieval Genealogy* 1.1 (2003), 51–53

—— 'Medieval Monarchs, Female Illegitimacy and Modern Genealogical Matters: Part I: Sybilla, Queen of Scotland, c.1090–1122', *Foundations: Newsletter of the Foundation for Medieval Genealogy* 1.2 (2003), 99–103

Mitchell, R. J., *The Laurels and the Tiara: Pope Pius II, 1458–1464* (London, 1962)

Mitterauer, M., 'Christianity and Endogamy', *Continuity and Change* 6 (1991), 295–333

Molho, A., *Marriage Alliance in Late Medieval Florence* (London, 1994)

Morgan, M., 'The Organisation of the Scottish Church in the Twelfth Century', *TRHS* fourth series, 29 (1947), 135–49

Mousourakis, G., *Fundamentals of Roman Private Law* (Berlin, 2012)

Mylne, J. R., *The Canon Law*, ed. J. Maitland Thomson (Edinburgh, 1912)

Neville, C., 'Widows of War: Edward I and the Women of Scotland during the War of Independence', in *Wife and Widow in Medieval England*, ed. S. S. Walker (Ann Arbor, MI, 1993), 109–39

Nicholson, R., *Scotland: The Later Middle Ages* (Edinburgh, 1974)

O'Brien, E., 'Arms and Letters: Julius Caesar, the Commentaries of Pope Pius II, and the Politicization of Papal Imagery', *Renaissance Quarterly* 62 (2009), 1057–97

Ó Cróinín, D., *Early Medieval Ireland 400–1200* (London, 1995)

Ollivant, S., *The Court of the Official in Pre-Reformation Scotland*, Stair Society 34 (Edinburgh, 1982)

Oram, R., 'Continuity, Adaptation and Integration: the Earls and Earldom of Mar, c.1150–c.1300', in *The Exercise of Power in Medieval Scotland c. 1200–1500*, ed. S. Boardman and A. Ross (Dublin, 2005), 46–66

—— 'Dividing the Spoils: War, Schism and Religious Patronage on the Anglo-Scottish Border, c. 1332–c. 1400', in *England and Scotland in the Fourteenth Century: New Perspectives*, ed. A. King and M. A. Penman (Woodbridge, 2007), 136–56

—— *Domination and Lordship: Scotland 1070–1230* (Edinburgh, 2011)

—— 'Lay Religiosity, Piety, and Devotion in Scotland c. 1300 to c. 1450', *Florilegium* 25 (2008), 107–13

—— *The Lordship of Galloway* (Edinburgh, 2000)

—— 'An Overview of the Reign of Alexander II', in *The Reign of Alexander II, 1214–49*, ed. R. D. Oram (Leiden, 2005), 1–47

Parish, H., *Clerical Celibacy in the West: c. 1100–1700* (Aldershot, 2010)

Payer, P. J., *The Bridling of Desire: Ideas of Sex in the Later Middle Ages* (Toronto, 1993)

Pedersen, F., 'Adventures in Law: The Danes and the Marriage Breakup of Philip II of France', in *Adventures of the Law. Proceedings of the Sixteenth British Legal History Conference, Dublin, 2003*, ed. P. Brand, K. Costello and W. N. Osborough (Dublin, 2005), 54–69

Penman, M. A., *David II, 1329–71* (Edinburgh, 2004)

—— 'David II (1329–1371)', in *Scottish Kingship 1306–1542: Essays in Honour of Norman MacDougall*, ed. M. Brown and R. Tanner (Edinburgh, 2008), 109–25

—— '*Diffinicione successionis ad regnum Scottorum*: Royal Succession in Scotland in the Later Middle Ages', in *Making and Breaking the Rules: Succession in*

Medieval Europe, c. 1000–c. 1600, ed. F. Lachaud and M. Penman (Turnhout, 2008), 43–59

—— '*A fell coniuracioun agayn Robert the douchty king*: the Soules Conspiracy of 1318–1320', *IR* 50 (1999), 25–57

—— *Robert the Bruce: King of the Scots* (New Haven, CT, 2014)

—— 'The Scots at the Battle of Neville's Cross', *SHR* 80 (2001), 157–80

Pennington, K., *Popes, Canonists and Texts, 1150–1550* (Aldershot, 1993)

Pollard, A. J., *Late Medieval England 1399–1509* (New York, 2000)

Pollock, F. and Maitland, F. W., *The History of English Law before the Time of Edward I* (Cambridge, 1923)

Ravilious, J. P., 'Maria Stewart, Illegitimate Daughter of Robert II, King of Scots', *The Scottish Genealogist* 56 (2009), 29–30

—— '"Nephew of the Duke": the Danielstons of that Ilk, and a Hitherto Unknown Daughter of Robert II, King of Scots', *The Scottish Genealogist* 54 (2007), 134–7

Reid, R. C., 'The Scottish Avenels', *TDGNHAS* 37 (1958–9), 70–8

Renouard, Y., *The Avignon Papacy 1305–1403*, transl. D. Bethell (Hamden, 1970)

Reynolds, P. L., 'When Medieval Theologians Talked About Marriage, What Were They Really Talking About?', in *Law and Marriage in Medieval and Early Modern Times. Proceedings of the Eighth Carlsberg Academy Conference on Medieval Legal History 2011*, ed. P. Anderson, K. Salonen, H. M. Sigh and H. Vogt (Copenhagen, 2012), 11–42

Robinson, O. F., 'Canon Law and Marriage', *JR* new series 29 (1984), 22–40

Rolker, C., 'Kings, Bishops and Incest: Extension and Subversion of the Ecclesiastical Marriage Jursidiction around 1100', in *Discipline and Diversity*, ed. K. Cooper and J. Gregory (Woodbridge, 2007), 159–68

Ross, A., 'The Identity of the "Prisoner of Roxburgh": Malcolm Son of Alexander or Malcolm MacHeth?', in *Fil súil nglais: A Grey Eye Looks Back. A Festschrift in Honour of Colm Ó Baoill*, ed. S. Arbuthnot and K. Hollo (Ceann Drochaid, 2007), 269–82

—— *The Kings of Alba c. 1000–c. 1130* (Edinburgh, 2011)

—— 'Men for All Seasons? The Strathbogie Earls of Atholl and the Wars of Independence, c. 1290–1335', *Northern Scotland* 20 (2000), 1–30

—— 'Moray, Ulster and the MacWilliams', in *The World of the Galloglass. Kings, Warlords and Warriors in Ireland and Scotland, 1200–1600*, ed. S. Duffy (Dublin, 2007), 24–44

Ross, C., *Edward IV* (London, 1974)

Rousseau, C. M., 'Innocent III, Defender of the Innocents and the Law: Children and Papal Policy (1198–1216)', *Archivum Historiae Pontificiae* 32 (1994), 31–42

Rüdiger, J., 'Married Couples in the Middle Ages? The Case of the Devil's Advocate', in *Law and Marriage in Medieval and Early Modern Times. Proceedings of the Eighth Carlsberg Academy Conference on Medieval Legal History 2011*, ed. P. Andersen, K. Salonen, H. M. Sigh and H. Vogt (Copenhagen, 2012), 83–109

Salonen, K., 'Nine Marriage Disputes in the Consistorial Court of Freising in the Late Middle Ages', in M. Korpiola, ed., *Regional Variations in Matrimonial Law and Custom in Europe 1150–1600* (Leiden, 2011), 189–209

—— *The Penitentiary as a Well of Grace in the Late Middle Ages: The Example of the Province of Uppsala, 1448–1527* (Saarijärvi, 2001)

Salonen, K. and Schmugge, L., *A Sip from the "Well of Grace": Medieval Texts from the Apostolic Penitentiary* (Washington, DC, 2009)

Scanlan, J. D., 'Husband and Wife: Pre-Reformation Canon Law of Marriage of the Officials' Courts', in *An Introduction to Scottish Legal History*, Stair Society 20 (Edinburgh, 1958), 69–81

Schmugge, L., 'Cleansing on Consciences: Some Observations Regarding the Fifteenth-Century Registers of the Papal Penitentiary', *Viator* 29 (1998), 345–61

—— 'Female Petitioners in the Papal Penitentiary', *Gender and History* 12 (2000), 685–703

—— *Kirche Kinder Karrieren: Päpstliche Dispense von der unehelichen Geburt im Spätmittelalter* (Zürich, 1995)

Schmugge, L., *Marriage on Trial. Late Medieval German Couples at the Papal Court*, transl. A. A. Larson (Washington, DC, 2012)

Scofield, C. L., *The Life and Reign of Edward IV*, 2 vols (London, 1923)

Seabourne, G., *Imprisoning Medieval Women: The Non-Judicial Confinement and Abduction of Women in England, c. 1170–1509* (Farnham, 2011)

Sellar, W. D. H., 'Courtesy, Battle and the Brieve of Right, 1368 – A Story Continued', in *Miscellany II*, Stair Society 35 (Edinburgh, 1984), 1–12

—— 'The Family', in *A History of Everyday Life in Medieval Scotland, 1000 to 1600*, ed. E. J. Cowan and L. Henderson (Edinburgh, 2011), 89–108

—— 'Hebridean Sea-Kings: The Successors of Somerled, 1164–1316', in *Alba: Celtic Scotland in the Medieval Era*, ed. E. J. Cowan and R. A. McDonald (East Linton, 2000), 187–218

—— 'A Historical Perspective', in M. C. Meston, W. D. H. Sellar and T. M. Cooper, *The Scottish Legal Tradition* (new enl. edn), ed. S. C. Styles (Edinburgh, 1991), 29–64

—— 'Marriage, Divorce and Concubinage in Gaelic Scotland', *TGSI* 51 (1978–80), 464–93

—— 'Marriage, Divorce and the Forbidden Degrees: Canon Law and Scots Law', in *Explorations in Law and History: Irish Legal History Society Discourses, 1988–1994*, ed. W. N. Osborough (Dublin, 1995), 59–82

Sheehan, M. M., 'The European Family and Canon Law', *Continuity and Change* 6 (1991), 347–60

Smith, B., 'In the Tracks of Bishop Andrew Pictoris of Orkney, and Henry Phankouth, Archdeacon of Shetland', *IR* 40 (1989), 91–105

Spufford, P., *Handbook of Medieval Exchange* (London, 1986)

Stewart, D., *A Short Historical and Genealogical Account of the Royal Family of Scotland* (Edinburgh, 1739)

Stringer, K. J., 'A Cistercian Archive: The Earliest Charters of Sawtry Abbey', *Journal of the Society of Archivists* 6 (1980), 325–34

—— *Earl David of Huntingdon 1152–1219* (Edinburgh, 1985)

—— 'Kingship, Conflict and State-making in the Reign of Alexander II: the War of 1215–17 and its Context', in *The Reign of Alexander II, 1214–49*, ed. R. D. Oram (Leiden, 2005), 99–156

—— 'A New Wife for Alan of Galloway', *TDGNHAS* 49 (1972), 49–55

—— 'Nobility and Identity in Medieval Britain and Ireland: the de Vescy Family, c.1120–1314', in *Britain and Ireland, 900–1300: Insular Responses to Medieval European Change*, ed. B. Smith (Cambridge, 1999), 199–239

—— 'Periphery and Core in Thirteenth-Century Scotland: Alan Son of Roland, Lord of Galloway and Constable of Scotland', in *Medieval Scotland: Crown, Lordship and Community: Essays Presented to G. W. S. Barrow*, ed. A. Grant and K. J. Stringer (Edinburgh, 1998), 82–113

Tanner, R., 'Cowing the Community? Coercion and Falsification in Robert Bruce's Parliaments, 1309–1318', in *Parliament and Politics in Scotland, 1235–1560*, ed. K. M. Brown and R. J. Tanner (Edinburgh, 2004), 64–73

—— 'James III (1460–1488)', in *Scottish Kingship 1306–1542: Essays in Honour of Norman MacDougall*, ed. M. Brown and R. Tanner (Edinburgh, 2008), 209–31

Taylor, A., 'Historical Writing in Twelfth- and Thirteenth-century Scotland: the Dunfermline Compilation', *Historical Research* 83 (2010), 228–52

—— *Laws of Medieval Scotland*, Stair Society 66 (Edinburgh, 2019)

—— 'Robert de Londres, Illegitimate Son of William, King of Scots, *c.* 1170–1225', *Haskins Society Journal: Studies in Medieval History* 19 (2008), 99–119

—— *The Shape of the State in Medieval Scotland, 1124–1290* (Oxford, 2016)

Thomas, S., 'Bishops, Priests, Monks and Their Patrons: the Lords of the Isles and the Church', in *The Lordship of the Isles*, ed. R. Oram (Leiden, 2014), 123–45

—— 'Clerical Illegitimacy in the Diocese of Sodor – Exception or Rule in the Late Medieval Church?', in *Heresy and the Making of European Culture: Medieval and Modern Perspectives*, ed. A. P. Roach and J. R. Simpson (Farnham, 2013), 313–31

Tierney, B., '"*Tria Quippe Distinguit Iudicia*..." A Note on Innocent III's Decretal *Per Venerabilem*', *Speculum* 37 (1962), 48–59

Treggiari, S., *Roman Marriage* (Oxford 1991)

Watt, D. E. R., *A Biographical Dictionary of Scottish Graduates to A.D. 1410* (Oxford, 1977)

—— *Medieval Church Councils in Scotland* (Edinburgh, 2000)

—— 'The Papacy and Scotland in the Fifteenth Century', in *The Church, Politics and Patronage in the Fifteenth Century*, ed. B. Dobson (Gloucester, 1984), 115–32

Watt, D. E. R. and Shead, N. F., *The Heads of Religious Houses in Scotland from Twelfth to Sixteenth Centuries* (Edinburgh, 2001)

Watt, J. A., *The Theory of Papal Monarchy in the Thirteenth Century: The Contribution of the Canonists* (New York, 1965)

Weiler, B., 'William of Malmesbury on Kingship', *History* 90 (2005), 3–22

Wertheimer, L., 'Children of Disorder: Clerical Parentage, Illegitimacy, and Reform in the Middle Ages', *Journal of the History of Sexuality* 15 (2006), 382–407

Willock, I. D., *The Origins and Development of the Jury in Scotland* (Edinburgh, 1966)

Winroth, A., *The Making of Gratian's* Decretum (Cambridge, 2001)

Witte Jr, J., *The Sins of the Fathers: The Law and Theology of Illegitimacy Reconsidered* (Cambridge, 2009)

Woolf, A., 'The Diocese of the Suðreyar', in *Ecclesia Nidrosiensis 1153–1537: søkelys på Nidaroskirkens og Nidarosprovinsens historie*, ed. S. Imsen (Trondheim, 2003), 171–82

—— 'The "Moray Question" and the Kingship of Alba in the Tenth and Eleventh Centuries', *SHR* 79 (2000), 145–64

—— *From Pictland to Alba, 789–1070* (Edinburgh, 2007)

—— 'The Song of the Death of Somerled and the Destruction of Glasgow in 1153', *Journal of the Sydney Society for Scottish History* 14 (2013), 1–11

Wormald, J., *Court, Kirk and Community: Scotland 1470–1625* (Edinburgh, 1981)

Wright, J. R., *The Church and the English Crown 1305–1334* (Toronto, 1980)

Zutshi, P. N. R., 'Proctors Acting for English Petitioners in the Chancery of the Avignon Popes (1305–1378)', *Journal of Ecclesiastical History* 35 (1984), 15–29

Index

Page numbers in **bold** refer to tables.

Printed and bound by CPI Group (UK) Ltd, Croydon, CR0 4YY
15/09/2026
14962417-0003

Printed and bound by CPI Group (UK) Ltd, Croydon, CR0 4YY
15/09/2026
14962417-0003